AMERICA'S VICTORIES

Why America Wins Wars and Why They Will Win the War on Terror

BY LARRY SCHWEIKART

T0336356

AMERICA'S VICTORIES: Why America Wins Wars and Why They Will Win the War of Terrorism

By Larry Schweikart

To Captain Steve Battle and Captain Craig Bender, United States Army, and all my former students now serving in the finest military in history

Cover by V.W.Rospond
Cover Image from the US Army
Edited by Vincent W. Rospond
Winged Hussar Publishing, LLC, 1525 Hulse Road, Unit 1, Point Pleasant, NJ 08742

This edition published in 2015
Copyright ©Larry Schweikart 2015

ISBN 978-0-98903649-6-2
LCN 2015940358
Bibliographical references and index
1. United States - History, Military. 2. United States - Civilization. 3. National characteristics

Knox Press in conjunction with Winged Hussar Publishing, LLC
All rights reserved

For more information on Winged Hussar Publishing, LLC, visit us at:
https://www.WingedHussarPublishing.com

Acknowledgments

== * ==

An old Army saying is that amateurs talk tactics, while professionals talk logistics. When it comes to writing a book, the public sees the writer, but there are numerous people whose efforts helped make it possible. First, thanks to my agent, Roger Williams at New England Publishing Associates, and his predecessor, the late Ed Knappman, who, through his dedication to my early works opened the door for whatever success met *America's Victories*. I'm grateful to Vincent Rospond for re-energizing the book.

For this book in particular, I'm indebted more to professional soldiers, sailors, airmen, and Marines than to professional historians. One group, whom I called my military brains trust-some retired vets, some currently serving-ignored the military's maxim, "Never volunteer for anything," and willingly helped me out, offering important viewpoints, corrections, and supplemental information. My cousin, Lieutenant Colonel Michael Jackson (USMC, Ret.), has been a consistent critical reader of my manuscripts. Professor Jeff Hanichen, USMC (Ret.), provided a thorough reading and great encouragement. Captain Chris Koren, USMC, Sergeant Christopher Cliukey (USAF, Ret.); Major Adrian DeNardo (USAF, Ret.); and Captain Danjel Bout, U.S. Army all made important contributions.

Two reviewers were particularly thorough and thought provoking: Clayton Cramer, a specialist in firearms in the early Republic, and Robert Lynn, a military history book reviewer. They saved me from innumerable errors, introduced many concepts I had not thought through (or thought of at all), and sharpened my arguments. Military historian Loren Gannon (USA, Ret.), at the University of Dayton, and civilian consultant to the U.S. Army and the U.S. Air Force Jeff Head also enhanced my understanding with long talks about tactics, strategy, and equipment.

Also at the University of Dayton, as always, the late Cynthia King provided original typing and editing support, and is a proofreader with an excellent eye; student researchers, including Danielle Elam and Carl Ewald, helped dig out articles and maps; and Ron Acklin, of UD's Print and Design–a true virtuoso of computer imagery-drew and created all the maps. My wife, Dee, stayed out of my hair for hours on end while I wrote this, and my son, Adam, who contributed research assistance to the "Hollywood Heroes" section, are also due a debt of gratitude and, of course, my love.

Larry Schweikart
Centerville, Ohio

Contents

Acknowledgments 4

List of Figures 6

Foreword to 2015 Edition 7

Introduction 11

1. Gitmo, Gulags, and Great Raids 21

2. Learning from Loss 48

3. Citizens as Soldiers 75

4. Pushing Autonomy Down 106

5. If You Build It, We Will Win 135

6. All for One 176

7. Protesters Make Soldiers Better 200

Conclusion 245

Index 257

List of Figures

Figure 1. The Death March of Bataan   **23**

Figure 2. The Battle of Ia Drang Valley   **50**

Figure 3. The Battle of New Orleans   **98**

Figure 4. The Battle of Baghdad   **108**

Figure 5. The Battle of Hoover's Gap   **137**

Figure 6. The Arsenal of Democracy   **163**

Figure 7. The Battle of Leyte Gulf   **193**

Figure 8. The "Battle" of Chicago   **201**

Foreword to the 2015 Edition

== * ==

When America's Victories first came out in hardcover, then later paperback, the war in the Iraq and Afghanistan fronts was still raging. As the paperback edition came out, the U.S. had just increased combat troop levels in the "surge" and in many ways, with considerable help from the "Anbar Awakening," we seemingly had turned the corner in Iraq especially. What a difference a few years makes. The election of Barack Obama, who expressed a clear goal of disengaging from Iraq and Afghanistan, changed the entire equation not only of the war, but of the very stability of the Middle East. A new group, ISIS (Islamic State of Iraq and Syria), has threatened the fragile stability of Iraq, taking such cities as Tikrit. ISIS accelerated and, if possible, increased the level of terror from that of al-Qaeda, unleashing horrific acts from the beheading of Christians to the live immolation of a Jordanian pilot on camera. The fact that al-Qaeda drifted into the background (even though some al-Qaeda moved in and out of ISIS seamlessly) suggests that, in fact, we had largely defeated al-Qaeda when Obama reversed course.

One cannot separate the military and its success or failure from its leadership. Obama's administration refused to even acknowledge that ISIS was "Islamic" (despite the fact that it's part of that organization's title), and has banned terms such as "Islamic terrorism" from any official utterance. It goes without saying that if you are afraid or unwilling to even name your enemy, you cannot defeat him. I still believe that everything I saw that was positive in the American military itself in the paperback edition of this book in 2006 remains true, but American military prowess and success is inexorably dependent on the presidency as a singular source of leadership. Without engaging in the diversion of whether Obama's policies intentionally weakened American military strength, or whether our strategic losses have come from mere incompetence is a debate for another time.

Some other observations I had in the earlier iterations of the book I think are today no less valid. For example, different people I spoke with, especially in the 2006-07 timeframe, frequently compared Iraq or Afghanistan with Vietnam. On one side of the political spectrum, there was the belief that the United States is once again a feckless invader trapped in a quagmire halfway around the world that the public opposes. On the other side, some worried that the same political timidity that restrained America's mighty military in the jungles of Southeast Asia was evident in the deserts and mountains of the Middle East.

But since the War on Terror began, I have been convinced that the Vietnam/Iraq comparison didn't hold up against history. In Vietnam, we were fighting a foreign government with unfettered access to South Vietnam via the Ho Chi Minh trail—especially after Tet. There was no effort made to destroy this pipeline, and certainly no attempt at invading Cambodia and putting an end to the infusion of supplies once and for all. Nor was there any effort made to seriously diminish the influx of supplies to North Vietnam, which on its own could not have supported such a war effort for more than a few months.

We also pretended that China and the USSR, for all intents and purposes, were not a part of the Vietnam conflict. Moreover, the United States never delivered any direct threats to the regime in Hanoi—nothing representing President George W. Bush's famous utterance of "*you're either with us or with the terrorists*" directed at the Viet Cong, Ho Chi Minh, and later, other relief pitchers in dictators' garb, never feared the loss of their control, let alone their lives.

Such has not been the case in Iraq and Afghanistan. While in both countries, porous borders enable foreign terrorists to cross at their leisure, there was a less effective Ho Chi Minh Trail to supply the enemy, although Iran sought to fill that role. Nevertheless, there was never a single nation-state backer such as China or USSR exists in the War on Terror. Until recently, Iran had been forced to choose between exporting terrorists or developing its own nuclear weapons, and, for the most part, it has chosen the latter with the full blessing of the Obama administration. As of this writing, there is virtually no concern by the American government about Iran developing nuclear weapons, let alone its intention to use them on Israel. As a result, Saudi Arabia, out of fear of a "nuclear-ified" Iran, has suggested that it too needs nukes. Indeed, as of this writing, the U.S. has just entered into a negotiation with Iran all but ensuring that it will get nuclear weapons.

At any rate, there was another aspect of the Vietnam analogy that was supremely troubling, and that is that the Vietnam conflict was actually a "war." Was Korea? In one sense, of course. Each had a beginning and end, with fairly well-defined areas of operation. Yet in a more important sense, each was in reality a "battle" within a much larger war—the ongoing Cold War. The real enemies in Korea were China and Russia, and their objective was expanding communism. They failed in Korea, and tried again in Vietnam. Despite having captured South Vietnam with its Communist puppets, the Soviet Union lost the larger contest and collapsed in 1991. One might even liken it to the Alamo, where Santa Anna achieved a tactical victory but was critically delayed, and suffered a strategic, and fatal, defeat.

A far better analogy to what happening in Iraq from 2003 to 2009 would be the Filipino Insurrection of the early 1900s including the "Moro Wars." In that conflict, wherein the "insurgents" sought to free the infant Philippines from U.S. governance long before the islands were ready, Americans occasionally fought Muslim fundamentalists who beheaded their enemies and who terrorized any villages siding with the Yanqui. As in Iraq, we competed, successfully, for the "hearts and minds" of the people, building hospitals and roads on one hand while killing terrorists on the other. That is not to say that "nation building" is the main goal---it never is in war. But there must be a realization that when one structure, government, or social organization disappears, something will take its place.

It's worth noting that the U.S., and to a somewhat different degree, western Europe, developed with basic systems of human rights, stability, property rights, and so on that are not either natural or comfortable for some other cultures. Japan, for example, had to be forced to allow women into the political sphere by Douglas MacArthur. It would be unrealistic to expect Iraq, Afghanistan, or any other country not steeped in constitutional government, common law, equality, and other western concepts to "get it" immediately. It took the west hundreds of years. But similarly we should not expect that nations could move into such stable, western-style structures without making some substantial change---just as Japan did when it recognized female equality. This will not happen immediately, and it won't happen without some discomfort.

Two particular similarities made the conflict in the Philippines an appropriate comparison and contrast. The first is that the total percentage of U.S. ground troops involved in the combat, as a share of all U.S. ground troops available, was very close to the percentage of ground troops we had in Iraq and Afghanistan. Depending on whether Navy and Air Force support personnel are included, the United States has around 17 percent of its ground forces in Iraq and Afghanistan combined, whereas in the Philippines it was about 12 percent, deployed against a numerically smaller enemy.

The second is that in the Philippines, the stated objective of guerrilla leader Emilio Aguinaldo was not so much to defeat American combat troops but to defeat William McKinley and successfully swing the election of 1900 to the "peace candidate, William Jennings Bryan. That echoed al-Zarqawi's goal of removing George W. Bush from the presidency in 2004, which also failed, Aguinaldo expressed what most terrorists today admit in private: they cannot match the U.S. military. Their only hope is to make Americans think "Vietnam" when they need to be thinking "Philippines."

That's where the similarities end, however. In the Philippines, the American military was far less restrained than it is in the War on Terror. Our forces burned down suspected enemy villages in their entirety. Torture was routinely employed in that engagement, unlike now-despite the overheated rhetoric and accusations of politicians such as Richard Durbin (D-IL) or Charles Rangel (D-NY). Whether the use of torture is a strength or a weakness for the U.S. military remains an issue for debate, even though some might rule it out entirely. Water-boarding and other types of information acquisition however highlight another difference between the Filipino Revolt and the wars in the Middle East: the press was almost entirely on the side of American victory in the former. As will be seen throughout, the U.S. media (and the world media as a whole) demonstrably hate the possibility of American victory in foreign wars. To them, the United States has become the major destabilizing force in the world at best and a villain at worst. This was made all the more clear by the election of Barack Obama, who was grounded in assumptions from his father and mentors that America was imperialistic and needed to be knocked down a peg or two. It has become obvious in his foreign policies that he wanted to follow through on those assumptions.

As to the question of whether we can defeat an ideology such as radical Islam begins with the observation that anyone who maintains the U.S. military can only defeat nation-states with regular armies and that it "cannot defeat an ideology" is essentially stating that radical Islam is, in fact, a violent ideology, and that the U.S. military is simply too weak to whip it.

If, indeed, radical Islam is an "ideology" that needs suppression, the United States has shown convincingly in the past century that with the public's support, our military can indeed crush an ideology—as we did fascism, Japanese bushidoism, and communism. Ultimately, the question of whether radical Islam is a "violent" ideology like these others will be answered in the cauldrons of Iraq, Afghanistan, and, sometime down the road, in Iran and Syria.

But this debate has a critical implication: if—as most liberals and even many conservatives suggest-the average Middle Easterner pines for human liberty and freedom from political oppression, then the number of those opponents in Iraq and Afghanistan is not only finite, but must be diminishing daily, and rapidly. The paperback volume in fact contained one of the only estimates of which I am aware that sought to quantify the number of enemy killed, wounded, and deserted since the War on Terror began. High-ranking U.S. government sources have admitted to me that there is little effort made to get these statistics out, which are highly indicative of progress in the war, because of the public's sensitivity to "body counts," dating back to the Vietnam era.

I disagree with our government's reticence on this matter. It is useful, even necessary, for the rest of us to know that we were winning. More recently, the rise of ISIS as a replacement for al-Qaeda suggests that, in fact, al-Qaeda was fairly well gutted. But the unwillingness of the Obama administration to take seriously ISIS (calling them, at one time, "the jayvee team") shows the utter incapacity of the current administration to fight, let alone win, a war on terror. But then again, since it refuses to even acknowledge that these are Islamic terrorists, it is likely irrelevant.

.

Larry Schweikart
Centerville, Ohio
April 2015

Introduction

== * ==

Why do Americans win wars? Even granting that Vietnam was a loss (although the military was never, ever defeated in an actual battle), and Korea was a "tie," over the course of two hundred years the armed forces of the United States have whipped the British Empire (twice), beaten a Mexican army (against all European expectations), fought a fratricidal civil war that resulted in higher casualties than all previous wars put together (due to the fact that officers and soldiers on both sides were deadly effective), and crushed the Plains Indians with a minimal number of troops. American forces then dispatched the Spanish in less than a year (when, again, most Europeans thought Spain would win), helped the Allies evict the Germans from France, and dominated an international alliance that simultaneously beat the Nazis, Japanese warlords, and Italian fascists. During the Cold War, we battled the North Koreans and their Chinese allies to a draw on the Asian mainland, then staved off a Soviet-supported invasion of South Vietnam for more than a decade. After the fall of the USSR, the U.S. military twice decisively crushed the biggest armed force in the Middle East, after which we essentially invited every foreign terrorist in the region to enter Iraq and join the fight. Squeezed in between two victories over Iraq, American forces did what the British and Russians could not do by invading Afghanistan and staying. Mix in with this credibly impressive record the fact that even before the United States had a large standing army, a handful of Marines and their mercenary allies spanked the Lilliputian pirates; then while still on the road to superpower status, we soundly defeated a Filipino "insurgency"; and for good measure kicked the Cubans out of Grenada in 1982. Probably the most astounding success was that the United States defeated the "superpower" Soviet Union in the Cold War without firing a Shot-or releasing a nuclear weapon.

Why is the American military so successful, not just recently, but historically? Why do Americans win wars? Are there distinctly (or predominantly) American characteristics that define what Russell Weigley once called an American Way of War? If so, are these not common to all "western" nations, and, if not, what makes us even more successful than historically great western military powers such as Great Britain, France, or Germany?

Some attribute American military success to luck (sheer nonsense), and a larger number point to the U.S. economy and our natural resources, claiming "*Of course, such a large, rich nation ought to win wars*". Yet other nations in their prime have had a proportionally greater dominance in resources, or in numbers of troops, but have not matched our success. Indeed, our enemies often acquire or imitate our technology, and occasionally even seek to copy our training, yet without success. Why? What are the secrets of America's Victories?

"Americans love a winner, and will not tolerate a loser," exclaimed George C. Scott in his famous portrayal of Patton. Patton was right when he said that to troops in 1943. Even Vietnam was winnable with the proper strategy and political commitment: in July 1986, asked if the United States could have won in Vietnam, retired general Curtis LeMay retorted, "In any two-week period you want to mention." [1] This "winners mentality" is not arrived at in all societies-and not at all in some-nor is it the result of luck or the roll of some geopolitical dice. Rather, the American soldiers, officers, and culture (including our remarkable free-enterprise system), which undergird the American culture of combat, produce a distinct fighting style that has almost always ended in victory. But the character and training of the American fighting man (and, recently, woman) is not the only factor that shapes our military success, nor is the presence of a free-market system. Some of the most unexpected sources of victory involve how Americans deal with defeat. Even in loss, American military thinkers have tolerated such open analysis and discussion that the lessons are quickly adopted, usually accomplishing even more lopsided victories the next time out. Unlike some European countries bound by class structures that did not permit, until recently, serious critical thinking about tactics and operations, the class-free American military has, with some exceptions, willingly learned from its mistakes.

Without a doubt, however, it is the American soldier (and sailor, and airman, and Marine) who has proven the difference maker. The American military culture has emerged from a militia-based volunteer force in the early Republic into a small, competent, but underequipped body of professionals in the late 1800s, evolving into the draftee armies of World Wars I and II, Korea, and Vietnam, and culminating in the highly skilled professionals who make up the modem volunteer armed forces. Although Victor Hanson has developed his well-regarded thesis about a "Western Way of War," the U.S. military has eclipsed and surpassed other practitioners to create a distinct American approach to warfare that is sui generis. It is a distinctly American military character replete with individual initiative and unprecedented autonomy for soldiers and officers, all supported by free-market production concepts that have made it the most potent force in the world. America's victories have been buttressed by the principles establishing the sanctity of life that permeate our founding documents, and that temper our treatment of enemies and inspire us to save fallen or captured warriors like no other society in history has done.

An ironic unintended consequence has arisen from this success. Despite every victory, new military actions are greeted by even greater and more unrealistic predictions of failure from the Left and, more recently, the "mainstream media." These prophecies are followed by "analysis" of how the triumph isn't as complete as the public thought, how we are "mismanaging the peace," for how we

---

[1] Quoted in Mark Clodfelter, The Limits of Airpower: The American Bombing of North Vietnam (New York: Free Press, 1989), p. 206.

are "creating more enemies" by our actions. Inevitably, then, come the exposes of "near catastrophes," intelligence screw-ups, troops run amuck, civilian casualties, and the Pentagon's incorrect predictions. Naturally, there is no room for context, of how in the last three major wars combined (Gulf War, Afghanistan, and Iraq), the United States lost fewer troops than at Okinawa in World War II. Nor does the media provide any discussion of a "greater good" achieved by military action, and rarely is there offered any sense of the overall competence of the American armed forces. One is left to conclude that our soldiers triumph in spite of themselves their officers, their government, and even their own culture—that they stumble and bumble along, from victory to victory, in the process abusing prisoners and spawning ever-growing numbers of enemies.

There are, in fact, good reasons for America's victories. One might call them "secrets" of American military success, except they are not hidden and often are so obvious that they are overlooked. The American culture of combat relies on several distinctly American elements:

• A fundamental principle of the sanctity of life that permeates combat operations and that shapes everything from how we treat prisoners to the emphasis we place on rescuing fallen wounded and our own captured POWs.

• Unparalleled self-criticism and reassessment, combined with civilian oversight and critical evaluation by the rest of society, including antiwar protesters, which has only made the American military more effective.

• A volunteer force of free citizens, originally represented by the militia, who enjoy personal liberties and private property rights at home. This force has at times been enhanced and expanded by a draft during wars that are perceived to threaten national existence.

• Personal autonomy unseen in any military force in history, spread throughout the ranks, generally impervious to class, background, or education.

• An affinity for technology, combined with an appreciation for using it in shock combat, produced by a free-market system that routinely supplies more, and usually better, weapons than our enemies possess.

• Unprecedented levels of unit and service unity, coordination, and cooperation, blurring the lines of service "fingers" and unifying them into a multiservice "fist."

• The ironic dynamic by which antiwar protesters, through their emphasis on American casualties as their primary means to change public opinion, have actually forced the U.S. military to relentlessly labor to keep our casualties down while making our soldiers more efficient. And the protesters have paradoxically helped make the American armed forces the most lethal in the world.

It is, however, impossible to separate these combat characteristics from the causes for which Americans have fought, for the American soldier is a liberator, not a conqueror, and millions of people around the world know it by personal experience. From Kuwait City to Kabul, from Germany to Grenada, a generation of free foreign citizens, live every day with the knowledge that their liberty was purchased by the blood of American patriots. Modern-day Marxists routinely claim past interventions have been on behalf of the "sugar interests," or "big oil," Halliburton, or Exxon. The truth is that in most cases, the United States has used its military reluctantly and, in Jefferson's words, only after "repeated injuries and usurpations." Our soldiers fight precisely because they understand the causes for which they are committed-and the stakes. Ulysses Grant, briefly a slave owner himself, who married into a slave-owning family, nevertheless willingly waged war on the South-after reluctantly participating in what he saw as an unjust war with Mexico--because he came to see slavery as an evil that had to be checked militarily.[2] George Patton's feelings about "the Hun" reflected his view that the dictatorships his men faced were the worst of humanity. Ask any of our soldiers, sailors, airmen or airwomen, or Marines in Iraq why they are fighting, and you will get a remarkably sophisticated, yet unmistakable message. The liberty they purchase for Iraqis there translates directly to our freedom from attack here.

Winston Churchill said, *"Great battles … create new standards of value, new moods, in armies and in nations."* [3] America's great battles, from New Orleans to San Juan Hill, from the Argonne to Fallujah, have defined its fighting men and women, reinforcing the Revolutionary assumptions that there is good and evil in the world, and that evil must be resisted. These military tests and others, such as Trenton, Hoover's Gap, the Kasserine Pass, and Baghdad, have provided vital information, even when resulting in temporary defeats or setbacks that the American armed forces have used to further improve themselves, becoming stronger even in defeat. Protesters wrongly believe they achieved a great victory over the military in the Vietnam era by "forcing an end to the war." In truth, they imposed a rugged self-evaluation on the Army, Marines, Navy, and Air Force that only made them more powerful and more effective, while at the same time touching off civilian reevaluation of the use of power that led to more skillful consensus building before troops were committed. There would be no more sending young men and women to die without first making a significant effort to convince a large majority of the public that the task was worth the sacrifice.

And yet even that "lesson" has been modified. The Reagan Doctrine (also called the Powell Doctrine) of only committing American forces under certain

[2]"A Slave Owner?," http://.mscomm.com/~ulysses/page160.html. Grant first encountered slaves in the 1840s in Missouri, and his wife held four slaves until the Emancipation Proclamation. Grant took one of his in-laws' slaves with him in 1858–59, at the request of his father-in-law. Grant paid the slave a wage and freed him after a year, even though he could have sold him for $1,000 and even though Grant was in severe financial circumstances. See William S. McFeeley, Grant: a Biography (New York: Norton, 1981).

[3]Victor Davis Hanson, Ripples of Battle: How Wars of the Past Still Determine How We Fight, How We Live, and How We Think (New York: Doubleday, 2003), p.11.

conditions-with overwhelming force, with a substantial public consensus about their use, and with a clear exit strategy—has itself been reevaluated in light of 9/11 In the process, some who gave Ronald Reagan a pass on the Lebanon withdrawal have critically revisited that event. Yet the fact that American policy makers, and the military, constantly review, refine, and, when necessary, overturn obsolete doctrine sets us apart from most of our foes (and a few of our friends).

Great battles illuminate, and America's greatest battles have often revealed the fundamental undergirding of military power that lies in free institutions and property rights. The Success of the 3rd Armored Division's race to Germany was as much owed to inventors and industrialists such as Andrew Jackson Higgins and Henry Kaiser as it was to George Patton's own exceptional generalship or his men's fighting abilities. For a man who celebrated winners, Patton's success-and that of MacArthur, and before him, Pershing and Grant—was as much due to the failed dreamers in the American economy as it was to the successful survivors. Modern warfare involved supplying ammunition, fuel, and food to the 5 percent of soldiers who do the fighting and dying, and a market economy's dynamic ability to out produce command-and-¬control economies means that America could be the great arsenal of democracy in World War II—and the great technology leader thereafter. By their willingness to take risks and demonstrate what was not possible, those who tried and failed may have played almost as important a role as those who succeeded. That was a characteristic inherent in the system, and it promoted the social value of encouraging geniuses to attempt great things, no matter the outcome.

Only the American economic and political culture tolerated such free-market failure, spurring a young Samuel Colt to tinker with a revolving pistol that no one wanted until a Single Texas Ranger pleaded his case to the government, and years later, providing the Union Army with Christopher Spencer's repeating rifle only after numerous unsuccessful sales pitches to the War Department. Where else would one of the most successful military vehicles in wartime, the Jeep, have come from the designs submitted by the private sector rather than a government facility? Where else would merely the potential of American technological dominance to create a "Star Wars" missile defense bring the "Evil Empire" to its knees, breaking its economy over the threat posed by a system not yet built, with gizmos not yet proven?

Americans win wars because they have wedded their own free-market principles and concepts of human worth to a national purpose that is relentlessly checked by civilian audit. Americans win wars because we tolerate and accept as a fact of life an ongoing antimilitary segment of society whose constant criticism, much to their dismay, pushes our armed forces to even greater economy with our soldiers' lives and to even greater efficiency of destroying our enemies. America's victories also often result because we are constantly sold short. Mao Zedong stated, *"The U.S. has a population of 200 million people, but it cannot stand wars,"* and Joseph Stalin snorted, *"Americans don't know how to fight."*[4] The American military has been underestimated by British imperialists (twice), Barbary thugs, a Mexican tin-pot dictator and a pompous Spanish monarch, German Imperial aggressors and then lunatic Nazis, Japanese warlords, Communist mass murderers of both the Russian and Chinese variety, Middle Eastern Islamofascists and their terrorist puppets, and most recently an autocratic homicidal Mesopotamian brute. In the Revolution, British commanders confidently expected to rout the peasants in the militias and the Continentals under George Washington. Seventy years later, both Mexican and European observers predicted that Santa Anna would march into New Orleans and Mobile-maybe even Washington-within weeks. A half century after that, Spain had what the world thought was a first-class navy, while the United States had not fought at sea since the War of 1812. When war broke out in Europe in 1914, German strategist Erich Ludendorff gambled that American forces would collapse when confronted by the professionals of the German army, and twenty-five years after Ludendorff was proven wrong, Adolf Hitler confidently laid plans to send waves of his new Amerika bomber to force the United States into surrender. For half a century, Communist dictators such as Stalin and Mao poured manpower and treasure into "brush wars" in Korea, Vietnam, Nicaragua, and Grenada, confident that lazy Americans, comfortable with their homes and entertainment, could not muster the will to stop them; (Even Mao admitted he was wrong: *"I never thought [the Americans] would attack North Vietnam,"* he told Pham Van Dong in 1968.)[5] And most recently, Osama bin Laden devised a strategy, based on a faulty reading of American actions in Somalia that he willingly shared with Saddam Hussein: that Americans would not tolerate casualties in order to enforce national policy.

One of the reasons the enemies of the United States consistently underestimate the American soldier is that they mistake the carping of a few for the common sense of the many. America's enemies look at antiwar leftists and assume their views are those of the majority. Those images can indeed be damaging in a number of ways. Jane Fonda posed publicly on an antiaircraft gun that had been used to shoot down-and kill-American pilots. Peter Collier, a onetime Communist activist, recalled in his biography that his cadre of antiwar fellow travelers would sit in front of the television set nightly and cheer as Walter Cronkite announced the latest American casualties from the war.[6] (This seems light years away from Americans at the home front in World War II who cheered enemy casualty numbers). Few nationally prominent liberals, for example, have disavowed Ward Churchill's comparison of the people inside the World Trade Center to "little Eichmanns"; little outrage can be found on the Left over the comments of a professor to a student that soldiers in Iraq should turn their guns on their own officers; and only a handful on the Left have denounced "war mom" Cindy Sheehan's

---

[4]Michael Lind, Vietnam: The Necessary War (New York: Touchstone, 1999), inside flyleaf.
[5]Lind, Vietnam, p. 47.
[6]Peter Collier and David Horowitz, Destructive Generation: Second Thoughts About the Sixties (New York: Summit, 1989), p. 264.

claims that Americans are the real terrorists—presidential aspirant Hillary Clinton being one of the main exceptions. Increasingly, the message from the Left is that 9/11 was an act of desperation brought on by the oppressive American presence in the world-especially the Muslim world. Or, put bluntly, in their view, we deserved it.

The actions of "Gold Star mom" Cindy Sheehan, an antiwar activist long before her son Casey (a volunteer) was killed in combat, prompted the mainstream media to invoke the Vietnam Template. According to the Vietnam Template, a war becomes a "quagmire" (especially if a Republican is president) if within a few days of the insertion of American troops, the enemy doesn't throw up his hands and beg for mercy. For example, on October 30, 2000 just in time for Halloween, the *New York Times's* R. W. Apple, Jr., admitting that fighting had only started three weeks earlier, gleefully asked, *"Could Afghanistan become another Vietnam?"*[7] (In this, Apple was joined by the esteemed, and somewhat nutty, Libyan dictator Muammar Gaddafi, who prophesied a—you guessed it—"quagmire.")[8] Consider that as George H. W. Bush edged closer to sending troops to Kuwait in 1991, Senator Ted Kennedy hysterically warned that a Gulf war would result in 45,000 American deaths.[9] Prior to the invasion of Afghanistan to root out the Taliban and destroy al Qaeda, Leftist pundits proclaimed that the United States was walking into another "quagmire." USA Today obligingly published solemn articles about the difficulty of the terrain in Afghanistan, and commentators soberly pointed out that both the British Empire and the Soviets had failed to take the country. American and allied forces crushed the Taliban and al Qaeda terrorists in record time, bombing Osama bin Laden either into hiding or the infernal regions. An estimated two thirds of al Qaeda fighters were eliminated in Operation Enduring Freedom in a matter of weeks, all in a country that "could not be taken." Today, the same "quagmire" comments are thrown out routinely to describe ... Iraq. A Lexis-Nexus search of the terms Vietnam, Iraq, and quagmire yields more hits than Jessica Simpson would get at a high school dance.

According to the Vietnam Template, de facto application of military force by the United States (especially against a Communist foe) is immoral, and therefore the cosmic sense of justice demands that we lose. If Americans are successful in such wars, it only results in "hubris" according to this template; and if we do not lose, then the Vietnam Template insists that there must be a nefarious explanation, such as "torture camps" or massacres of civilians. For that reason, when the Abu Ghraib prison scandal surfaced, the mainstream media was convinced it had found the smoking gun that would also convince the American public that our presence in Iraq was unjust and ill fated. In April and May of 2004, the New York Times alone had thirty consecutive page-one stories on the prison "scandal."

Above all, the Vietnam Template reserves its most vehement criticism for those occasions when the United States acts unilaterally to protect its interests.

[7] R. W. Apple, Jr., "Quagmire Recalled: Afghanistan as Vietnam," New York Times, October 30, 2001.

[8] Giles Trequesser, "Gaddafi Says U.S. Risks Quagmire in Afghanistan," Afghan News, September 17, 2001.

[9] Jennifer Verner, "Ted Kennedy's Jihad," http://www.frontpagemag.com/Articles/ReadArticle.asp?ID=13510.

Calls for the United States to develop coalitions and "work with others" sounds sincere, but often they are attempts to deliberately water down our incredibly effective military with, to be blunt, minor-leaguers from other nations. While no one doubts the commitment of these nations and the sacrifices of their troops—some of which, such as the Britons, Australians, and New Zealanders, are exceptionally good-too often these forces exist as second-tier units to free Americans for the hard work of killing the enemy. In his famous Gulf War briefing, General Norman Schwarzkopf lauded the Saudi and Kuwaiti units for their hard fighting without stating the obvious: they achieved much of their success because American air and sea power had already "attrited" (in the general's words) up to 75 percent of the forces they would encounter.

Concerns about unilateral action, however, more often than not reflect a concern about the moral authority to use troops, not the efficiency with which they will operate. To many on the Left, any decision to deploy troops in our own self-interest constitutes a form of "bullying" and arrogance toward the "international community." Moreover, unilateral use of troops suggests that we, in fact, know what is good for us without having to rely on the opinions of others, some of whom have long quietly been our enemies.

Further, when it comes to the Vietnam Template, it is unfair to demonize your enemies: An oppressive Soviet dictatorship must not be referred to as an "Evil Empire." Homicidal killer Saddam Hussein must be "humanized," hence we have video footage of him eating Doritos. Terror mastermind al-Zawahiri is pictured as suave and mysterious, in a classy suit, no different from a European businessman selling software. Suspects at Gitmo are portrayed as naive, innocent, and almost childlike, wanting only to read their Korans and pray to Mecca, not understanding why they are detained in such a "hell hole." Hard-core propaganda, such as the cartoons and comic strips produced by Walt Disney and Dr. Seuss in World War II, is verboten. CNN cannot even call terrorists "terrorists;" the language of reporting the Iraq war is that imported foreign terrorists are "insurgents," and suicide bombers who march into London subways are "suspects." Labeling Osama bin Laden, al Qaeda, or other terror sponsors "evil" is viewed as "incendiary" and "counterproductive," and may result in alienation of people around the world by the United States. Seeking out the source of suicide bombers' funding or locating the state providers of their bombs is "unnecessarily widening the war." "Who, after all, is a terrorists we frequently hear the pundits ask.

One fact stands out: privately, those who employ the Vietnam Template know Americans can't be beaten on the battlefield, so they rely on a stealth campaign at home. They raise "concerns" by "serious observers," "defense analysts," and former military officers (mostly promoted up the chain in the Clinton administration) about any perceived weakness in the strategy or conduct of the war.

More than in earlier periods of American history, antiwar activists have been largely unable to fan any moral outrage over American military operations abroad, mainly because our interventions have liberated millions. Unable to play the morality card, all that has remained for the mainstream media's Vietnam Template is to emphasize the cost in the form of casualties. Thus, there was a truly ghoulish death watch approaching, first, the thousandth death in Iraq, then the two thousandth. Yet by historical military standards, these are phenomenally low numbers, which required the media to produce articles asserting that the superior health care wounded soldiers are receiving has actually contributed to a lower quality of life for those with serious wounds-ignoring entirely the obvious fact that more wounded are surviving than in any previous military conflict. Focusing solely on the dead also requires that reporting ignore the motivations of why we have gone to war, and why these gallant fighters signed up in the first place. The Vietnam Template commandeth: Remember the casket, forget the cause.

And if you really want to go off the deep Left end, look at the scribblings of Frances Fox Piven, who maintains that *military aggression ... paved the way for ... plundering Americans. The predatory beast is turning on its own.*[10] For the Left, you see, every war comes down to money—a "war for oil" or some other resource. Vietnam, the New Left revisionists told us, was all about expanding the influence of "multinational corporations" in newly developing regions of the world. By Marxist definition, after all, only capitalist countries can engage in "imperialism."

Fortunately, these phrases don't resonate quite as well today as they did forty or fifty years ago. Too many Americans (and citizens of other countries) have seen the United States liberate country after country—then leave. Only the United States Congress would pass a resolution requiring that we leave a conquered country (Cuba) after the Spanish-American War within five years. We were out of Grenada so fast American troops didn't even have time to paint KILROY WAS HERE on a Grenadian wall. In the past sixty years, American military forces have voluntarily withdrawn from "occupied" countries- Saudi Arabia, the Philippines, France, the Benelux countries, Haiti, and Liberia-so many times that the local motels are considering seasonal rates. In still other nations occupied by American forces, such as Japan and Germany, small contingents of troops remain with the host country's permission, and attempts to scale down or remove them have been met with desperate pleadings that they remain. When U.S. forces withdrew from Subic Bay Naval Base in the Philippines in 1991, a protester waved a sign that said, YANKEE GO HOME—AND TAKE ME WITH YOU![11] To the extent that there are any "permanent" bases abroad-as there are in Germany or South Korea-watch the local angst if we so much as hint at pulling out. It's much the same at home: about the only time you can find Ted Kennedy acting friendly toward the Pentagon is when it is considering dosing a military base in Massachusetts. When the blue-ribbon base-dosing panel made its recommendations in 2005, the howls of protests from senators who rarely have a good word for the U.S. military could

---

[10]Frances Fox Piven, The War at Home: The Domestic Costs of Bush's Militarism (New York: New Press, 2004), p. 12.
[11]Max Boot, Savage Wars of Peace: Small Wars and the Rise of American Power (New York: Basic books, 2002), p. 125.

be heard as far away as Timbuktu.

Previous generations of Americans would not have tolerated the antics of the Left, nor allowed America's military operations to be defined by the Vietnam Template. Andrew Jackson would have shot Abbie Hoffman and David Dellinger (probably personally); George Washington likely would have hanged them-after a fair military tribunal. The more generous Abraham Lincoln might have met with Cindy Sheehan, but certainly Ulysses Grant would have jailed her and the press as well. The bombastic Teddy Roosevelt can be pictured personally giving Ward Churchill a sound pummeling, and turning Jane Fonda over his knee for a turn-of-the-century spanking!

Yet, ironically, it is this very freedom of expression that ensures still more American victories. The very antiwar activism that infuses a substantially antimilitary media results paradoxically in a high profile for leftist sentiments that are not shared by the majority. In turn, the antimilitary Left feeds the tendency of others to underestimate the American willingness to fight, and, if we stick it out, usually to win.

America's victories reflect the fact that the sanctity of life remains at the heart of the American soul. While casualties are unavoidable in any combat situation, and while almost certainly noncombatants will be killed in wars, the American view that all life has value has imposed a rigid economy of human life on our military. The motto "Leave no man behind" would be unthinkable among the Islamic terrorists or in Japan's Bushido code. It was equally inapplicable on behalf of the Nazi youth squads armed with Panzerfaust antitank weapons who were being annihilated in droves as Joseph Goebbels heartlessly wrote them off as "unworthy" of National Socialism, or when Adolf Hitler demanded the 6th Army not retreat from Stalingrad. Likewise, Mexican dictator Santa Anna dismissed the lives of his men at the Alamo as so many "chickens," ordering a costly frontal assault when he easily could have reduced the walls by cannon fire. The American emphasis on human life, even when it comes to the treatment of prisoners, has inexorably pushed the United States military toward greater and greater combat efficiency, for in the end, war is all about who lives and who dies. And, as Patton said, *"No one ever won a war by dying for his country...."* In short, the American obsession with casualties has consistently produced fewer of them.

America's victories affirm the principles that make America great: free expression yields better ideas; a free market outperforms planned, collectivist economies; individual freedom and autonomy produce better soldiers; admitting mistakes and learning from them only makes you stronger; and the sanctity of life that makes U.S. forces the most casualty conscious in history has, at the same time, made them the most deadly. Americans win wars because what makes us free also makes us fierce, and that ferocity will ultimately propel us to victory in the War on Terror.

CHAPTER ONE
Gitmo, Gulags, and Great Raids

The United States military has a higher regard for human life—American and foreign, friend and foe—than any other force in history. And no other military has gone to such lengths to treat enemy prisoners well and to rescue its own prisoners in enemy hands.

On, paper, the 78,100 American and Filipino soldiers who squared off against the 200,000 Japanese troops on Bataan in late March, 1942, seemed a solid, if not formidable, force. Although they had abandoned most of Luzon as indefensible, the Americans and their Philippine allies had taken up positions along a line stretching through jungle and over mountains from Bagac on the western coast of Bataan to Orion on the eastern side. Dug in, with General Jonathan Wainwright's 11,000-strong force holding the island fortress of Corregidor at their backs, under normal conditions the two sides might have been nearly equal.

In reality, most of the Americans and their allies were already whipped, perhaps with the exception of the 4th Marine Regiment. Only one regular United States Army regiment, the 31st Infantry, opposed the Japanese. A handful of American tanks and a hodgepodge of other special units augmented a mostly ill-trained Filipino force. These men were starving—down to fifteen ounces of food a day each—devoid of any air support at all, and low on ammunition and other supplies. Food, above all, was the main problem. Men were already reduced to eating "wallpaper paste," a tasteless gummy rice unaccompanied by meat, vegetables, or fruit. Two meager rice mills the Americans had constructed earlier now labored unsuccessfully to feed the troops that, Wainwright warned Washington, would soon be "starved into submission." [1] Wainwright, however, was under orders not to surrender, and he had dutifully commanded his subordinate on Bataan, Major General Edward P. King, Jr., not to surrender either. But King was out of options. His men were deteriorating by the day, and soon many would be too sick even to move to a prison camp. King therefore drew up a list of points raised for "Japanese consideration"—a surrender document—including care for the many in two major Bataan hospitals and how and where American troops should surrender. Communication was difficult beyond degree, with roads choked by retreating soldiers, Japanese fighter planes strafing and bombing troops in the open, and another fleeing 20,000 Filipino civilians adding to the chaos. As a result, the Americans received inconsistent and uneven orders to assemble at Balanga, on the western coast of Manila Bay. Soon more than 100,000 soldiers and civilians wandered

---

[1]Stanley L. Falk, Bataan: The March of Death (New York: W. W. Norton, 1962), p.32.

northward to their "official" processing point, most guarded, some not.

Immediately the Japanese engaged in brutality, massacring the 400 men of the Filipino 91st Division, who, hands tied behind their backs, were lined up along a narrow ravine, and shot. Imperial soldiers marched into the two main field hospitals, defecating and urinating next to the wounded, observing no medical protocol at all. Japanese infantry, used to abusive training, grueling marches, and low rations, expected the starving GIs and their allies to keep pace, and many were bayoneted where they fell. Treatment varied with the guards because there had been almost no formal instructions issued by Lieutenant General Masaharu Homma, and one column, marched to Cabanatuan in the hot sun, had a single two-hour rest period with no water for a journey of almost a hundred miles. Most fell out due to hunger or thirst, or simple exhaustion. Sometimes Japanese troops rode by in trucks and shared water; sometimes they beat or tortured the prisoners where they fell. One group of Americans marched all the way to Balanga without guards. Colonel John Ball, told to set the pace for his column of Americans, tried to slow down as the men struggled to keep up, until the Japanese caught on to this tactic and smashed him in the back of his head with a rifle butt.[2]

Many who dropped to the ground out of exhaustion continued to crawl on knees and elbows, aware that if they stopped, they could expect a bayonet or a slow death by starvation or thirst. Japanese guards on bicycles swung batons or heavy wooden sticks, shouting *Bakayaro!*" (Stupid idiot!). At all points they took personal items: watches, rings, or anything else of value. Although one American officer persuaded a Japanese private to trade watches, rather than just take his, another protesting American was yanked out of line and shot instantly. Oddly enough, the Japanese seemed disinterested in items that might be truly valuable militarily, including diaries, manuals, plans, and photographs. Woe to the American found with any Japanese souvenirs on his person, which earned an immediate beating, if not a bayonet, for sealing from the dead. Some who possessed Japanese yen were beheaded, but the constant walking in the burning sun with no water was torture as well. Prisoners testified after the war that they had not been given water for several days at a time, and when they were allowed to drink, it was from rice paddies full of local Philippine carabao (cow) dung.

It took days for prisoners to arrive in Balanga, and yet the Death March of Bataan had only started. The Japanese intended to move the assembled prisoners to Camp O'Donnell, more than fifty miles north of Balanga as the crow flies, but much farther by the winding trial or road the men would have to take. As thousands of new prisoner arrived at Balanga, the filth and stench became unbearable: men passed out trying to relieve themselves in the thickets designated by the Japanese as "bathrooms." Malaria and dysentery ravaged the prisoners. At bayonet point, the Japanese forced a detail of Americans to dig a slit trench and bury alive ten sick Filipinos. One man who sat up was instantly bayoneted.[3]

Out of Balanga, the Japanese finally attempted to move men by truck,

---

[2]Falk, March of Death, pp.122-23.
[3]Falk, March of Death, p. 147.

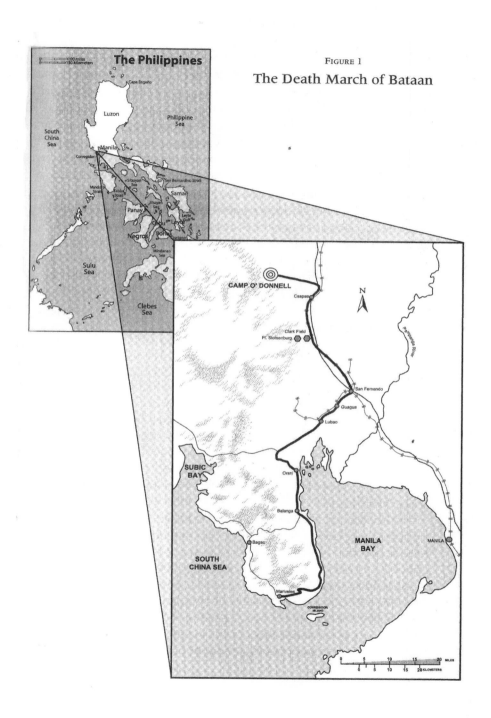

FIGURE 1

The Death March of Bataan

but only between one seventh and one third of the prisoners were transported in such a manner, depending on whose testimony you accept. Among the marchers, anyone falling out for any reason was shot, including a weakened colonel who fell down behind the column. When the prisoners came into a mango grove, and one of them tried to climb the tree for the fruit just above their heads, he, too, was shot. One group, defying Japanese rifle fire, ran into a sugarcane field, stripped the bark from the cane and put it in their mouths, then ran back into line before their captors could kill them. Officers, especially, drew the Japanese guard's ire. Soldiers riding by on trucks or bicycles routinely smacked anyone with stars on his shoulders, but clubbing all prisoners from trucks appeared to be a favorite sport.

At Lubao, about a third of the way to Camp O'Donnell, the Japanese finally furnished meals. Then, at San Fernando, halfway to their final destination, the men were crammed into steamy railroad cars, packed so densely that once a man was in place, he was locked in that position for the duration. The steel sides of the metal boxcars seared the flesh of anyone unfortunate enough to touch them, and men racked by dysentery relieved themselves on their fellow prisoners. There was no choice. Unloaded at Capas, the troops faced a final march to Camp O'Donnell. There, Filipino civilians braved Japanese guards to give the prisoners food and water, then went on to their prison. Japan's "humanitarian principles of Bushido" had resulted in about 650 American dead out of the approximately 10,000 who had begun the march, and between 5,000 and 10,000 Filipino dead of the approximately 42,000 prisoners who left Bataan.[4] By any definition of the word, what the Japanese did on Bataan was torture.

And if that didn't qualify as torture, perhaps what followed in December 1944, at Puerto Princesa Prison Camp in the Philippines, did. When American Liberator bombers appeared overhead, the Japanese guards herded 150 American prisoners into "dark, poorly ventilated pits" that served as air-raid shelters.[5] But on that day the prisoners were not put there to protect them from air attacks, but to execute them. Moments later Japanese soldiers burst into the compound carrying buckets filled with high-octane aviation fuel, which they flung into the pits. Then before the Americans could react, the Japanese hurled in torches, roasting the prisoners alive.

---

[4] Falk, March of Death, p. 191. Numbers are difficult to validate because no one knows for certain how many escaped, how many actually began the march, and so on. The Japanese lack of organization made numbers meaningless from their end. Among other sources, see Louis Morton, The Fall of the Philippines (Washington: Government Printing Office, 1953); Donald Knox, Death March: The Survivors of Bataan (New York: Harcourt Brace Jovanovich, 1981); William E. Dyess, The Dyess Story (New York: G.P. Putnam's Sons, 1944); and evidence in the war crimes trial of General Homma, "United States of America vs. Masaharu Homma, before the Military Commission convened by the Commanding General, United States Army Forces Western Pacific, (1946)" in the World War II Records Division, National Archives, Alexandria, Virginia. Some maintain that the Death March was contrary to the principles of Bushido (David Bergamini, Japan's Imperial Conspiracy, New York: William Morrow, 1971), but, in fact, officers and men who did not act brutally were punished by the military in some cases; and in any event, the overall record does not support the more "honorable" view of Bushido.

[5] Hampton Sides, Ghost Soldiers: The Forgotten Epic Story of World War II's Most Dramatic Mission (New York: Doubleday, 2001), p. 10.

Club Gitmo

On June 14, 2005, Senator Dick Durbin (D-IL) made a speech on the floor of the United States Senate in which he quoted an FBI report about conditions at the Guantánamo Bay prison for terror suspects. After describing these conditions, which ranged from air-conditioning not working to playing pop songbird Christian Aguilera and rap music as "torture techniques" (to which no rappers apparently took offense), Durbin set off a firestorm by comparing the experience of the prisoners to the death camps of *Nazis, Soviets in their gulags, or some made regime—Pol Pot or others—that had no concern for human beings.*" [6] Despite evidence disproving him, Congressman Charles Rangel continued well into the war to maintain that American aircraft had bombed "innocent women and children." On the one year-year anniversary of the Abu Ghraib scandal, Senator Ted Kennedy repeated the claim that there were "torture techniques" used at Guantánamo prison, and described "cruel interrogation tactics" used in Iraq, Afghanistan, and Guantánamo, including the *use of painful stress positions, sexual humiliation, threatening prisoners with dogs, and shipping detainees to countries that practice torture.*"[7] Abu Ghraib, Professor Frances Fox Piven claimed, *"was nearly emptied in the last days of Saddam's regime [but] in filling up again."*[8]

    And was there torture? If you consider forcing a terrorist to "wear a bra, dance with another man and behave like a dog," then perhaps torture existed at Guantánamo Bay prison. Even then, the chief investigator, Air Force Lieutenant General Randall Schmidt, said flatly that "no torture occurred." His report concluded there was no *evidence to support the allegation that the detainees were denied food and water.*" One of the most common forms of "abuse" was continuous "loud music." When contrasted with shocking portraits of Holocaust victims, starved to skeletal depths, and mass graves and ovens, the definition of Christina Aguilera as "torture" has reached new heights. Perhaps one of the most astounding examples of American "torture" involved Abdullah M., who was missing a leg when he got to "Gitmo," where he was fitted with a prosthetic leg and rehabbed before being released and repatriated to Afghanistan. He is now sought for involvement in the 2004 bombing of the Islamabad Marriott.

    Actually, however, the official report was incomplete because it did not include the abuse at Gitmo—of American guards by the prisoners. One anonymous eyewitness, who spent time investigating Gitmo but who, as an intelligence analyst, could not reveal his name, visited there in June 2005. The writer encountered the following incidents: American guards had to black out their name tags because terrorists threatened to tell al Qaeda operatives still not in custody to

[6]U.S. Senate, floor statement by Senator Dick Durbin on Guantánamo Bay, June 14, 2005, http://durbin.senate.gov/gitmo.cf.

[7]Senator Ted Kennedy, "Abu Ghraib—One Year Later,: http://tedkennedy.com/journal/59/abu-ghraib-one-year-later.

[8]Frances Fox Piven, The War at Home: The Domestic Costs of Bush's Militarism (New York: New Press, 2004), p. 92.

"look you up on the Internet" and "slaughter you and your family in your homes at night." Guards were routinely bombarded with feces, urine, and semen as the attempted to deliver food or water. Worse, guards were assaulted by prisoners, hit with chairs, bitten, scratched—all without permission to retaliate. When on soldier did smack a detainee with a handheld radio, trying to get him off another MP, the soldier was dropped in rank; and in another incident, when an MP sprayed an inmate with a hose after the detainee doused the MP with water from his toilet, the guard was charged with assault. Most Americans would find such retaliation not only understandable, but probably desirable under the circumstances.

Then there were the tall tales of one Marine Staff Sergeant, Jimmy Massey, which the mainstream media (MSM) scooped up uncritically. Massey claimed to have shot and killed peaceful Iraqi protesters, seen Americans shoot a four-year-old girl in the head, and observed tractor trailers filled with the bodies of Iraqi civilians killed by Americans. He even published a book (appropriately enough, released in France) called Kill, Kill, Kill. It should have been entitled, Lie, Lie, Lie. Even as news organizations rushed to broadcast Massey's claims, they never bothered to find out if they were true. Even a simple phone call to the Marine Corps would have revealed that his claims were false, yet it wasn't until late 2005, when the St. Louis Post-Dispatch investigated his allegations, that they were found baseless. Editors later shook their heads at how they had been hornswaggled by a self-avowed Cindy Sheehan supporter, but at the time it never crossed their minds to verify the claims. The horrific stories just fit the MSM's template for the Iraq war too well.

Antiwar activists, reporters, and protesters well know that Americans' deep concern for human rights can be used against the military. What they miss is the very truth of that concern: we believe in justice when dealing with our enemies, and in showing mercy whenever practical. These beliefs are ingrained in all Americans, especially those in the military, and contrary to popular notions, they are even inherent in the American military tradition of demanding unconditional surrender, for Americans assume that there is no need for legitimate military foe to worry about submitting when he will be dealt with justly. Such was the case in the Civil War, where virtually entire armies were paroled, released, exchanged, or otherwise sent on their way—with one major exception. At Fort Pillow, in April 1864, Confederate troops under General Nathan Bedford Forrest (who would later become the first Imperial Wizard of the Ku Klux Klan) massacred black Union troops who had surrendered. And in almost any war, including those fought by Americans, individual incidents of brutality occur. Reports (many of which remain undocumented) of individual American soldiers taking the gold teeth of dead Japanese, or shooting prisoners, or adorning a jeep with a Nazi skull emerged after World War II, but official policy and overall military practice dealt harshly with those who violated the principle of mercy for prisoners.

Paroling prisoners in the nineteenth century was a Western principle that evolved for three reasons: first, there was no adequate means to control, feed, or shelter them; second, officers could often by ransomed; and third, simply murdering them was out of the question due to the strictures of Christianity and the Western notions of right to life. Hence, in the twenty-first century, America's terrorist prisoners at Gitmo eat better and have facilities far more comfortable than their "free" civilian counterparts in Cuba, just across the wire.

Durbin's accusations became so ludicrous that talk show host Rush Limbaugh alluded to "Club G'itmo," a "Caribbean vacation resort" for jihadists, and offered Club G'itmo gear on his Web site. Among the items for sale was a T-shirt that said:

MY MULLAH WENT TO GLUB G'ITMO AND ALL I GOT WAS THIS LOUSY T-SHIRT, I GOT MY FREE KORAN AND PRAYER RUG AT G'ITMO or YOUR TROPICAL RETREAT FROM THE STRESS OF JIHAD,

as well as Club G'itmo Soap-on-a-Rope. His original "Club G'itmo Brochure" featured pictures of captured jihadists on sailboats, jet skis, and in fancy beach hotel rooms. The phenomenon caught on so quickly that people soon were appearing with the Club G'itmo T-shirts in highly public places, such as baseball games, and sending their photos to Rush. The parody was stinging. When only a few years ago Saddam was literally murdering dissidents at Abu Ghraib, then later, when American prisoners of al Qaeda, such as Nick Berg, were beheaded (with the grisly execution videotaped), here was a prison facility where inmates were given three square meals a day, provided with prayer rugs and Korans at federal expense (when courts had ruled that Bibles could not be distributed in schools due to "separation of church and state), and pop icons. The notion that Americans were "abusing" much less "torturing" al Qaeda terrorists at Gitmo was laughable when the United States was going out of its way to provide religious liberties often denied American school children!

One of the main reasons Americans do care for their prisoners, and even respect the human rights of terrorists like José Padilla and Richard Riady, is that the United States adheres to Western concepts of sanctity of life, derived from the Bible and from the Greco-Roman traditions of individual worth or purpose (telos). These principles did not develop instantly, and well into the Roman Republic, captured people were enslaved and males worked to death in mines. Unquestionably, there were limits to these concepts. To the Jews, Gentiles were goyim; to the Greeks, non-Greeks were barbarians. Almost all of these cultures accepted the concept of natural slaves, and everyone believed that those defeated in battle entered into subjugated status de facto. Still, Jewish law called for just economic and political practices for strangers or Gentiles, and slaves were to be offered freedom after seven years—a remarkable change in human affairs that defied practices elsewhere. Most Western cultures provided means by which those in servitude could acquire freedom and even citizenship in some cases, and the Romans realized that a carrot of civic participation was worth several sticks of punishment by crucifixion. Alexander and Caesar both pragmatically applied the principle that treating prisoners well sent a message to enemy forces still in the field that there was no need to fight to the death. Romans even extended selected citizenship to some captured peoples. Under Roman law, military service of thirty years automatically made one a full citizen, and applied to some foreign mercenaries. This concept mixed with the practices of Germanic tribes wherein anyone who participated in the hazards of war had a voice in the decision to go to war, a sort of protodemocracy from the Thüringen Forest. [9] Throughout the Middle Ages, Christian doctrines continued to refine and temper combat, especially because it was still all too common for knights to kill innocent peasants during individual battles. And without question there were murderous rampages during the Crusades, though these often had far more complex causes than mere bloodlust.[10] To be sure, the transition from the rights of nobles to the rights of man was slow and (literally) tortuous. It was common for kings to slaughter the inhabitants of enemy towns that fell to them (though nobles were saved for ransom). Excesses in the name of the Church were plentiful. Still, by the millennium, a link was forged between church and state in which knights gained their titles no only through the grant of the lord or king, but also with the blessing of the Church. Investiture became a religious ceremony, and while many (even, perhaps, most) took their sacred vows with a grain of salt, the underlying assumptions that even peasants had worth permeated Western Europe, and lay behind efforts to control carnage among knights with such clerical edicts as the Truce of God and the Peace of God.

Whether good or ill for the long-term health of Western civilization, rights as emanating from Good soon gave way to concepts of natural rights, to which all were entitled— even one's enemies—and after the Magna Carta, such rights (whether applied to commoners or not) started to seep into the fabric of the entire system. Treatment of prisoners started to fall under both religious and political strictures, which, of course, were not always followed. At Agincourt, Henry's troops, afraid the French knights had circled behind them, slashed the throats of dozens of French noblemen held captive. (This was bad business, as well as sinful, in that captives were routinely ransomed back to the prisoners' families.) And while certainly a wide berth was permitted in areas of religion, as with Joan of Arc's execution, treatment of prisoners improved unless one engaged in what was viewed as outright treason (in the case of William Wallace, aka Braveheart, where the response still included lengthy torture sessions). By the 1700s, this gradual transformation had resulted in "civilized" armies whose prisoners were held in facilities that met at least some minimal standards at the victor's expense or were repatriated in an exchange.[11]

This did not prevent the British from essentially killing some 13,000

---

[9]Reinhard Bendix, Kings or People: the Mandate to Rule (Berkeley: University of California Press, 1980).

[10]See Christopher Tynan, God's War: A New History of the Crusades (Harvard: Belknap, 2006), especially pp. 477-560 and the discussion of the slaughter in Byzantium during the Fourth Crusade.

[11]Armstrong Stuckey, The Military Experience in the Age of Enlightenment (Westport, CT: Prager, 2003).

American patriots on their "hell ships" in New York Harbor under the direction of Provost Marshal William Cunningham. The British prison ship Jersey alone, the largest prison hulk, held some 10,000 men who were (most say deliberately) underfed ad given no medical treatment, leading to thousands of deaths by malnutrition and disease. Many were buried near the site of the Brooklyn Navy Yard. Other British prisons at churches, poorhouses, and schools accounted for perhaps another 2,500 dead revolutionaries. Cunningham, who was executed for forgery in England in 1791, gave a full confession of the atrocities under his command just before he was hanged, admitting to secret executions of "*275 American prisoners and obnoxious persons.*" [12] In his confession, he wrote:

> *A guard was dispatched from the Provost about half after 12, at night, to Barrack Street and the neighborhood of Upper Barracks, to order the people to shut their window shutters, and put out their lights, forbidding them not to presume to look out of their windows or doors, on pain of death; after which the unfortunate prisoners were conducted, gagged, just behind the Upper Barracks, and hung without ceremony and there buried by the lack pioneers of the Provost.* [13]

In addition to the infamous Jersey, the British held hundreds of patriots on Whitby, Good Hope, Prince of Wales, Falmouth, Scorpion, Strombolo, and Hunter. Out of the 20,000 held captive, however, fewer than 6,000 were actually soldiers, while another 9,000 sailors could be considered military personnel if the government determined they were acting in the interests of the Revolution. This behavior was recognized as contrary to "civilized" behavior by then.

For his part, George Washington simply pardoned most British prisoners because he had no facilities for keeping them long, although some, such as the Ticonderoga prisoners, were retained and fed. Many of the Hessians taken prisoner at Trenton and Princeton remained in America and became citizens. Loyalists and Tories were expected—but not forced—to leave after the Revolution. Otherwise, by the time of the Republic, the United States had started to surpass in its treatment of prisoners its British forefathers. Hellholes like Andersonville still marred prisoner treatment in the Civil War, and instances of American soldiers' shooting surrendering enemy combatants in the field occurred in both world wars, but the concept of human worth and rights—even of prisoners—was at work more frequently than not. [14]

Benign and humane treatment by American captors, however, was seldom reciprocated. After the Japanese conquest of Wake Island—a thorn in the side of the Japanese Empire for several weeks—several soldiers were beheaded on the Nitta Maru in retaliation for the garrison's staunch defense of Wake. Later, civilian prisoners were kept on the island to prepare defensive positions against the Americans. When they finished, Rear Admiral Shigematsu Sakaibara had

---

[12]Provost Marshal William Cunningham quoted at http://longislandgenealogy.com/prison.html.

[13]Cunningham's statement appears on http//longislandgenealogy.com/prison.html.

[14]John S.D. Eisenhower, Yanks: The Epic Story of the American Army in World War I (New York: Free Press, 2001), p.172.

ninety-eight American contractors lined up on the beach and machine-gunned, then, for good measure, bayoneted. American military prisoners from Wake held in Japan were told by their guards that if the U.S. forces came ashore, *"we would be the first to go,"* said one survivor.[15] A document that surfaced after the war revealed that the Japanese planned a massive extermination program—a "final disposition," as it called the killing of prisoners—which instructed that "whether they [prisoners] are destroyed individually or in groups ... with mass b*ombing, poisons, drowning, decapitation, or what, dispose of them as the situation dictates ... [and] annihilate them all, and do not leaves any traces."* [16]

In his second trip to Iraq after Saddam's fall, writer Karl Zinsmeister argued that American goodness and restraint was the main reason the United States has succeeded in Afghanistan and Iraq when the Soviets failed in similar battles against Islamic insurgents in Afghanistan and Chechnya.[17] Word got out that the Americans took prisoners and treated them well, meaning there was little reason to fight to the death. Zinsmeister repeatedly observed American commanders exercising patience beyond all reason, and yet it produced fruit: it was not unusual, he reported in 2003, for Iraqis to *"criticize Americans for being insufficiently ruthless in dealing with the insurgents* (emphasis in original)."[18] (This echoed the complaint by Manuel Quezon, a lieutenant in Emilio Aguinaldo's Philippine insurgency in the early 1900s, that it was impossible to stoke the fires of anti-Americanism because of the Yankees' benevolence: *"Damn the Americans! Why don't they tyrannize us more?"*)[19] Despite some polls that showed Iraqis disapproving of American forces, when pollsters go to the nitty-gritty question "How long should the Americans stay?" they were stunned to find in almost every poll that large majorities thought the United States needed to remain in Iraq at least two years. Surveys also revealed that the Iraqis were fed up with the insurgents: 78 percent found attacks on Coalition forces "unacceptable."[20] In an Arab world where, in some nations, more than 90 percent lionized Osama bin Laden, 57 percent of Iraqis viewed him unfavorably—and 41 percent of those, "very" unfavorably!

Most Western armies engage in extensive planning to receive and process prisoners, and one of the biggest problems of the Gulf War in 1991 was that Iraqis were surrendering too fast. Tankers enveloping Saddam's army recalled they would throw MREs (meals ready to eat) and bottled water to the Iraqi prisoners and pint them toward the rear, where someone else would eventually process them. Nearly 100 Iraqi soldiers surrendered to a CNN news crew!

But that is the humorous side of what can often be a deadly situation:

[15]John Wukovits, Pacific Alamo: The Battle for Wake Island (New York: New American Library, 2003), pp.208, 236, 242.
[16]Wokovits, Pacific Alamo, p.242
[17]Karl Zinsmeister, Dawn Over Baghdad: How the U.S. Military Is Using Bullets and Ballots to Remake Iraq (New York: Encounter Books, 2004), p.107.
[18] Zinsmeister, Dawn Over Baghdad, p.93.
[19] Max Boot, Savage Wars of Peace: Small Wars and the Rise of American Power (New York: Basic Books, 2002), p. 125.
[20]Zinsmeister, Dawn Over Baghdad, p.88

in Sicily in 1943, American troops found a number of German soldiers faking surrender, then attacking the U.S. troops. In response to these reports, Americans behaved more aggressively toward prisoners, such as in the two incidents near Biscari where 73 Italian POWs were massacred by a captain and sergeant of the 45th Division. Prior to the invasion, based on reports by Canadians of feigned-surrender ambushes, Patton, in "one of his most dynamic pep talk," spoke to men of the 45th Division ad warned them to *"watch out for this treachery"* and to *"kill the s.o.b.s unless they were certain of their real intention to surrender."*[21] After the Biscari events, Patton himself was under fire (and under investigation by the inspector general), even though when he learned of the episode, his orders had been "Try the bastards," meaning the Americans.[22] Patton was cleared entirely by the investigation, which concluded that the defense attorneys had brought his name in unfairly and inaccurately. Patton wrote his wife that the Germans and Italians had *"pulled the white flag trick four times. We take few prisoners."*[23] (This was not the first time German troops pulled such stunts: in World War I an American colonel witnessed a German officer "pretend to surrender, then throw a bomb at an approaching lieutenant.")[24]

   Some journalists, it seems, saw a much different war: in the Atlantic Monthly of 1946, Edgar L. Jones claimed, in John Kerry-esque style, *"We shot prisoners in cold bold, wiped out hospitals, strafed lifeboats ... [and] boiled the flesh off enemy skulls to make table ornaments."* [25] Jones's article has become a stock citation among leftist critics of the American military. One can find individuals who engage in bizarre or ghoulish behavior in any group of people, especially in every military that has ever existed. But what were some of the facts of Japanese "surrenders?" What was their version of the "white flag trick?" Historian Samuel Eliot Morison wrote of innumerable incidents of treachery, such as a wounded Japanese soldier who stabbed to death a surgeon working to save his life; a drowning Japanese sailor who reached for a gun and shot this American rescuer as he turned to give him a cup of coffee.[26] Marines fresh off combat at Saipan and Iwo Jima told of Japanese who surrendered in pairs, the first concealing the second, who had a grenade. The Bushido-trained enemy, however, had no such concerns about prisoners. In the Gilberts, twenty-two Americans were beheaded by a single commander, and at Ballale, Japanese guards bayoneted ninety.[27] Even with those incidents clearly in mind, Americans remained willing to take prisoners, although they were cautioned to take no chances.

   In contrast to the Japanese, or Muslim jihadists in Iraq, American com-

---

[21]General Albert C. Wedemeyer, who witnessed the speech, recorded this, as cited in Carlo D'Este, Patton: A Genius for War (New York: harper Perennial, 1995), p. 509.

[22]D'Este, Patton, p.509

[23] D'Este, Patton, p.510.

[24]Eisenhower, Yanks, p.130.

[25] Jones, "One War Is Enough," pp.48–53.

[26]Samuel Eliot Morison, The Two-Ocean War (Boston: Little, Brown, 1963), p. 273

[27] Gavin Daws, Prisoners of the Japanese: POWs of World War II in the Pacific War (New York: Quill, 1994), passim.

mitment to the sanctity of life (Leave no man behind) has produced, at times, remarkably costly results in attempts to rescue wounded comrades or to liberate prisoners. The efforts to rescue the crews of downed Black Hawk helicopters in Mogadishu, for example, accounted for most of the 18 dead and 70 wounded. None were killed directly by enemy fire in the initial raid that was the objective of the mission, although one man did fall from a helicopter while rappelling down.

An even more costly rescue attempt involved the 77th Division task force under Major Charles Whittlesey that became separated far ahead of American forces in the World War I Argonne offensive. Surrounded by the Germans, the Lost Battalion held out for a week against German forces that used mass assaults, artillery, and even flamethrowers to try to root out Whittlesey's Americans. Yet the true lost battalions were those men who tried to extricate the 77th: relief forces ordered in by General John Pershing that sustained as many as 5,000 casualties before the 77th was rescued. Put another way, the Americans willingly lost 5,000 to save 550 (of whom only 194 survived).[28]

Contrast that with the scenes witnessed by Mark Bowden in Black Hawk Down, where Somalis who were attacking U.S. troops were gunned down, yet Bowden recorded not a single incident when the Somalis attempted the rescue of a wounded man. American memoirs from Iraq, from David Zucchino's Thunder Run to Ray Smith and Bing West's The March Up, do not relate a single incident of Iraqi fighters attempting to rescue their own wounded. Quite the contrary, enemy strategy from the Boxer Rebellion to Iraq has resembled the infamous banzai charge more often than not. During the Boxer Rebellion, a British war correspondent, describing the attacks on American and allied troops, observed the Boxers, "in a state of hysterical frenzy," charging straight into the allied positions. [29]Such was certainly not the American way if it could be helped. *"From Antietam to Hamburger Hill,"* notes Robert H. Scales, *"a victory won with too many lives was not considered a victory at all."* [30] Virtually all of the Army's literature between 1920 and 1940 emphasized reducing casualties. A series of papers compiled into Infantry in Battle, written for the Infantry School in 1934, dealt with such aspects of command as how to limit losses during the approach march to a combat zone, and the phrases "minimum losses" or "best way to avoid losses" reappear constantly, indicating the seriousness of the issue.[31]

The message this sends to many societies is that Americans are cowards or, at the very least, soft. During World War II, Marshal Zhukov, who headed the Soviet army's assault on Germany, told Eisenhower that the best way to clear a minefield was to march an army through it. Certainly the Japanese before 1942 thought the American was weak, and Osama bin Laden, looking at Soma-

---

[28]Hunter Liggett, Commanding an American Army (Boston: Houghton Mifflin Company, 1925), pp. 181–90; John J. Pershing, My Experiences in the World War, vol. 1 (New York: Frederick A. Stokes Company, 1931).
[29]Boot, Savage Wars of Peace, p.7.
[30]Robert H. Scales, Firepower in Limited War (Washington, D.C.: National Defense University Press, 1990), p.4.
[31]Evan Andrew Huelfer, The "Casualty Issue" in American Military Practice: The Impact of World War I (Westport, CT: Praeger, 2003), pp. 95–96.

lia, mocked that when *"tens of your soldiers were killed in minor battles and one American Pilot was dragged in the streets of Mogadishu, you left the area carrying disappointment, humiliation, defeat and your dead with you."*[32] In fact, once the bullets start flying, Americans, always cognizant of death, focus on the objective. Colonel David Shoup, issuing a situation report from Tarawa Atoll in November 1943 summarized this dynamic when he said, *"Casualties many; percentage dead unknown; combat efficiency: We are winning."* [33]

Shame, Honor, and Military Strategy

It is neither possible nor worthwhile to try to convince mad killers and lunatic jihadists, intent on blowing their entrails all over Madrid and London trains, buses, and subways, why life has value, or why those societies who believe in the sanctity of life are not inherently cowardly. (One would think a jihadist in good standing might actually look at the incredible effort to rescue the downed helicopter pilots in Mogadishu and see the valor of those acts, but then that would be asking a jihadist to think sanely.) From that perspective alone then, the war on terrorism can never rely primarily on diplomacy, "understanding the enemy," or other such nonsense, but must always rely on force. As General Walter Boomer, who directed Gulf War air operations, noted, "You can only be compassionate on the battlefield if you are operating from a position of strength." [34] Put another way, an enemy who has no concept of the sanctity of life is impressed only by power.

For that reason—and virtually no one in the press has investigated this aspect of Abu Ghraib—the news coverage of "abuses" at the Iraqi prison and at Gitmo may actually have backfired on Western liberals and instilled no small degree of fear among the terrorists themselves. It is common for Western analysts such as Andrew Bacevich to misread the situation and claim that the Abu Ghraib "scandal blew a gaping hole in the Bush administration's policy in Iraq … [showing] American soldiers not as liberators but as tormentors, not as professionals but as sadists getting cheap thrills." [35] That, of course, is how Westerners and some non-Arab Muslims might see it. But in most Arabic Islamic societies, and certainly in those frequented by the loopiest of suicide bombers, women have no standing. They are slightly above dogs, and nowhere near the level of personhood attributed to men. What do you think was the response among these types of men when they saw pictures in the news of American women holding Iraqi terrorist prisoners by dog chains? To some, undoubtedly, anger. But to others, respect. While critics of Abu Ghraib rightly claim the former has created more jihadists, the images had

[32] Osama bin Laden, "Declaration of War Against the Americans Occupying the Land of the Two Holy Places," August 23, 1996, quoted in Andrew J. Bacevich, The New American Militarism: How Americans Are Seduced by War (Oxford: Oxford University Press, 2005), p.196.

[33] James R. Stockman, "The Battle for Tarawa" (1947), in Peter G. Tsouras, ed., The Greenhill Dictionary of Military Quotations, p.240.

[34] Tsouras, ed., The Greenhill Dictionary of Military Quotations, p. 240.

[35] Anthony J. Bacevich, The New American Militarism: How Americans Are Seduced by War (Oxford: Oxford University Press, 2005), p. 67.

a profound effect on non-Western minds and in all likelihood gave pause to many would-be insurgents.

On May 9, 2005, *Newsweek* published a story that there was Koran abuse at Gitmo, claiming, among other things, that guards at the facility flushed a Koran down a toilet (a physical impossibility due to the size of the book—not to mention the insufficient water pressure). By May 16, *Newsweek* had backpedaled and retracted the story, but no before rioting broke out in Jalalabad, Afghanistan, and other parts of the Muslim world.[36] (Note, however, that no rioting ever took place after the Abu Ghraib photos were released, and not that the Muslim world responded to prisoners being shamed in far different way than it perceived attacks on its holy book!) *Newsweek* issued a weak apology, but otherwise took no responsibility for the deaths of at least a dozen people. The magazine had inflamed the Muslim world over a lie, harmed U.S. public relations, and probably extended the war. In contrast, a December 12 issue of *Newsweek* , headlined *"Women and Terror,"* acknowledges that al Qaeda's "core organization in Afghanistan and Pakistan and its avant garde in Iraq need more recruits," and "Jordanian researcher Hassan Abu Hanieh, an acquaintance of Abu Mussab al-Zarqawi, "is goading Muslim men" by using female martyrs.[37] *"Are there no men, so that we have to recruit women?"* asked Zarqawi on a web site. [38]

The Abu Ghraib pictures, however, had a much different impact, and probably had greater propaganda value in "terrordom" than did all the images of dead jihadists and captured Fedayeen put together. Those photos had an effect on Muslim terrorists, steeped in a jihadist culture of shame and honor, that was staggering and which was completely missed by the mainstream media in the United States. Here were fairly small American women blatantly giving orders to "brave" Islamofascist thugs, forcing them to simulate sex—a pure power act in Islam, with the only acceptable outcome a pregnancy with a man-child—and making them wear women's underwear on their heads. In a column I wrote called *"Iraqi Abuse and the Arab 'Street,'"* I suggested, *"The submissive positions of these 'tough' Iraqi men under the heels and attached to the leashes of WOMEN ... sends a very powerful message to the 'street.'"* One of the abused prisoners said that *"he will go home to his family in Nasiriyah, but his shame will not allow him to stay."* [39] (It should be noted that the so-called hooded man from Abu Ghraib, Haj Aki al Aaisi, was identified by Vienna's Die Presse in its December 13 edition as a "henchman" for Saddam who presided over at least thirty-eight murders. At least one of the victims was tortured before being killed).

The experience of dealing with a shame/honor culture in Bushido-ridden Japan was instructive. As John Lynn explained, *"Originally bushido was a chi-*

[36]"Newsweek Retracts Quran Story,: http://www.cnn.com/2005/WORLD/asiapcf/05/16/newsweek.quran/.

[37]"Women and Terror" Newsweek, December 12, 2005, http://www.msnbc.msn.com/id/10315095/site/newsweek/page/4/.

[38]Ibid

[39] Larry Schweikart, "Iraqi Abuse and the Arab 'Street,'" http://www.frontpagemag.com/Articles/Printable.asp?ID=13305; Andrew Buncombe and Justin Huggler, "The Humiliated Man Beneath the Hood," New Zealand Hearld, July 4, 2005.

valric code that incorporated humanity, modesty, and consideration [but by World War II, the Japanese military culture] stripped it down to a few deadly virtues.[40] Basically, those "deadly virtues" came down to soldiers sacrificing themselves without a thought, offered up for the "benevolent Emperor." If necessary, Japanese warriors were to engage in gyokusai, or "glorious self-annihilation."[41] Field manuals instructed Japanese soldiers not to be taken alive, and as early as 1908, regulations ordered the execution of commanders who surrendered their units. In the 1930s, on Japanese major, who was captured by the Chinese while unconscious and then later released, committed suicide over his dishonor.[42] After the stunning defeat at Midway, the Imperial Japanese Navy dispersed uninjured sailors who had witnessed the humiliation, putting some in secret hospitals or quarantining them, lest they give away the magnitude of the loss.[43] When the United States took Saipan in the summer of 1944, Americans had to kill 97 percent of the defenders, including 3,000 men who engaged in a suicidal charge (some with no more than bamboo sticks). Even then, battle-hardened GIs were horrified to see civilians leaping to their deaths at Marpi Point cliffs, warned by the Japanese military that Americans would rape and torture them. Mothers and fathers threw screaming children into the ocean, and those who hesitated where shot by Japanese snipers. All the while, American interpreters and even a few Japanese prisoners shouted through bullhorns to stop, promising good treatment, and U.S. Navy vessels hauled many from the sea who had survived the fall.

At Okinawa in 1945, kamikaze pilots—human-guided cruise missiles—plunged themselves into more than 250 ships, sinking 30, and inflicting severe damage of 11 U.S. carriers and killing 7,000 Americans. The battleship Yamato was on a suicide run when it was sunk by American aircraft. Such fanatical "honor death," unseen even among most of the Plains Indians, was simply outside the war mentality of the U.S. military.

Understanding the terrorist mind—in this case, the Islamic terrorist mind—demands an objective and cold-eyed look, not a view of Arab terrorism seen through the Western lens that focuses on a political solution, as in Northern Ireland, or independence, as in Basque Spain. Rather, it demands a dispassionate examination of honor and shame as understood by the society in question. This concept of honor was not lost on General Douglas MacArthur, who, before the Japanese surrender at the end of World War II, issued an order forbidding the confiscation of Japanese officers' swords. Admiral Bull Halsey confronted MacArthur, arguing that the swords kept the spirit of militarism alive. MacArthur replied that he had been guided by Grant and his treatment of the Rebels at Appomattox, but Halsey responded, *"Grant was dealing with an honorable foe. We are not."* MacArthur considered Halsey's words and said, *"You're right! I'll revoke the*

---

[40]Lynn, Battle, p.247.

[41] Ibid, p.247. See also Saburo Ienaga, Pacific War, 1931–1945 (New York: Panteon, 1979.)

[42]All examples from Ienaga, quoted in Lynn, Battle, p. 247.

[43]Jonathan B. Parshall and Anthony P. Tully, Shattered Sword: The Untold Story of the Battle of Midway (Washington, D.C.: Potomac Books, 2005), p. 386.

order." [44]

Whereas overcoming the mind-set of the Bushido Japanese warriors required some understanding of honor and the role of the emperor as Japanese soldiers understood it, so too does success against Arab terrorists require an understanding of the codes of shame and honor that have defined Arabs for centuries. After the fall of Saddam, for example, Arab protesters who were interviewed on the street expressed outrage that they had believed Baghdad bob and were ashamed of the ease with which American forces had overthrown the "strong man of Iraq." MSNBC reported in *"The Secret War"* that *"as American armored columns pushed down the road to Baghdad, 400-watt loudspeakers mounted on Humvees would, from time to time, blare out in Arabic that Iraqi men are impotent."* The Fedayeen, the article reported, could not bear to be taunted (especially about their manhood) and rushed out to attack ... and be killed. *"What you say is many times more important than what you do in this part of the world,"* says a senior U.S. psyops warrior. [45]

David Gutmann, a professor of behavioral psychology, has analyzed the psychological elements of Islamic terrorists, concluding (as did T.E. Lawrence in his Seven Pillars of Wisdom that the central, traditional objective of Arab males in Bedouin societies was to acquire sharraf, or honor, while avoiding humiliation or shame. [46] Honor s acquired through combat, thus intertribal conflict "should never really end." [47] More important, Arab shame/honor cultures have concocted a rationale by which they "cannot lose." When terrorist guerrilla armies fight powerful nations such as the United States, goliath "only adds to his own shame" by defeating a lesser foe, while "David only adds to his honor." [48] The *"modern Arab world,"* Gutmann argued *"resembles Japan of World War II ... [wherein] psychic wounds, the wounds inflicted by defeat and evident inferiority ... inspire suicide bombers."* [49] Worse, from the Arab shame/honor perspective, a terrorist's actions impose shame—not on himself, but on the enemy whom he kills, civilian or not. Driving people to avoid airplanes, buses, or normal life through terror achieves the Muslim terrorist's ends in a twofold fashion by disrupting life and by enhancing the killer's own honor and his enemies' shame. Or, in reverse, from a psychological perspective, the "abuse" inflicted at Abu Ghraib was precisely the right kind of shame and humiliation that struck at the psychological core of terrorists!

According to Sania Hamady, an Arab authority on Bedouin psychology, *"modern Arab society is ruthless, stern and pitiless ... [It] worships strength and has no compassion for weakness."* [50] John Laffin, in The Arab Mind Considered,

[44]E. B. Potter, Bull Halsey (Annapolis: Naval Institute Press, 1985), p. 362.
[45]Evan Thomas and Martha Brant, "The Secret War," Newsweek, April 21, 2004, http://msn.com/id/3068575/.
[46]David Leo Gutmann, "Shame, Honor and Terror in the Middle East," http://frontpagemagazine.com, October 24, 2003.
[47]Gutman, "Shame, Honor, and Terror in the Middle East."
[48]Gutman, "Shame, Honor, and Terror in the Middle East."
[49]David Gutman, "Saving Arabs from Themselves," www.frontpagemagazine.com, August 12, 2005.
[50]Hamady quoted in John Laffin, The Arab Mind Considered: A Need for Understanding (New York: Taplinger Publishing Company, 1975), p. 22.

writes on the Arab's *"sexual frustrations and obsessions, his paralyzing sense of shame."*[51]   Another analyst of the terrorist mind, Patton Howell, argues that impotence feeds a constant sense of humiliation, which turns to self-hate. The *"Terrorist Rule,"* he suggests, *"is hate others as your hate yourself."*[52]   As a religion, Islam has had little impact on these perceptions, and is some ways exacerbated Middle Eastern feelings of impotence and self-hate. It has brought humiliation, shame, and honor to the forefront of geopolitics, due in no small part to the fact that Islamic societies have, for the most part, excluded women and treated all sexual relations as statements of power. One opponent of the United States in Iraq feared the U.S. invasion was *"part of a plan ... to castrate us."*[53]   Arab writers include women in novels only to create sexual situations—women can never have an opinion, think, or act independently.[54]   Indeed, an incredible commentary on the role of female Palestinian bombers was the conclusion by religious scholars that a woman could be a martyr, but was limited in how long she could be out without a chaperone before she blew herself to bits![55]   It is not by accident that one of George W. Bush's quiet policy objectives—ostensibly influenced by Laura Bush, Condoleezza Rice, and Karen Hughes—has been to unleash the power of Muslim women in Afghanistan and Iraq, so far with great success, despite the claim by Democratic National Committee chairman Howard Dean that *"as of today it looks like women will be worse off in Iraq than they were when Saddam Hussein was president."*[56]   Indeed, it is one of the high ironies of the twenty-first century that the ultimate expression of male chauvinism that was so reprehensible to the feminists of the 1970s and 1980s is found in the Muslim societies that conservative American foreign policy seeks to reform—a policy that the ultraliberal American feminists virtually have opposed universally!

Bushido has been replaced with the ideology of jihad, Shintoist shame and honor repackaged in Islamic theological terms, exaggerated and perverted by the madrassas. It is worth noting; in passing, that while concepts of shame and honor as motivating factors are downplayed by the media, liberals' favorite explanation for terrorism—"poverty and ignorance"—don't wash at all. Marc Sangeman's study of 400 terrorists, mostly al Qaeda, found an astonishing 75 percent came from the middle class and nearly two thirds were college educated. They were older, as well, averaging twenty-six years of age.[57]   Nasra Hassan found similar characteristics about Palestinian terrorists: *"None of them were uneducated, desperately poor, simple-minded or depressed. Many were middle class.... Two were*

---

[51]Laffin, Arab Mind Considered, p. 24.
[52]Patton Howell, The Terrorist Mind in Islam and Iraq (Dallas: Saybrook Publishing, 2003), p. 79.
[53]"Women and Terror."
[54]Laffin, Arab Mind Considered, p. 78.
[55]"Women and Terror."
[56]"Dean: Women in Iraq Were Better Off Under Saddam," Washington Times, August 15, 2005.
[57]Marc Sangeman, Understanding Terror Networks (Philadelphia: University of Pennsylvania Press, 2004), quoted in Richard Minitier, Disinformation: 22 Media Myths That Undermine the War on Terror (Washington: Regnery, 2004), 126–127 and Sangeman's paper, "Understanding Terror Networks," Foreign Policy Research Institute, November 1, 2004.

the sons of millionaires."[58]

What kind of education they are getting is another matter. In Arab societies, which remain largely illiterate, the spoken word has disproportionate power. Merely to say something is true makes it so in the Arab mind. To say Americans or Jews were killers to Arab children is a true statement to someone who has grown up with a madrassas as his only education. Moreover, the Koran can only be legitimately read in Arabic according to Muslim fundamentalists: no other language is even capable of capturing the ideas. Recitation and memorization replace analysis or critical thinking in Arab schools because conformity bestows honor. All dialogue between Arabs must be considered in terms of subtext, that is, not what it stated, but what the two parties are concealing. Above all, the value of Arabic-Bedouin honor—as the inverse of shame—is paramount, and failure to conform is dishonor.

"We are a people that never forgets if it has been injured," said Egyptian president Nasser in 1955. But if an act resulting in shame is bad, revealing it is a double disgrace, so Arab society represses shame and conceals wrongdoing. If exposed, a shameful act must be avenged because in Arab society, *"the shamed individual could lose his influence and power and through him the group will similarly suffer."*[59] In Christendom, shame is removed by public or semipublic confession and forgiveness, both of the person who was shamed and if another party was involved, by the transgressed against the transgressor. (Matthew 6:15, *"But if you do not forgive men their trespasses, neither will your Father forgive your trespasses."*) Proverbs says to feed your enemy and give him a drink if he is thirsty, *"for in so doing you will heap coals of fire on his head"* (Proverbs 25:21-22). Solomon, the author of Proverbs, obviously had dealt with the Arab mind: in Judeo-Christian teaching, forgiveness empowered the forgiver, but to Arab Muslim teachings, the person forgiven was only indebted and shamed further, thus had "coals of fire" heaped on his head. One 1972 study in Egypt of murder cases where the perpetrator was caught found an astonishing 85 percent in some way related to shame and honor![60] Failure in any way leads to shame in Arab society, making learning from loss in a military sense particularly difficult. When Egyptians purchased Soviet-built MiG fighters, an Egyptian air force officer candidly noted that it was *"too much responsibility"* to fly the planes, meaning, the Egyptian pilots might fail several times before mastering the new technology.

One critical aspect of Arab thinking and Muslim teaching has changed, however, since John Laffin wrote The Arab Mind Considered in 1975. At that time, of course, exceptions, including the Assassins cult, as well as the cult of Hasan bin Sabbah, a truly debauched group that practiced oral sex and ingested drugs before embarking on their mission, but these actions were not condoned by Koranic scholars.[61] Sometime between 1975 and the 1990s, however, it became

[58]Nasra Hassan, "An Arsenal of Believers," New Yorker, November 19, 2001.
[59]Laffin, Arab Mind Considered, p. 84.
[60]Laffin, Arab Mind Considered, p. 85.
[61]Wes Moore, "Hasan bin Sabbah and the Secret Order of Hashishins," http://www.disinfo.com/archive/pages/dossier/id985/pg1/index.html.

acceptable to kill oneself in the process of destroying one's enemy, a new theological strain driven largely by the ramblings of Sayeed Qutb, an existentialist and virulent anti-American leader of the Muslim Brotherhood who was hanged in Egypt in 1966. Qutb's influence as a Salafist, or "pious forbearer," lived on, unfortunately, evolving into an "anarch Islam." He argued that when a Muslim fights in an occupied area, his death under any circumstance could not be considered a violation of the Koran. His ideas were reinforced by Abdullah Azzam, who recruited Osama bin Laden into the mujahedeen and maintained that all land ever occupied by Muslims that has since been taken over by another power was "occupied." Politically, the Muslim Brotherhood practice of suicide bombing received support within Yasser Arafat's Palestinian Liberation Organization (PLO) and its intifada (waking up) against Israel in 1987, when the first wave of suicide bombings were institutionalized and blessed by some Muslim clerics. All the suicide groups were theologically united under the Salafiyya Jihadiyya group, which claimed that the new type of terror was legitimate.[62] Out of support for Hamas, Sheikh Yusuf al-Qaradawi and a group of ulama ruled that suicide operations against civilians were one of the "glorious" types of jihad.

After the deadly bombings in Iraq between 2004 and 2005, however, even the anti-American clerics started to see there was a problem with suicide bombers killing masses of civilians. A conference of Islamic scholars in 2005 debated the Koran's instructions on the subject. The Koran says, *"Do not kill yourself, surely Allah is ever merciful to you,"* said Muhammad Rafat Othman, Egyptian professor of Islamic law, and *"a person who blows himself up is committing suicide. This opinion is based on sources that categorically forbid self-killing."*[63] *"What Islamic religious law does permit is for a person to wage jihad, facing one of two options—victory or martyrdom. He may risk being killed by someone else, but may not kill himself."* Another "progressive" cleric argued, *"We are dealing with an angry Islam that is hostile to the world through its sons, whom we have not educated or taught well, and in whom we have not inculcated culture. [They] bear a hatred of life and of the living (emphasis mine). ...Our religious curricula have not succeeded in planting in their hearts the humane values of love."*[64]

Such sensible voices, however, were countered by other imams, such as Sheikh Yusuf al—Qaradawi:

> This has nothing to do with suicide. This man does not want to commit suicide, but rather to cause great damage to the enemy, and this is the only method he can use to cause such damage. Since this method did not exist in the past, we cannot find rulings about it in the ancient jurisprudence. We may find rulings about plunging into the [ranks of the] enemy and risking one's life, even in cases of certain death—so be it. The truth is that we should refrain from raising this issue, because doubting it is like joining the Zionists and American in condemning our brothers in Hamas,

---

[62]"Leading Progressive Qatari Cleric: By Permitting Suicide Operations," Al-Qaradhawi and His Ilk Have Caused a Moral Crisis in Islam," http://memri.org/bin/articles.cgi? Page=subjects&Area=reform&ID=SP96805.

[63]"Islamic Scholars Debate Suicide Operations in a Counter-Terrorism Conference," MEMRI, August 26, 2005, at http://memri.org/bin/latestnews.cgi?ID=SD97105.

[64]"Leading Progressive Qatari Cleric."

the Jihad, the Islamic factions, and the resistance factionsin Iraq. It is as if we are joining them. [65]

    This took on its own form of honor, so much so that Middle Eastern women raised sons specifically to someday blow up Jews.[66] *"The hatred which we indoctrinate into ... our children from their birth is sacred,"* said Syrian minister of education, Suleiman al-Khash.[67] Such comments underscored the aspect of honor at the heart of such suicide missions. *"Are we avenging our honor by murdering Muslims?"* asked Sharia law professor Abd al-Hamid al-Ansari from Qatar.[68] If honor and shame are at the root of the new interpretations of Islamic law that promote suicide bombings, then fire must be met with fire. And perhaps it has been, unintentionally. Right after the Abu Ghraib photos became public, in which the humiliation of terrorists by women was on display for the entire Arab world to see, the situation on the ground in Iraq became remarkably calm. After weeks of threats from Ayatollah al-Sadr, American troops walked into Najaf without incident. The number of roadside bombings dropped. Apparently the message got through: *"Don't screw with the Americans. They'll turn their women loose on you!"*

Here a Nazi, There a Nazi

Durbin's reference to Nazi death camps reflected a recurring theme with the Left, which is to invoke Hitler and fascism in the context of the American military at every possible opportunity. Consider ultra-leftist academic Frances Fox Piven, whose diatribe against the war on terror accused Bush of "follow[ing] Goring's age-old formula for leading a people into war."[69] (Piven, predictably, calls Iraq a quagmire, too.) Slinging the term Nazi at George Bush is so common on the Left that a Google search linking Bush and Nazi yields an astounding 1.9 million hits. The antiwar *Dallas Libertarian Post's Draheim Report* claims a *"Bush Nazi Connection"* gave the family its money; while the "progressive" *Online Journal* announced that its "time for Nuremberg II."[70] Former vice president Al Gore, whose 2003 speeches (while he thought he was still a viable candidate) reached Yoko Ono-esque screech levels, told supporters in 2004 that Bush and his staff were comparable to Nazi "brownshirts." [71] John Stanton's Web site *Counter-Punch* ties the Marines and Nazis together:

    In the Pentagon, Hitler's ideology, has a friend in the form of US Marine Corps Lieutenant General William Boykin who believes that "God supports the US military because we're a Christian

[65]"Islamic Scholars Debate Suicide Operations."
[66]Howell, Terrorist Mind, passim.
[67]Quoted in Laffin, Arab Mind Considered, p. 106.
[68]"Leading Progressive Qatari Cleric."
[69]Piven, The War Home, p. 91.
[70]Richard M. Draheirm, "The Bush-Nazi Connection," http://www.lpdallas.org/features/draheim/dr991216. htm; "Time for Nuremberg II," Online Journal, http://www.onlinejournal.com/Special_Reports/030905Madsen/030905madsen.html.
[71]Noelle Straub, "Gore Slams Bush 'Brown Shirts,'" Boston Herald, June 25, 2004, http://news.bostonherald. com/national/view.bg?articleid=33260.

nation, because our foundation and our roots are Judeo-Christian ... Our spiritual enemy will only be defeated if we come against them in the name of Jesus." [72]

The Blanket, a *"Journal of Protest and Dissent"* in Fox-like fashion quotes Herman Goering on war.[73]   Foothill College professor Leighton Armitage said that "Nazis" control the U.S. government, and he has likened the security wall in Israel to the "Ghetto Wall" in 1940 Warsaw used by the Nazis to contain the city's Jews.[74]

When not invoking the Nazi reference, the Left has found other interesting descriptions of "totalitarianism" in America. Dan Rather, claiming after 9/11 on the David Letterman show that he *"would willingly die for my country at a moment's notice"* changed his tune and said he feared being "necklaced here," where *"you will have a flaming tire of lack of patriotism put around your neck."*[75] The media darling Cindy Sheehan, an antiwar activist long before her son, Casey, died in Iraq, staged a sit-in at Bush's Crawford ranch in August 2005 when Bush was on vacation there, telling reporters *"The biggest terrorist in the world is George W. Bush"* and referring to bin Laden as "allegedly" behind the 9/11 attacks.[76]   Prodded on by such organizations as *MoveOn.org* and funded by George Soros, Sheehan's hysterical rant concluded, *"We want our country back and, if we have to impeach everybody from George Bush down to the person who picks up dog sh—t in Washington, we will impeach all those people."*[77]   When other Gold Star Mothers (by the dozens) countered Sheehan, she accused them of being *"as brainwashed as the rest of America,"* and called them *"murder and mayhem moms."*[78]   It seems the only mother who lost a son or daughter in combat who is worthy of attention is one who opposes the war. The mainstream media barely noticed the large numbers of peaceful counter-protesters in Crawford, including the parents or loved ones of other fallen soldiers who had trekked there to demand Sheehan take their sons' and daughters' names off her symbolic crosses.

Called on their outrageous claims, the media had to back off assertions that American were "killing civilians." *Newsweek's* Rod Nordland, in July 2005, grudgingly admitted that while occasionally Iraqi civilians were killed in checkpoint incidents—usually tragic mistakes—such civilian deaths at the hands of Americans happened "not very often." Rather, the *"scourge of Iraqi civilians"* was, *"hands down ... the insurgents."* [79] The *"Iraq Body Count,"* a running "to-

[72]John Stanton, "Hitler's Ghost Haunts America," October 25, 2003, http://counterpunch.org/stanton10252003.html.

[73]Karen Cox, "Dancing at the Edge of an Abyss," The Blanket, November 30, 2004, http://lark.poblacht.net/klc05122g.html.

[74] "Foothill College Prof Says Jewish 'Nazis' Control U.S. government," http://www.discoverthenetwork.org/individualProfile.asp?indid-1453.

[75]Rather quoted in Piven, The War at Home, p. 117.

[76] "Cindy Unleashed," www.drudgereport.com/flash3.htm, August 17, 2005; Stephen Spruill, "Crawford: Sheehan Calls bin Laden Alleged Terrorist," NRO.com, August 25, 2004.

[77] "Cindy Unleashed."

[78] Joe Kovacs, "Sheehan: Other Moms of slain 'Brainwashed,' Cindy Labels Them Supporters of 'Murder and Mayhem,'" www.worldnetdaily.com, August 19, 2005.

[79]Rod Nordland, "Truth Is the First Civilian Casualty," Newsweek, July 23, 2005, at http://msnbc.com/

tal" of civilians killed in Iraq, claims that a minimum of 23,000 civilians have been killed since Operation Iraqi Freedom, and a maximum of 26,000 have died.[80] Yet as even *Newsweek* discovered, such numbers rely heavily on estimates and family members who unerringly refer to dead insurgents or terrorists as civilians. Indeed, the Iraq body count labels anyone who is an unknown agent as a civilian, when a more accurate word might be terrorist. An even more ridiculous "estimate," from the British medical journal *Lancet,* of 98,000 Iraqi civilian deaths had an astounding variance of "confidence" of between 8,000 and 194,000 civilian deaths—in other words, civilian Iraqi deaths could just as easily have been as low as 8,000![81] This supposedly peer-reviewed "scholarly" article then cites as its source for the higher figure the Iraq Body Count, which is equivalent to someone trying to "prove" visitation by flying saucers by citing the *MUFON* (the Mutual UFO Network).

Admiral Isoroku Yamamoto warned the Japanese government in 1942 that distortions and falsehoods in the name of "boosting morale" were harmful. *"All [you] need to do really is quietly let people know the truth. There is no need to bang the big drum. Official reports should stick to the absolute truth—once you start lying, the war's as good as lost."*[82] To the extent that the antiwar movement had sloganized the terms Nazi or fascist and applied them to American soldiers, Yamamoto's advice seems prescient for the protesters: they lost the (anti) war.

The Great Escape

One of Hollywood's few summer successes in 2005 was a film called *The Great Raid*, starring Benjamin Bratt, about the 1945 rescue by the 6th Ranger Battalion of 500 Americans, many of them Bataan Death March survivors, at the Japanese Cabanatuan POW camp. After detailed scouting with Filipinos, Lieutenant Colonel Henry Mucci sent Filipino guerrilla fighters to hold the roads while a P-61 Black Widow fighter buzzed the camp to create a distraction. Crawling under the wire, Mucci's men were surprised to find that many of the Americans did not believe they were being rescued because Mucci's team wore different uniforms from what the prisoners had worn years earlier, and the challenged their rescuers. Finally, Mucci persuaded (in some cases, by physical force) the survivors to leave the huts.[83]

As the Rangers and former prisoners trekked out, they encountered a Hukbalahap (Huk) village, which disliked both Americans and Japanese, and especially the Filipino Scouts under Captain Juan Pajota. After dispatching one of Pajota's lieutenants to negotiate passage through the Huk village, the officer came

id/8679662/site/newsweek/.
[80]http://www.iraqbodycount.org.
[81]"Mortality Before and After the 2003 Invasion of Iraq: Cluster Sample Survey," http:www.thelancet.com/journals/lancet/article/PIISO140673604174412/abstract.
[82]Quoted in Tsouras, The Greenhill Dictionary of Military Quotations, p. 387.
[83] Sides, Ghost Soldiers; and Forrest Bryant Johnson, Hour of Redemption: The Heroic WW II Saga of America's Most Daring POW Rescue (New York: Warner Books, 2002).

back and told Mucci it was safe. The colonel pulled his pistol and warned the lieutenant that he would head the column, and if the Huks attempted anything, he would be the first casualty. The column moved through without incident, and Mucci apologized to the Filipinos for doubting them. Several hours later, the weary men arrived at Talavera, which the 6th Army had just captured. History's greatest POW raid was in the books, although it certainly was not the only one.

In July 1864, General William T. Sherman dispatched General George Stoneman and his force of 5,000 cavalry to Macon, Georgia, to destroy rail lines and cut off supplies to Atlanta. Stoneman also requested permission to take his regiments to free the prisoners at nearby Andersonville Prison. As Sherman noted, "There was something most captivating in the idea, and the execution was within the bound of probable success."[84] He wrote Stoneman, "*If you can bring back to the army any or all of those prisoners of war, it will be an achievement that will entitle you, and your command, to the love and admiration of the whole country.*" Although the raid started out well, Stoneman ran into trouble when 3,000 Georgia militia met the 2,200-strong Yankee force. Meanwhile, Confederate General Joseph Wheeler had his own cavalry, six times the size of the Union force, hot on Stoneman's heels. Finding himself surrounded, Stoneman's troops staged several dismounted charges against the Rebels before they were forced to surrender … and become prisoners themselves at Andersonville.

More recently, in 1970, Colonel Arthur "Bull" Simons lead a group of Special Forces volunteers to rescue POWs spotted by an SR-71 Blackbird reconnaissance plane in May. However, by the time Simons's men set down in November, the camp was empty.[85] The POWs had been moved in July. Simons led another rescue effort—this one successful—in 1979, when he was hired by Electronic Data Systems founder H. Ross Perot to free two EDS employees held in a prison in Iran. He infiltrated Iran and provoked a mob in Tehran into storming Gazre prison, where the employees were held hostage. This riot freed the two Americans, along with 11,000 Iranian prisoners, and Simons successfully transported the EDS employees to Turkey, in the process providing the plot to a Ken Follett best-selling book, On the Wings of Eagles.

All of these examples are provided in order to ask these questions: Can you name a single attempt by the Japanese in World War II to free POWs? Or even the Germans? How about the North Vietnamese during the Vietnam War? Can you find any example of the North Koreans' seeking to liberate their own prisoners in the Korean War? The answers are obvious. In our more than two-hundred-year history, not one of our opponents—not even the British—conducted a raid, or made any attempt whatsoever (except prisoner exchange, to free their own prisoners. That is an astounding comment on the American way of war.

Recently, more false media reports swirled around mortar attacks on Abu

---

[84]Robert W. Philbrook, "Albert Philbrook & the 14th Illinois Cavalry," http://www.philbrick-genealogy.org/Civil%20War/albert_philbrook_story.htm.
[85]Benjamin F. Schemmer, The Raid (New York: Harper & Rowe, 1976); and John L. Plaster, SOG–The Secret Wars of American Commandos in Vietnam (New York: Simon & Schuster, 1997).

Ghraib, which were initially described as attempts to rescue some of the prisoners. However, correspondence from the front suggests otherwise. Members of the 333rd Military Police Company, Illinois National Guard, "who arrived there a few days after the [escape] story broke ... were mortared frequently." Most of the rounds, the guardsmen noted, landed among prisoners being kept in outside areas—hardly an indicator of a rescue attempt. "None of the mentioned attempts to break prisoners out, and blamed media hyping of the Abu Ghraib scandal for the attacks."[86]   One soldier from the 333rd said the media "did a lot of damage."

Americans value life, and rescuing our own prisoners, so much so that General Douglas MacArthur cited freeing POWs as a key reason to invade the Philippines. Locked in a fierce debate with Admiral Chester Nimitz as to the best strategy for defeating Japan in mid-1944 after the Battle of the Philippine Sea (also known as the Great Marianas Turkey Shoot, in which 346 Japanese planes and two carriers were sunk, compared to just 30 American aircraft), MacArthur sent a message to the Joint Chiefs in which he argued "purely military considerations" justified retaking the Philippines. Even if that were not the case, however,

practically all of the 17,000,000 Filipinos remain loyal to the United States and are undergoing the greatest privation and suffering .... We have a national obligation to discharge. Moreover, if the United States should deliberately bypass the Philippines, leaving our prisoners, nationals, and loyal Filipinos in enemy hands ... we would incur the gravest psychological reaction [and] probably suffer such a loss of prestige among all the peoples of the Far East that it would adversely affect the United States for many years....[87]

Still later, when he met with Franklin Roosevelt, MacArthur pointed out that America had not only abandoned loyal Filipinos, but more than 11,000 Americans, many of whom still languished in POW camps. In a private moment with the president, the general reminded FDF of his political exposure if he bypassed American POWs. Roosevelt agreed with MacArthur, and the Philippine invasion was on.

Americans win wars because we value the dignity and worth of the individual, because we leave no man behind, and because we find the loss or incarceration of a single POW unacceptable. Ultimately—again, always with a few exceptions, such as with the Plains Indians—our attitude toward life has tempered us into the most benign victors in history. Our enemies consistently misread this concern for human life as weakness or softness. It is just the opposite. Americans will risk a company to save a private, a division to save a company. Americans win wars because, unlike the Japanese, we do not conduct death marches and because, unlike the jihadists, no shame or honor is worth strapping on a suicide vest to blow up a marketplace full of women and children. At their worst, our Gitmos are never gulags.

---

[86]E-mail from Sergeant Christopher Cliukey, (USAF, Ret.), November 20, 2005, quoting his column in the Freeport Ink, August 25, 2005.
[87]Quoted in Thomas J. Cutler, The Battle for Leyte Gulf, 23–26 October 1944 (Annapolis: Naval Institute Press, 1994), p. 23.

The Left constantly reminds us of the Japanese relocation in World War II, equating temporary detention centers with Hitler's horrific gassing camps. On March 18, 1942, Franklin Roosevelt created the War Relocation Authority, which oversaw the relocation of 110,000 Japanese Americans on the West Coast (not the East Coast or anywhere else) on the grounds that they might be a security risk if a Japanese invasion of the United States occurred, as many in government feared would happen. As the 1943 public statement of relocation program noted, the relocation camps were never intended to be "internment" camps, and as soon as individuals could pass through proper security, the would be released.[88] Lieutenant General J. L. DeWitt summarized the Japanese relocation in his final report of June 5, 1943: *"It is better to have had this protection and not to have needed it than to have needed it and not to have had it—as we have learned to our sorrow."* [89] Certainly some racism was involved, and western state governors also pleaded with the federal government to remove the Japanese in part because the governors thought they could not provide proper security for them, or from saboteurs among them. But Canada issued similar orders for Japanese living in British Columbia, and the concerns about Japanese invasions of the West Coast—and the role of fifth columnists—were genuine. The United States even built air bases behind the Cascades, to conduct bombing raids on the West Coast, should the Japanese invaders have achieved a beachhead.[90] Twenty years later, following two Supreme Court cases, the U.S. government began reparations to Japanese who had been interned, and the U.S. Congress passed legislation that awarded formal payments of $20,000 each to the 60,000 surviving internees.[91] To date, Japan has not issued so much as an apology to China, Korea, or the Philippines for atrocities committed during its occupation of those lands and confirmed in the war crimes trials.

Unjust as the internment of Japanese citizens may have been, the potential for a fifth column justified interring West Coast Japanese until security risks could be sorted out. But if that was how Americans treated the "Japanese" (even though most were U.S. citizens), how did the Japanese treat prisoners? Lord Russell's classic, The Knights of Bushido, records many instances of the Japanese performing vivisection on POWs, of an officer slicing off a young woman's breasts and a young man's genitals, of another officer hacking off a prisoner's hands and legs.[92] Russian troops fighting the Japanese in 1938 were found with cartridges hammered into their eyes. In one case a pilot was not only beheaded, but the Japanese sliced up his flesh and cooked it—a practice more common than was let on during the war, as was revealed in the war crimes transcripts.[93] The Rape of Nanking is

[88]"Relocation of Japanese Americans," War Relocation Authority, May 1943, http://www.sfmuseum.org/hist10/relocbook.html.
[89]Lieutenant General J. L. DeWitt, Letter of Transmittal to the Chief of Staff, U.S. Army, June 5, 1943, http://www.sfmuseum.org/war/dewitt0.html.
[90]http://www.fallon.navy.mil/history.asp.
[91]Michelle Makin, In Defense of Internment: The Case for 'Racial Profiling' in World War II and the War on Terror (Washington, D.C.: Regnery, 2004).
[92]Lord Russell, The Knights of Bushido: A Short History of Japanese War Crimes (London: Greenhill Books, 2002), pp. 233–35.
[93]Russell, Knights of Bushido, pp.236–37.

infamous, but similar slaughters occurred in Java, Borneo, and other cities in China besides Nanking. Between 300 to 400 "undesirables" in Singapore were shot under the orders of the Tiger of Malaya, Tomoyuki Yamashita. When Manila was about to be liberated, Fleet Orders commanded, "When killing Filipinos, assemble them together in one place … saving ammunition and labour."[94]   Hundreds of civilians were buried alive at Fort Santiago, and still more at the German Club, where soldiers shot or bayoneted women and children fleeing the flames. Hospital patients at the Red Cross building were likewise mercilessly murdered.[95]

"Racist" America, in fact, celebrated Chinese, Filipino, and Korean allies in World War II, depicting them as heroic and proud—it was only the Japanese who got the caricatures with slanteyes and buckteeth. It was Japan, not the United States, whose racism against other Asians was manifestly obvious, and had been even before Pearl Harbor. In 1923, Japanese mobs tortured and killed 6,000 Koreans in Japan, convinced the Koreans helped cause the earthquake of that year.[96] Japanese militarists in Asia killed more Asians than Americans ever did—some estimated 15 million to 35 million Chinese alone![97]   Japanese in china during the war adopted the "three-all" policy of *kill all, burn all, destroy all.*" [98]   It is true that American soldiers in the Second World War demonized the "Jap bastards" while at the same time risking life and limb to rescue Burmese, Filipinos, and Chinese. American aviators in China, the famed Flying Tigers under Claire Chennault, volunteered long before Pearl Harbor. Racism? Where is the racism that produced volunteer American pilots who arrived in China in the summer of 1941 to defend the Chinese?

By any stretch on the imagination, can the treatment of terrorists at Gitmo or Abu Ghraib in any way compare to atrocities committed by the Empire of Japan? Does the playing of Aguilera CDs in any way equate with the Nazis' gassing of innocent Jews or the Japanese performing vivisection on prisoners in China? Can any rational person compare the three meals a day given to prisoners at Gitmo (which, by the way, are better than the MREs given to the troops who guard them) with Alexander Solzhenitsyn's accounts of intentional starvation of gulag exiles in One Day in the Life of Ivan Denisovich? The worst military prison in America offers better food and living conditions than the average citizen enjoys in most of the world's countries.

When a Lieutenant Calley is discovered, he is prosecuted, as were four American soldiers in Sicily in July 1943 after they gang-raped an Italian woman. When those soldiers were arrested and their identities proved beyond all reasonable doubt, all four were tried and hanged within two months. Two soldiers con-

---

[94]Russell, Knights of Bushido, p. 253.
[95]Iris Chang, The Rape of Nanking (New York: Penguin, 1998); Bergamini, Japan's Imperial Conspiracy, passim.
[96] John W. Dower, War Without Mercy: Race and Power in the Pacific War (New York: Pantheon Books, 1986). p. 284.
[97]Lynn, Battle, p. 235, and http://www.edu.cn/history/www.arts.cuhk.hk/NanjingMassacre/NMchron.html.
[98]Lynn, Battle, p. 227.

victed of rape in France in 1944 were also hanged.[99] Although the United States and her allies prosecuted Japanese for war crimes related to the mass rapes in Nanking, is there any evidence that the Japanese punished their own soldiers for these atrocities? The reader knows the answer.

Americans win wars because as a society, as a culture, we value life. We take unprecedented steps to free our own POWs, even making efforts that few other Western countries have ever made. With a few highly unusual exceptions, prisoners who surrender to the United States face a safe incarceration with good food, decent conditions, exceptional medical care, and, today, remarkable toleration of their (often violent) religious practices. Americans win wars because most people—except the most deeply brainwashed of Nazis, Islamofascists, or Japanese militarists—see that a regard for the sanctity of life is a desirable trait. A culture of life will always prevail over a culture of death, and Americans win wars because they intuitively understand that principle.

---

[99] B. G. Burkett and Glenna Whitley, Stolen Valor: How the Vietnam Generation Was Robbed of Its Heroes and Its History (Dallas: Verity Press, 1998), pp. 125–26.

CHAPTER TWO
Learning from Loss

*Concern for casualties in American military efforts has nurtured a reverse hu-
bris, which has produced a culture in which past successes—and failures—are
studied and analyzed without regard to whether or not we look good.*

The North Vietnamese machine gunner rolled the GI over to use as a
sandbag for his weapon, pushing the tripod up against the soldier's ribs. But
Private Jack Smith wasn't dead—he was covered with blood, playing possum as
best he could because his life depended on it. Smith remembered the feel of the
Vietnamese gunner's knee in his side. Although he trembled with fear, Smith's
ruse was not discovered because the teenager blasting away at the Americans was
shaking in fear worse than he was.

Smith's battalion was the first in Vietnam to be overrun. Now the Viet-
cong and PAVNs (People's Army of Vietnam) fought hand to hand with the
Americans of the 2nd Battalion, 7th Cavalry. When the teenage PAVN soldier
started firing, Smith's men shot back with rifle grenades. *"Oh, my God,"* Smith
thought. *"If I stand up, the North Vietnamese will kill me; and if I stay lying
down, my buddies will get me."*[1] Instead, the aim of the 7th troopers were true.
Although Smith was wounded, The American troops killed the machine gunner,
but the Communist attack had nearly destroyed the company. By the time American air power and reserves had driven off the North Vietnamese, Smith's unit
had 93 percent casualties. PAVNs had infiltrated as far as the American mortar
pits—generally well behind the front lines—and fighting was so close that Smith,
lying close to another enemy machine gunner, "simply stuck out my rifle and
blew off his head." [2]

Ninety-nine years after Custer led his ill-fated attack at the Little Big
Horn, the 7th Cavalry again found itself surrounded and infiltrated. This time
the troopers had ridden into action with helicopters instead of horses; and this
time the enemy was the Vietnamese army, not the Sioux and Cheyenne. But as
had occurred almost a century earlier on that Montana plain, the 7th Cavalry in
November 1965 was in danger of being overrun as it lost its fire superiority and
unit cohesion. Again it appeared that an American cavalry unit in enemy territory would be over whelmed and massacred, but Colonel Hal Moore had learned
the lessons of the past, studying Custer's battle. Above all, he knew that he had
advantages Custer did not: precision artillery and, above all, air support. Within
minutes, Moore called in curtains of artillery fire. When he shouted "Broken Ar-
row" into the radio, planes were stacked up above the battlefield at thousand-foot
increments, raining down bombs and napalm in a murderous assault that saved

[1]Quoted at "Death in the Ia Drang Valley," http://www.mishalov.com/death_ia_drang_valley.html
[2]http://www.mishalov.com/death_ia_drang_valley.html

Moore's command. Even as the Communist forces surrounded Moore's men and cut off one unit temporarily, superior firepower, brought in almost on top of the 7th, proved a life saver.

Although the United States "lost" the Vietnam War, its battles provided plenty of examples of how the American military learned its own lessons—and those of others—and adapted. At Khe Sanh, for example, in January 1968, Marine battalions defended a long airstrip set in the middle of several hills. The situation was an approximation to Dien Bien Phu, where the Communists had had their great victory over the French just fifteen years earlier. Like the French, General William Westmoreland was confident he could hold the base but unlike the French, Westmoreland had unprecedented air power. He also had made extensive provisions for supporting Khe Sanh, moving 17,000 troops to within thirty minutes of the besieged base. Viet Cong and North Vietnamese (NVAs) shelled the base relentlessly, to the point when air resupply was reduced to pushing pallets off transports moving a few feet off the ground. Wounded were hustled to a bunker a few feet from the airstrip so helicopters could rapidly evacuate them.

The situation was grim: NVA mortars and rockets decimated almost everything above ground and forced the Leathernecks—who had no chance to bathe and limited fresh food—into *"living a life more similar to rats than human beings,"* noted one officer. Forays away from the camp during the day could go no farther than thirty or forty yards, and pounding by B-52s right on top of the Marines seemed not to deter the Communists. Finally, after four months of hell, the siege was lifted. Unlike the French at Dien Bien Phu, the Americans were not pushed off the high ground: the knocked the NVA back in every assault. More important, American commanders applied air power liberally, flying twenty-four thousand sorties that dropped one hundred thousand tons of bombs, denuding the entire forest around the base. Although U.S. forces counted only 1,602 dead enemy, Westmoreland estimated that the NVA death toll alone was at least ten time that. When wounded were included, General Vo Nguyen Giap probably lost close to 30,000 men while failing to take the base. When piled on top of the staggering losses of the Tet Offensive—which, ironically, produced something of a lull for Khe Sanh—the Communist losses for January through April of 1968 easily exceeded 50,000 men, or more than half of all troops committed. No army in history has survived such battlefield losses, but Giap and Ho Chi Minh were trading the lives of their troops for critical coverage in the American media. What the Marines won on the hills around Khe Sanh, the New York Times and CBS took away in the homes of Americans.

No More Vietnams

American military forces have experienced their share of defeats, some of them shocking. Custer's destruction at the Little Big Horn stunned the nation and in the long term forced a review of the entire Indian policy. Wake Island,

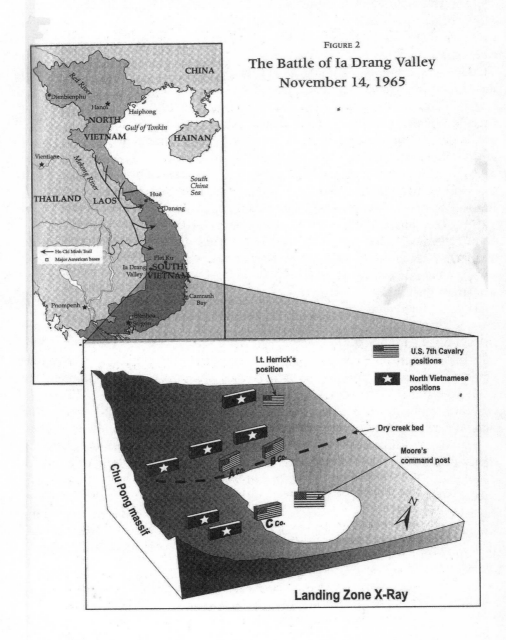

FIGURE 2

The Battle of Ia Drang Valley
November 14, 1965

eventually taken by the Japanese, held out from December 8 through December 23 of 1941, but because of its dogged defenders, the battle became an inspiration to a reeling nation. Its famous radio message after driving off one Japanese attack ("Send us more Japs") was a mistake in which the innocuous words Send us and more Japs were added unwittingly as mere boilerplate code words to another message, but to Americans back home it appeared that the Marines and their civilian contractor allies were begging for more attackers![3]

To this day, references to Pearl Harbor provoke head shaking and comments like "We should have been prepared." More than any other military episode, however, the "Vietnam Syndrome" has shaped the American culture of combat with its implications for strategy, tactics, and fighting.[4] Defined as *the intangible loss of confidence*" that the United States suffered after withdrawing from Vietnam, the Vietnam Syndrome suggests an equally dangerous commandment, namely, Thou shalt not take casualties. Leaders as respected and diverse as Ronald Reagan, Colin Powell, and Wesley Clark have outlined several criteria for the commitment of American military force—a litmus test—which all boil down to one imperative: keep the nation united by keeping casualties low.[5] General Robert Scales, commenting on the 1990 Gulf war preparations, noted that "the real issue was the prospective human cost of the operation," and, again, noted that "concern over casualties prevailed" in planning.[6] An increasing amount of scholarship on casualties in wars has surfaced as well, including articles in the Army's technical journal, Parameters, by Harvey Sapolsky and Jeremy Shapiro, and Karl Eikenberry.[7]

Of course, the concern for combat deaths does not date from Vietnam, but first became a public issue during the Civil War, and then again in World War I. Even though America's participation in the First World War was brief—just over a year of substantial combat—it greatly shaped the American concern for combat casualties. Prior to the war, in 1912, General James McAndrew, who would be General John J. Pershing's chief of staff in the American Expeditionary force, delivered an address to the American Historical Association (AHA) that "*urged his-*

[3]When the defenders themselves discovered that the message had been made into a propaganda slogan, they were outraged. "Who I the crap said that!" asked one corporal. The last thing the men on Wake wanted after one invasion attempt was another invasion force. (John Wukovits, Pacific Alamo: The Battle of Wake Island (New York: New American Library, 2003), p. 112.

[4]Michael Pearlman, Warmaking and American Democracy: The Struggle over Military Strategy, 1700 to the Present (Lawrence: University Press of Kansas, 1999), pp. 334, 397.

[5]See Ronald Reagan, An American Life (New York: Pocketbooks, 1990), pp. 266–467; Colin Powell, My American Journey (New York: Random House, 1995); Secretary of Defense Caspar Weinberger to the National Press Club, November 28, 1984; and Wesley Clark, "The United States and NATO: The Way Ahead," Parameters, 29, Winter 1999–2000, pp. 2–14.

[6] Robert Scales, Certain Victory: The U.S. Army in the Gulf War (Fort Leavenworth: U.S. Army Command and General Staff College Press, 1994), pp. 35, 36, 126, 140; Bernard Trainor and Michael Gordon, The Generals' War: The Inside Story of the Gulf Conflict (New York: Little, Brown and Co., 1995).

[7] Karl Eikenberry, "Take No Casualties," Parameters, 26, Summer 1996, pp. 109–118, and Harvey Sapolsky and Jeremy Shapiro, "Casualties, Technology, and America's Future Wars," Parameters, Summer 1996, pp. 119–22. Nothing could be further from the truth than the comment that "the officer corps that came back from Southeast Asia devoted precious little energy to dissecting the defeat it had just endured." (Andrew J. Bacevich, The New American Militarism: How Americans Are Seduced by War (Oxford: Oxford University Press, 2005), p. 42.

torians to enlighten the American people about the nation's history of peacetime unpreparedness."[8] (One might consider the remote chances that the modern AHA would allow a general to speak at all, let alone in favor of military preparedness!) Major General Leonard Wood, based on his experience in the Spanish-American War, warned that the United States had shown that it typically failed to prepare for foreign wars. After the war, the comments of Wood and McAndrew would prove prescient, and many would agree with Pershing that "participation in the Great War should teach our people the cost in life and treasure of unpreparedness."[9]

Even as Doughboys headed for Europe in June 1917, by which time headlines had for three years detailed the bloody gore of the trenches, the military and the American public were unprepared. U-boats lurked off the Atlantic coast, dealing death from below, and if the troops were fortunate enough to land in France, they faced the as-yet unsolved conundrum of the trenches, barbed wire, and machine guns. Before a single American soldier planted his feet on French soil, the Army was concerned with mortality statistics. Early subordination of American troops under French command made casualties worse, with one postwar study concluding that Americans serving under their own officers "*advanced farther and under greater resistance in less time*" with fewer casualties than those under the French.[10]

American commanders, however, provided only slightly better results. In July 1918, during one of its first offensive operations at Soissons, the 26th Infantry Regiment suffered 90 percent casualties, and the 1st and 2nd divisions lost 12,000 men. Poorly trained infantry bunched up, which only made them bigger targets. After action reports agreed that the Yanks were courageous but unskilled, or as a lieutenant soberly acknowledged, "*We learned small unit tactics from the Germans. They were costly teachers.*"[11] The then lieutenant George Patton added, "Untutored courage proved useless in the face of educated bullets."[12] More than a decade later, Chief of Staff George Marshall pointed out that the Army had suffered "a great many unnecessary casualties" in World War I due to "the clumsy handling of men."[13] Indeed, American training (or, more appropriately, retraining) occurred during the conflict, and another lesson was learned in that context, namely, there was only so much young officers could absorb in school without experience. Many seasoned officers were yanked out of combat and sent to school, depriving the units of the best leaders the Army had. But the military learned those lessons, too.

After the war, a number of writers who had served in the ambulance corps, including Ernest Hemingway, John Dos Passos, and E. E. Cummings, pro-

[8]Evan Andrew Huelfer, The "Casualty Issue" in American Military Practice: The Impact of World War I (Westport: Praeger, 2003).

[9]General John J. Pershing, "Graduation Address to the General Staff College Class of 1920," cited in Huelfer, The "Casualty Issue," p.70

[10]Quoted in Huelfer, The "Casualty Issue," p.5

[11]Pearlman, Warmaking and American Democracy, p. 210.

[12]Pearlman, Warmaking and American Democracy, p. 209.

[13]Larry Bland, ed., The Papers of George Catlett Marshall, 2 vols. (Baltimore: The John Hopkins University Press, 1986), 2:64.

duced a string of antiwar books, such as *Three Soldiers* (1921) or *The Enormous Room* (1922).[14] "Disillusionment literature" drenched the writing market, to the extent that Samuel Eliot Morison later wrote that it affected the "*generation of youth which came to maturity around 1940 [leaving them] spiritually unprepared for the war they had to fight*."[15] Along with the works that promoted pacifism, a wave of personal monographs, memoirs, articles written for military publications such as the Army and Navy Journal, and other writings soon saturated the martial market. These works provided a wealth of firsthand accounts of combat and the tactics that worked, and those that did not. Open publication of that type was not seen in Stalin's Soviet Union or, later, in Hitler's Germany. Technical writing, including casualty assessments, circulated inside the U.S. military, and while by some comparisons the World War I casualties were less horrific (say, when placed next to those at Gettysburg or alongside those of the other major belligerents), the overall numbers do not lie. More than 53,000 Americans died in the war and close to 180,000 were wounded. Congress, naturally, had to launch an investigation after the war, spending millions of dollars for "inconclusive results."[16]

Analysis after the war focused on the cost of unpreparedness, and the role of preparation and training in reducing casualties. Although Congress reduced defense budgets during the 1920s, the national Defense Act of 1920 was called by General Hunter Liggett "*one of the finest and best thought out pieces of legislation ever enacted*."[17] Defense budgets in Harding's and Coolidge's' small-government-oriented administrations remained tight, and in the 1930s, while the Germans built more than 2,500 tanks, the entire stockpile of the United States was a meager 329. Still, the U.S. military enacted critical changes in the 1920s, among them bringing West Point up to date. After declaring the U.S. Military Academy "*forty years behind the times*," U.S. Army chief of staff General Peyton March assigned Brigadier General Douglas MacArthur to become the new superintendent of West Point in 1919.[18] The youngest man in nearly a century to head the academy, MacArthur struggled against public opinion that wanted to demilitarize, isolate, and reap a "peace dividend." MacArthur flatly stated that the old system had failed and that "a new type of officer was necessary," one who could lead well and save the lives of his men. Mathematics and engineering were deemphasized as tactics, doctrine, and military arts were given more attention. For the first time, West Point began teaching management courses, and MacArthur instituted physical conditioning and summer training with regular army units.

Infantry officers specifically studied measures to reduce combat losses, as

---

[14]See Paul Fussell, The Great War and Modern Memory (New York: Oxford University Press, 1975); David Kennedy, Over Here: The First World War and American Society (New York: Oxford University Press, 1980); George Mosse, Fallen Soldiers: Reshaping the Memory of the World Wars (New York: Oxford University Press, 1990); John Dos Passos, The Soldiers (New York: Modern Library, 1921): E. E. Cummings, The Enormous Room (New York: Modern Library, 1922); and William March, Company K (Concord, NY: American Mercury, 1931).

[15]Samuel Eliot Morison, "Faith of a Historian," American Historical Review, 56, 1951, pp.266–67.

[16]Huelfer, The "Casualty Issue," p.69.

[17]Hunter Liggett, Commanding an American Army (Boston: Houghton Mifflin Company, 1925), pp.155–56.

[18]Quoted in D. Clayton James, The Years of MacArthur, 2 vols. (Boston: Houghton Mifflin, 1970), 2:261

well as ways to increase firepower on the battlefield—the characteristic American "force multiplier" approach. Here the American army differed from its British or European counterparts, who "augmented firepower by increasing a unit's number of light machine guns." [19] Americans, however had a marksmanship tradition. Soldiers were expected to be good shots, so the Infantry Board looked for ways to increase the rate of fire of the individual soldier, ditching the 1903 Springfield rifle for the new M1 Garand. This provided a rate of twenty to thirty rounds per minute, or double that of the Springfield, and it reflected the continued American emphasis on individual performance within the group.

To augment West Point, the Command and General Staff School at Fort Leavenworth, Kansas, emphasized tactical decision making, operations, and combined arms. Although not noted for developing original thinking, Fort Leavenworth produced officers who proved not only effective but economical with the lives of their men.[20] It created a *common doctrine, language, and outlook* for American officers, and even though it emphasized "uniformity," it allowed officers to be "used as interchangeable parts," and made the graduates professional. [21]Even in a uniform, it was seldom difficult to get Americans to express their individuality. Taken together, the military schools democratized and equalized the educational base of the American officer corps, and provided tremendous opportunities for career advancement.

A few of the old guard, like their counterparts in France, clung to the notion that marksmanship and bayonet skill alone could prevail in the next war. Well into the 1920s, cavalry retained a primary mission, and tanks were subordinated to the infantry. Aside from a few lone voices, such as Billy Mitchell's in the Army Air Corps and Billy Moffatt's in the Navy, air power's role remained undetermined, unrefined, and outside the general strategic planning. The Italian general Giulio Douhet's Command of the Air had already influenced thinkers on both side of the Atlantic, but despite the potential savings of infantry lives gained by massive bombing campaigns, few saw strategic bombing as a new magic key to defeating an enemy with minimal losses. An exception was Billy Mitchell's *Winged Defense* (1925), which claimed that bombing could shave "months and even years off contest of ground armies" with a savings of "millions of lives." [22]

Mitchell's views were not shared by many, but the Army did slowly incorporate air power doctrine into its education, staring with a 1926 manual Employment of Combined Air Forces, which echoed Mitchell's call for strikes deep in the enemy's heartland as a means of reducing infantry losses. Although the concept was nothing new, the phrase *destroy the enemy's will to resist* started to come into vogue. American thinkers rejected Douhet's population bombing, but

[19]Huelfer, The "Casualty Issue," p.95.
[20]Huelfer, The "Casualty Issue," p.97.
[21]Timothy Nenninger, The Leavenworth Schools: Education, Professionalism, and the Officer Corps of the United States Army, 1881-1918 (Westport, CT: Greenwood Press, 1978), 147–49; Huelfer, The "Casualty Issue," 100; Martin Blumenson, "America's World War II Leaders in Europe: Some Thoughts," Parameters, 19, December 1989, pp. 2–13
[22]Billy Mitchell, Winged Defense (New York: G. P. Putnam's Sons, 1925), p. 127.

did accept the premise that enemy military and industrial targets could be crushed by strategic bombing, an approach made possible by the 1935 introduction of the B-17 and the Norden bombsight. MacArthur acknowledged the key role of air power in the next war when he said that in a future conflict, *"the nation that does not command the air will face deadly odds."*[23] Even then, however, air planners started to calculate ways to reduce casualties, including producing tactics that would guarantee target destruction on the first mission so that additional missions would not be necessary. Before the first bombs fell at Pearl Harbor, American planners had developed a thoroughgoing paper campaign to reduce Germany without the insertion of ground forces by using more than 6,800 heavy bombers.[24]

Some, such as Sherwood Ross, argue that a combination of factors, including Walt Disney's animated film *Victory Through Air Power* (1943), swung the policy toward bombing of civilians as well as military targets, without acknowledging that productivity of war goods was disrupted by leveling acres of housing, and German workers were taken from factory work to fighting fires and other emergency work.[25] The fact is, however, that well before Pearl Harbor, the American World War I experience of high battlefield losses among infantry had made an indelible impact on virtually all observers. This partially enabled Winston Churchill to convince Franklin Roosevelt that the easiest way for the United States to enter the war against Germany was through air power. Not only was it economical with human life (although the early B-17 raids experienced tremendous losses as a percentage of planes committed), but it played to the American strength of production. Build, build, build, and the Nazis would be swept under. Unrealistic authors were already making such argument, including William Ziff, who claimed in 1942 that air power could save the United States for a "war of attrition," and even General Henry "Hap" Arnold who knew ground operations could not be avoided, nevertheless preached that air power could "save millions of lives in ground combat."[26] Whatever the appeal of air power, however, top commanders like MacArthur and Eisenhower realized that it was merely one component of the overall force, and increasingly they worked to incorporate air power into combined arms operations—in other words, using airplanes to support men on the ground, not take their place. What remains impressive about the big thinkers was how they grasped the integrated nature of war and the necessity—utterly

---

[23]Douglas MacArthur, Reminiscences (New York: McGraw-Hill, 1964) ,p. 99
[24]Huelfer, The "Casualty Issue," p. 124; James Gaston, Planning the American Air War: Four Men and Nine Days in 1941 (Washington: National Defense University Press, 1982); R. J. Overy, "Air Power and the Origins of Deterrence Theory Before 1939," Journal of Strategic Studies, p.14, 1992, 73–101; Michael Sherry, The Rise of American Air Power (New Haven: Yale University Press, 1987); Williamson Murray, "Strategic Bombing: The British, American, and German Experiences," in Williamson Murray and Allan Millett, eds., Military Innovation in the Interwar Period (New York: Cambridge University Press, 1996), pp.96–143; and Robert Futrell, Ideas, Concepts, and Doctrine: A History of Basic Thinking in the United States Air Force, 1907-1964 (Maxwell Air Force Base, AL: Air University Press, 1971).
[25]Ross Sherwood, "How the United States Reversed Its Policy on Bombing Civilians," The Humanist, 65, July/August 2005, pp.14–22.
[26]William Ziff, The Coming Battle of Germany (New York: Duell, Sloan, and Pearce, 1942), pp. 160, 187, 272; Arnold quoted in Sherry, Rise of American Air Power, p.127. See also Arnold's book, Global Mission (New York: harper & Bros., 1949).

missing in the First World War—of mating tactics to technology.

British use of tanks in the Great War was a classic example of how tactics failed to keep up with technology. Although joining the war late, American military planners had their interest in the tank aroused, and Patton's armored brigade at Saint-Mihiel proved extremely effective, losing only two tanks to enemy fire, with only two men killed. In later action, Patton's brigade took heavier losses, however, prompting (typically) American studies and examination that revealed that mechanical difficulties, improper coordination, and poorly trained crews contributed to the losses.[27] During the interwar years, Patton, Eisenhower, and chief of infantry Major General R. H. Allen all continued to tout the value of the tank, which, Allen maintained, "had paid for themselves many times over" in combat. Tanks, he continued, would restore the infantry's power by enabling an attack *"without prohibitive losses."* [28] Although the fire-breathing Patton is most associated with armor, it was none other than the more reserved Ike who wrote an article in 1920 for the Infantry Journal extolling the value of tanks. Eisenhower's article was so radical in it concepts and arguments that Chief of Infantry Charles Farnsworth threatened him with court-martial if he did not cease such writings![29]

Whether tanks or aircraft, doctrine or dogma, the Army and Navy discovered after World War I that they had absorbed an evolution in managerial structures that had already taken root in business. Already in the nineteenth century, most large-scale firms had adopted hierarchies of managers (top level, middle managers, and so on) to handle the daily business of large companies. This new approach had originated during the separation of ownership from the management of railroads in the 1850s, and by 1900 it had spread to processed foods, cigarettes, paint, meatpacking, kerosene, and virtually all other production and manufacturing. Professional managers, who had specialized training, had taken over these companies with the single-minded goal of increasing efficiency (usually through lowering cost). No one did that better than Andrew Carnegie, but all the titans of industry practiced efficiency methods in some form, which usually involved a commitment to slow but steady growth with low risk (as opposed to rapidly increasing profits if it also meant higher risks). Companies, and the men who ran them, became risk averse, which is why so few major breakthroughs ever come from an industrial leader in the field.

Although the military services "professionalized" somewhat slower than private industry, they nevertheless adopted a similar structure and, already possessing a managerial hierarchy of sorts, the Army and Navy soon started to reflect the same conservatism—and even stodginess— when it came to new technologies or practices. Whether it was General John Thompson's submachine guns, Preston Tuckers' forty-mile-per-hour armored car, or Lieutenant William Sims's

[27]Captain George Patton, "Light Tanks," December 12, 1917, in Dale Wilson, "The American Expeditionary Forces Tank Corps in World War I: From Creation to combat," M.A. Thesis, Temple University, 1988, p.23; Dwight Eisenhower, At Ease: Stories I Tell to Friends (Garden City, NY: Doubleday, 1967), p. 136.
[28]Quoted in Huelfer, The "Casualty Issue," pp.128–29.
[29]George Hoffman, "The Demise of the U.S. Tank Corps and Medium Tank Development Program," Military Affairs, 37, February 1973, pp. 20–25

revolution in naval gun sighting, new weapons and tactical concepts struggled to find a home against entrenched bureaucracies—an unfortunate fellow traveler of professional management.[30]

Consequently, Eisenhower's rebuke over tanks was hardly surprising. In business you can always quit as a leader in the field and start a small competitor. The challenge for the American military was to find a way to encourage radicals and revolutionary thinking within the confines of established doctrine and structures. Fortunately, the Army War College and the Naval War College provide forums in which new ideas percolated, keeping tanks alive conceptually until new tests again showed their worth. MacArthur, having played a prominent role in modernizing and improving infantry tactics, now slowed the trend toward mechanization by allowing both the infantry and cavalry to develop their own mechanized forces. Worse, a number of other factors shaped tank development, including the cargo capacity of the flatbed trucks that had to transport them over long distances, which limited the United States to light tanks. Not until the Army saw the success of the Germans in 1939 and 1940 did the War Department seriously reassess its tank policies.

The result, as Russell Weigley observed, was that the Army to some degree retained an emphasis on mass and power, but had developed weapons that emphasized speed and mobility. I World War II, tanks especially would reflect this dichotomy, as even the medium Sherman tank could not stand toe to toe with heavy German armor.[31] Naval amphibious doctrine, however, started to blend the two in its 1931 Tentative Manual for Landing Operations, whose ideas included island-hopping, air and naval superiority, and amphibious assaults at weaker points.[32]

While the military attempted to adjust to the lessons of World War I, the politics of the New Deal intervened. Roosevelt slashed appropriations for the Army to what MacArthur described as *"below the point of safety."*[33] The U.S. Army fell to seventeenth in size among the world's military forces, and the warnings about preparation and training became faint echoes. No money existed for new models of tanks, trucks, or aircraft, let alone for joint exercises. Having briefly learned the lessons of unpreparedness in World War I, the United States applied some of the solutions, shelved a few others, and ignored still others. Nevertheless, the casualty issue had so shaped American thinking that it pushed military doctrine down several lines that would, in the long run, reduce losses and increase battlefield performance by instilling the paramount place of mobility and speed, the very keystones of Patton's and MacArthur's offensives, in military doctrine; shaping the desirability of air campaigns in reducing the enemy's abilities to maintain supply, transportation, and morale; and bringing about changes in

[30]William J. Helmer, Thompson, The Gun That Made the Twenties Roar (New York: Macmillan, 1969); Elting Morrison, "Gunfire at Sea: A Case Study of Innovation," in Morrison, Men, Machines, and Modern Times (Cambridge, MA: MIT Press, 1966), pp.17–44.
[31]Russell Weigley, Eisenhower's Lieutenants (Bloomington, IN: Indiana University Press, 1981), pp. 2–12.
[32]Holland Smith, Coral and Brass (New York: Charles Scribner's Sons, 1949).
[33]Huelfer, The "Casualty Issue," p.151.

infantry and amphibious tactics that would prove economical later. The trick was not to miss the tipping point, where employing military forces sooner rather than later would save lives.

"If You Encounter Steel, Withdraw"

In December 1937, the clearly marked *USS Panay* was sunk on the Yangtze River in broad daylight by Japanese aircraft. Whereas in the 1900 Boxer Rebellion Americans demanded that an immediate expeditionary force punish the perpetrators of the attack on the American embassy, in 1937 isolationist public attitudes called for a full withdrawal from China. Roosevelt slapped sanctions on Japan, and the public turned away. As tensions mounted with Germany over the Nazis' war on England, in October 1941 the destroyer *Reuben James* was torpedoed by a U-boat and sunk, killing 115 crewman. Once again, an overt act of war was ignored—by virtually all but singer Woody Guthrie, whose song "The Sinking of the Reuben James" asked if anyone knew the names of those who died in the attack.

Vladimir Lenin once said that the Communist expansionist policy was to *"probe with the bayonet. If you encounter steel, withdraw, and if you encounter flesh, continue."* From 1937 to 1941, both the Japanese and the Germans had probed American will and encountered flesh. Blinded into believing that disengagement and isolation would reduce casualties, American policy makers—supported by the public—had only ensured greater losses when the war came.

Similar lessons could have been applied to Mogadishu, where 18 dead Americans led President Bill Clinton to withdraw American forces from Somalia. Osama bin Laden, soon to be the world's greatest terrorist, watched closely and told reporters that the events in Mogadishu and the 1983 withdrawal of the Marines from Lebanon after a truck bombing of the Marine barracks, in which more than 240 Marines were killed, typified the unwillingness of Americans to suffer casualties. *"The extent of your impotence and weakness became very clear [in Somalia],"* he concluded in the *"Declaration of War Against the Americans for Occupying the Land of Two Holy Places."*[34]

In each case—the *Panay*, the *Reuben James*, the Beirut Marine barracks, and the Black Hawk Down incident—Americans feared that material and physical preparation for combat would, in turn, drive policy decisions and even encourage military action. Yet in each case it was the failure to prepare that ultimately ensured far higher loss of life, including civilians. Roosevelt was swimming against a public opinion tide, but he certainly knew by early 1941 that matters were nearing the point when American involvement in Europe was nearly assured. Kent Greenfield, the U.S. Army's chief historian, described Roosevelt's position as desiring to "confront his enemies with a rapidly growing weight of material power,

---

[34]Osama bin Laden, "Declaration of War Against the Americans Occupying the Land of the Two Holy Places," August 1996, http://www.meij.or.jp/new/Osma%20bin%20Laden/jihad1.htm

then crush them with a minimum expenditure of American lives."[35]   By May, secretary of war Henry Stimson wrote in his diary, *"I feel more up against it than ever before. It is a problem whether this country has it in itself to meet such an emergency. Whether we are really powerful enough and sincere enough to meet the Germans is getting to be more and more of a real problem."*[36]

The War Department could not sit without plans if war came, and by September 1941 it had a Victory Plan that dealt with a two-front war, emphasizing a strategic offensive in Europe and a holding action in the Pacific. Planners even anticipated losing some ground to Japan in the short run in order to defeat Germany.[37]   The same planners knew that neither a naval blockade alone nor a combination with air power would win a European war. Although they held out a faint hope that strategic bombing might make a land invasion unnecessary, their main emphasis remained preparation of land forces so that when they were committed, they would be trained and used in force. The Chicago Tribune, in an effort to derail any movement toward war, published the Victory Plan in December 1941, just three days before Pearl Harbor.[38]   (This incident was remarkably similar to the massive protest marches against globalization and big business that were planned for the World Trade Center just days after 9/11). Ultimately, having learned the casualty lessons of World War I—despite the sluggish progress during the New Deal—military planners had prepared a cohesive strategy of annihilation that would employ naval and air power first, then us American manpower to deliver the coup de grace, minimizing losses through attrition. Even now, the lessons of World War I remain vivid in the minds of planners. As the Army's current doctrine states: *"the American people expect decisive victory and abhor unnecessary casualties."* [39]

Collapse at Kasserine

Partly due to the American concern about high casualties, and partly due to shrewd maneuvering by British Prime Minister Winston Churchill, the United States entered the war in Europe through the cellar: Africa. A relatively bloodless landing in North Africa kicked off Operation Torch in November 1942. There are the halfhearted resistance consisting of French troops under the command of the Vichy collaborationist government fooled some American commanders into thinking the Germans, under Field Marshal Erwin Rommel, might be just as easy. They were wrong.

---

[35]Kent Roberts Greenfield, American Strategy in World War II: A Reconsideration (Baltimore: Johns Hopkins University Press, 1963), p.74.
[36]Henry Stimson and McGeorge Bundy, On Active Service in War and Peace (New York: Harper Publishers, 1948), 371, and Stimson's "Diary," quoted in Huelfer, The "Casualty Issue," p.191.
[37]Huelfer, The "Casualty Issue," p. 189.
[38]Thomas Fleming argues that Roosevelt leaked the memo to the press, which makes little sense: the Victory Plan would have, if anything, galvanized forces against war. See The New Dealers' War: FDR and the War Within World War II (New York: Basic Books, 2001).
[39]United States Army, FM100-5 Operations (Washington: Government Printing Office, 1993), pp. 1–3.

Confronted with their first major ground combat of World War II, the U.S. soldiers and equipment performed poorly at best. Command under Major General Lloyd Fredendall never clearly delineated zones of authority with the French allies, nor among Fredendall's subordinates. (One officer literally struggled to determine which of six superior officers, including a Briton and a Frenchman, he took orders from.) Fredendall issued bombastic yet cryptic orders so lacking in specificity that some officers thought they were in code. Telling his air commanders *"Don't wait for us to order air missions, you know what the situation is, just keep pounding them"* explained nothing about the actual battlefield needs for air support. [40] Mostly armed with completely ineffective M3 light tanks, Fredendall's troops were scattered over a front of more than 125 miles, trying to protect desert passes. His units were mixed, hodgepodge collections—not the kind of self-contained fighting volunteers who had stood with Andrew Jackson at New Orleans, but unequal conglomerates of men who had never fought or trained together. When needed replacements arrived, they had full duffel bags but no weapons: "some had never fired a rifle, none had entrenching tools or bayonets, and many were not even trained infantrymen."[41]

Out of some 50 American tanks to engage the German armor in the first serious exchange, only 4 escaped destruction. Yet American commanders, especially Fredendall, completely misjudged the extent of the defeat, leading to still further losses. About 6,000 of the 30,000 Americans who fought at Kasserine were wounded or missing, and another 300 were killed—20 percent of the force. Germans captured or destroyed more than 183 tanks, nearly 200 half-tanks, 208 artillery pieces, and 512 trucks and Jeeps in the II Corps alone, not counting other various American units assigned to Fredendall. It was a disaster, and especially disheartening for the first time out of the box for the U.S. Army. *"The defeat,"* wrote Marin Blumenson, *"shook down the command and the logistical establishment."* [42]

Kasserine stoked the fires of the gravest British concerns about whether or not the Yanks could fight. It was a revival of the same approach the British and French had used in World War I, attempting to relegate G.I.s to mere replacement roles within British or French units, rather than using them as intact, self-contained units. Of course, that didn't fly in 1917 and it wasn't seriously broached in 1942, although the doubts did not go away. After the war, the British concerns seemingly were validated by American historian S.L.A. Marshall, whose famous book *Men Against Fire* claimed that 75% of American troops did not fire their weapons, even though they were engaged in combat. However, Marshall's methods---not to mention his conclusions---were disproven by Roger Spiller.[43]

[40]Martin Blumenson, Kasserine Pass: Rommel's Bloody, Climactic Battle for Tunisia (New York: Cooper Square Press, 2000), p. 85.

[41]Blumenson, Kasserine Pass, pp. 138–39.

[42]Blumenson, Kasserine Pass, pp. 312.

[43]S.L.A. Marshall, Men Against Fire: The Problem of Battle Command (Norman, OK: University of Oklahoma Press, 2000 [1947]), vs. Roger Spiller, "S.L.A. Marshall and the Ratio of Fire," RUSI Journal, Winter 1988, 63-71; No. 2. Also see Paul Addison and Angus Calder, eds., Time to Kill: The Soldiers' Experience of War in the West, 1939-1945 (London: Pimlico, 1997), esp. Reid Mitchell, "The GI in Europe and the American

Ultimately, American units suffered from the very elements of freedom and democracy that required defending: their units were polyglot, made up of different levels of experience and different ethnic groups; they could not be indoctrinated the way German troops could; and the replacement system prevented the kind of unit maturation that the Germans had. Or, as Dave Dougherty and I put it in *A Patriot's History of the Modern World, vol. 1,* "Having evolved from a militia tradition where units elected their own officers and thought independently, Americans represented the epitome of the Western War of War for better or worse on the battlefield."[44]

Nevertheless, the debacle at Kasserine was not a decisive victory for Rommel. Not only did it cost the Afrika Korps 1,000 men—dead, wounded, and missing—but the Germans failed to achieve any semblance of a knockout blow. Worse, the Americans quickly reassessed everything from doctrine to training to deployment. George Patton was given command of the II Corps, and he immediately changed their demeanor, attitude, and above all, training. He trained units together and kept them together so that they fought together, building cohesion. Patton ended ad hoc assignment of forces. New equipment, which had already started to come ashore before Kasserine (especially the Sherman M-4 tank, which, while still limited, was a vast improvement over the M-3), soon reached the troops. Within months, the United States had analyzed every aspect of its defeat, and it never looked back, driving the Germans out of Tunisia at a total loss of almost 320,000 men for the campaign. Ironically, *"the turn of the tide at Kasserine proved actually to be the turn of the tide in all of Tunisia,"* wrote Ike.[45]

Quick Learners

If Americans are, as they were at Kasserine, unprepared and caught off guard at times, and if at other times, they are overconfident and reckless, they generally learn quickly from their defeats. At Wake Island, after Marines figured out that the Japanese had targeted their five-inch gun positions at the end of the first failed assault, they spent their nights moving the guns to new positions and making dummy cannons to draw fire. Adaptation and improvement have characterized the American soldier since Washington's time. Shortly after the main combat operations began in the American Revolution—when the Continental Army under George Washington was defeated in consecutive battles—British and Hessian of-

---

Military Tradition," 306-07. The debate eventually encompassed the notion of how good the G.I.s were, with the common view being that American infantry were not as good as their German counterparts. This was challenged by Peter Mansoor, The GI Offensive in Europe: The Triumph of American Infantry Divisions (Lawrence, KS: University of Kansas Press, 2002), but Martin van Creveld (Fighting Power: German and U.S. Army Performance, 1939-1945, [Santa Barbara, CA: Praeger, 2007]) and others have concluded that the American replacement/rotation system prevented the kind of experience from being built in American units than existed in German infantry. See Larry Schweikart and Dave Dougherty, A Patriot's History of the Modern World, vol. 1., From America's Exceptional Ascent to the Atomic Bomb: 1898-1945 (New York: Sentinel, 2012), pp.179-80.

[44]Schweikart and Dougherty, Patriot's History of the Modern World, p.180.

[45]Blumenson, Kasserine Pass, p.313

ficers observed that the American had already started to improve based on their experience. At White Plains, a Hessian lieutenant found *"they had excellent positions ... [and] had made their defenses better than usual, and maintained their posts with extraordinary tenacity."*[46]

Yet if American commanders have a weakness, it is that too often they have too much confidence in their troops—a trait their European counterparts rarely suffered from. Neither the Duke of Wellington nor Frederick the Great could be accused of overestimating the abilities of their men. Yet during the Civil War, both Ulysses S. Grant and Robert E. Lee made open-field assaults on entrenched positions more than once, resulting in horrific casualties for the Union at Cold Harbor and in the near destruction of the Army of Northern Virginia at Gettysburg. Each time, the commander put inordinate stock in the courage, perseverance, and fighting abilities of his forces. Lee's previous experience in the Mexican War gave him false confidence in the success of a frontal assault against a heavily defended position. At Chapultepec, in the Mexican War, George Pickett and James Longstreet had smashed the Mexican defenders despite overwhelming odds, but they had yet to face General George Meade and the Army of the Potomac.[47] Lee ordered the attack on Cemetery Ridge on July 3 despite having seen Yankee artillery shred his units crossing an open field at Malvern Hill just a year earlier. Grant, on the other hand, vowed never to repeat his mistake after assaulting the slopes of Vicksburg in his attempt to take that city, a promise he forgot at Cold Harbor. Custer's overconfidence in his cavalry against the Plains Indians spelled his doom. In each case, disaster ensued because the commanders thought their men capable of almost anything.

Part of the problem stems from commanders who forget that all soldiers are not trained alike. To say that the American soldier is the best trained in history is true; nevertheless, there are many levels of competence. Rangers, the Army's elite, look down upon those is the regular Army, just as the inter-service elite Delta Force looks down on the Rangers. At the other end of the scale are the maintenance units, such as the unfortunate 507th Maintenance Unit, which took a wrong turn and drove straight into a congested city full of Iraqi militia. Many of the 507th had not fired their weapons since basic training. Eleven were killed, six captured.

The experience of the 507th provided a sobering lesson that everyone in the armed forces is a potential combatant, and that anyone not well trained in weapons was at more serious risk than those who were. The Marines, given their superiority in combat training and despite their youth (the marines are the youngest, on average, of the enlisted troops), generally fared far better than the regular Army in combat situations. Both were less vulnerable than the reserves or Guardsmen who made up a significant portion of the convoy drivers. It didn't take long for the Army to figure this out: by the summer of 2004, the Army announced

---

[46]David Hackett Fischer, Washington's Crossing (Oxford: Oxford University Press, 2004), p. 111.
[47]See Mark Perry, Conceived in Liberty: Joshua Chamberlain, William Oates, and the American Civil War (New York: Penguin, 1997), pp. 228–29.

sweeping changes in its basic training program, including an increased emphasis on combat skills. *"Soldiers of all specialties will face direct contact with an adversary,"* stated Colonel Bill Gallagher, commander of Fort Benning's training brigade.[48] More, and more realistic, live-fire training, longer field maneuvers, and combat survival would now draw more attention. Cooks, mechanics, radio operators, and intelligence specialists would receive new instruction, previously not offered support personnel, in such areas as urban combat, quick-fire techniques, clearing a room, and other fighting techniques.

Many veterans complain that the feminization of the military has diluted training even further. The Army has twice as many females as the Marines; the Reserves and National Guard have three to four times as many. Certainly, the disaster with the 507th Maintenance Unit did not advance the cause of feminists arguing for women in combat. The more important breakdown was not sex, but training. America's military is diverse, but it is not great because it is diverse. It is great because it is deadly efficient, and diversity shows that anyone, from any background, can perform well within the system if properly trained. Whether a well-trained American female soldier was "as capable" as a heavier and stronger male, the real divergence was between well-trained Americans of either sex … and everyone else. Since 1976, that system has increasingly refined itself, studying lessons learned from every engagement, then improving tactics and training.

American successes and failures warrant study, and one of the most important episodes examined by the marines was the Russian experience in crushing the Chechnyan terrorists in Grozny. Among the essential lessons learned from Grozny's streets is that cultural differences can alienate a local population and turn neutrals into enemies. The *"Russians admit they underestimated the effect of religion and culture on the conflict."*[49] RPGs and booby traps were effective against Russian units, and the ferocity of urban combat took a high mental tool on Russian troops (in one survey, 72 percent had some psychological disorder after Grozny). The Chechnyans learned how to "hug" Russian troops to neutralize the Russians' superiority in air power, and exploited cell phones and the Internet to win the information war. After studying Grozny, the Marines devised entirely new tactics for pacifying and controlling Iraq's cities.

Prior to the Iraq War, critics—especially from the Left—wrung their hands and gravely prophesied that even if American forces reached Baghdad, the battle for the city would result in a bloodbath and Stalingrad-style house-to-house fighting. However, the chief of staff of the Army had already ordered a massive study of urban combat that drew upon the analysis of roger Spiller, whose 1999 paper, *"Sharp Corners,"* was published two years later.[50] Spiller maintained that urban warfare could be won by striking the right targets with precision. His anal-

---

[48]Thom Shanker, "Army Pushes a Sweeping Overhaul of Basic Training," New York Times, August 4, 2004.
[49] Lester W. Grau and Timothy L. Thomas, "Russian Lessons Learned from the Battles for Grozny," Foreign Military Studies Office, http://fmso.leavenworth.army.mil/FMSOPUBS/ISSUES/Rusn_leslrn.htm.
[50]Roger J. Spiller, Sharp Corners: Urban Operations at Century's End (Fort Leavenworth, Kansas: Combat Studies Institute, 2001); Russell Glen, Heavy Matter: Urban Operations Density of Challenges (Santa Monica: RAND, 2001).

ysis was expanded by others who saw cities as possessing "centers of gravity" that could be tipped by simultaneously striking at economic, political, and cultural points. Although these views were *"admittedly theoretical and wholly untested,"* both the Marines and the Army considered them sound enough to implement in training manuals.[51]   Among the other techniques that were employed, the Coalition decided not to invade a city prior to taking Baghdad so as not to reveal their tactics before the main battle.   This was true in Basra, where the media harped on the "difficulty" the British had in taking the city.   Commentators repeatedly questioned why Basra had not fallen, when, in fact, the purpose all along was to encircle the city and wait until Bagdad fell.

Yet even as Americans changed tactics, adapted, improved, and changed again (occasionally within the course of days), Americans on the ground in Operation Iraqi Freedom noted of their attackers, *"They never changed the way they fought, so we were able to use appropriate tactics to counter."*[52]   Describing the enemy fighters in An Najaf, Lieutenant Colonel Christopher Hughes noted that those he called *"the stupid"* would *"fire from a window and come back and fire from the same window."*[53]

Operation Iraqi Freedom was not without its own battlefield errors, the most serious of which was the attempt to destroy the Iraqi Medina Division with the 11th Attack Helicopter Regiment (AHR) on March 23, 2003.   Illuminated by the lights of Baghdad, and delayed at the outset by insufficient fuel, the 11th AHR encountered a wall of enemy small arms fire.   Iraqi tactics had been developed in the twelve years after the first Gulf War—and were initially effective, using widely decentralized antiaircraft weapons and tracking systems.   Yet it only took the single setback of the 11th AHR for the Army to adapt; and its next attack, by the 101st Aviation Brigade, just five days later, already had applied the lessons learned from March 23.

Studies such as *"Sharp Corners"* continued a tradition within the U.S. military of encouraging self-criticism and scholarship as opposed to merely self-serving propaganda.   First among the service journals to engage in such exchanges was the U.S. Naval Institute Proceedings, started at the United States naval Institute under Alfred Thayer Mahan for the purpose of discussing tactics, history, and politics as they applied to naval affairs.   Mahan, whose interest in navies throughout history later formed the basis of his book *The Influence of Seapower Upon History* (1890), thought the past provided important lessons for officers in the present.   Over the years, Proceedings proved to be the most self-critical of the military journals, in the 1980s debating the judgment of the commander of the USS *Vincennes*, which shot down an Iranian airliner by mistake in 1988.   Later, in the 1990s, Proceedings carried heated articles on gays in the military and women aboard ships.

[51]Gregory Fontenot, E. J. Degan, and David Tohn, On Point: The United States Army in Operation Iraqi Freedom (Washington, D.C.: U.S. Army chief of Staff, 2004), p.50.
[52]Fontenot, On Point, p.279.
[53]Fontenot, On Point, p. 269.

The U.S. Army's Parameters, established in 1971, provided a similar *"forum for mature thought on the art and science of land warfare, joint and combined matters, national and international security affairs, military strategy, military leadership and management, military history, ethics, and other topics of significant and current interest to the US Army and the Department of Defense."*[54] Parameters has been called "one of the causes of the intellectual renaissance of the US Army since Vietnam."[55]   Several journals—Parameters, U.S. Naval War College Review, and Proceedings—all feature scholarly articles (although Proceedings less so), in contrast to the least self-critical of the military journals, *Air Force Magazine*, which is really more of a glossy public relations monthly. Even *Air Force Magazine,* however, occasionally publishes challenging and original works. Added to that, the *Journal of Military History* provides a private-sector academic journal specifically devoted to military history. In short, the American armed forces have a number of sources of intellectual analysis and criticism that feature a degree of self-criticism rarely found in other Western militaries and almost never among recent terrorist enemies, where self-evaluation invites accusations of shame and dishonor.

More important than the journals are the military schools that originated them. Early in its history, the United States developed schools to train officers for its armed forces, despite an antipathy against standing armies. Over the objections of Secretary of State Thomas Jefferson, the Federalist congress required military instruction by organizing a corps of artillerists and engineers, and *"supplying it with the necessary books, instruments, and apparatus in 1794."*[56]   George Washington urged a permanent institution of military arts in his final address and, finally, under considerable pressure from Federalists, President Jefferson established West Point as the nation's military school in 1801. An act of March 1802 legally established the academy by dividing artillerists from engineers and assigning the latter to West Point, where cadets were to be taught by officers not on duty.[57] West Point emphasized mathematics and engineering, although by the 1820s the curriculum had shifted strongly in favor of civil engineering. Indeed, during a six-year period, no live-fire exercises wee even conducted, and board members complained that cadets lacked a basic understanding of tactics. This emphasis on civil engineering increased as the young Republic passed the General Survey Act of 1824, requiring more civil engineers than ever. The study of military topics fell even more in the 1820s, from 42 percent to 26 percent, as both mathematics and engineering courses increased.[58]   By 1836, critics were labeling West Point a

---

[54]"Mission Statement," http://carlisle-www.army.mil/usawc/Parameters/.

[55]"Our Story So Far," Parameters, Summer 1995, pp. 5–6.

[56]Robert G. Angevine, The Railroad and the State: War, Politics and Technology in Nineteenth-Century America (Stanford: Stanford University Press, 2004), p. 23.

[57]Sidney Forman, "The First School of Engineering," The Military Engineer, 44, March–April 1952, pp.46–68; George S. Pappas, To the Point: The United States Military Academy (Westport, CT: Praeger, 1993); Thomas J. Fleming, West Point: The Men and Times of the United States Military Academy (New York: William Morrow, 1969); Stephen E. Ambrose, Duty, Honor, Country: A History of West Point (Baltimore: John Hopkins University, 1966).

[58]Angevine, Railroad and the State, p.58.

"great place to make preachers." [59]

War with Mexico changed all that, converting the school from a training ground for engineers to one that created military officers capable of performing necessary engineering and scientific tasks. In the Mexican War, more than 450 West Pointers received honors or promotions, leading Sylvanus Thayer to rightly boast that *"the sons of West Point have covered themselves with glory."* Captain Robert E. Lee assessed the war as a *"glorious thing for West Point."* In fact, both the motivational training common to preachers and the analytical thinking necessary for engineers tended to combine in officers to create excellent leaders. General Winfield Scott said the war might have lasted several more years without the expertise of the West Point officers. Over time, as we have seen, even more specialized schools at Carlisle Barracks and at Fort Leavenworth appeared to further improve officers' skill in tactics, general education, and management.

Rewriting the Last Stand

Although Colonel Hal Moore had read several histories of the Custer massacre before he took his new 7th Cavalry (air) into the Ia Drang Valley, he did not have the advantage of recent advanced technological research by Richard Fox that revealed a much different story about Custer's Last Stand. But the results of Fox's study probably wouldn't have surprised him, for it showed that the destruction of Custer's force derived from its inability to maintain discipline, cohesion, and superior firepower.

Thirty years after Moore's troops defeated the North Vietnamese, the lessons of the Custer battle were once again relevant. This time, they were applied by Americans at Fallujah, Iraq. After President Bush declared the conclusion of "major ground operations" in Operation Iraqi Freedom in April 2003, terrorists, foreign fighters, and Saddam loyalists flooded into Iraq, and gradually they came to hole up in the outlaw city of Fallujah. Even under Saddam, Fallujah was the real-life equivalent of the Moss Eisley Spaceport in Star Wars films—"a greater hive of scum and villainy" could not be found in Iraq, to paraphrase Obi Wan Kenobi. Simply put, every thug in the Middle East had set up shop in Fallujah, intimidating locals and creating a hub of terror support for anti-U.S. activities. In April 2004, American forces massed to crush the terrorists in Fallujah, then suddenly pulled back in the same month. The offensive did not come for months. To many observers, this constituted a loss of will—a replay of Vietnam or Mogadishu—and to others, it indicated a "PC takeover" of the military effort by the administration. In fact, as Bing West recounts in his book on Fallujah, Bush wanted Fallujah seized immediately after the murder of four civilian contractors, and sent down the order for the Marines to *"go get those responsible."* He was not told that the Marines disagreed with the order, and that they had a different plan. [60] The Marines began a war of attrition in preparation to take the city. Before they could move in force,

[59] Angevine, Railroad and the State, p. 107

[60] Bing West, *No True Glory: A Frontline Account of the Battle for Fallujah* (New York: Bantam, 2005), p.7

however, the Marines were replaced by the 82nd Airborne.

When the Joint Task Force (the Coalition's headquarters unit in Baghdad) ordered a block-by-block operation to clear the insurgents, Lieutenant Colonel Brian Drinkwine, commanding the 82nd Airborne, which would have to fight its way through the city, protested, arguing that it would drive unaligned youths over to the terrorists. General John Abizaid, who flew to Fallujah, agreed with that assessment. The attack was called off. Back in the United States, conservative Web sites were ablaze with "Vietnam redux" rhetoric, not realizing that the commanders in the field had made the decision based on the dynamics of the situation. Editorialists demanded a *"strong response,"* and the respected retired lieutenant general Bernard Trainor warned that America would lose control of the situation if it backed off.[61]

In fact, two key allies had all but mutinied. First, the Iraqi governing council had expressed the strongest opposition to an invasion of Fallujah, with some members threatening to resign if a full-scale attack went ahead. Second, the British resisted what they saw as a public relations disaster. The 82nd, then new Marine replacements, halted in the siege of the city as a seemingly endless line of "negotiators" stepped forward to claim they could achieve a peaceful settlement. Certainly the Americans wanted, if possible, an Iraqi face on the security forces that took the city, but several experiments with former Iraqi generals had proved fruitless.

Restrained from a full-scale offensive, the U.S. military continued to winnow, infiltrate, "attrit," snipe, and wait for the orders to attack. For months, snipers and Special Operations Forces picked off enemy combatants. According to one report, a single Marine sniper doing his third tour of duty had more than 100 confirmed kills (although not all in Fallujah.)[62] As one sniper put it, *"A head will pop up in a window, they'll hit them, ranges up to 2,000 yards .... Very rarely will they miss."* [63] Special Ops worked at night, often with tips from local residents sick of being bullied. Typically, a young boy would approach an American unit on the edge of Fallujah in the dark, pass along a sheet of paper with an address or a name, then disappear. Shortly thereafter, the terrorist would "disappear" as well, and although the physical perimeter of Fallujah did not shrink at all, the terrorist structure within started to teeter. Staff Specialist Khaled Dudin, Colonel Drinkwine's right-hand man, noted that residences of the city's biggest jihadist leaders were identified, and American forces would enter their homes at night, then leave if the person in question was not home. *"Some nights,"* he recalled, *"we'd search their houses and not even wake up their kids. We got that skilled."* [64] Members of the 82nd Airborne, then the Marines and Special Ops who surrounded Fallujah, blended into the night, leaving the foreign fighters in terror. Still, for months a stark dilemma was posed to innocent Fallujans who wanted to rid their city of

[61]Quoted in West, *No True Glory*, p.114.
[62]Jack Wheeler, *"Allah's Waiting Room,"* To the Point, http://www.ivanyi-consultants.com/articles/awr.html.
[63]Matthew Stannard, "U.S., Iraqi Troops Mass for Assault on Fallujah ...," San Francisco Chronicle, November 6, 2004.
[64]West, *No True Glory,* p.41

terrorists. *"Fallujah is controlled by two powers—the Americans and the mujahedeen,"* said one resident. *"If we cooperate with the mujahedeen, we get raided. If we cooperate with the Americans, we get killed."*[65]

Other new weapons increased the threats to the jihadists in Fallujah: one was a small robot called the Dragon Runner, a four-wheeled surveillance drone with sensors and a camera that could see around corners and is sturdy enough to be dropped out a second-story window.[66] The marines also used a flying robot called Dragon Eye, a five-pound battery-powered surveillance drone launched by bungee cord or by hand. Dragon Eye can fly at thirty-five knots for nearly an hour on one charge and can see with low light and infrared cameras. A controller could point and click to a spot on the map, and Dragon Eye would send back the real-time pictures. But more fearsome was Slayer One, and Air Force C-130 armed with two 20 mm Gatling guns and a 105 mm howitzer, all equipped with infrared sights. When Slayer saw a group of twenty insurgents approaching American positions in the dark, it cut them down in seconds.

All of this battlefield shaping, including psyops, wherein highly visible media displays of the morgue areas intended for the jihadists were beamed into Fallujah, increased the pressure on the remaining fighters. Two other elements were necessary to shape the battlefield, both political. First, the Iraq government needed to be formed in early 2004, which could then place an official Iraqi stamp of approval on the assault. Second, the U.S. presidential election needed to be out of the way. President Bush could not afford the possibility of a long, bloody siege going on during a campaign. Consequently, as soon as the Iraqis had an interim government and Bush had been reelected, the crushing of the Fallujah jihadists was a done deal.

In the meantime, however, the situation threatened to deteriorate into *"faint echoes of Tet,"* as Bing West referred to the reporting debacle. Al Jazeera, the anti-American Arab television network, sent reporters into the insurgent-held areas, transmitting pictures of wounded and bleeding children—all of whom, Al Jazeera hoped, would be assumed by viewers to be wounded or killed by the Marines. Western news organizations, most of them hostile to the military to begin with, picked up the Al Jazeera reports. Those images, West reported, resulted in *"political pressures [that] constrained military actions both against Fallujah and against Moqtada al-Sard."* [67] Actions in Ramadi provided a model for the campaign against Fallujah. The news media had completely missed the story of the Ramadi battle, which was not the dozen Marines killed, but the shattered insurgent offensive, which had been well supplemented by hundreds of foreign fighters.

Whereas George Washington's Continentals had stepped off to drums and fifes, and George Meade's Army of the Potomac to brass bands and bugles, the Marines surrounding Fallujah were partial to Jimi Hendrix and Eminem. What

---

[65] West, *No True Glory*, p.42.
[66] Stannard, "U.S., Iraqi Troops Mass for Assault on Fallujah."
[67] West, No True Glory, p.93.

had not changed from Washington's time, however, was the propensity for the chain of command to distort information from the battlefield. Bush, once anxious for a final assault, sought, "options," preferably with the involvement of Iraqis. His military commander in Iraq, Abizaid was hesitant to order an attack, as was the head of the Coalition Provisional Authority, L. Paul Bremer. In short, Bush was not getting battlefield knowledge from the commanders in Fallujah, who thought they could take the city in a few days, and the normally decisive Bush anticipated a public relations disaster if there were heavy casualties, especially among civilians.

But Americans had been willing to try to several options, from the failed Fallujah Brigade (a brigade of Iraqis, led by former Iraqi officers) to bundles of money for reconstruction. Most important, Ayad Allawi, the prime minister of the interim Iraqi government, did not have the political capital to throw his weight behind an assault until after September, when Sadr's revolt peaked. At that point, Allawi confronted and backed down a fellow Shiite, setting the stage for the final curtain in Fulljah. He closed al Jazeera's bureau in Iraq, and silenced the main propaganda organ of the terrorists, then sent many of the Iraqi governing council members to Fallujah to meet with city leaders. This time, even those who had threatened to resign agreed that the city had to be taken. When Bush was reelected, both leaders had the political support they needed to end the Fallujah fiasco. Even the British redeployed units to free up more Marines for the attack.

On November 7, 2004, the American and Iraqi forces began their assault. Iraqi forces trained by General David Petraeus of the 101st Airborne furnished three battalions. Real troops, not faux soldiers like the Fallujah Brigade, participated in the operation. Combat was bloody, but in a week in was over, with more than 1,000 insurgents killed and virtually all driven out. Abu al-Zarqawi's bomb-making factory had been destroyed, and his organization in the city shattered. The Fallujah episode illustrated the multifaceted nature of modern war: while it may have been militarily more efficient in the short run to plow into Fallujah, the certain collapse of the interim Iraqi government, the animosity of the British, and the absence of a long-term Iraqi presence to police the city afterward would have been counterproductive. Important lessons learned, once again, about the critical nature of decision makers having the best available facts from all involved, including the grunts on the ground, were factored into preparations for future Fallujahs. Just as Patton seethed about his divisions' gasoline going to "Monty" (the British field marshal Bernard Alexander Montgomery) during World War II, so, too, in Iraq were multinational political considerations necessary.

Applying lessons from the past failures characterize many aspects of Operation Iraqi Freedom. General Tommy Franks noted that this was the first war that effectively integrated Special Operations forces into the combat plan. (A few words of clarification are in order here: Special Forces is a term that specifically refers to the Army's Green Berets, while Special Operations Forces includes all elite special units, such as the Rangers, Delta force, SEALs, Marine Recon, and others. Both are referred to in shorthand as Special Ops). Ironically, it was a de-bacle—the Iranian rescue mission, more than twenty-five years ago—that revived and improved the Special Operations Forces. Operation Eagle claw, infamous for its burning aircraft and scenes of Iranians picking over the corpses of eight servicemen, "*shocked the Pentagon and congress*" into building up Special Oper-ations forces to deal with future terrorist activities.[68] The squadron commander of Operation Eagle Claw, Colonel Roland Guidry of the U.S. Air Force, pointed out that the missions in Afghanistan and Iraq applied the lessons learned in the Iranian desert.

All learning doesn't come from battlefield setbacks alone. By the late 1990s, even without Afghanistan and Iraq, the Army was finding that many of its West Point graduates were leaving after their fire-year hitches were up. Surveys showed that one of the leading causes of unhappiness was not the regimen, or even the dangers: it was officers' dissatisfaction over not getting the branch they had requested. West Point's solution was Branch for Service, a market-oriented innovation that exchanged extra service time for a guarantee of service branch. Cadets were asked for bids on how much extra time they would put in, and after reviewing the bids, anyone who had offered time beyond the two years of Army service automatically go his or her first choice was 10 percent more likely to stay beyond the minimum service. After tallying the additional time in the Branch for Service exchange, the Army found that it had more than fifty-one years of officer service from the cadets.[69]

Learning from Others' Mistakes

As American forces prepared to invade Afghanistan, the predictable hysterical warnings from the Left arose: it would be a "*quagmire,*" or "*another Vietnam.*" R. W. "Johnny" Apple, who apparently could not get Vietnam off his mind—he would later write almost the same thing about Iraq—asked, "*Could Afghanistan become another Vietnam?*" The Los Angeles Times chimed in: "*The United States is not headed into a quagmire; it's already in one.*" Britain's In-dependent published a column by Kennedy iconographer Arthur Schlesinger, Jr., who asked, "*Are We Trapped in Another Vietnam?*" Realize that each of these came after only a few weeks' worth of ground operations.[70] American troops couldn't fight in the cold (and later, in Operation Iraqi Freedom, critics would say they couldn't fight in the heat!). Most of all, the pessimists cautioned, the Soviets had failed there just fifteen years earlier. The message was clear: if the "great" Soviet army could not subdue the Afghans, how could the United States?

[68]Bill Kaczor, "Failed Iran Rescue Mission 25 Years Ago Let to Later Success," Associated Press, April 22, 2005.

[69]Nancy Gibbs and Nathan Thornburgh, "*The Class of 9/11*," Time, May 30, 2005,pp. 28–43.

[70]Quoted in Richard Minitier, ***Disinformation: 22 Media Myths That Undermine the War on Terror*** (Wash-ington: Regnery Books, 2005), p.77.

Americans dislike military losses, especially their own. Usually the military planners review every aspect of a lost battle, from technology to leadership, to identify the determining factor. The failed Soviet invasion of Afghanistan was no different. As Tommy Franks and Secretary of Defense Donald Rumsfeld prepared for the invasion, they agreed that *"we should not flood the country with large formations of conventional troops."* Franks told Rumsfeld, *"We don't want to repeat the Soviets' mistakes."*[71] President Bush had already put the military on notice: the struggle against terrorists would be a "new kind of war." Perhaps the most important change in the military occurred after 9/11: the mission of the military was now defined by the Bush Doctrine. Incorporated into top-level military documentation, the Bush Doctrine, according to the Army, *"fundamentally changed the way the United States would ensure its domestic security."* Rather than "respond" and "prepare," the doctrinal mandates of the Clinton administration, the Army now was to "dissuade forward" and "decisively defeat" America's enemies, noted On Point, had "fundamental implications" for how the military trained and equipped itself. It involved being able to deploy an expeditionary force capable of imposing America's will on hostile foreign soil, then maintaining a presence there long enough to secure the change. It was nothing short of a revolution in doctrine.[72]

Equally as important as learning from battlefield situations has been the ability of most American political leaders to avoid putting the military in losing situations. Once again, Vietnam stands as the classic example of what not to do. Secretary of defense Robert McNamara and President Lyndon Johnson, in the summer of 1965, established the objectives of the bombing campaign known as Rolling Thunder: *"The purpose of the program ... have been, first to give us a better bargaining counter [emphasis added] across from the North Vietnamese, and second, to interdict the flow of men and supplies from the North to the South."*[73] Note that nowhere was the purpose of the bombing to defeat the North Vietnamese, but merely to gain a better negotiating position. As air historian Mark Clodfelter points out, by using bombings as a tool of negotiation rather than an instrument of war, McNamara and Johnson necessarily became involved in target selection and the timing of missions. Fearing the accidental death of Russian personnel on scene, American bombers were prohibited from attacking North Vietnamese surface-to-air (SAM) missile sites while under construction! In a nation with seven thousand to ten thousand antiaircraft guns and two hundred SAM sites, the fact that the United States lost only eighty air-craft was something of a miracle.[74]

Clodfelter recounted the ridiculous, but predictable, course of events when negotiations—not the destruction of the enemy—became the main purpose

[71]Tommy franks with Malcolm McConnell, *American Soldier* (New York: Regan Books, 2004), p. 324.
[72]Fontenot, *On Point*, p.23.
[73]Mark Clodfelter, *The Limits of Air Power: The American Bombing of North Vietnam* (New York: Free Press, 1989), p. 70.
[74]Benjamin Lambeth, *The Transformation of American Air Power* (Ithaca: Cornell University Press, 2000), pp. 17–18, 297, passim.

of air missions:

> *Johnson also stopped Rolling Thunder completely on eight occasions be-*
> *tween March 1965 and March 1968.... In May 1965, he halted the*
> *campaign for six days as a "propaganda effort" to demonstrate that he*
> *sought a peaceful solution to the war.... [I]n December 1965 and Feb-*
> *ruary 1967 ... [there were] bombing pauses of thirty-seven days and*
> *six days, respectively. Johnson stopped Rolling Thunder briefly during*
> *Christmas and New Year's in 1966 and 1967, and for twenty-four*
> *hours on Buddha's birthday in May 1967.*[75]

Soon Johnson's bombing policies were a morass: member of the admin-istration (not the military) battled over definitions of "acceptable" interdiction, disagreed over whether a highway with no moving traffic was a target, and could not agree even on the precise meaning of a *convoy*![76] These vagaries, as might be expected, led to the formation of committees to reach consensus—a sure harbinger of high American losses and ineffective bombing.[77] Recently, North Vietnamese military documents acquired by researchers found that during the bombing pauses and "peace initiatives," the North Vietnamese not only repaired their radars and antiaircraft batteries, but also reviewed and improved tactics to defeat the Americans. Put another way, every one of Johnson's bombing pauses directly contributed to additional U.S. deaths.

Leftists, having failed to turn Afghanistan into Vietnam, desperately want to make Iraq another Vietnam, which is hardly likely under any circumstances, given that no Muslim nation can supply the Iraqi terrorists with weapons in the same way the Chinese supported the North Vietnamese. From 1956 to 1963 alone, China poured 270,000 guns, 200 million bullets, 10,000 pieces of artillery, and thousands of trucks into North Vietnam.[78] Between 1965 and 1969, Chinese engineers built "20 new railway stations, 39 new bridges, 14 tunnels, and 117 kilometers of new rail lines and repaired 326 kilometers of existing rail lines" for North Vietnam, sending an astounding 327,000 troops to work in the North in order to free up North Vietnamese to go south![79] On top of that, North Vietnam absorbed 50 percent of all Soviet aid to all satellite regimes. Put another way, the United States faced a massive Sino-Soviet-North Vietnamese coalition when it fought "only" the Viet Cong in the South.

What often goes unnoticed, however, is that prior to Vietnam, the United States had already fought and won a guerrilla war in Asia: the aforementioned Philippine counterinsurgency of 1899-1902. In the Philippines, American forc-es battled an enemy that substantially outnumbered the estimated terrorists in Iraq (where maximum estimates suggest about 20,000 terrorists/insurgents are

---

[75]Clodfelter, *Limit of Air Power*, p.119
[76]Clodfelter, *Limit of Air Power*, p. 121
[77]Wallace M. Greene, "The Bombing 'Pause': Formula for Fairlure," Air Force, April 1976, 36–39; Robert N. Ginsburgh, "Strategy and Airpower: The Lessons of Southeast Asia," *Strategic Review*, 1, Summer 1973, pp.18–24.
[78]Michael Lind, *Vietnam: the Necessary War* (New York: Touchstone, 1999), p.10.
[79]Lind, *Vietnam*, p.19.

fighting). The forces of Emilio Aguinaldo and other insurgent leasers exceeded 80,000, and perhaps reached as high as 100,000, and, like today, the United States fielded a relatively small army, about 74,000 men, of whom about 25,000 to 45,000 were combat troops, now outfitted in the new khaki uniforms (although some cavalry still wore blue jackets).[80] Aguinaldo, like Ho Chi Minh and Osama bin Laden after him, did not expect to defeat the American military, but rather to "sour Americans on the war and ensure the victory of the anti-imperialist William Jennings Bryan in the presidential elections." [81]

As the jihadists did in 2004, Aguinaldo guessed wrong in 1900. William McKinley won, and the new commander on the scene, Major General Arthur MacArthur (Douglas's father), proved more draconian than his predecessor. MacArthur declared martial law and issued a new general order that subjected combatants not in uniform—the same kinds of people that are held at Guantánamo prison—to execution. Within a year, Aguinaldo was captured and the resistance fizzled as the population chose sides. As one historian of the war concluded, "*The Filipino insurgents accurately targeted the US strategic center of gravity—the national willpower*" expressed by the president and the voters.[82] American commanders, however, used a technique the British employed successfully in the Boer War (and the Spanish less successfully so in attempting to put down the Cuban revolution) that is more difficult to use today: they built large camps for the anti-guerrilla civilians, similar to Indian reservations and, in fact, called concentration camps by the British. This isolated the guerrillas from popular support (as it did the Boers) and was followed up by the establishment of hundreds of small garrisons that tracked the insurgents and killed them. However, learning from the British policy, which resulted in great suffering among Boer civilians, American strategy involved determined efforts to improve hygiene, education, and life within the compounds, essentially creating an early 1900s version of secure communities. It was a strategy later described by the famous baseball manager Casey Stengel as keeping the "*guys who hate you away from the guys who are undecided.*"

But American strategy went beyond merely separating the "guys who like you" from the "guys who hate you." The military governor held local mayors, or principales, responsible for attacks that emanated from their towns or for atrocities that occurred in their villages. (Early on, this would have been a useful technique in, say, Fallujah). As with the war on terror, insurgents were not allowed to remain in country, but were packed off to Guam so as not to infect others with their antigovernment sentiments. And, as in Iraq and Afghanistan, rebuilding the local infrastructure, especially by building schools, proved quite valuable. Major

[80]Timothy K. Deady, "Lessons from a Successful Counterinsurgency: The Philippines, 1899–1902," Parameters, Spring 2005, pp. 53–68; John P. Langellier, *Uncle Sam's Little Wars: The Spanish-American War, Philippine Insurrection and Boxer Rebellion, 1898–1902*, (London: Greenhill Books, 1999). Teddy Roosevelt's Rough Riders actually put aside the brown uniforms in favor of the earlier 1883 blue flannel shirts.
[81]Deady, "Lessons from a Successful Counterinsurgency," quoted in the online version: http://carlisle-www.army.mil/usawc/Parameters/05spring/deady.htm. For Aquinaldo's comments, see John Morgan Gates, *Schoolbooks and Krags: The United States Army in the Philippines, 1898–1902* (Westport, CT.: Greenwood Press, 1973), pp.162–63.
[82]Deady, "Lessons from a Successful Counterinsurgency," quoted online

John Parker, whose wife ran schools for two thousand students, thought her work was equal to a regiment's. Some one thousand Americans traveled to the Philippines as teachers, and the United States founded a university in Manila. General Elwell Otis, MacArthur's predecessor, had already started a Filipino army that could defeat the insurgents without American help. Economic and medical help poured in. Over time, even the pesos-for-guns program worked, although early on it was a flop. Still, as other pacification policies kicked in, *"it was common for hundreds of rifles to be surrendered by disbanding insurgent groups."* [83]

Looking at the Philippine Insurrection, some techniques clearly are inapplicable in the modern world. Concentration camps (in the British sense of the word) would be viewed as violations of civil rights, even in hot spots like Iraq or Afghanistan. But regional pass systems, strict curfews, and isolating specific neighborhoods can work effectively. Essentially, Fallujah was an experiment in this type of cordoning off an entire city. The Army also found that six hundred small garrisons were more effective than fifty—a lesson that was often ignored in Vietnam, where large firebases encouraged less contact with the friendly civilian population. Above all, every sort of tool—propaganda, economic and medical aid, money, and heavy "sticks" against those who support the insurgents—must be used. As one analyst of the Philippine Insurrection put it, *"Identify where to insert, and how to hammer, wedges between social, ethnic, and political groups"* as well as terror leaders and their followers. [84]

Whether Ap Bac or An Najaf, the Philippines or Fallujah, Brooklyn Heights or Bull Run, Corregidor or Kasserine, Americans study their losses and immediately apply the lessons learned. We do not do so perfectly, and occasionally we need a refresher course when forgetting past instruction. Whereas other societies would require the lives of failed commanders when shame or honor is an issue, Americans routinely give second, and even third chances for redemption, optimistic that success is an intrinsic quality in every American. This has produced remarkable turnarounds, from Grant's near disaster at Shiloh to his magnanimous acceptance of Lee's surrender at Appomattox; from the ragtag GIs chased out of Kasserine to the confident troops that stormed Sicily. And when commanders and their units have paid the ultimate price, as Custer and his men did at Little Big Horn, Americans learned from them as well. No other cavalry disasters followed his. Americans win wars because even though losses are embarrassing and deadly for many of the combatants, we have never treated them as shameful. American military forces have been willing to put pride aside and learn from their mistakes. When the Duke of Wellington was told at Waterloo that Napoléon's troops were "coming on in the same old way," it testified to the fact that one of history's greatest generals had not yet learned from loss. Americans win wars because more often than not we will admit, *"We screwed up ... but you won't fool us twice."*

---

[83]Deady, "Lessons from a Successful Counterinsurgency," quoted online
[84]Deady, "Lessons from a Successful Counterinsurgency," quoted online

CHAPTER THREE
Citizens as Soldiers

The strength of America's armed forces comes from a reservoir
of free men and women who willingly become professional soldiers.

On December 1, 1814, acting on intelligence that the British intended to invade New Orleans, General Andrew Jackson assembled a veteran force of more than 4,000 soldiers, mostly militia, but including local Creoles, Baratarian pirates, the Native Guard—a group of "free men of color"—and Indians, as well as regular units of the United States Army. Some of Jackson's men had marched all over the Southeast with him. Many came from Tennessee (including young Davy Crockett, whose enlistment ended before the battle of New Orleans), but there were plenty of Mississippians, Alabamians, Louisianans, and Kentuckians who had fought with General Jackson off and on for the better part of two years. Even though many had seen extensive combat, and were thoroughly reliable in the field, most of them volunteered under a state militia enlistment process that allowed men to sign up for periods of months, not years; and between battles Jackson watched hundreds of men depart and hundreds more new faces arrive. It was a problem that did not afflict his red-coated enemy, who derided the American militia "dirty shirts" as lacking the cool professionalism of the smartly dressed Europeans.

For two years, Americans had waged a seesaw war against England in North America. A handful of successes—the battles of Chippewa, Lundy's Lane, and Oliver Hazard Perry's remarkable victory on the Great Lakes—had been overshadowed by utter failure in America's Canadian campaign. By late 1814 the American navy was virtually bottled up in its home ports, thoroughly outnumbered and outgunned by the British, who, thinking they were finally finished with Napoléon's France, could turn their weight against the irreverent upstarts across the pond. The most humiliating moment for the United States came just four months before Jackson arrived in New Orleans. A British force had sailed up the Potomac and landed less than twenty miles from Washington, D.C. The British then swept away a larger force of American defenders, including many militia who ran, and burned the city.

Yet even as British troops ransacked the White House, Jackson's reputation in the southern theater was growing. He was already known to his men as Old Hickory because of his toughness—the man had survived smallpox, the flat blade of a British officer across his face in the Revolution, and a brawl with the Benton brothers back in Tennessee that had put a pistol ball into his shoulder.[85] Still re-

---

[85]See Robert V. Remini's three-volume biography: *Andrew Jackson and the Course of American Empire, 1767–*

covering from his gunshot wound, the gaunt Jackson was not in good health; his arm was still in a sling and his "complexion was sallow and rather unhealthy-looking." [86] But an aura of defiance clung to him, and men followed him loyally. He had come to the Deep South from Tennessee because of British intrigues with Indian tribes there. The Red Stick uprising had led to a massacre of more than 250 settlers at Fort Mims, near Mobile, Alabama, in August 1813. These Red Sticks, a renegade element of Creek Indians loosely affiliated with Tecumseh's Shawnee resistance in Indiana, were egged on by promises of British support. States raised militia forces, and the United States ordered the commander of the Sixth Military District, Major General Thomas Pinckney, to take command of the operation so that Jackson, a major general in the militia, would not be the highest-ranking officer.[87]

Pinckney, however, knew a leader when he saw one. He loosed Jackson, and the Tennessean aggressively marched on the hostiles. Following bloody sparring with the Red Sticks for months, Jackson finally fielded a formidable army and struck the Indian camp from two sides at Horseshoe Bend in March 1814, crushing the Creek resistance for good. Having criticized the performance of some of his militia units in the past, Jackson noted that at Horseshoe Bend, *"the militia of the venerable Genl. [George] Doherty accompanied [the 39th Regiment] in the charge, with a vivacity & firmness which would have done honor to Regulars."*[88] Having dispatched the Red Sticks, Jackson received the regular army rank of major general in the Seventh Military District, leaving him in charge of the Mobile-New Orleans sector.

The men who marched with Jackson knew hardship. Some had not been paid since Fort Mims—almost a year—and they were chronically short of equipment and powder. Mississippi volunteers returned home after eight months in the field *"almost literally naked,"* according to Louisiana governor William Claiborne.[89] Georgia governor David Mitchell said his state's militia was *"destitute of all supplies"*—no *"camp equipage and ... very little ammunition."*[90] When Claiborne asked the federal government to provide four thousand muskets to arm the state militia, he received only six hundred. Militia men often looked forward to defeating the Indians just to acquire their enemy's stock of powder. At first, Jackson hotly complained about the units' overall lack of skill, but under his command, like the Continental Army under George Washington more than thirty years earlier, the undisciplined dirty shirts were forged into an army, and next time they encountered the Creeks, he had a crack fighting force.

1821 (New York: Harper and Row, 1977); Andrew Jackson and the Course of American Freedom, 1822–1832 (New York: Harper and Row, 1981); and Andrew Jackson and the Course of American Democracy, 1833–1845 (New York: Harper and Row, 1984).
[86]Robert V. Remini, The Battle of New Orleans (New York: Penguin, 1999), p.11.
[87]C. Edward Skeen, Citizen Soldiers in the War of 1812 (Lexington: University Press of Kentucky, 1999), p.160.
[88]Skeen, Citizen Soldiers in the War of 1812, p.166
[89]Claiborne to Secretary of War John Armstrong, January 24, 1814, in Skeen, Citizen Soldiers, p.162.
[90]Skeen, Citizen Soldiers, p.162.

Nevertheless, the problem of the short-term volunteers still plagued Jackson's army. Jackson found that after defeating the Red Sticks and marching to New Orleans from Alabama, the number of his men had dwindled from 4,100 men (1,200 regulars) to only 2,300 troops (500 to 1,000 regulars). Fortunately for Jackson—and America—thousands more were already marching to join him in New Orleans under an astonishing array of circumstances. There were 500 Mississippians, although only 200 had muskets and the rest had rifles or shotguns. The problem lay not in the lack of weapons, but in the militia's unwillingness to use inferior muskets when they had requested rifles. Jean Laffite's Barataria Bay pirates threw in their lot with the Americans, adding a thousand guns and considerable powder, flints, and supplies, and no small amount of intelligence on British movements. A Negro corps of free men of color was also formed in New Orleans, joining the Tennessee and Kentucky militia who stayed loyal to Jackson, and the Louisiana militia. Jackson allowed this motley array to sweep through the buildings and warehouses of New Orleans in search of powder, muskets, flint, pickaxes, and hoes. Literally thousands of soldiers waited in the ranks unarmed—some of them unwilling to bring their own valuable weapons into combat and risk losing or damaging them. Moreover, there was a grim understanding that casualties would inevitably free up guns. As British warships approached the city, Jackson and his polyglot dirty shirts prepared to do what no other militia-dominated army of any size had ever done before: defeat a relatively equal number of British regulars in an open field of battle.

Americans win wars because from our earliest history we adopted the view that a free people defends themselves, at first through militias, then later through professional full-time service. The principle that our armies reflect us and come from a representative cross section of the American population (and not a few elite families or from slaves or mercenaries) constitutes on of the most important advantages U.S. armed forces possess.

Citizen Soldiers

Andy Jackson's militia came out of a tradition that dated from colonial times, when England lacked sufficient manpower to garrison forts throughout her North American colonies. Every English colony mandated that locals serve in a militia in order to provide their own protection.[91] The resulting colonial militias have often been ridiculed as inefficient and even cowardly. While that may have been the case in some instances during the War for Independence, colonial militias of citizen soldiers proved more than a match for Indian tribes in a series of wars. They also effectively augmented British regulars during the French and Indian War. Washington, for one, thought that his regiments were the equal of any Europeans.[92] Indeed, Washington and his commanders studied British regular army

[91]See http://www.claytoncramer.com/ArmedAmericaTeaser.pdf, and his review of colonial militia laws in http://www.claytoncramer.com/primary.html#MilitiaLaws.

[92]Don Higgenbotham, George Washington and the American Military Tradition (Athens, GA: University of

procedures, implementing European-style drill.

The man most responsible for changing the reputation of the American militia was Nathanael Greene, the Revolutionary War general credited with directing America's greatest campaign during the conflict. Greene, wrote Russell Weigley, *"remains alone as an American master developing a strategy of unconventional war."* Greene's partisans fought a running (often, literally) war with Lord Cornwallis's British army in the southern United States until he lured the Redcoats deep into South Carolina, inflicting serious losses on them. Despite Greene's successes, his best militia still could not defeat British regulars in European-style line fighting, but Greene already had demonstrated a trait that would come to characterize American officers, namely, constantly adapting to both his own strengths and his enemy's weaknesses, mixing European fighting styles with those of Native Americans and anything else that worked. He perceived that in a war of maneuver, fewer troops—even militia—could avoid crushing defeats of the type that dominated European set-piece battles, while a maneuvering army could inflict such constant damage on his British foes they would inevitably make a crucial mistake. Moreover, militia could be replaced far faster than regular troops could be sent from England; and they were experts at harassing, posing a constant threat to British troops.

After the Revolution, the United States continued to rely on calling up state militias for most serious military undertakings, usually fighting Indians.[93] These militias laced three key ingredients for making effective soldiers over the long haul: consistently good arms, uniform training, and a long-term contractual enlistment that kept them in the field for extended campaigns. For the short haul, however, they could be potent, if not downright deadly. Naturally, the tiny regular army denigrated the volunteers. In the Mexican War, regulars were called volunteers, Mustangs, and Mohawks, or even referred to derisively as the Continental Army.[94] Winfield Scott complained to the secretary of war that *"a regiment of regulars, in 15 minutes from the evening halt, will have tents pitched & trenched around ... arms & ammunition well secured ... fires made, kettles boiling,"* while *"volunteers neglect all these points; eat their salt raw meat raw ... lie down wet ... leave arms & ammunition exposed to rain, mud & dews."* [95]

But American militia units had important strengths, not the least of which was their independence and autonomy. During the dark months of the Revolution as Washington retreated from New York to New Jersey, the Redcoats in hot pursuit, John Cadwalader's Pennsylvania Associators, some 1,800 men had urged their commander to cross the Delaware River to assist Washington. Here was a volunteer unit that acted on its own initiative, marching to the sound of the guns

Georgia Press, 1985), chap. 1.

[93]Richard Kohn, Eagle and Sword: The Beginnings of the Military Establishment in America (New York: Free Press, 1975).

[94]Robert W. Johannsen, To the Halls of the Montezumas: the Mexican War in the American Imagination (New York: Oxford University Press, 1985),p.41.

[95]George Winston Smith and Charles Judah, eds., Chronicles of the Gringos: The U.S. Army in the Mexican War, 1846–1848 (Albuquerque: University of New Mexico Press, 1968), p.30.

and providing Washington with the crucial troops he needed to follow up his attack on the Hessians at Trenton. No similar unit, with such radical autonomy, existed anywhere in the world: these men, even to the point of mutiny, had demanded that their commander take them to battle. This autonomy stemmed, in part, for the sincere, if romantic, Americanized view of the Revolutionary militia fighting for freedom. Such a warrior was described by the *New England Chronicle*: "*he that is a soldier in defense of such a cause, needs no title; his post is a post of honor, and although not an emperor, yet he shall wear a crown—of glory—and blessed will be his memory!*"[96] These militiamen of Puritan New England elected their own sergeant majors and voted for the office of major general.[97] Free-market principles, especially the sanctity of contract, played no small role in determining how—and for how long—soldiers served. From the Seven Years' War onward, units objected to being used in ways not specifically stipulated in their enlistment contracts. In 1756, when Lord Loudoun, the British commander in chief in North America, tried to incorporate units formed only to attack Crown Point and Ticonderoga, he unleashed a firestorm of resistance on the grounds that he was violating their contracts.[98]

Far too often, however, militia performed less commendably than the Associators.[99] Washington never missed an opportunity to condemn militia troops: "*They come in you cannot tell how; go out you cannot see when; act you cannot tell where ... and leave you at last in a critical moment.*" [100] "*No militia,*" he argued, "*will ever acquire the habits necessary to resist a regular force.*"[101] Of course, Nathanael Greene was already proving the general wrong, but the weaknesses of non-professional soldiers was apparent. They could break an attack, but lacked the cohesion to follow up a victory (which is why the actions of Cadwalader's troops were so impressive). Militia were excellent at harassing and defeating guard units and supply trains, but they had trouble facing up in open field, where only the repetition of firing—and being fired at, at a range of thirty yards—could steel men's tendency to cut and run. And militia could crush Indians, who did not fight in the Western tradition. While the military still relied on volunteers, turning them into professionals remained the central challenge. This had been done on an ad hoc basis under Washington, then later in the young Republic. "Mad" Anthony Wayne, by the 1790s, had distinguished his Wayne's Legion by rigorously training his troops in "*precision maneuver, skill and marksmanship, and esprit.*"[102] Most

---

[96]Writer known as "The Freeman" quoted in David McCullough, 1776 (New York: Simon and Schuster, 2006), p.63.

[97]T. H. Breen, Puritans and Adventurers: Change and Persistence in Early America (New York: Oxford, 1980), pp. 25–45.

[98]Fred Anderson, A People's Army: Massachusetts Soldiers and Society in the Seven Years' War (Chapel Hill, NC: University of North Carolina Press, 1984), chap. 6, and his "Why Did Colonial New Englanders Make Bad Soldiers? Contractual Principles and Military Conduct During the Seven Years' War," William and Mary Quarterly, 38, 1981, pp. 395–417

[99]Mark V. Kwasny, Washington's Partisan War, 1775-1783 (Kent, OH: Kent State University Press, 1996).

[100]Washington quoted in Peter G. Tsouras, ed., The Greenhill Dictionary of Military Quotations (London: Greenhill Books, 2000), p. 306.

[101]Tsouras, The Greenhill Dictionary of Military Quotations, p. 307.

[102]Edward M. Coffman, The Old Army: A Portrait of the American Army in Peacetime, 1784-1898 (New York:

units, however, did not measure up to the professionalism of Wayne's Legion. In 1861, when calls went out for volunteers in the Civil War, training officers received what *"can only justly [be] called a mob and one not fit to face the enemy."*[103] Would-be Union cavalry, drilling with swords, terrified their horses into running off, while infantry, attempting to fix bayonets in a drill, inflicted wounds on each other.[104] The truth was that when a conflict subsided, and Congress (as it always did) reduced the size of the army and navy, in many outposts there were scarcely enough men to handle daily chores and still take any number of troops on maneuver. In the 1820s, there were not enough artillery officers to train gunners to fire their weapons; and throughout the antebellum period the army *"had difficulty concentrating enough troops to conduct and large-scale exercises."*[105] "Mad" Anthony Wayne, Winfield Scott, and Andrew Jackson all understood that the nation's hope for military success lay in disciplined forces—if enough of them could be maintained in peacetime.[106]

Regulars and Militia

While Jackson marched against the Indians in the South, Jacob Brown had spent months training his men in Buffalo, readying them for the British invasion force they would soon meet. He eliminated desertions and drilled them in forming lines and attacking with the bayonet. When they took the field in 1814 against the British at the Battle of Chippewa, brown formed his men, wearing their gray uniforms (later traditionalized at West Point as the cadet's uniform), into a concave line around the British, who still struggled in a column, thoroughly outgunning the Redcoats. The stunned British commander, General Phineas Riall, exclaimed *"Those are Regulars, by God."* [107] Twenty days later, at Lundy's Lane, the scene was repeated, and it was the British commander—not the American general Winfield Scott—who reported that his men "displayed an unpardonable degree of unsteadiness."[108]

Peacetime, however, brought a romanticized assessment of militia units, especially when Congress could defray the costs of a standing army by touting the achievements of militia forces. Even Alexis de Tocqueville gushed about the tendency of the American citizen to combine with fellow citizens to defend the nation, arguing that in Europe, one would never see such spontaneous combinations, as there men were bound by compulsory association. Without question, Americans just naturally seemed to join together to solve problems in contrast to the class-stifled Europeans. But a political component also played a role in muffling

---

Oxford, 1986), p. 20.
[103] John Keegan, The Mask of Command (New York: Penguin Books, 1987), p.188.
[104] Keegan, Mask of Command, p.18.
[105] Coffman, The Old Army, p.161.
[106] Donald R. Hickey, The War of 1812: A Forgotten Conflict (Urbana, IL: University of Illinois Press, 1989), p.187.
[107] Harry L. Coles, The War of 1812 (Chicago: University of Chicago Press, 1965), p.157.
[108] Hickey, War of 1812, p.188.

the criticism of militias because the memories of the threat posed by a standing army still remained fresh in Americans' minds.

Sooner or later, though, governors and legislatures had to confront come unpleasant realities. In colonial times, the struggle between militia roughly trained in the "Western way of war" with Indians ended with Indian defeat. But twice, in conflicts with a top-rate European army, the militia had proved incapable of regular victories or of sustaining a campaign to its conclusion. Ironically, the poor performance of the militia had proved incapable of regular victories or of sustaining a campaign to its conclusion. Ironically, the poor performance of the militia became something of a self—reinforcing circle: regular army advocates hesitated to spend money training militia when the same resources could be put to better use with the regular army, hence providing even less training for the militia. Slowly, states had ended compulsory militia training by the 1840s. In the Mexican War, the 12,000 militiamen composed only 12 percent of the total force, compared to 88 percent in the War of 1812. Partly due to foreign perceptions of the army as militia based, foreigners were unimpressed when they observed American units. In 1775, one British surgeon described the American fighters as "*a drunken, canting, lying, praying, hypocritical rabble without order, subjection, discipline, or cleanliness.*"[109] Similar descriptions in the War of 1812 were even applied to regulars. One Englishman visiting a U.S. post watched regular companies of the Second Infantry as they drilled:

> *There is nothing very imposing in the appearance of the American troops. Their dress consists of a short blue jacket ... grey trousers, and a leather shako, with an eagle, the number of the corps, and the letters "U.S." upon it.... Their movements are loose and slovenly, but, like the French, they are taught to make their formations with celerity and precision.*[110]

Style, not substance, repeatedly caused foreigners to underestimate the Americans. As war with Mexico approached in 1846, Mexican officers expressed confidence that they could easily defeat the Americans and march into New Orleans and Mobile. General/President Santa Anna, before he was deposed, boasted he would plant the Mexican flag in Washington, D.C.[111] Other Mexican leaders thought American citizen soldiers "*totally unfit to operate beyond their [own] borders,*" and overseas experts agreed: the English weekly Britannia sneered, "*America, as an aggressive power is one of the weakest in the world ... fit for nothing but to fight Indians.*"[112] Mexican newspapers agreed: *La Voz del Pueblo* insisted, "*We have more than enough strength to make war. Let us make it, then, and victory will perch upon our banners.*"[113]

A detailed analysis by the British minister in Texas in 1845 listed the reasons an American invasion would fail, including an inability of U.S. soldiers to

---

[109]Kwasny, Washington's Partisan War, p.3.
[110]Francis Wyse, in the 1840s, quoted in Coffman, The Old Army, p.166.
[111]Justin H. Smith, The War With Mexico, 2 vols. (New York: Macmillan, 1919), 1:106.
[112]Mexican officials and Britannia quoted in Smith, War With Mexico, 1:105.
[113]Quoted in Smith, War With Mexico, 1:107.

"resist artillery and cavalry," and the fact that the Americans were *"not amenable to discipline ... [and] cannot march on foot."*[114] A correspondent for the *London Times* stated flatly in 1845 that Mexican troops *"are superior to those of the United States."*[115] Other Europeans shared that sentiment: the *Paris Globe,* beginning what seems to be a perennial French misjudgment of American military prowess, prophesied that an American war with Mexico would be *"ruinous, fatal"* to the United States.[116] Even the stodgy *London Times* itself joined the chorus, asserting that *"the invasion and conquest of a vast region by a state which is without an army and without credit is a novelty in the history of nations."*[117] It seems the news media's "embedded generals" were no more accurate in their judgments in the 1840s than in the twenty-first century!

One way in which the U.S. military has been consistently underestimated is that few non-Americans understand that the United States does not take war lightly, and when committed, the solider in every citizen rises up. It is no different from ancient Sparta, where, when asked why Sparta had no walls, the king pointed to the citizens under arms and said, *"These are the Spartans' walls."*[118] In April 1861, Abraham Lincoln found that when he issued a call for 73,000 volunteers, he got almost 92,000. Then, as before, it seemed that the war would be fought by militia units. Regulars in the Union Army in 1860 numbered only just over 16,000, and only increased to 25,000 by 1863. Four drafts added another 162,000 (even though 249,000 were drafted, almost 87,000 paid a commutation fee to be relieved of service, raising more than $26 million).[119] An additional 178,000 black troops enlisted, more than half of them from seceded states. State militia volunteers made up the balance of the 2.1 million soldiers who fought for the Union, affixing their names to the muster rolls that Joshua Chamberlain described as *"pledges of honor—redeemable at the gates of death."*[120] The Confederacy employed the draft even sooner, in April 1862; in desperation, in 1864 it allowed blacks to enlist as laborers with the promise of freedom at the end of their terms, but its total number of men in uniform reached only 900,000 during the war.

Only a handful of blacks voluntarily fought for the Confederacy,[121] but in an oft-missed fact, some 100,000 white Southerners fought for the Union, including the 1st U.S. Alabama Infantry, the 1st U.S. Mississippi Mounted Rifles, the 4th U.S. Arkansas Infantry, the 2nd U.S. Florida Cavalry, and some 40,000 men from Tennessee.[122] At any rate, significant percentages of both Northern and Southern society flocked to the state militia banners and on both sides, volunteers

[114]Captain Elliot, quoted in Smith, War With Mexico, 1:105.
[115]Captain Charles Elliot, in the London Times, July 5, 1845.
[116]The Globe quoted in the Charleston Mercury September 8, 1845.
[117]London Times, April 5, 1845.
[118]Plutarch, on Sparta, in The Lives, quoted in Tsouras, ed., *The Greenhill Dictionary of Military Quotations*, p. 211.
[119]http://www.civilwarhome.com/themen.htm.
[120]Joshua L. Chamberlain, *The Passing of the Armies* (Dayton, Ohio: Morningside Bookshop Press, 1974), p. 23.
[121]Charles Barrow, J. H. Segars, and R. B. Rosenburg, *Forgotten Confederates: An Anthology About Black Southerners* (Atlanta, GA: Southern Heritage Press, 1995).
[122]Michael Zak, *Back to Basics for the Republican Party*, 3rd ed., (Chicago: Thiessen Printing, 2003), p. 69.

accounted or the majority of troops. To General Thomas "Stonewall" Jackson, these motivated men had no equals. Writing in his memoirs, he gushed, "*The patriot volunteer, fighting for his country and his rights, makes the most reliable soldier on earth.*" [123] (In Mexico, Jackson had a different view, noting that the professionals were much better, and volunteers less reliable.)[124] One hundred years later, American soldiers—most of them volunteers—likewise surprised North Vietnamese officers with their "fanaticism" and tenacity.[125]

Slowly, however, from 1790 onward, a small professional army with trained regulars came into being. A somewhat larger standing army was used on the frontier after the Civil war and then, after the Spanish-American War, as part of a constabulary force in American overseas possessions. Between 1899 and 1916, the army's strength fluctuated from a low of 54,000 in 1907 to 107,000 in 1916, which still placed it at a fraction of the size of its major potential adversaries. Germany and France had half a million men under arms; England, a quarter million; and Japan, 230,000. American regulars fought in China at the Boxer Rebellion; on Mindanao and the Sulu Archipelago; and in Mexico, on a futile chase after Pancho Villa. There troops were led by commissioned officers who saw combat, mostly in Cuba, 15 percent of whom were West Point graduates.[126] Unfortunately, the officer corps aged and tended to get promoted by seniority prior to World War I. By the time of the Philippine Insurrection of 1899-1902 and the Moro Campaigns of 1902-1913, many observers, including Theodore Roosevelt, were arguing for more promotion from the ranks. Still, the professional army developed an esprit de corps, leading a spokesman for the American Expeditionary Force in France in 1918, when asked if the Americans could really hold the Germans, replied, "*General, these are American regulars. In a hundred and fifty years they have never been beaten. They will hold.*" [127] Hyperbole aside, the German 7th Army commander General Max von Boehm was one of the first foreign officers to take the Americans seriously. He remarked after his first battlefield encounter with the Yanks, "*In the coming battles ... it is not a question of the possession of this or that village or woods ... it is a question of whether the Anglo-American claims that the American Army is the equal or even the superior of the German Army is to be made good.*"[128] After the Second Battle of the Marne, Lieutenant Kurt Hesse concluded the claims were valid:

---

[123]Tsouras, *The Greenhill Dictionary of Military Quotations*, p. 506.

[124]G. F. R. Henderson, *Stonewall Jackson and the American Civil War* (London: Longmans Green, 1898), pp. 36–37.

[125]B. G. Burkett and Glenna Whitley, *Stolen Valor: How the Vietnam Generation Was Robbed of Its Heros and Its History* (Dallas: Verity Press, 1998) p.62.

[126]Edward M. Coffman, *The Regulars: The American Army, 1898-1941* (Cambridge: Belknap, 2004), pp. 27, 50.

[127]John S. D. Eisenhower, *Yanks: The Epic Story of the American Army in World War I* (New York: Free Press, 2001) p. 140

[128]Eisenhower, Yanks, 146; Ernst Otto, "*The Battles for the Possession of Belleau Woods, June 1918,*: U.S. Naval Institute Proceedings, November 1928, pp. 146–80.

The American ... had nerve; we must give him credit for that; but he also displayed a savage roughness. "The Americans kill everybody!" was the cry of terror on July 15th, which for a long time stuck in the bones of our men.[129]

Hesse was not far off in his assessment, since 60 percent of the forces he led were dead or wounded. By 1918, Crown Prince Rupprecht of Bavaria lamented the soldiers the Germans had once doubted, *"The Americans are multiplying in a way we never dreamed of."*[130]

By the Second World War—the "Good War"—the nation still had to draft two thirds of its soldiers, even after movie director Frank Capra was dragooned by FDR into making eight pro-enlistment films. (Walt Disney, too, contributed several pro-enlistment cartoons.) Yet only one third of Vietnam vets had been drafted, and volunteers accounted for a surprising 77 percent of battle deaths. Only 101 eighteen-year-old draftees died in the entire war, or less than 1 percent. Some 97 percent of the eighteen-year-olds who were killed had volunteered for service. When the media focused on the 10,000 Americans who fled to Canada to avoid the draft, it ignored the fact that nearly 30,000 Canadians entered the U.S. military, and 10,000 of them served in Vietnam.[131] Perhaps even more surprising, the Army's desertion rate was 55 percent higher in World War II than in Vietnam.[132]

From the Shores of Tripoli to ... Hollywood?

Standing behind their barricades outside New Orleans in 1815, Andrew Jackson's polyglot force typified in their diversity American armies before and since. Militia, regulars, Indians, Creoles, free men of color, and Baratarian pirates all waited for the Redcoats to assault their positions. This odd assortment might have seemed improbable had not, just a decade earlier; a similar force won a key victory in what has been called America's "first war on terrorism."[133] Facing continued hijackings and ransom demands by the Barbary Pirates, Thomas Jefferson dispatched William Eaton, the consul to Tripoli, with arms and cash, and then ordered the vessels of the U.S. navy to the Mediterranean. In a scenario that might sound familiar, Jefferson first sought support from England, France, and Germany, all of whom turned him down. He decided to act unilaterally, and obtained a joint resolution from Congress that empowered him to end the pirates' depredations. Eaton, an ambitious and largely unrestrained diplomat, along with Marine lieutenant Presley O'Bannon, landed in Alexandria and recruited *"a rogue's gallery of Turkish, Greek, French, English, Spanish, Indian, and Eastern European mercenaries,"* all herded by eight marines toward Tripoli, where they were to overthrow

---

[129]Quoted in Eisenhower, *Yanks*, p. 161.
[130]Marc Wortman, *The Millionaires' Unit: The Aristocratic Flyboys Who Fought the Great War and Invented American Air Power* (New York: Public Affairs, 2006), p. 234.
[131]Harry G. Summers, Jr., *Vietnam War Almanac* (New York: Facts on File, 1985), p. 108
[132]Summers, *Vietnam War Almanac*, p. 140.
[133]Joseph Wheelan, *Jefferson's War: America's First War on Terror, 1801-1805* (New York: Carroll and Graf, 2003).

the bey.[134] Eventually, Easton's command numbered more than 1,000, including large numbers of Egyptian and Bedouin horsemen. At one tense point, a dispute over pay and supplies saw the eight marines and the Greeks square off against the entire Arab contingent until Eaton won his point. This unconventional force closed in on Tripoli and routed a garrison of 800 Tripolitan troops at Derna, where the Marines charged enemy forces that outnumbered them ten to one, providing the Marines with one of their most inspired lines in "The Marines' Hymn." Eaton and O'Bannon, with their highly unorthodox fighting force, temporarily ended the demands for tribute.[135]

As a matter of course, Americans routinely encourage locals to take up their own fight, and do not denigrate anyone who wants to join our cause. In 1899, battling guerrillas in the Philippines, the United States recruited the Philippine Scouts and the Philippine Constabulary, two forces of local troops. The Scouts, whose members included many who had served in the Spanish army, helped capture Emilio Aguinaldo, and in 1913, the Scouts remerged to help the Moros.[136] And in 2001, a force as unorthodox as Eaton's Arabs or the Philippine Scouts stormed Mazar-e Sharif during Operation Enduring Freedom, when General Tommy Franks sent a handful of Special operations soldiers and CIA operatives to join with the northern Alliance, a mixture of northern Afghan tribes, to rout the Taliban that protected Osama bin Laden.

Jackson's, Eaton's, and Franks' forces were the extreme illustration of American military diversity, but until Vietnam, it was common to see Americans of all social ranks and backgrounds volunteering to fight. John Shy's study of colonial militia revealed a wide cross section of the social order in the military, and he notes that as early as 1713, some 400 (apparently free) blacks joined with white militia forces to defeat the Yamasee Indians in the Yamasee War.[137] Even slaves turned out as armed members of the South Carolina militia in the late 1600s. During the Indian wars on the Great Plains 260 years later, Crow and apache scouts routinely rode with the troopers in blue to fight the Sioux, Cheyenne, and Comanche. In the 1890s, one young lieutenant in charge of Brule Sioux soldiers noted that despite a language barrier, they were intelligent and well disciplined, and *"if you think my Brules don't know their duties, just go down [to their guard post over the hay supplies] some night and try to steal some hay."*[138]

Generally speaking, men from the lower social orders and recent immigrants often made up large numbers of the infantry units, and as late as 1904, a booklet called The Life of an Enlisted Man in the United States Army bemoaned the fact that *"there seems to prevail the idea that to be a soldier ... is to be in a*

---

[134]Mark S. Longo, "To the Shores of Tripoli," *Military Heritage*, June 2005, pp. 40–49, quotation on p. 47; Donald Barr Chidsey, *The Wars in Barbary: Arab Piracy and the Birth of the United States Navy* (New York; Crown, 1971).

[135]Max Boot, *The Savage Wars of Peace: Small Wars and the Rise of American Power* (New York: Basic Books, 2002), pp. 3–29.

[136]Coffman, *The Regulars*, p. 35.

[137]John W. Shy, "A New Look at Colonial Militia," *William and Mary Quarterly*, 20, April 1963, pp. 175–85.

[138]Coffman, *The Old Army*, p. 260.

position which is below that of the ordinary citizen."[139] But in most conflicts, the political, social, and cultural elites were in the midst of action, and indeed, both Army and Navy recruiters rejected a substantial number of applicants from 1900 to 1913, ranging from 70 percent all the way to 81percent![140] Many were turned away due to illiteracy, alien status, or physical causes. Social status may have played a less important role than region in determining who served. Americans agreed with early Whig writer John Trenchard that a national army should consist of *"the same persons as have the property.*"[141] Mark Lender's study of New Jersey troops in the Revolution seemed to confirm that enlisted men came from the upper levels, but he also showed a wide distribution of landholding among the militiamen, including estates of more than four hundred acres.[142] However, the West and South provided a disproportionate number of men, and the North Atlantic, North Central, and South Atlantic Divisions, the fewest.[143] One could find Americans of all professions, social ranks, and ethnic backgrounds in the Army or Navy, although a regional bias against military service had started to afflict the Northeast.[144] Except for the American Revolution and the Civil War, the Northeast has been the only consistently antimilitary section of the country.

If the Northeast as a region has a long history of antimilitary positions, such a bias was missing among any particular occupational group. Charles Whittlesey, the Medal of Honor winner who led the Lost Battalion in World War I, was a Harvard-trained New York lawyer; and in the Spanish-American War, the cream of New York society, including Hamilton Fish and Dudley Dean, whom Teddy Roosevelt called "The best quarterback ever to play on a Harvard Eleven," volunteered for the Rough Riders.

Even Hollywood—which today is the bastion of the Left's antimilitary propaganda machine—sent its best to wars prior to Vietnam. Indeed, in World War II, a new class of cultural icons—this time from Hollywood—were as thoroughly represented in the military services as any other group. Among those who were drafted or volunteered to fight were almost all of the movie industry's leading actors.[145] Topping the list was Clark Gable, who was technically too old to serve. Yet he joined up, enlisting as a private before being promoted up the ranks

[139]Alfred Reynolds, *The Life of an Enlisted Man in the United States Army* (Washington, D.C.: Government Printing Office, 1904), p. 7.
[140]Coffman, *The Regulars*, p. 97.
[141]Trenchard quoted in Marke Edward Lender, "The Social Structure of the New Jersey Brigade: The Continental Line as an American Standing Army," in Peter Karsten, ed., *The Military in America: From the Colonial Era to the Present* (New York: Free Press, 1980), pp. 27–44 (28).
[142]Lender, "Social Structure of the New Jersey Brigade," pp. 30–31.
[143]Coffman, *The Regulars*, p. 98.
[144]Michael Lind, Vietnam: the Necessary War (New York: Touchstone, 1999), chap.4. Lind maintains that an isolationist "Greater New England, including Ohio, Wisconsin, much of the upper tier of the Midwest, and even Oregon has been antiinterventionist" and antimilitary. This is not true—Ohio supported President Bush in both 2000 and 2004, and the presidential elections in Wisconsin, Michigan, and Pennsylvania were very close. This point is particularly important when one considers that in 2004, the war in Iraq was a central issue. California voted for Ronald Reagan in both 1980 and 1984, and for Richard Nixon in 1968 and 1972. Nixon won "Greater New England" Oregon twice, Michigan twice, Wisconsin twice, and Oregon twice. If there is a "Greater New England" antimilitary/isolationist pattern there, I fail to see it.
[145]http://www.palletmastersworkshoop.com/flipside.html.

and attending Officer Training School. Gable and Jimmy Stewart both saw action in bombers over European skies. After starting as a "buck private peeling potatoes," Stewart attained officer rank and led hundreds of men, including another future Academy Award winner, Walter Matthau, who won six campaign ribbons gained in hundreds of bombing runs over Germany.[146] William Holden, already cast in a number of roles, also served as an officer in the Army Air Force, where he made training films. Another airman, Charles Bronson, was a tailgunner on B-29 bombers in the Pacific. Star Trek creator Gene Roddenberry flew C-46s with the 8th Army Air Force and received the Distinguished Flying Cross. Jack Palance, famous for his role as Curley in City Slickers, underwent facial reconstruction surgery after his B-17 crash-landed in Britain in 1943. Burgess Meredith, Cameron Mitchell, Kevin McCarthy, Oscar winner Martin Balsam, Jackie Coogan (a glider pilot), Dale Robertson, George (Superman) Reeves, Russell Johnson (the professor on Gilligan's Island), Robert Preston, George Gobel, Gene Raymond, Karl Maulden, Red Buttons, and Robert Taylor also put in time with the U.S. Army Air Force.

Humphrey Bogart, who had already fought in World War I, tried to enlist but was turned down because of his age, Jason Robards, who became an actor after the war, was already serving aboard the USS *Northhampton*, which was stationed at Pearl Harbor, but he was a radioman at sea on December 7, 1941, and went on to receive the Navy Cross. Fellow swabbie, and another Academy Award winner, Henry Fonda, already an established star for his role in *The Grapes of Wrath*, was in uniform by 1943. The Navy wanted him to make training films, but he insisted on combat, saying *"I don't want to be in a fake war in a studio."* He served on a destroyer in the Pacific. Oscar-winner Ernest Borgnine, already serving in the Navy, joined them in the South Pacific in 1943. Eddie Albert was awarded a Bronze Star while serving as a U.S. Navy landing officer at Tarawa and friends Robert Montgomery and Douglas Fairbanks, Jr. —both already stars—applied for admission to the U.S. Naval Reserve. Fairbanks was a Navy officer from 1941 to 1946 and put in time with Lord Mountbatton's Commando staff in England. William Conrad was an F4U pilot, and Richard Boone, a TBF flight crewman. Comedian Shecky Greene sailed aboard the aircraft carrier *Bon Homme Richard*. The list of Hollywood actors who served in the Navy is extensive, and includes Paul Newman, Jack Lemmon, Bob Barker, Jackie Cooper, Rock Hudson, Tony Curtis, Kirk Douglas, Tom Poston, Cliff Robertson, Rod Steiger, Dennis Weaver, and Robert Stack. In addition, Dennis Hopper, Gilligan's Island Alan Hale, Victor Mature, and Arthur Godfrey all served in the Coast Guard.

Many leading men joined the Marines, including George C. Scott, Glen

---

[146]Rob Edelman and Audrey Kupferberg, Matthau: A Life (Lanham, MD: Taylor Trade Publishing, 2002), pp. 39–46. See also Flint Whitlock, "Insight: In the 1940s, the American Film Industry Rallied Like Never Before or Since to Support the War Effort," WW II History, November 2006, pp. 16–25; James E. Wise and Paul Wilderson, III, Khaki: Movie Actors in the Army and Air Services (Annapolis, MD: Naval Institute Press, 2000); James Wise and Ann Rehill, Stars in Blue: Movie Actors in America's Sea Services (Annapolis, MD: Naval Institute Press, 1997); Michael Munn, Stars at War (London: Robson Books, 1996). Thanks to research help from Adam Schwiekart for this material.

Ford—who would go on to serve in Korea as well—plus Brian Keith, and pilots Tyrone Power, who obtained the rank of major before his death, and Ed McMahon, who also flew in Korea and eventually became a colonel. Bob Keeshan, who after the war would gain fame as the children's who host Captain Kangaroo, joined up just before the war ended. It is an urban legend that he fought alongside Academy Award-winner Lee Marvin, who did survive fierce combat on Saipan. Don Adams, who later starred in the television series *Get Smart,* contracted malaria at Guadalcanal and was out for the war. Lee Powell, the first silver screen Lone Ranger, was killed invading Tinian with the 2nd Marine Division. Both Robert Reed and Sterling Hayden were Marines assigned to the Office of Strategic Services (OSS) in Europe. John Russell, a prototypical cowboy, was wounded and decorated for valor at Guadalcanal. James Whitmore, a law student at Yale, interrupted his education to join the Marines, finishing his degree while in boot camp.

The creator of the *Twilight Zone,* Rod Serling, jumped out of airplanes with the 11th Airborne Division, and was awarded a Purple Heart, and actor Jack Warden was a paratrooper with the 101st Airborne. James Arness, television's Marshall Dillon in Gunsmoke, was wounded at Anzio and received a Bronze Star; his brother Peter Graves, who starred in Mission: Impossible, served two years in the Army Air Corps; and the whiny, simpering Ted Baxter (Ted Knight), on The Mary Tyler Moore Show, cleared land mines and was awarded five Bronze Stars. Perennial Academy Award-nominee and circus acrobat Burt Lancaster joined the Army and served in North Africa and Italy. Stalwart actor George Kennedy served under Patton in France, Jackie Gleason's costar in the *Homeymooners*, Art Carney, was wounded by shrapnel invading Normandy and walked with a limp from that point on. Tony Award-winner Charles Durning, having received a Silver Star for heroism at Normandy and three Purple Hearts, was one of the few survivors of the Malmedy, France, massacre of American POW's.

John Agar, Jeff Chandler, Ossie Davis, Carl Reiner, and impressionist actor Frank Gorshin all served in the U.S. Army. Werner Klemperer, who enlisted, and who would later go on to a famous role in Hogan's Heroes as Commandant Klink, the head of a German stalag, in real service was a military policeman in Hawaii. Some, like Charlton Heston, a sergeant, were assigned to such remote places as Kodiak, Alaska. Future president Ronald Reagan, an officer in the Army Air Corps, was not assigned to combat due to severe hearing loss, and instead made training films. Telly "Kojak" Savalas received a Purple Heart in action, but was released from the Army in 1943 after suffering a near-critical injury in an off-duty head-on collision—he was told he would not walk again. Rick Jason, who would later star in *Combat,* the longest-running war series on television, came from a wealthy background. His stockbroker father bought him a seat on the New York Stock Exchange, but when war came, he enlisted in the Army Air Corps.

Future directors included Marines Sam Peckinpah (stationed in China), George Roy Hill (a transport pilot who later serve in Korea as a fighter pilot), and

Robert Altman, who flew B-24s. John Ford filmed combat operations. Then directors Daryl Zanuck, Frank Capra, William Wyler, and producer Jack Warner worked for the Army's Film Unit along with actors Joseph Cotten, Lee J. Cobb, and Van Heflin.

As great as the heroism of some of these men was, two stories of tenacity stand out: Robert Montgomery, already an Oscar winner, did not wait for the war to come to America. He joined the American Field Service, driving ambulances in Europe until Dunkirk. Then, when the United States declared war on Japan and Germany, he came home to join the Navy, becoming a PT boat captain and receiving a Bronze Star. Desidero "Desi" Arnaz, Lucille Ball's partner and famous Cuban husband, was offered a commission in the Cuban navy, where he would have been relatively safe on Caribbean patrols. Instead, he attempted to enlist, but was rejected as a noncitizen. But that did not keep him from being drafted—and he was—and despite failing the physical, he went into the infantry, where he injured his knees. He finished the war entertaining troops.[147]

Other veterans went onto become celebrities in literature and theater after the war. Norman Mailer invaded the Philippines with his infantry regiment; Louis L'Amour, later a famous Western writer, fought ashore at Normandy in his tank destroyer; and Alex Haley, before he conceived of Roots, protected the coasts with the U.S. Coast Guard. William Manchester, a Marine sergeant on Okinawa, suffered serious wounds, one of which left a Japanese bullet next to his heart that went undetected when he was in a hospital recovering from previous wounds. Manchester had been unconscious and lying in a triage area when he was hit by a stray enemy round. Others were spared such traumas. Tony Bennett, serving as an infantryman in Europe, got his first chance to sing while in the Army. Funnyman Don Knotts served in a special Army entertainment unit, future director and actor Mel Brooks was practicing his Al Jolson routine and becoming a stand-up comic. Science fiction writer Ray Bradbury honed his writing skills for the War Department's propaganda office. Hollywood women served as well: Nancy Kulp, "Jane Hathaway" on the Beverly Hillbillies, was a lieutenant in the WAVES; Bea Arthur, later of Maude, served in the Marines' women's auxiliary; Martha Raye entertained troops with the USO and was a part-time nurse; black cabaret singer Josephine Baker was a spy; teenage Audrey Hepburn risked her life as a messenger for Dutch resistance groups; and Marlene Dietrich—soon after becoming a U.S. citizen—promoted war bond sales and made anti-Nazi propaganda broadcasts in German. Al Hirt, jazz trumpeter, entertained troops during the war. Of course, the story of bandleader Glenn Miller, who died flying to Europe to entertain troops, is well known, as is that of Carole Lombard, the beautiful actress whose plane crashed en route to Los Angeles to sell war bonds.

While it is true there was a draft—and many of these famous men were inducted—a large number joined up, some lying about their ages and/or leaving comfortable surroundings and certain exemptions. Long before the World War

---

[147] See Larry Schweikart and Michael Allen, *A Patriot's History of the United States: From Columbus's Great Discovery to the War on Terror* (New York: Sentinel, 2004), chap. 17.

II draft could effectively kick in, civilian contractors on Wake Island voluntarily joined with the Marines to hold off the Japanese invasion. Construction workers from Morrison-Knudsen manned machine guns, hurled grenades, stood guard, and loaded shells, often with only a few minutes' training. (Of these civilians, ninety-eight were kept on the island after the Japanese shipped off the military prisoners, and they were slaughtered in a mass execution after the civilians completed their work).[148]

One key difference between the Hollywood of World War II and the Vietnam generation is that while many Vietnam vets became performers or artists, including Patrick Duffy and Steve Kanaly of Dallas fame, and Dennis Franz and Pat Sajak, and the writer William Broyles, who co-created the television show *China Beach*, many actors in 1942 became veterans. It is also true that the Vietnam experience provided a fertile ground for writers: fiction authors Winston Groom (Forrest Gump), John Del Vecchio, Tobias Wolff, and others. Tim O'Brien's *Going After Cacciato* (1978) was a Vietnam novel that won the National Book Award. It is also an irony that one of the most celebrated icons of the late 1960s, guitarist Jimi Hendrix, famed for his heavy-metal version of "The Star-Spangled Banner," briefly served in the 101st Airborne in 1962. At first, he took pride in the fact that he was a paratrooper: *"I'm in the best division: the 101st Airborne. That's the sharpest outfit in the world."*[149] All Hendrix wanted to do at the time was play his guitar, which soon led him to seek a discharge, although the explanations of how he actually left the military remain in dispute.[150] However, in 1969, when European interviewers badgered him about the Vietnam War, hoping he would make inflammatory statements, Hendrix shocked them by comparing Vietnam to D-Day: *"Did you send the Americans away when they landed in Normandy? ... No, but then that was concerning your own skin. The Americans are fighting in Vietnam for the complete free world.... Of course, war is horrible, but at present, it's still the only guarantee to maintain peace."*[151] Another supposed 60s-era radical, Frank Zappa, actually made fun of "peaceniks" more than he ever attacked Richard Nixon or LBJ.[152]

In the post-Vietnam era, Marines, soldiers, sailors, and airmen and women still constitute a remarkable cross section of American citizens, with the exception of those who were in the entertainment industry or in journalism. While reporting from Iraq, Karl Zinsmeister ran into a Russian who had moved to New York at age seventeen and was now a brigade commander; a paratrooper sergeant with a Ph.D. in philosophy from Fordham; and a Columbian-born helicopter mechanic, among many others. Evan Wright of Rolling Stone was stunned to find a Dartmouth grad among the Marines he observed. The spectrum of soldiers and Marines serving in Iraq like in Vietnam and the Gulf War, includes every walk of life save one:

[148]John Wokovits, *Pacific Alamo: The Battle for Wake Island* (New York: New American Library, 2003), pp. 74, 236.
[149]Charles R. Cross, *Rooms Full of Mirrors: A Biography of Jimi Hendrix* (New York: Hyperion, 2005), p. 91.
[150]Cross, *Room full of Mirrors*, pp. 93–94.
[151]Cross, *Room full of Mirrors*, p. 248.
[152]Barry Miles, *Zappa: A Biography* (New York: Grove Press, 2004).

virtually no members of the entertainment medium. (Comedian Drew Carey, a Marine from 1981 to 1986, regularly entertained troops on USO tours.) No Hollywood leading men signed up for duty in the wake of 9/11, in stark contrast to the patriotic outpouring after Pearl Harbor. Not a single major actor or actress gave up a motion picture career to fight for the country, and only a handful, including James Woods, Gary Sinese, and Ron Silver, made the talk-show rounds to support the war. (Contrast that with World War I, when the most prominent movie stars of the day—Mary Pickford, Douglas Fairbanks, and Charlie Chaplin—held Liberty Bond rallies, at one time bringing out thirty thousand to support the war!)[153]

Aside from Pat Tillman, virtually no modern celebrities have served or fought in any of the conflicts in the last fifteen years. Tillman, the NFL star who resigned from the Arizona Cardinals and a multimillion dollar contract to enlist in the Army, became a Ranger and was assigned to Afghanistan, where he was killed in a tragic friendly fire incident. A few others can be singled out, such as Josh Holden, a 2003 West Point graduate who held down two jobs as a first lieutenant and as an outfielder for the Billings Montana Mustangs, a farm team of the Cincinnati Reds organization, and Kyle Eckel, a 2005 Naval Academy graduate who was a free-agent fullback for the New England Patriots.[154] Three of the most famous athlete-warriors, Roger Staubach, David Robinson, and Chad Hennings all served their time in the military before joining their professional sports. Staubach served in Vietnam; Hennings flew A-10s in combat in the Gulf War; and Robinson's seven-foot-one-inch frame led the Navy to issue him an unusual waiver from active duty and to feature him in recruiting instead. Others have fulfilled their obligations to the military before their professional careers, though unlike Staubach and Hennings, none have done so during an active war in the all-volunteer military.

Several members of Congress had sons serving in the military during the War on Terror, including representatives Duncan Hunter (R-CA), Joe Wilson (R-SC), Todd Akin (R-MO), and senators Kit Bond (R-MO), Tim Johnson (D-SD), and others. (Surprisingly, this works out to about 1.1 percent of the 535 members of the 2005 House and Senate, compared to the 0.5 percent of the total U.S. population.) In addition, the son of Chicago mayor Richard Daley, who joined the Army, and the eldest son of New York governor George Pataki, commissioned a second lieutenant in the Marines, constituted other members of the "political class" who signed up. Perhaps more surprising to some antimilitary critics, Ivy Leaguers and honor students were continuing to sign up. Contrary to New York Times reporter Chris Hedges's assertion that *"poor kids from Mississippi ... who could not get a decent job ... joined the Army because it was all we offered them,"* thousands of top honor students annually took the military entrance exams. Karl Zinsmeister found *"Cornell grads, Ph.D. candidates, and high-tech wunderkinds"* in his three tours of Iraq.[155]

---

[153]Eisenhower, *Yanks*, p. 20.

[154]Jill Lieber, "Soldier-Athlete Being All He Can Be," and "Naval Academy Graduate Takes Leave to Join Patriots' Camp," USA Today, August 19, 2005.

[155]Lynn Vincent, "Unusual Recruits: Ivy Leaguers and Honor Students Are Signing Up to Serve," World Magazine, August 27, 2005.

Having the participation of the "elites" in the military is a fairly common American characteristic. After war broke out in Europe in 1914, there was enough concern that various National Guard units began to recruit. When President Arthur Hadley of Yale called for students to join the Yale Battery of the Connecticut National Guard, he hoped to get 135 volunteers. Instead, 950 showed up the first day.[156] In fact, the Yalies went far beyond signing up for National Guard duty. One group, distressed by American unpreparedness for war—most of them Yale students and all of the "*sons of America's early twentieth-century aristocracy [and fabulously wealthy]*"—purchased their own seaplane and paid for lessons to learn to fly it. Most of them went to Europe and several saw action after the war broke out. At least one was shot down and killed. Their foresight in preparing the nation's first aviation unit—when the U.S. Navy had a total of twenty-two operable seaplanes, while Germany was producing one thousand aircraft a month—led Admiral William Sims to label them "twentieth-century Paul Reveres."[157] Their sacrifices were common among America's privileged and wealthy. When Quentin Roosevelt, Teddy's son, was killed in a dogfight, the former president delivered a speech in Saratoga where he said, "*The finest, the bravest, the best of our young men have sprung eagerly forward to face death for the sake of a high ideal; and they have brought home to us the great truth that life consists of more than easygoing pleasures, and more than hard, conscienceless, brutal striving after purely material success.*"[158] Even groups of wealthy girls from the top of society formed the Girl's Radio Unit, which inspected radios at military contractor factories, earning only $20 a week for a six-day week.

Just under a century later, Americans from all walks of life still joined the Army, Navy, Air Force, and Marines and many fought in Afghanistan or Iraq, including graduates of Harvard's ROTC program. A recent study found that, on average, American recruits were more highly educated than the population as a whole. The same study compared enlistees before and after 9/11, finding that after 9/11, demographic regions in the highest-income quintile provided the greatest positive proportional increase in recruits![159] And contrary to the theme of so many modern war movies, such as Black Hawk Down or We Were Soldiers, where soldiers only fight "*for each other*," America's servicemen and women are "*quite conscious of the titanic clash of moral universes that lies behind today's U.S. venture into the Middle East,*" and many are "*not only aware of the historic importance of this fight, but quite proud of their role in it.*"[160]

Moreover, if some of the media, Hollywood, and social elites no longer enlist the way they used to, America still gets the cream of the crop into its military academies. If West Point and Annapolis don't quite compare with Harvard

---

[156]Wortman, Millionaires' Unit, p. 26
[157]Wortman, Millionaires' Unit, pp. xiv-xv.
[158]Ibid., p. 218.
[159]Tim Kane, "*Who Bears the Burden? Demographic Characteristics of U.S. Military Recruits Before and After 9/11,*" Center for Data Analysis, Heritage Foundation, CDA05-08, November 7, 2005, pp. 2–3.
[160]Karl Zinsmeister, *Dawn over Baghdad: How the U.S. Military is Using Bullets and Ballots to Remake Iraqi* (San Francisco: Encounter Books, 2004), p. 10.

and Yale when it comes to SATs, they more than make up for it with dedication and desire. After 9/11, West Point faced an unusual problem: many cadets were quitting—not because they were afraid to go to war, but because they couldn't wait. As more and more reports of cadets quitting to enlist came across Lieutenant General William Lennox's desk, he addressed the entire corps on September 13, with a message he titled *"Tactical Patience." "I told them that they'd be needed. As officers,"* he explained.[161]

Training, Training, Training

Differences between regulars and militia units stood out starkly in the Civil War, when not only did enlisted men have to master the military arts, but commanders such as Colonel Joshua Chamberlain went to sleep each night with the officer's drill book in their hands. Indian fighting on the frontier kept the tiny regular army's skills somewhat honed, even though at the turn of the twentieth-century, units were limited to a thousand rounds of live-fire practice per year. Infantry tactics pretty much resembled those used by Joshua Chamberlain and Ulysses Grant until 1911, when the **Infantry Drill Regulations** stressed *"flexibility and realism,"* and emphasized physical fitness and marksmanship.[162] Although the regular army remained small on the eve of World War I, its regulars "trained up" quickly and saw battle well ahead of expectations by the British or French, and the presence of the Reserves and the National Guard allowed a continuity of command whereby officers and men remained at least somewhat in the loop even while not on full-time active duty. It reiterated the message that possibly more than any other factor, training minimized losses. Of the post—World War I lessons learned, Lieutenant Colonel Paul Malone, advocating an infantry training school, wrote, *"Losses of American lives will bear a close but inverse ratio to the extent which training of infantry in time of peace is given to the leaders of infantry units."*[163] At a relatively early point, then, Americans came to view training as a key to reducing casualties.

Eight years later, in Iraq, the United States found that increasingly casualties were incurred because of hit-and-run attacks, roadside bombs, and even suicide trucks, as opposed to traditional combat attacks. A pattern soon became clear: the Marines, given their superiority in infantry combat training, generally fared far better, even in convoy situations, than regular Army. Both were less vulnerable than reserves or Guardsmen, who made up a significant portion of the convoy drivers, but as the losses of 17 Marines from the same reserve unit in Ohio in August 2005 showed, even better-trained troops were vulnerable to explosive devices and mines. Still, the message was clear: all men and women in a war zone needed to be combat trained, first and foremost.

By the summer of 2004, the Army had adapted, announcing sweeping

[161]Nancy Gibbs and Nathan Thornburgh, "The Class of 9/11," Time, May 30, 2005, pp. 28–43, quotation on 32.
[162]Coffman, *The Regulars*, p. 108.
[163]Paul Malone, "The Need for an Infantry School," Infantry Journal, 16, November 1919, pp. 347–59.

changes in its basic training program. Including an increased emphasis on infantry combat skills. *"Soldiers of all specialties will face direct contact with an adversary,"* stated Colonel Bill Gallagher, commander of Fort Benning's training brigade.[164] All officers had to think of themselves as infantrymen first.

Historian John Keegan said of Ulysses Grant that he valued *"a day of drill higher than a week of oratory"* because training involved not only lots of practice time, but a mental attitude—a different posture of aggression, alert constantly to the possibility of enemy attacks and of their own response. Grant also concluded that *"drill and discipline were, worth more to our men than fortifications."*[165] Whether it was the fighting civilian volunteers on Wake Island in the opening days of World War II or the National Guard units in Iraq, a lack of training could turn courageous men and women into ineffective targets. The contractors on Wake Island literally received only a few minutes' of instruction on how to fire three-inch guns and machine guns, throw grenades, and otherwise fight.[166] Even with the professional Marines on the island, lack of sufficient training due to 1930s cutbacks became obvious, as when the company bugler, Alvin Waronker, forgot the proper "general quarters" tune and began playing whatever music "tumbled into his mind."[167]

More than fifty years later, military analysts emphasized the value of training more than ever. Trained combat units suffered far fewer casualties than reserves or National Guard forces. Virtually all Marines and Rangers in Iraq constantly cleaned and rebuilt their weapons. Prior to the decision to go to war in 2003, Marines on board ship regularly practiced rebuilding their M16s blindfolded, with all the other members of the squad screaming at them. It was not only their training, but their aggression that made the Marines different. One officer proudly called his Marines *"the most demented young people our society can produce."*[168] He meant it as a compliment.

Education and literacy made training easier through drill manuals and writer policies. As Davin Hackett Fischer noted, in 1776 the *"Yankee regiments may have been the most literate army in the world. Nearly all New England privates could read and write."*[169] American soldiers from the ranks read Common Sense. Of course, training officers who could understand tactics differed from teaching them mere literacy, but even after the establishment of military schools such as West Point and Annapolis, the American military wanted officers to be as well educated as possible, and in the twentieth century, officers were routinely funneled through the best universities, where they attained advanced degrees in business, engineering, history, and political science. Despite overt hostility to the military on many campuses, many of the nation's leading institutions, including

---

[164]Thom Shanker, "Army Pushes a Sweeping Overhaul of Basic Training," New York Times, August 4, 2004.
[165]Ulysses s. Grant, *"Personal Memoirs, 1885-1886,"* at http://www.bartleby.com/1011/25.html
[166]Wukovits, Pacific *Alamo*, passim.
[167]Wukovits, *Pacific Alamo*, p. 50.
[168]Williamson Murray and Robert H. Scales, Jr., *The Iraq War: A Military History* (Cambridge, MA: Belknap Press, 2003), p. 113.
[169]David Hackett Fischer, *Washington's Crossing* (New York: Oxford, 2004), p. 21.

MIT and John Hopkins, still maintain ROTC programs. Combat officers frequently observe that their graduate degrees in social sciences or the humanities provided them with excellent preparation for the challenges they found in Iraq and Afghanistan.

Critics who claimed that military service, particularly in Vietnam, "militarized" those who served, making them more authoritarian and violent, have produced no evidence to support their claims, much to their surprise.[170] To the contrary, American officers are expected to be instructed in the arts and letters as well as the ways of war. A reading list for each level of officer provided by the Army ranges from works on history to the latest on corporate management. America's economic advantages, which demand higher-skilled and more educated employees at almost every level, enable the military to train soldiers faster; and, once released from military duty (in every war but Vietnam), the veteran has been viewed as having obtained valuable skills in the Army or Navy that would enhance his performance in a civilian job. (Vietnam vets, it seems, were frequently discriminated against due to the Left's incredible depictions of them as "baby killers," or drug-addicted, imbalanced psychopaths.)[171] The ability of highly skilled civilians to enhance military operations was evident during the Civil War, when Herman Haupt's Union railroad agency gave the North a decisive edge because he could employ, with virtually no additional training, thousands of Yankee soldiers, who had prewar experience in railroads. Telegraphers on both sides could begin work immediately upon joining. On the other hand, cavalry recruits who had never ridden a horse took more time to develop.[172]

Early in the twentieth century, sergeants started to assume that all American males could drive automobiles, and were surprised when any could not. When tanks were introduced to the 66th Infantry, the sergeant told one of the trainees, *"Drive the damn tank, it's just like a truck except for the steering levers."*[173] The soldier did not want to tell the sergeant he did not know how to drive a car, and promptly ran into a building. But that changed. By World War II, Americans, far more than the citizens of any other country in the conflict, were more likely to have driven a car or operated a motor vehicle. There was a car for every four Americans, contrasted with Italy, where the ratio was 1:138, or even Germany, where it was 1:28.[174] This meant an American needed only a few minutes to learn the basics of a truck gearbox, and perhaps only a few hours to figure out the idiosyncrasies of a tank or half-track. Germany, on the other hand, had to specially create the Motor Sport School just to train some 187,000 tank and truck drivers

---

[170]Alan Lizotte and David Bordua, "Military Socialization, Childhood Socialization, and Vet's Firearms Ownership," *Journal of Political and Military Sociology*, 1980, 243–56; James Fendrich and Michael Pearson, "Black Veterans Return," in Martin Oppenheimer, ed., *The American Military* (Chicago: Aldine, 1971), 163–78; M. K. Jennings and G. B. Markus, "Political Participation and Vietnam-Era War Veterans: A Longitudinal Study," in Nancy Goldman and David Segal, eds., *The Social Psychology of Military Service* (Beverly Hills: Sage, 1976), pp. 175–200.

[171]See Burkett and Whitley, *Stolen Valor*: passim.

[172]Quoted in Coffmann, *The Old Army*, p. 157.

[173]Coffman, *The Regulars*, p. 310.

[174]James F. Dunnigan and Albert A. Nofi, *Dirty Little Secrets of World War II* (New York: Quill, 1994), p. 26.

between 1933 and 1939.[175]

Diversity, 1800s Style

Because Americans tended to come from such a background of equality and to suffer less than other countries from class distinctions, training became even more important. Yet it was equally important that Americans willingly accept any group whose cause was our own. Andrew Jackson, following in the tradition of William Easton and Presley O'Bannon, demonstrated this at New Orleans. There he used whomever he found for the defense of the city, although at first there was a lone exception: he had no intention of allying with Jean Lafitte's pirates of the Barataria region. Both the British and the Americans had simultaneously courted and attacked Jean Lafitte's renegades prior to 1815. Yet both sides also knew that whatever the pirates' criminal background, they were valuable local military assets. Their spies permeated the West Indies, providing them with crucial information on ship and troop departures. Recognizing this, the British sent envoys to Jean Lafitte to forge an alliance, but with typical British heavy-handedness, the ministers threatened to "*destroy Barataria unless [the pirates agreed to] help her invade the United States.*"[176]

Lafitte, however, was too French and too criminal to ally with England. Yet neither could he risk running into American arms: Louisiana governor William C. C. Clairborne had issued a warrant for Lafitte's arrest with a reward of $500, prompting Lafitte to issue his own "reward" of $500 for Claiborne! While Lafitte still pondered his options, all the while expecting an attack by the British, his men were shocked when he was shelled by the USS *Carolina*. The pirates withdrew inland, but Lafitte, even after the attack, still distrusted the British so much that he thought the Americans a more natural ally. Moreover, he thought of himself as a citizen of New Orleans, obviously not having heard about Andrew Jackson's reference to the Baratarians as "hellish banditti!"[177] Fortunately for Lafitte, a local group, the New Orleans Committee on Defense, sought to change the general's mind. They knew Jackson needed every available gun and, more important, that he had few trained sailors and little artillery. Lafitte had lots of both. Further, the committee persuaded a federal district judge to drop all charges against the pirates, and the state legislature voted a resolution suspending all actions against the pirates for four months. Jackson no longer had any legal justification for rejecting the pirates' aid. Jean Lafitte and his brother, Dominique, personally met with Jackson and convinced him of their eagerness to fight for the city. Impressed, Jackson relented and invited the "hellish banditti" to help build the defenses and to supply all the war materials they could. Immediate-

---

175   Kenneth Macksey, *Why the Germans Lose at War: The Myth of German Military Superiority* (New York, Barnes & Noble, 1996), p. 68

[176]Jane Lucas de Grummond, *The Baratarians and the Battle of New Orleans* (Baton Rouge: Louisiana State University Press, 1961), p. 39.

[177]Remini, *Battle of New Orleans*, p. 38.

ly, they organized three companies of badly needed artillery. Jackson appointed Lafitte to his staff, and the pirate's possession of maps and his knowledge of geography proved critical. Lafitte's pirates joined the Creoles, Indians, mulattoes, militia, and regular army units that defended the city, adding yet another element of color and diversity to the American defenders, and further distinguishing them from the flinty professionals in red who marched to meet them. Men continued to arrive daily, but even with Lafitte's pirates, Jackson's troops numbered only slightly more than 4,000, and they faced some 15,000 of England's finest regulars.

Vice Admiral Sir Alexander Cochrane commanded the fleet that advanced toward New Orleans, arriving at Chandler Island some seventy miles from the city on December 8. Cochrane, unable to get by American gunboats and forts protecting New Orleans, landed his force at Bayou Bienvenue—a process that involved switching vessels at two points and a painstaking process of rowing men from Pea Island. British troops began an excruciatingly difficult landing operation from their ships docked off Cat Island. They had to row troops from the ships first to Pea Island, where they reassembled, then the entire body rowed another thirty miles to Bayou Bienvenue. The journey to Pea Island alone took ten hours one way, hauling 2,000 soldiers per trip. After three days, all the troops were finally ready for the second part of the journey. On December 22, the invasion on the mainland began, and after sweeping aside some light American resistance, Admiral Cochrane promised to eat Christmas dinner in New Orleans. [178]

Jackson possessed a good tactical mind as well as an aggressive character, but he did not know the full disposition of the enemy, so he moved cautiously to the Lacoste Plantation within range of the British camp. There he began to form the first of several lines. He put the dismounted Mississippi Dragoons on the extreme left along with General John Coffee's 800 Tennessee volunteer mounted rifles and the New Orleans rifle company. Jackson commanded all the artillery, 66 Marines, two battalions of volunteers, the 7th and 44th U.S. Infantry regiments, a battalion of 287 New Orleans volunteers, the company of free men of color, and the Choctaw Indians to the right, from the river stretching across to Coffee. More important, Jackson had the guns of the Carolina from the Mississippi, which opened the battle on the night of December 23 by shelling the British troops as they advanced. Jackson moved his forces forward, despite ferocious—but largely ineffective—fire from the British. Coffee sensed the opportunity and charged, threatening to drive the British back into the sea.

The Tennesseans could fire their long rifles more accurately than the British could, yet the Redcoats grimly held their ground. One captain remarked that there was no record *"since the invention of gunpowder ... of two opposing parties fighting so long muzzle to muzzle."*[179] When a British counterattack threatened to capture Jackson's six-pounder guns, a tenacious defense by the Marines drove off the Redcoats until the guns could be pulled back. Across the battlefield, dirty shirts and Redcoats squared off in hand-to-hand combat. Tomahawk met bayonet,

[178]Remini, *Battle of New Orleans*, p. 69.
[179] Remini, *Battle of New Orleans*, p. 77

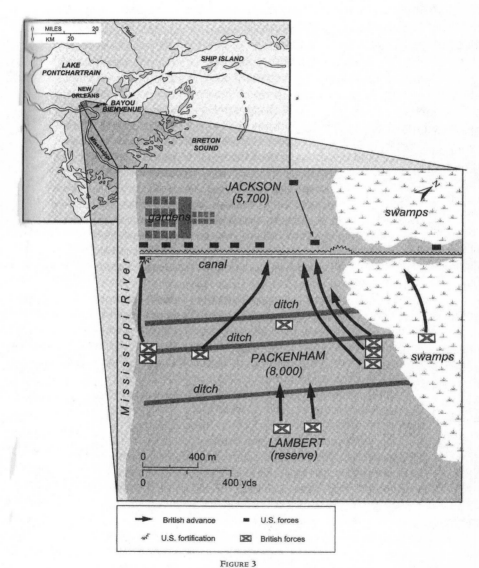

FIGURE 3

The Battle of New Orleans
January 8, 1815

hunting knives struck swords. The contest continued until 9:30 at night, when Jackson decided the superior discipline of the British would favor them if he continued the fight. He ordered a withdrawal two miles back to Rodriguez Canal near the Chalmette Plantation.

Each side lost about 250 men killed, wounded, missing, or captured, but Jackson's troops had advanced five hundred yards against regulars in triple line formation. Among the British war councils that night, officers and enlisted men alike were convinced they had faced 15,000 Americans rather than a force of less than half that size.[180] Any notion that militia units could not fight with discipline and determination vanished in Jackson's advance. A Frenchman working for the Americans snorted, "*The heroes of Wellington*" were made "*to appreciate the prowess of those warlike sons of the western country.*"[181] It was a remarkable performance for Jackson's dirty shirts, who had stood toe to toe against the British. Jackson was disappointed that he had the good ground. And, most important, he knew the British were all in front of him.

Jackson's men now occupied a narrow strip between the Mississippi River and an impenetrable cypress swamp. With American gunboats on the river, the British would have to advance against him head-on. His men immediately worked to deepen and strengthen the canal; they built a rampart and brought up sufficient ammunition. All through Christmas Eve, American forces placed their artillery strategically in four batteries, and reinforced the earthworks, bringing additional soil in to strengthen the four-foot high rampart. General David Morgan's men set up positions on the west bank of the Mississippi, their left flank protected by another swamp.

Meanwhile, a new British commander, Lieutenant General Sir Edward Pakenham, had arrived, fresh from campaigning with his brother-in-law, the Duke of Wellington, against Napoléon. Pakenham thought the setback on December 23 was due to incompetent leadership, and mistakenly assumed there were not sufficient forces in front to oppose him. He ordered his artillery brought up and directed at the Carolina and the Louisiana, destroying the first and forcing the second to reposition farther back. After another failed reconnaissance in force on December 28, Pakenham ordered up still more artillery. The Americans endured the barrage for several minutes, then fired back. Once again—to the astonishment of the British—not only was the fire from American guns accurate, but it was at least as rapid as the fire from the trained British batteries.

When the British guns fell silent, only Jackson saw that his own artillery had been effective beyond imagination. Major C. R. Forrest, the assistant quartermaster of the 34th regiment, glumly reported, "*Our Batteries made no impression on the Enemy's parapet, the Order for the assault was not therefore carried into Effect.*"[182] After the battle, Jackson glanced over his shoulder at his most

---

[180]Donald Barr Chidsey, *The Battle of New Orleans: An Informal History of the War That Nobody Wanted: 1812* (New York: Crown, 1961), p. 128.

[181]Remini, *Battle of New Orleans*, p. 80.

[182]C. R. Forrest, *The Battle of New Orleans; A British View* (New Orleans: The Hauser Press, 1961), p. 38.

recent allies, the Baratarians, whose guns had outdueled the British, and his opinion of them became much more favorable. *"I wish I had fifty such guns on the line, with five hundred such devils as those fellows behind them,"* he muttered.[183] *"Too much praise,"* Jackson later wrote to James Monroe, *"cannot be bestowed on those who managed my artillery."*[184] Jackson's multiethnic troops still stood behind their ramparts, fully supplied with twenty-eight thousand cannonballs and fifty-six thousand pounds of gunpowder.

Pakenham had only one choice: a frontal attack on both sides of the river, beginning with the assault by 1,400 men under Colonel William Thornton on Morgan's west bank positions, whereupon the guns would be turned on Jackson's lines. One thin column would attack on the east bank, on Jackson's right, as a diversion, then the main attack of some 5,000 troops would come. The first 400 men would carry fascines (large bundles of sticks) to fill in the ditch, permitting a crossing, then three regiments, numbering 2,200 and constituting the main part of the assault on Jackson's center would attack while other elements hit Coffee on the flank. Pakenham stood Jackson and his men in the Rodriguez line, which stretched into the swamp before it refused backward at a ninety-degree angle. General John Adair held one regiment and one battalion in reserve.

On the morning of January 8, Pakenham's plan started to implode. First, the command sent across the river to attack Morgan had been carried down river by the Mississippi's current, and could not coordinate the attack with the main assault. Apparently unaware that his flank attack was already out of kilter, around 4:00 A.M. Pakenham ordered his troops forward through the dark on the east bank. Riding through the ranks to the front, he learned that the men carrying the ladders and fascines were not in place, forcing a delay. Finally, he ordered the advance, which was signaled by a Congreve rocket, just as a thick fog descended on the field, obscuring all movement.

Through the fog, Pakenham's Redcoats swept over the American pickets and outposts. Frantic lookouts ran back to Jackson's line to warn of the British advance. Then, just as the first British units passed the American forward redoubts, the fog lifted and the entire British army stood on an open plain in broad daylight, their red coats exposing them like targets in a monster shooting gallery. The Americans erupted with … cheers? Jackson's men shouted their approval that finally the British would have to take them on, army to army. Pakenham's men responded with their own cheers as they advanced. It was a splendid sight, but only for moments before Jackson's cannons opened up on the ranks, tearing huge gaps in British lines. Pakenham's veterans plowed ahead, coming in range of American muskets, Tennessee long rifles, and even pistols. At two hundred yards, Jackson's commanders yelled, "Fire! Fire!" They had pre-sighted a specific spot on the field that marked the perfect kill zone.

"Let's finish this business today," shouted Jackson as his men poured fire into the regulars. American ranks rotated to the line as they fired, stepping back to

[183]John Saxon, *Lafitte the Pirate* (New York: D. Appleton, 1930), p. 181.
[184]Remini, *Battle of New Orleans*, p. 113.

reload and letting others in. It was a maneuver that Maurice of Nassau, the inventor of musket drill, would have admired. A constant volley of fire raked British lines, heavy balls smashing bone and ripping flesh. Americans liked large-caliber weapons, and their musket balls would stop a man cold, like a sledgehammer to the chest. A Redcoat hit in the arm or leg faced almost sure amputation when the femurs and elbows were shattered beyond the abilities of the medical practices of the day to repair. Worst was the gutshot, which slowly bled a man to death because there was no hope of extracting the ball or suturing the wound. Cannon of the day fired both solid shot that bounced like deadly bowling balls, mowing down ranks like so many pins, or explosive case shot that had had fuses cut to allow shells to explode in the air or on the ground. Trained gunners, such as Lafitte's men, could by experience cut a fuse perfectly, so that an air burst occurred just a few feet above the enemy troops, raining hot, deadly casing pieces on them at intense velocity. While one could hope for a miracle—during the Revolution a Continental was once found with a musket ball smashed against his forehead; it had broken the skin but done no apparent damage—the reality was that heavy, sustained gunfire such as Jackson's men delivered that January day would shred the red lines arrayed before them. British soldiers fell by the dozens: "*we were mowed down by the hundreds*," said a British officer.[185] One Kentuckian recalled "*talking, swearing, and joking*" the entire time his unit delivered continuous fire. British officers who survived claimed they had never seen such devastating fire.

Meanwhile, those who were able to reach the American trench had no fascines, and they looked around desperately for their 44th regiment, which bore all the ladders and bridging equipment. Pakenham saw the confusion, but he could not locate the commander of the 44th, so, galloping to lead them himself, he was unhorsed and his arm shattered. As he struggled to his feet, he saw that even the fabled Highlanders were breaking, whereupon the general ordered up the reserve. Another volley struck Pakenham in the groin, and he went down, paralyzed. Carried to the rear, he died. General Gibbs took over before he, too, was shot. Then General Keane was hit, twice. A few officers led scattered remnants to the parapets, where they were repulsed.

The assault on the western bank against Morgan had gone much better for the British, but not well enough, and they, too had to withdraw. Pakenham's force had lost 291 killed (including Pakenham himself), 1,262 wounded, and 484 taken prisoner. The 93rd Highlanders lost 50 percent of their unit. Jackson's forces had only 7 killed and 6 wounded, although the four-day total was steeper: 55 killed, 185 wounded, and 93 missing. When the British left the field, they had 2,000 casualties of the 15,000 who had started the campaign. As historian Zachary Smith concluded, "*One of the best equipped and best disciplined armies*

---

[185]Lieutenant George Gleig, "A Contemporary Account of the Battle of New Orleans," *Louisiana Historical Quarterly*, 9 (January 1926), pp. 11–15; quotation is on 11; George Gleig, *Campaigns of the British Army at Washington and New Orleans Under Generals Ross, Pakenham and Lambert, in the Years 1814-1815* (London: J. Murray, 1827), pp. 334–35.

that England ever sent forth was defeated and shattered beyond hope by one half its number of American soldiers, mostly militia."[186]

Subsequent historians have attempted to demean the performance of the militia and volunteers, but Jackson's own after-action report to the secretary of war praised the volunteer units. Even Morgan's Kentucky militia was mostly exonerated in a later count of inquiry *"because of a lack of arms and poor troop displacement."*[187] Jackson had used whomever he had—blacks, pirates, Indians, militia, city volunteers, and regulars—to hand the British their most embarrassing—and last—defeat in North America.

Why Does the Left Hate America's Citizen Soldiers?

Andrew Jackson, William Eaton, and Tommy Franks proved the old maxim that an army of deer led by a lion is more to be feared than an army of lions led by a deer. The unorthodox mix of free blacks, militia, pirates, and regular Army troops that Jackson commanded in 1815 may seem to have little in common with the Doughboys of World War I or the GIs who stormed Normandy, but Americans have a knack for infusing conscripts with a spirit of liberty and purpose, then forging them into effective combat units—sometimes only for a few weeks, but long enough to do the job. For all their cutthroat ways, Jean Lafitte's pirates and Tommy Franks' mounted Afghans could see that the United States stood for liberty and her enemies did not. That, however, should not engender such vitriol on the part of the Left when it comes to the armed forces. What gives?

The plain fact is that America's military services are, and always have been, diverse. They represent all aspects of American society including—until very recently—the entertainment and political elites. Why is that so bad? Because it strikes at the very heart of Marxist/liberal notions of an oppressive society in which the poor wage the rich man's fight. The armed forces of the United States have always reflected the principle that large numbers of Americans know, and love, the essence of America, and that they are willing, if necessary, to die for the values that are American. That, in itself, raises another problem for the Left, for in radical liberal "relativism," no value is any better than another, and certainly no nation any more worthy of allegiance than another. It drives leftists crazy that decade after decade, for more than two hundred years, men, and now women, of all walks of life and all social stations have willingly, and even eagerly, said by their military service, *"America Is Good!"*

This can be seen even in American occupations and incursions, as in Haiti in the early twentieth century, where *"a couple of thousand Marines succeeded where a century earlier 27,000 of Napoleon's crack troops had failed."*[188] Compared to what they had experienced with their own dictators, American rule was benign and mild. Despite a sensationalized trail of a Marine who killed two Hai-

[186]Zachary F. Smith, *The Battle of New Orleans* (Bowie, MD: Heritage Books, 1988), p. 82.
[187]Skeen, *Citizen Soldiers in the War of 1812*, p. 171.
[188]Boot, *Savage Wars of Peace*, p. 176.

tians without provocation, three separate investigations found the few number of offenses against civilians "remarkable."[189]

Ultimately and paradoxically, the willingness of Americans to serve voluntarily is what lies behind most calls—certainly all of those from the Left—to reinstitute the draft. Liberals know that some elites (including conservatives) will find ways to evade the draft, although in World Wars I and II, the only major exemptions were for physical disability, family hardship, occupation (as a war necessity), and conscientious objector status. In the Civil War, men could purchase a substitute for $300, and John D. Rockefeller avoided service by hiring an unidentified man in his place. (It can be argued that he did more to win the war by supplying military goods than he ever could have done with a musket in his hand.) During Vietnam, deferments were granted for the same reasons as before, but also for enrollment in college. Muhammad Ali, musicians Jesse Winchester and Bill King—none of whom were in college—and thousands of draft-age students escaped the draft during Vietnam. It is not surprising that the Left seeks to revive the draft, which it sees as placing such burdens on the majority of middle-class (and a few upper-class) families that it would separate support for American military actions from the public. *Slate*'s Fred Kaplan argues that *"almost no one in the executive branch wants a draft, because it would instantly give every American family a stake in U.S. foreign policy ... [and] Bush could not possibly want the intense debate that even the prospect of a draft would inspire."* [190]Former senator Ernest "Fritz" Hollings (D-SC) introduced a resolution in 2003 to bring back the draft, saying *"One way to avoid a lot more wars is to institute the draft."*[191] Likewise, congressmen John Conyers (D-MI) and Charles Rangel (D-NY) have sponsored a bill to revive the draft, essentially viewing it as a means to end the war in Iraq. Yet far from showing how "hypocritical" conservatives are, the Hollings-Conyers-Rangel approach exposes the antimilitary bias of the Left, for their desire to bring back the draft is really a backdoor measure to ensure America's defeat in the War on Terror!

In fact, the Army (which is the service branch most affected by manpower shortages, as the Marines meet their quotas on a regular basis) has been extremely pleased with the performance of the all-volunteer force. It is more motivated, better trained, and more educated than any other force in history. As the war in Iraq dragged on, however, recruitment started to flag. Part of the reason may have been the revived economy, with unemployment falling by .4 percent since President Bush took office. Evidence that other factors, and not casualties in Iraq, were influential came from a report that fewer were applying to the U.S. military academies. Applications for West Point fell 9 percent in 2005, but applications to the U.S. Naval Academy dropped 20 percent, and the applications to the U.S. Air

---

[189]Boot, *Savage Wars of Peace*, p. 177.

[190]Fred Kaplan, "Who's in the Army Now? Why We Can't Send More Troops to Iraq," June 30, 2005, http://www.slate.comid/2121793/.

[191]Susan Piperato, "Sensing a Draft. Is Conscription in the Wind?" Chronogram, August 2004, http://www.chronogram.com/issue/2004/08/news/draft.php.

Force Academy fell even more, by 23 percent.[192]   If concern about combat—and potential death or injury—drove applications, then one would expect the Army would experience the greatest decline, not the Navy (which has, as ground forces, only the Medical Service Corps and the Seabees in Iraq or Afghanistan in addition to some SEAL teams) or the Air Force (which has had few casualties in Iraq or Afghanistan after the end of "major combat operations"). Reenlistment in the active Army since 9/11 has exceeded targets by 6 percent, and all active duty branches as of 2005 were at or above their goals. And the fact that enlistment in the Marines, who almost certainly will see combat deployment, remains high suggests that other factors are at work.

The most important of those factors is a booming economy. For generations, the military services (especially the high-tech Air Force) have offered young men and now women an exceptional free college education. Recent changes in higher education, however, in the form of higher levels of scholarship support from states, the federal government, and universities themselves have combined to reduce the premium offered by a West Point, Annapolis, or Colorado Springs education. Simply put, the combination of a free quality education offered by the service academies has diminished as it has become easier to get a free ride to state and private schools. High immigration rates may also contribute to lower recruitment levels and applications to service academies: contrary to popular myth, in the Civil War, native-born men were represented at higher rates than the foreign born. New research also suggests that the sons of unskilled workers, although the wealthiest classes were only slightly less likely to enlist than lower groups, leading a major researcher to conclude that the differences were not large enough "*to justify describing the war as a 'poor man's fight.'*").[193]

Of course, the generals who led these soldiers knew their value. *"The soldier is the Army,"* said George Patton.

> *No army is better than its soldiers. The soldier is also a citizen. In fact, the highest obligation and privilege of citizenship is that of bearing arms for one's country. Hence it is a proud privilege to be a soldier—a good soldier. To be a good soldier a man must have discipline, self-respect, pride in his unit and in his comrades and to his superiors, and self-confidence born of demonstrated ability.*[194]

In World War II, correspondent Ernie Pyle reiterated Patton's words, from a different perspective, writing *"The fighting soldier ... was fighting for his life, and killing then for him was as much a profession as writing was for me."* The American soldier wanted to *"kill individually or in vast numbers ... to see the Germans overrun, mangled, butchered in the Tunisian trap [or of] our bombers*

[192]Brian MacQuarrie, "Fewer Applying to U.S. Military Academies," Boston Globe, June 13, 2005.
[193]See Maris A. Vinovskis, "Have Social Historians Lost the Civil War? Some Preliminary Demographic Speculations," in Maris A. Vinovskis, ed., *Toward a Social History of the American Civil War* (New York: Cambridge, 1990), pp. 1–30 (quotation on 17).
[194]George S. Patton, Jr., *War as I Knew It* (New York: Houghton Mifflin, 1947), p. 355.

sinking whole shiploads of fleeing men" because he wanted the war to be over."[195] For Americans, war was abnormal, a perversion to be ended as quickly as possible. The *"rest of us,"* Pyle wrote, wanted *"terribly yet only academically for the war to be over. The front-line soldier wanted it to be terminated by the physical process of his destroying enough Germans to end it. He was truly at war."*[196]

Andrew Jackson's men at the Battle of New Orleans showed America's citizen soldiers at their best—men who hated war, yet who knew the only way to end their war was to eliminate the long red lines in front of them. There volunteers from all races, backgrounds, and skill levels stood behind a small barricade to embarrass the best military in the world. Americans win wars because her citizen soldiers are free men and women who own property, vote themselves into combat, and possess the legal means to protest military involvement. Americans win wars because they voluntarily submit to rigorous training to become deadly effective soldiers. And Americans win wars because war, to them, is an aberration, and the normal state of peace must be restored as quickly as possible.

---

[195]Ernie Pyle, *Here Is Your War* (Cleveland: World Publishing, 1945), p. 242.
[196]Pyle, *Here Is Your War*, p. 242

CHAPTER FOUR
Pushing Autonomy Down

Compared to any nation in history, the United States has a more democratized military that views individuals as capable and competent, and empowers them with unprecedented levels of autonomy and decision making at every rank.

Saddam stood right in the middle of al-Firdos Square, like a conqueror from the ancient world, arm upraised in a Caesar-esque salute. Except it wasn't Saddam himself. It was a twenty-foot-tall metal statue of the Iraqi dictator—on of thousands of icons to the butcher of Baghdad that dotted Iraq's cities—and it wasn't going to stay there long.

U.S. Marines of the 3rd Battalion, 4th Marines (in "Marineology," the ¾), under Lieutenant Colonel Brian McCoy, had responsibility for this zone during the invasion. One of them, Corporal Edward Chin of New York, climbed up Saddam's shoulders to drape a U.S. flag over the dictator's face—a red, white, and blue burka. Old Glory remained there briefly as a crowd cheered, then, according to the corporal's plan, he took an Iraqi flag from someone in the crowd and replaced the Stars and Stripes with it. But it wasn't just any Iraqi flag. Instead, Chin replaced the U.S. flag with the traditional Iraqi flag used before Saddam made "improvements" to it by cynically adding Koranic verse. Before Chin's flag raising, the Marines had swung a metal cable around Saddam's neck, tied it to an M88 tank retriever, and as soon as the flag ceremony ended, they put the vehicle in gear. Instead of ripping the entire structure out of the ground, the tank retriever pulled Saddam's torso over at a ninety-degree angle, yanking the legs off their long steel struts and making it look like Saddam-on-stilts. Finally, the statue broke, literally cutting Saddam off at the knees. Iraqi crowds took over, cutting off the head and dragging it around town behind a pickup as mobs beat on his face with the soles of their shoes—for generations symbolic of the genitals—and spit into his eyes amid shouts of "traitor," "torturer!" and "dictator!" Jubilant crowds of Iraqis poured into the streets to celebrate, leading Iraq's UN ambassador in New York, Mohammad al-Douri, to dourly state "the game is over." Already seeking to distance himself from the deposed fugitive dictator, he added, "I have no relationship with Saddam."[1]

In those few symbolic minutes, the regime died and the Iraqi nightmare was partially over as a new phase of terroristic warfare began. Yet the Marines' expedition into Baghdad was originally planned as only a temporary "probe"—on his own authority, Colonel Steve Hummer, head of Regimental Combat Team 7, one of three RCTs to storm the city, "forgot" to issue a withdrawal plan.[2] A

[1]"Baghdad Fall," USA Today, April 10, 2003.
[2]Bing West and Ray L. Smith, The March Up: Taking Baghdad With the 1st Marine Division (New York: Bantam, 2003), p. 233.

similar lapse in memory seemed to afflict members of the Army's 3rd Infantry Division, whose armored brigades had made two stunning "thunder runs" from the west, one slicing through Baghdad along Highway 8 before veering off on the Qadisiya Highway to the Baghdad International Airport, then, the next day, charging straight through the guts of the city to storm the Parade Grounds, Baath Party Headquarters, and the Sujud Palace. What made the latter so astonishing was that it was completely contrary to then-established military doctrine, according to the *U.S. Army Field Manual An Infantryman's Guide to Urban Combat,* that armor is vulnerable (if not helpless) in urban warfare. It therefore shocked the tankers of the Assassins, the 4th Battalion of the 64th Armored Regiment, when Captain Philip Wolford announced to them on April 6, *"Tomorrow morning, we're attacking into Baghdad. We are going into the heart of Saddam's regime and we are going to take it and keep it."* [3] Wolford advanced his suggestions up the chain of command, where General Buford Blount, who had already been revising his plan, approved them.

The fact that colonels in the field were sending suggestions upward to generals, or that officers adapted new tactics in the field without fear of reprisal, spoke volumes about a key American military trait—that of empowering the troops. Exercising their individual initiative not only presupposes that officers and troops have the training, education, and preparation to "freelance," but more important, assumes that they have incentives to exercise their own judgment. Unlike any other military culture in history, American fighters are trusted to adapt and overcome—the field manual be damned!

Parking for Eighty-eight Tanks?

Both the Marines and the Army share a remarkable trait, one virtually unseen in Saddam's military or, in the past, in armies from non-Western cultures: their commanders have the autonomy and the training to exercise command authority even directly contrary to accepted tactics, creating both new doctrine and political policy as the go. Trust in this kind of autonomy has not always proved well earned—debate still rages over the actions (or inaction) of General Richard Ewell at Gettysburg, or whether Lieutenant Colonel George Armstrong Custer exceeded his orders by attacking the Indian village at the Little Big Horn—but more often than not the system has endowed American officers with a flexibility and independence no other fighting forces have had. At the Battle of Palo Alto in 1846, American junior officers used mobile artillery tactics they individually adapted from the French, resulting in a lopsided victory in which some 300 Mexicans died while only five Americans fell. Just under a century later, General George Patton used this same remarkable autonomy that failed Ewell to swing an entire armored division to the rescue of Bastogne. Autonomy of the type displayed by <u>Patton's 3rd Army</u> or the Spartan Brigade in Baghdad characterized a combat

[3]David Zucchino, *Thunder Run: The Armored Strike to Capture Baghdad* (New York: Atlantic Monthly Press, 2004), p. 89.

108

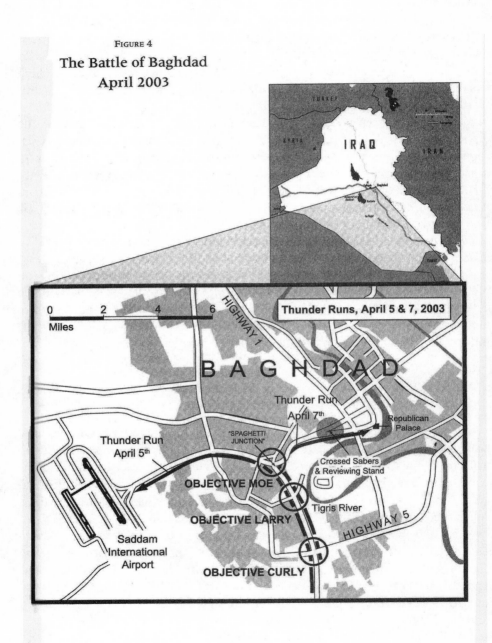

FIGURE 4

The Battle of Baghdad
April 2003

culture unique in history, and it was distinctly American. Because of this capable leadership and training, and the motivation of the troops, it is safe to say that in 1991 or 2003, if Iraq had had our equipment, and we, theirs, the outcome of each war, with slightly different casualty totals, would have been the same.

Saddam's fall (and undignified capture, eight months later, a few miles from his hometown of Tikrit) was accomplished by a remarkable, against-the-book charge into Baghdad by the 3rd Army to the west and the 1st Marine Division to the east, with support from Special Forces and airborne troops in Kurdish-held zones to the north. What was striking about Operation Iraqi Freedom was how much of the plan American forces modified, adapted, or discarded along the way. The original battle plan called for a northern invasion from Turkey by the 4th Infantry Division (4th ID), but at the last minute, the Turkish government reneged on previous promises, and the 4th ID had to be shipped to southern Iraq through the Suez, around Saudi Arabia. Like the Spartans at Marathon, the 4th arrived too late for the main fight, and, as at Marathon, their presence was not needed. In twenty-one days, the American military had moved through 350 miles of enemy territory, outflanked or defeated more than 200,000 enemy soldiers, and stolen the Iraqi capital right out from under Saddam's nose.

During the campaign, the Marines made up new tactics on the fly all the time, such as the Afak Drill, developed by the ¾'s Lieutenant Colonel Brian Mc-Coy. A traditional enveloping tactic had the Marines setting up a large base of fire, then using smaller teams of riflemen to flank the enemy. McCoy, however liked to send tanks along to envelop with the infantry. It proved exceptionally effective against poorly trained forces, and it brutally dispatched the Fedayeen (Saddam's martyrs). Riflemen actually disliked the drill because it gave all the action—and the glory—to the tankers.

Certainly the tankers had their greatest moment since World War II when Major General Buford Blount swung his armor against Saddam International Airport on the first of two thunder runs. The concept behind a thunder run was simple: drive as fast as you can, shoot everything that looks like it's going to shoot you, and get out. For this, Blount turned to the Spartans, the 2nd Brigade, 3rd ID (Mechanized)—thirty tanks and fourteen Bradley fighting vehicles. They were accompanied by the Desert Rogues, several armored personnel carriers detached from the 1st Battalion, 64th Armored. Already this marked a variation of the original plan, which was to surround Baghdad and engage in infantry penetrations of the city. On the fly, Blount was now coming up with a radical new combat doctrine, one that defied decades of lessons learned. Ever since Mogadishu, the Pentagon had been spooked about unban combat and shied away from sending armor into cities, with their tight streets and narrow alleys. (The inability of tanks to elevate their main gun made them vulnerable to antitank weapons from tall buildings.) But as mechanics repaired damaged tanks all through the night, Blount decided he was going to send his brigade to the airport.

On the morning of April 5, 2003, the entire battalion had its engines running along Highway 8, which ran to the west of Baghdad and circled west to the airport. Every tank had its own catchy name painted on the barrel—Crusader, Cry Havoc, apocalypse. Each Abrams tank represented the most lethal ground vehicle in the world: a turbine delivering 1,500 horsepower could propel the tank to speeds of more than fifty miles per hours; its powerful 120 mm main gun, using laser targeting systems, could fire a wide range of munitions with deadly accuracy on the run; and its armor was all but impenetrable to anything but the most advanced anti-tank missiles or anti-tank rounds fired from other tanks. For anti-infantry work, the Abrams carried a .50 caliber machine gun operated by the commander, while the loader had a 7.62 mm coaxial gun mounted on the right side. Supporting the tanks were M113 Bradley fighting vehicles, with their 25 mm chain guns and their own coaxial machine guns. The Bradleys could carry six infantrymen each, and could keep up with the tanks, providing quick infantry support if the tanks were in danger of being swarmed.

Second Brigand Commander David Perkins stated that mission's objective was to "*enter Baghdad for the purpose of displaying combat power ... and to simply show them that we can.*"[4] On the way in, the Iraqis got off a one-in-a-million RPG shot that hit an Abrams in the thin rear panel, setting it on fire and forcing the crew to abandon it. (Later, not wanting to leave it to the Iraqis, the crew scattered ammo and fuel inside and dropped thermite grenades down the hatch. Then U.S. forces hit the tank with multiple high-energy antitank rounds; and, finally, the Air Force struck it with a Maverick missile—but still the tank was virtually intact!) As the tankers rolled into town, they were stunned to see that average Iraqis were on the other side of the highway, going about their business, apparently brainwashed by their information minister, Mohammed Saeed al-Sahaf, better known as Baghdad Bob. A high-ranking Iraqi officer accidently drove right into the American column, where he became an instant POW and told his army interrogators that Baghdad Bob has said the Americans were stopped cold beyond the Euphrates River. Perkins nearly blew a gasket, and wanted to park his tanks right behind Bob.

Unfazed, the column rolled along, weathering thousands of rounds of small arms fire and dozens of RPGs, in the process cutting down hundreds of Iraqis and blowing up dozens of pickups outfitted with machine guns, or "technical," then made the left turn to the Baghdad airport, which had already been seized from the west by the 1st Brigade. Just outside the airport, Iraqis had erected concrete barriers and hunkered down with their machine guns and RPGs, but with little effect. The 2nd Brigade's tanks plowed through the barricades, killed the defenders, and continued on to the safety of the airport. Within a few hours, a reinforced American tank brigade had done the unimaginable: it had run the gauntlet through an urban combat zone, losing only a single tank and a handful of troopers. Told that "four or five" American tanks were at the airport, Iraqi General Mohammed Dash was sent to report on the fighting there. He returned to headquarters shaken: "*Four or five tanks!*" he screamed to his superiors. "*Are you out of your minds?*

[4]Zucchino, *Thunder Run*, p. 13.

The whole damn American army is at the airport!"[5]   Undaunted, Baghdad Bob broadcast that the infidels had been butchered at Saddam International.

That was the last straw for Perkins, who formulated a plan right there for a second thunder run to shut up Baghdad Bob. He would drive his tanks right up to the Ministry of Information. He planned a bold thrust right into the center of Baghdad, a new thunder run with each part of the advance preceded by slowly rolling (and ultra-accurate) artillery fire. His objectives were the military parade field and reviewing stand, with its pompous crossed-sabers gateway; Baathist Party headquarters; the Ministry of Information; one of Saddam's main palaces; and the Rashid Hotel. Perkins knew the armored force could exit to the east if things got really rough because the Marines were advancing rapidly and would soon control the opposite side of the Tigris River. Still, the prospect of taking fewer than 1,000 men, sixty tanks, and twenty-eight Bradleys into the center of a city of five million was a bit overpowering. As he detailed the plan, officers shook their heads at the risk—and the chutzpah—but none dissented. These were soldiers even more ambitious, thinking, If we can get to the heart of Baghdad, why not stay a night? And if we can stay one, why not two?

A key to the second thunder run was three Highway 8 interchanges, named Curly, Moe, and Larry. These interchanges had to be held to ensure a steady flow of ammunition and supplies. As one column blasted into Baghdad, Perkins proposed to send thirty Bradleys and fourteen tanks to hold the three exchanges and the ten miles of ground against thousands of attackers. He looked around the room for comments. "Hoo-ah!" came the response. The thunder was on.

Immediately, though, the tankers confronted a problem they had not seen on the run to the airport: a minefield. After scouts and engineers reported that the massive minefield lay in their path, sappers were dispatched to clear the field before the armor rolled. In less than two hours, a handful of engineers cleared 444 mines in darkness right in the middle of Iraqi positions. The sappers had started clearing the mines around 3:30 in the morning, and the tanks moved off at around 5:30, firing as they went, tearing apart SUVs and roadside bunkers. Some Fedayeen hid behind women and children. (*"They lack manhood,"* sneered Major General James Mattis when he had first seen this tactic. *"They're as worthless an example of men as we've ever fought."*)[6] As the tankers plowed ahead, officers called in 155 mm artillery for less than a mile ahead of their positions—a rolling barrage that whistled over their heads as they charged into Baghdad. At "spaghetti junction," a cloverleaf-type maze of highways, the Rogues split off down the parallel Kindi Highway while the main body charged up the Qadisiya Highway past the reviewing stand and the crossed sabers. At just past 8:00 A.M., the Assassins drove through the palace gates.

Only then did Perkins, in consultation with Blount, conceive of the new strategy. Originally the idea was to *"create chaos, to disrupt Iraqi defenses."*[7]

---

[5]Zucchino, *Thunder Run*, p. 66.
[6]West and Smith, *The March* Up, p. 74.
[7]Zucchino, Thunder Run, p. 128.

But the tankers had gotten completely inside the city and were fighting from the inside out. Perkins's men literally had injected themselves, like an antibiotic, right into the middle of the diseased Iraqi heart, and he started to think that if he could hold his position overnight, he could hold Baghdad. All the while, Baghdad Bob continued his litany of lies to the journalists, who by now were starting to get information flowing back to them from their "request" to the Information ministry for parking for eighty-eight tanks, even Sahaf knew the game was over.

At the time, however, few recognized that the scales of war had tipped. Through the night, the Iraqis mounted a deadly ground-to-ground missile attack on the tactical headquarters, killing several and disrupting communications; launched a counterattack with their own tanks; and tried to overwhelm Larry, Moe, and Curly. The battle to hold Curly was especially difficult, and the position was nearly overrun as minibuses pulled up to unload a dozen fighters, only to have a Bradley blast them apart. Curly's defenders killed so many of the enemy that they came close to running out of ammunition until a single company of largely disparate vehicles and troops rode to the rescue. *"With hatches open, every soldier in the column fired continuously from every hatch and gun port,"* protecting the twenty resupply trucks that were interspersed in the column that rescued Curly.[8] Iraqis rushed the column wildly, pouring fire from concealed positions in every building. But it was ineffective, undisciplined, and untrained fire. In the end, it was futile. With Curly secure, Blount pushed additional units into Baghdad, where Perkins's tanks had run perilously close to empty. Once again, the Iraqis were surprised by the audacity of the Americans' movement, and by the time they recovered, Perkins's tanks were already refueling, then linking up with the Marines, who had fought their way onto the east bank on April 9.

Competence, Not Class

Napoléon once remarked that in his French army, *"every soldier carries a Marshal's baton in his knapsack."* His willingness to advance soldiers on the basis of performance and competence was unique. His British and Prussian enemies still assigned command ranks largely based on titles and landholdings. As late as 1875, aristocrats made up half of the commissioned officers in the British army, and even after England abolished the purchase system in 1873, officers were still expected to have a private income. But Napoléon understood the vulnerabilities of relying on those who acquired wealth by inheritance over those who demonstrated talent in battle. Likewise, he broke with his own Revolutionary French army, which elected its officers. Napoléon's willingness to promote from within, based on competence gave his armies a significant advantage over their enemies.

Despite the memorable exhortation of Major General Adna Chaffee, Sr., in the Red River War, when he "inspired" his men by shouting *"Forward*! If any man is killed, I will make him a corporal: Americans enthusiastically adopted

[8]Willliamson Murray and Robert H. Scales, Jr. *The Iraq War: A Military History* (Cambridge, MA: Belknap Press, 2003), p. 216.

Napoléon's "knapsack" philosophy, ruthlessly applying the "law of results": get them or be replaced.[9] No one took this to heart more than Washington, who followed the advice of a bookseller, Henry Knox, a young junior officer lacking any military experience. Knox conceived the idea to transport the cannons from Ft. Ticonderoga to Boston and the fact that such a scheme was not only transmitted to Washington, but then acted upon, spoke volumes for a military in which *"almost anyone's ideas deserved a hearing."*[10] While militia units continued to elect their own officers until the Civil War, professional soldiers and sailors in the United States military could not count on money to always gain them a commission, and they could rely even less on connections to ensure promotion.[11] Nevertheless, the brevet rank proved cumbersome and confusing. On one occasion, a private, Frederick W. Stowe, was brevetted a 2nd lieutenant, jumping three ranks and during the Civil War, some 1,700 officers held the brevet rank of brigadier or major general, producing no small degree of confusion, especially about which rank insignia to wear. George Armstrong Custer held two separate ranks: one as a major general of volunteers, a lieutenant colonel in the regular Army, and the brevetted rank of major general in the Army. Ulysses S. Grant was promoted to a lieutenant and brevetted to a captain at Mexico City. Brevets were meaningless in terms of pay or authority and they did not become official until Congress acted on them. What it did illustrate, however, was the willingness of the American military to advance individuals based on performance, requiring protocol to catch up.

George Washington deserves considerable credit for developing this pragmatic tradition. He *"thought and acted like a military professional, and during the Braddock and Forbes campaigns, he took advantage of his opportunity to study closely the procedures of a regular army."*[12] Modeling his Virginia regiment on European examples, he emphasized strict discipline and required his officers to read European military literature, introducing "commoners" to the lofty altitudes once reserved for aristocrats.[13] By 1757, he was boasting that his regiment was equal to "any [British unit] on the continent," and thought the only thing separating his officers from those in the British army were the commissions.[14] Washington's faith in his officers, such as Knox, Hamilton, and Nathanael Greene was a strength, but typically the British viewed such reliance on "inferiors" as a weakness. Predictably, after the capture of General Charles Lee, Washington's second in command, a Hessian captain wrote *"We have captured ... the only rebel general whom we had cause to fear."*[15] Washington despised militias not because they

---

[9]Max Boot, *Savage Wars of Peace: Small Wars and the Rise of American Power* (New York: Basic Books, 2002), p. 90.

[10]David McCullough, *1776* (New York: Simon and Schuster, 2006), p. 60.

[11]Edward M. Coffmann, *The Old Army: a Portrait of the American Power* (New York: Oxford, 1986), p. 67.

[12]Don Higginbotham, "The Early American Way of War: Reconnaissance and Appraisal," *William and Mary Quarterly*, April 1987, pp. 230–73 (quotation on 236).

[13]Don Higginbotham, *George Washington and the American Military Tradition* (Athens, GA: University of Georgia Press, 1985), chap. 1.

[14]Washington to the Earl of Loudoun, March 23, 1757, quoted in Higginbotham, "Early American Way of War," p. 236.

[15]McCullough, *1776*, p. 266.

lacked courage, but because the conditions of their service prevented them from being steeled into professionals.

Perhaps intuitively, Washington sensed that Americans largely served for different reasons than their counterparts in the professional European armies (where, by the 1700s, enlistment was generally out of economic necessity or for social advancement) or in the non-Western mercenary/slave armies, where there was little or no choice about whether to fight. Studies of early American forces reveal that large numbers of those who enlisted were sons of the well to do, and served less out of economic necessity than out of concern for family, community, or religion. In close-knit New England units, for example, men responded to *"appeals from local dignitaries who might be friends or neighbors,"* and many were young men awaiting an inheritance who found solid temporary service in expeditionary forces as an alternative to hanging around the farm.[16] But since they served for family, friends, community, and ideas, and since they knew their officers, sometimes on a first-name basis, the provincial army developed new relationships of command, or *"an organic network of kinship and personal loyalties."*[17] The lowliest privates were always addressed by officers as "gentlemen," reflecting a *"moral condition rather than a social rank."*[18] In that sense, they started to bond into a much different force from the European model.

Put another way, by the Seven Years' War, American units had already introduced startling new levels of autonomy at the lower ranks, a predictable evolution, given Americans' distaste for class and aristocracy. Men willingly submitted to those they knew and trusted, rank or no rank, and likewise, superiors delegated freely to those they had already seen wield power responsibly in the community, courthouse, and church. This extended to free men of color, too, and in New England some blacks rose to the rank of colonel in Washington's army, although Washington himself warmed up slowly to the idea of black recruits.[19]

One key failure in the American system was that it did not integrate racially the way it had socially until after World War II. Black regiments in the Union Army were viewed as second-class units: they were initially paid less than white troops; and they were held out of battle until political pressure finally allowed them to fight, at which point they fought well. But the exceptional record of the Union's black regiments—the Buffalo Soldiers of the 10th Cavalry on the frontier and at San Juan Hill, or the 99th Fighter Squadron in the Second World War—does not compensate for, or excuse, a flaw in the system that was only overcome with great resistance and difficulty.

Race excepted—and it was an important exception—most Americans in the military are equal, as General George Patton learned in Sicily in 1943 when

---

[16]Fred Anderson, *A People's Army: Massachusetts Soldiers and Society in the Seven Years' War* (Chapel Hill, NC: University of North Carolina Press, 1984), chap. 2. Also see his "A People's Army: Provincial Military Service in Massachusetts during the Seven Years' War," WMQ, 3rd series, 15 (1983), pp. 499–527.

[17]Anderson, *People's Army*, p. 48. This is reinforced by the study by Harold Selesky, *War and Society in Colonial Connecticut* (New Haven: Yale University Press, 1990).

[18]David Hackett Fischer, *Washington's Crossing* (Oxford: Oxford University Press, 2004), p. 272.

[19]Fischer, *Washington's Crossing*, p. 22.

he struck a pair of enlisted men in two separate incidents at Army hospitals, label-ing the soldiers malingerers and cowards because they had no outwardly visible wounds. One of the two men Patton slapped, an artilleryman named Paul Bennett, had been ordered to the hospital by a surgeon but had begged to stay on with the unit; the other, Private Charles Kuhl also was at the hospital for battle fatigue. What is often unmentioned is that other soldiers in the hospital cheered after a nurse reported to them what the Patton had done.[20] After a firestorm in which Eisenhower maneuvered to save Patton's job, the general was ordered to make amends or apologize to *"individuals concerned as may be within your power."*[21] Patton met with Private Kuhl and explained his intent was only to make the pri-vate say to himself, *"'I'll show that SOB Patton that I am not a yellow coward, become brave and redeem myself.'"* But, Patton continued, *"I see now that I used the wrong psychology. If you will shake my hand in forgiveness, I'll be much obliged to you."*[22] Kuhl's face "lit up with a broad grin" and he shook the gener-al's hand, recalled a doctor who witnessed the scene. The doctor wrote, "I kept thinking, *'My Lord, here is a three-star general apologizing to a lowly private soldier.'* I could not imagine anything similar happening in any other army."[23]

Patton temporarily lost sight of the fact that despite rank, American sol-diers were first and foremost free men and viewed themselves as inherently equal to each other, officer or not. This has been apparent since colonial times, when Virginians enacted a conscription law during the Seven Years' War that exempted freeholders, producing a backlash by the *"Lowest Class of our People,"* as Gover-nor Robert Dinwiddie put it.[24] Unable to draft, Virginia offered more substantial bounties for enlistment, illustrating the inability of the elites to impose compulso-ry military service on others.

By the time of the Revolution, the shared values of the variegated classes contributed to the close communication and psychological support present be-tween officers and the ranks.[25] For the most part, leaders like Patton, who ex-posed himself to enemy fire alongside his men on several occasions, remembered that. It was more than just a philosophical principle of equality that linked officers and their troops. Quite often, American leaders came from the same places in society as those whom they commanded: in the Civil War, half the troops Grant and Sherman led were farmers, followed by large numbers of tradesmen.[26] This,

---

[20]Donald v. Bennett and William R. Forstchen, *Honor Untarnished: A West Point Graduate's Memoir of World War II* (New York: Tom Doherty, 2003), p. 147. It was not clear which of the two incidents Bennett refers to though

[21]Carlo D'Este, *Patton: A Genius for War* (New York: Harper Perennial, 1996), p. 536.

[22]D'Este, *Patton*, p. 538.

[23]D'Este, *Patton*, p. 538.

[24]Dinwiddie quoted in Higginbotham, "Early American Way of War," p. 243. See also James Titus, "Soldiers When They Chose to Be So: Virginians at War, 1754-1763," Ph.D. dissertation, Rutgers University, 1983

[25]Robert Middlekauf, "Why Men Fought in the American Revolution," Huntington Library Quarterly, p. 43, 1980, pp. 135–48, and his *The Glorious Cause: The American Revolution, 1763-1789* (New York: Oxford, 1982).

[26]Of the commandants of the USMC through 1983 for which there is information on the father's occupation, five were farmers; five were merchants or small businessmen; four were doctors, lawyers, or well to do; one was a judge; one was a minister; and seven were military officers. (Allan R. Millett and Jack Shulimson, Com-

in turn, prompted wiser commanders to pay attention to their men's gripes, suggestions, and even their illusions. For example, at Vicksburg, Grant indulged his troops; insistence on a bloody frontal assault rather than a siege, knowing that it would be costly. After it failed, his soldiers would be far more eager to use a more patient indirect attack if it meant holding down casualties. Their commitment to the monotonous and unglamorous work in the trenches, Grant noted later, arose out of his willingness to let them learn for themselves, then apply the lesson. Robert E. Lee probably gave in to exactly the same *"pressure of equality,"* when he committed to Pickett's Charge on the third day at Gettysburg, noting his troops were "up," and to order them to withdraw would be as great a defeat as the verdict of the battlefield. Sometimes, democracy and equality produce battlefield outcomes that even the most talented leaders cannot avoid.

Yet this, too, is more often than not an inherent strength, and to foreigners, such consideration of the will of the troops was anathema. English military observers consistently misunderstood the Americans' "unprofessional" behavior, first in the Seven Years' War, then in the Revolution, interpreting it as an indicator of "bad soldiering." Seeing officers mingle with the enlisted troops put them off (even though the Duke of Wellington practiced it routinely). In fact, Americans had so internalized British concepts of contractual rights that they based all of their arguments about military service on such principles, especially when they confronted any *"unwarranted pretension of superiors."*[27] Just as the rights of Englishmen defined the conflict between the colonies and the Mother Country, so too the rights of soldiers shaped the American military character beyond that practiced in other countries, not only cementing the notion of free men fighting voluntarily, but also leveling the differences between officers and enlisted ranks.[28]

American hostility toward classes, entrenched in the Revolutionary generation, over time produced a democratization of military forces unmatched elsewhere. From the American Revolution until well into the 1850s, for example, it was common for British aristocrats to purchase a command in the army, ensuring that the aristocracy controlled the military. A captaincy in 1776 cost 1,500 pounds, a colonelcy 3,500 pounds. Of the 102 regimental colonels in 1769, *"more than half came from an aristocracy of two hundred families in a nation of seven million people."*[29] But while some American officers still tended to come from the ranks of the educated and the privileged, an increasing number of leaders were entering the military from all occupations. It is interesting how many great soldiers were teachers or professors at one time, with probably the most famous being Gettysburg hero Colonel Joshua Chamberlain. After working on his family farm, Cham-

mandants of the Marine Corps (Annapolis: Naval Institute Press, 2004).

[27]F. W. Anderson, "Why Did Colonial New Englanders Make Bad Soldiers? Contractual Principles and Military Conduct During the Seven Years' War," WMQ, 38, July 1981, pp. 395–417 (quotation on 396).

[28]Robert A. Gross, *The Minutemen and Their World* (New York: Hill and Wang, 1976); Charles Royster, A *Revolutionary People at War: The Continental Army and the American Character, 1775–1783* (Chapel Hill: University of North Carolina Press, 1979).

[29]Fischer, *Washington's Crossing,* p. 34.

berlain attended Bowdoin College, then became a professor there. John "Blackjack" Pershing, whose father was a failed store owner, taught school before being accepted at West Point. Andrew Jackson, raised in the backwoods on the North/South Carolina border, joined the army as a courier in the Revolution, and then later taught school briefly before studying law. Winfield Scott Hancock's father was a teacher, as was Omar Bradley's. William Tecumseh Sherman, too, worked in education, becoming the administrator of what is today Louisiana State University, leaving that post when the Civil War loomed.

Other great American leaders came from similarly humble origins. General Victor "Brute" Krulak, the Vietnam Marine legend, was the son of a watchmaker; Indian fighter George Crook was raised on a farm. Ulysses Grant's father was a tanner; Jimmy Doolittle's dad, a carpenter; Nathanael Greene's father was a Rhode Island minister; and Henry Knox's, an Irish-born shipmaster. Stonewall Jackson's lawyer father died when he was six, after which the family was impoverished, while Sherman's dad, a judge, died when he was nine, although he had the good fortune of being raised by prosperous Missouri friends of the family. The lives of other storied American soldiers reveal a similar absence of aristocracy: General John Buford of Gettysburg fame had a well-to-do father, but he attended a trade school before finally gaining admittance to West Point. Similarly, George Marshall left his family's wealth to enroll in Virginia Military Institute. George Meade's father was a maritime agent, and although Meade went to West Point, he resigned his commission after the Mexican War to be a civil engineer. "Mad" Anthony Wayne came from a family of soldiers, as did George C. Patton, but Wayne worked as a surveyor before returning to the military. Tommy Franks grew up in Midland, Texas, a setting not too different from Dwight Eisenhower's Abilene, Kansas. And color proved a minor barrier to qualified people: Dunbar High School, which had an exceptional record of producing high-achieving students, turned out the nation's first black general, and during World War II, when black officers were still rare, Dunbar graduates included a brigadier general, nine colonels and lieutenant colonels, and a "score of majors."[30] The first black to graduate from Annapolis also came from Dunbar, yet this school was hardly the domain of "elite" blacks: as late as 1893, the occupations of Dunbar parents included, *"51 laborers, 25 messengers, 12 janitors, but only one doctor."*[31] Achievement came from expectations, standards, and above all, discipline, just like in the military.

Of course, a few exceptions to the pattern of humble origins stand out. General Alfred Terry, a Yale-educated lawyer, was the clerk of the Superior Court of New Haven County before he joined the Connecticut militia in the Civil War. Patton married wealth, Leonard Wood was a doctor's son and attended Harvard Medical School, and James Longstreet lived on a plantation. Smedley Butler, the Marine who won the Congressional Medal of Honor twice, rising to major

---

[30]Thomas Sowell, *Black Rednecks and White Liberals* (San Francisco: Encounter Books, 2005), p. 208.
[31]Sowell, *Black Rednecks*, p. 204.

general, was the son of a congressman from Pennsylvania.[32]   Robert E. Lee, the Confederate hero, grew up in comfortable means, thanks to his mother (his father's second wife), Ann Hill Carter. But Lee's dad, Henry "Light-Horse Harry" Lee, lost all his money in land speculation and wrote his war memoirs from a twelve-by-fifteen-foot debtors' prison cell. In short, Americans had anything but an aristocratic military tradition.

If anything, it was remarkable that even during Vietnam, volunteers came from all walks of life, despite characterizations of that war as a poor man's fight. In the Mexican War, the sons of Henry Clay and Daniel Webster both volunteered, along with Edward Everett's nephew. Robert Johannsen observed, *"Well-to-do professional men, merchants, and farmers joined the ranks as common soldiers,"* while entire companies were formed out of occupational groups such as law students in Nashville or clerks in New Orleans.[33]   Yale formed a volunteer unit, the Yale College Regulars, and one Illinois volunteer, looking at the crowd of men who had gathered for induction during the Mexican War, found no aristocracy nor a place for *"professional pomposity or pretended fastidiousness."*[34]   He observed lawyers, politicians, doctors, farmers, lead miners, and plain old "hard-fisted Suckers." Kentuckian broad-brimmed hats, buckskin coats, and work clothes mixed with regulation blue denim jackets, causing Mexicans to comment that they looked like *"clowns at a carnival."*[35]   An Englishman, George F. Ruxton, who, observing the volunteers, scoffed, *"The American can never be made a soldier. His constitution will not bear the restraint of discipline,"* later ascribed American victories to the number of German, English, and Irish soldiers in their ranks![36]

Even Vietnam, constantly mischaracterized as a "working class war," was no such thing.[37] Almost 80 percent of those who served in Vietnam had graduated from high school (compared to only about 65 percent of those military-age males who did not serve). A 1992 study of 58,000 men killed in Vietnam, compared to 58,000 randomly selected contemporaries, showed an almost even distribution between those in the top third of the income range (26 percent) and those in the lowest third (30 percent).[38]   Some 35 Yale graduates died in Vietnam, a casualty rate per population about equal to the rest of the nation.[39]   Draftees actually tend-

---

[32]Hans Schmidt, *Maverick Marine: General Smedley D. Butler and the Contradictions of American Military History* (Lexington, KY: University of Kentucky Press, 1987).

[33]Robert W. Johannsen, *To the Halls of the Montezumas: The Mexican War in the American Imagination* (New York: Oxford, 1985), pp. 27–28.

[34]Johannsen, *To the Halls of the Montezumas*, p. 28

[35]Johannsen, *To the Halls of the Montezumas*, p. 30.

[36]George Frederick Ruxton, *Adventures in Mexico and the Rocky Mountains* (New York: Harper, 1848), pp. 178–9.

[37]Contrast the claims of Myra MacPherson, *Long Time Passing: Vietnam and the Haunted Generation* (New York: Doubleday, 1984); James Fallows, "What Did You Do in the Class War, Daddy?" Washington Monthly, October 1975; and Christian Appy, *Working Class War: American Combat Soldiers in Vietnam* (Chapel Hill: University of North Carolina Press, 1993), and with Arnold Barnett, Timothy Stanley, and Michael Shore, "America's Vietnam Casualties: Victims of a Class War?" Operations Research, 40, September–October 1992, pp. 856—66.

[38]Barnett, "America's Vietnam Casualties," passim.

[39]B. G. Burkett and Glenna Whitley, *Stolen Valor: How the Vietnam Generation Was Robbed of Its Heroes and Its History* (Dallas: Verity Press, 1998), p. 59.

ed to have more education than volunteers, meaning that infantry units tended to be more educated as a share of the U.S. population than previous armies. This meant the U.S. Army was, in an unprecedented fashion, using brainpower on the front.[40] Certainly the Air Force did: virtually all of the Air Force's casualties were college grads. And casualty rates for ground units in Vietnam were skewed in the first place because GIs served three months longer in combat zones than during World War II.

Not only has an absence of class distinction facilitated a sense of community in American armies that was often absent in other Western forces, it also enhanced and empowered the critical positions of corporals and sergeants—NCOs, or noncommissioned officers—more than anywhere else in the world. These men (and much later, women) almost always came from the middle and lower classes because, especially later, one had to have a college degree to be an officer, but at the same, NCO pay was substantial and competitive, and NCOs could expect promotion according to their abilities. While it remained uncommon until well after the Civil War for NCOs to be recommended for officer training schools, the principles were already established, and reinforced a characteristic that defined the American fighting forces, that of pushing autonomy downward. Writers in the **Army and Navy Journal** complained that the boards of officers who had to approve promotions sent up the names of too few noncoms, and there was a particular concern that civilians of means might purchase a position. In 1879, **The Nation** argued for an overall elevation "*of the character of the service that there be no gulf between rank and file which cannot be bridged by intelligence and training ... and [instead is viewed] as offering a career to the sons of these sterling citizens from whom other professions draw their best blood*" (emphasis mine).[41]

Qualifications to become an officer remained open to virtually all: as of 1892, "*any unmarried soldier under the age of thirty and with two years of service could apply for a commission.*"[42] A regional examination followed, and if the candidate was successful, he moved into an Army-wide exam. The exam material covered mathematics, grammar, history, law, and, of course Army drill and regulations. In 1901, the largest number of officers ever (215) came from the ranks of the regulars, although the percentage of regular soldiers receiving commissions declined, so that by 1909 only about 10 percent still came from lower ranks. (The Navy tended to promote fewer sailors from the ranks.) Nevertheless, for the most part, the door was open, and not just to military men: civilians could obtain commissions, and, indeed, the largest segment in the year 1909 (160) came from civilian life, including four civilians who had graduated from the U.S. Naval Academy! Oddly enough, from 1909 on, while uncommon, several Annapolis

---

[40]George Q. Flynn, *The Draft: 1940–1973* (Lawrence: University of Kansas Press, 1993), p. 234. See also "Vietnam Warriors: A statistical Profile," VFW Magazine, March 1993.

[41]The Nation, quoted in Coffman, *The Old Army*, p. 225.

[42]Edward M. Coffman, *The Regulars: The American Army, 1898–1941* (Cambridge: Belknap Press, 2004), p. 123.

men received Army commissions.[43]

After World War II there was some hesitancy about quickly promoting noncoms to 2nd lieutenant. These concerns were practical rather than class directed, stemming from wartime experience that such promotions drained the NCO cadre of talented and experienced soldiers in ranks, where they were most needed. Combat, however, has often brought noncommissioned officers into command roles: at Soisson in 1918, a U.S. battalion, *"a major's command, was being commanded by a sergeant—and commanded well."* [44] Stephen Ambrose recounts in his Band of Brothers that the 1st sergeant of Easy Company was given a battlefield commission to 2nd lieutenant. General Al Gray, USMC, began his career as an enlisted man and worked his way up the ranks to be selected commandant of the Marine Corps in 1987. Lieutenant General Lewis "Chesty" Puller enlisted in 1918, fought in actions between the wars, in World War II, and in Korea, earning an unprecedented five Navy Crosses. As far back as the 1960s, U.S. Army Special Forces relied so heavily on noncoms that if a commissioned officer decided to tag along, and lacked the experience of the unit's sergeant, it was standard operating procedure for the sergeant to assume operational command. Most modern Special Operations Forces routinely defer to the most experienced person, regardless of rank, during a operation.

While the modern Army and Marines move men and women up in select situations, it is only done after careful review of their overall record. Nevertheless, although enlisted personnel proceed up their own path to a top rank of sergeant major or master gunnery sergeant, they can be recommended for Officer Candidate School if they meet the same age and education requirements of those who enter the Reserve Officer Training Corps (ROTC), the service academies, or Officer Candidate School directly. They also can be selected to attend Limited Duty Officer School or Warrant Officer School, and as such could be promoted to (but not above) the rank of lieutenant colonel. In short, Americans have developed a system with a full range of opportunities, wherein the lowliest private can become the head of an entire service branch, while at the same time recognizing that the career paths and attitudes of those who enlist in the ranks, as opposed to those who, from the moment they sign up, wish to lead, are quite different. It is precisely that flexibility that has produced both autonomous soldiers and officers.

As had started to occur in Europe, in the United States military leaders also gained respect by standing at the front with the troops. Officer casualties were nothing new to Western armes. At Austerlitz, Napoleon lost 1 general (killed) and 13 wounded; at Eylau, 23 killed or wounded; and at Borodino, 12 killed and 37 wounded.[45] At Gettysburg, George Pickett lost almost all of his regimental commanders, while across the low stone wall, General Winfield Scott Hancock fell from his horse badly wounded when a round shattered his saddle

[43]Coffmann, The Regulars, p. 124

[44]John. S. D. Eisenhower, Yanks: The epic Story of the American Army in World War I (New York: Free Press, 2001), p. 169

[45]John Keegan, *The Mask of Command* (New York; Penguin, 1987), p. 116.

and sent pieces flying into his body. The previous day, Colonel Vincent Strong, Joshua Chamberlain's regimental commander and a Yale graduate, fell at Little Round Top. And, of course, two of the Confederacy's brightest lights had been killed earlier in the war, Stonewall Jackson and Albert Sidney Johnston. Less than a year after Gettysburg, Jeb Stuart would die from wounds he received at Yellow Tavern; and A.P. Hill, Robert Rodes, and William Pender, along with many others holding general officer rank, died before the war was over.

Likewise, in other conflicts, officers experienced high casualty rates. Captain Bucky O'Neill, the famed Arizona sheriff and Rough Rider, fell to a Spanish bullet at San Juan Hill. In World War I, at Soisson, *every battalion commander of the 26th Infantry was a casualty, and the 3,500 man regiment, a colonel's command, had been taken over and directed smoothly by a captain with only two years of service in the Army.*[46] Admiral Isaac Kidd was killed at Pearl Harbor aboard the USS Arizona (and was posthumously awarded the Medal of Honor), and rear admirals Daniel J. Callaghan and Norman Scott were killed aboard their ships, the San Francisco and Atlanta, respectively, during the Battle of Savo Island, off the coast of Guadalcanal, in August 1942. Brigadier General Kenneth Walker was reported missing after leading a bombing mission over Rabaul. Lieutenant General Simon Bolivar Buckner, the highest-ranking Army officer killed in the Pacific in World War II, was mortally wounded directing troops during the Okinawa invasion. A higher percentage of Army officers died in Vietnam than in World War II, including 12 generals. Most recently, Lieutenant General Timothy Maude, who did not know he was in a war zone, was a victim of the terrorist attack at the Pentagon on 9/11.[47]

Neither fame nor rank differentiates American troops on the battlefield, a fact that tends to reinforce the democratization process still further. With officers willing to share risk, trust runs both ways. During Operation Iraqi Freedom (where the highest-ranking soldier killed as of 2005 was a colonel), Lieutenant General William Wallace, Major General David Petraeus, and Brigadier General Benjamin Freakley were standing near a Humvee and using it as a desk when mortar rounds dropped a few hundred meters away and started "walking" toward them. They calmly continued their meeting until the rounds were only thirty meters distant, then backed up a few feet to continue. Small arms and mortar fire erupted and the generals moved in the direction of the fire so rapidly that the military police protecting them had to run to keep up. Before the generals could engage the enemy, a helicopter spotted the mortar tube and artillery took it out, but the troops were impressed by the instinctive reaction of their corps leaders to move to the sound of the guns.[48]

What Not to Do

[46]Eisenhower, *Yanks*, p. 169.

[47]Burkett and Whitley, *Stolen Valor*, p. 48.

[48]Gregory Fontenot, E. J. Degen, and David Tohn, *On Point: The United States Army in Operation Iraqi Freedom* (Washington, D.C.: U.S. Army Chief of Staff, 2004), p. 220.

American's trust in its soldiers from the top down stands in remarkable contrast to the cultures of other nations. In Operation Iraqi Freedom, General Tommy Franks relied on the fact that Saddam had never developed autonomy among his officers. Quite the contrary, Saddam had divided crucial assignments between his Republican Guard (under the command of one of his two sons, Qusay) and the "Special Republican Guard," made up solely of men from villages north of Baghdad whose families were loyal to Saddam's. Far from distributing information freely among commanders, Saddam compartmentalized intelligence to discourage any thought of revolt. Ever since the first Gulf War, observers had commented on the differences in training between American soldiers and their Iraqi counterparts. Captain Harry Hornbuckle marveled that they had "*no tactics at all.*" Instead of concentrating fire, gunmen shot "haphazardly, almost casually," and never coordinated a single attack.[49]

Major James Lechner, training new Iraqi soldiers new Samarra, found Iraqi soldiers "*both in training and in battle to be courageous, smart, motivated and willing to endure harsh and difficult conditions to accomplish their missions.*" But "*the old Saddam-era officers were both reluctant to assume responsibility and to share authority, so they resisted American efforts to train competent Non-Commissioned Officers (NCOs).*" Decisions were "*passed up the chain of command by field officers unwilling to take risks.*"[50] Much of the Iraqi officers' reluctance to exercise autonomy is a product of their own recent history, when during the Iran-Iraq War, a general who lost twenty kilometers was executed, and any Air Force general who lost more than his quota of planes was also killed. Needless to say, Iraqi Air Force generals hesitated to fly their planes at all, especially on training missions, leaving their pilots woefully inexperienced when the hostilities erupted. [51] (Contrast that mind-set to the mild reprimands of Patton, who was once criticized by a war-games umpire for failing to mass his tanks according to doctrine: Patton was already flanking the enemy by using new tactics.)[52] All of this, of course, flies in the face of American doctrine, as expressed by Commander Holloway Halstead Frost, the youngest officer ordered to the Naval War College, at age twenty-seven, and the author of several prizewinning papers in Proceedings. "*Every mistake in war is excusable,*" observed Frost, "*except inactivity and refusal to run risks.*"[53]

The openness of the American system, whereby anyone could have a good idea, was apparent in World War II when, after the aircraft carrier Lexington sank, Machinist Oscar W. Myers, the fuel officer for the USS Yorktown, concluded that the Lex sank in part because of a gasoline fire on her deck. He conceived of draining the fuel system after use and filing the pipes with inert CO_2 gas, and

---

[49]Zucchino, *Thunder Run*, p. 179.

[50]Mark Bowden, "When Officers Aren't Gentlemen ..." Wall Street Journal, February 8, 2005.

[51]Bob Woodward, *The Commanders* (New York: Simon and Schuster, 1991), p. 286.

[52]Martin Blumenson, *Patton Papers: 1940–1945,* vol. 2 (Boston: Houghton-Mifflin, 1974), p. 37.

[53]Holloway H. Frost, "The Spirit of the Offensive," U.S. Naval Institute Proceedings, 49, February 1923, pp. 97–110. (quotation on 285).

Captain Elliot Buckmaster concurred. The installation of this system on the York-town likely prevented a calamitous fire on June 4 at Midway following a direct bomb hit.[54]

After Operation Iraqi Freedom, critics of the Bush administration policy in Iraq claimed that it was a mistake for the Coalition Provisional Authority to disband Saddam's army after American forces took Baghdad, oblivious to the fact that the old Iraqi army was neither efficient nor reliable as a genuine peacekeeping force. If Major Lechner's experience is typical, then retaining the old force would have created a different set of problems.[55] Instead, a new, truly westernized Iraqi force could not resemble the defeated Arab armies, but had to be introduced to the same underlying assumptions that permeated the American fighting forces. In retrospect, the issue of unemployed soldiers was significant. There was no easy answer to westernizing a force while at the same time ensuring that marginal Sun-ni Saddamites had work.

However, instilling western doctrines and assumptions had not come eas-ily or quickly. Even in the American army, the constant need to push autonomy downward came only with great resistance. Going as far back as Vietnam, top of-ficers still micromanaged the details of individual firefights, depriving field com-manders of initiative and creativity. In contrast, the post-cold war military empha-sized flexibility and training, what the Army called Future Force, and leadership had to be more decentralized than ever. Junior officers and NCOs were now allowed—and expected—to make decisions based on changing battlefield condi-tions, exploiting opportunities when they arose. This was institutionalized in the army's *Field Manual 100-5,* the basic rule book for military operations, and was soon followed by the Marines' *Fleet Manual 1: Warfighting.*[56] Taken with the Marines' internal reassessment, the Army documents represented a revolutionary shift from Vietnam, and nowhere was this more evident than in command decision making, which was steadily pushed down through the grades to junior officers. In some cases, change had already occurred in the ranks before it was institutional-ized in the books. Colonel Hal Moore, who wrote *We Were Soldiers Once ... and Young,* told his troops in 1963 when he set up the 11th Air Assault (which would soon be renamed the 7th Cavalry), *"decision-making will be decentralized: Push the power down. It pays off in wartime. Loyalty flows down as well."*[57]

It only made sense: command and control from behind the lines had been superseded by advanced communications. Captains and colonels had only to be given the proper information and they could make on-the-spot decisions. Both the Army and the Marines trusted their officers' judgment—and even more, their training—to issue orders to properly adapt to any situations. One of the best examples of such on-the-fly decision making came when 101st Airborne soldiers

---

[54]Jonathan B. Parshall and Anthony P. Tully, *Shattered Sword; The Untold Story of the Battle of Midway* (Washington, D.C.: Potomac Books, 2005), p. 407.
[55]Bowden, "When Officers Aren't Gentlemen."
[56]Fontenot, *On Point,* pp. 21–22.
[57]Harold G. Moore and Joseph L. Galloway, *We Were soldiers Once ... and Young* (New York: Ballantine, 1992), p. 19.

prepared to guard the Mosque of Ali (a sacred Muslim site). At one point a crowd that had been friendly started to turn ugly, fearing that the troops had come to arrest the mosque's Ayatollah Sistani. Rocks began to fly, and one hit Lieutenant Colonel Chris Hughes in the helmet. Seeing his men slipping the safeties off their weapons, Hughes commanded, *"Take a knee and point your weapon to the ground. Smile, and show no hostility."* This ran counter to crowd-control training, but Hughes's quick thinking and the discipline of the troopers sucked the anger right out of the crowd, and he and his men were able to move out without a shot fired.[58]

Such company-level autonomy reflected a radical change in the delivery of information to and from the battlefield, which itself reflected a transformation in command and control throughout the armed forces.[59] As General Tommy Franks, CENTCOM commander during Iraqi Freedom, put it, the U.S. Army was *"the trailing edge of industrial-age warfare and the leading edge of knowledge-based, information-age warfare."*[60] Decentralization of command depended on training, but it also required communications systems not available in earlier eras. Only revolutionary advances in computers-another essentially American technology—and satellites improved communication, command, and control to the degree that officers in the field could obtain instantaneous reports on combat conditions around them. The military even changed its famous C3 terminology (Command, Control, and Communications) to C4, adding computers. As microprocessors' size and costs plummeted, it became possible to wire individual soldiers similarly to the way they'd carried walkie-talkies, or to monitor ground units through UAV spy planes, and to follow every armored unit in the invasion through a computer monitoring system called Blue Force Tracker, which displayed the position of every tank and armored personnel carrier on screens at headquarters. Thanks to ultra-sophisticated video and digital photography, this technology painted live enemy units in red, which became the Red force, and if they entered blue areas, they could be tracked. However, as General Peter Pace, the current chairman of the Joint Chiefs of Staff pointed out, too much communication can lead to a practice of deferring decisions: senior leaders, he maintained, had to start saying, *"Look, if it's not dying or burning, don't call me."*[61]

Autonomy vs. Arrogance

If the American penchant for pushing autonomy downward produces officers and enlisted personnel capable of unprecedented levels of decision making

---

[58]Rick Atkinson, *In the Company of Soldiers: A Chronicle of Combat* (New York: Henry Holt, 2004);p. 232; Karl Zinsmeister, *Boots on the Ground: A Month with the 82nd Airborne in the Battle for Iraq* (New York: Truman Talley Books, 2003), pp. 192–93.

[59]According to the U.S. Army's history of Operation Iraqi Freedom, the army went through three separate stages in its post–Cold War evaluation. See Fontenot, *On Point*: 1.

[60]Fontenot, *On Point*, 1

[61]"How the Marine Corps Trains Leaders," *Fortune* 75, June 27, 2005, http://www.fortune.com/fortune/fortune75/articles/0,15114, 1070964-9,00.html.

at lower ranks, it also has a dark side, which is that he same freedom to freelance and interpret orders loosely can be abused. Two of the most infamous examples of autonomy improperly used involved cavalry: the 7th Cavalry under Lieutenant Colonel George Armstrong Custer, attached to General Alfred Terry in the Little Bighorn campaign of 1876, and the Confederate cavalry commanded by J.E.B. Stuart attached to the Army of Northern Virginia under General Robert E. Lee at Gettysburg. Five companies of Custer's force were annihilated at the Battle of the Little Big Horn, and the remainder of the regiment separated from Custer's command was fortunate to survive. Thirteen years earlier, Stuart's impetuousness had led him on a raiding mission deep into Pennsylvania at the very moment that Lee was stumbling quite blindly into the Battle of Gettysburg.

In the Spring of 1876, three columns of soldiers moved to force the Sioux and Cheyenne Indians back onto their reservations. The Indians had gathered in Montana to fight against continued white intrusions of their Black Hills lands. One column, led by Colonel John Gibbon, headed eastward from Fort Ellis (near modern-day Bozeman) with about 450 men. A second column of about 1,000 men, led by General George Crook, headed north from Fort Fetterman in Wyoming. Crook had some 300 Crow and Shoshone Indian allies as well. General Terry's force, with 300 infantry and some Gatlin guns, as well as the entire 7th Cavalry of about 650 men (counting scouts and hangers-on), went westward from Fort Abraham Lincoln in Dakota Territory. Terry, in command of the entire operation, estimated that his 2,300 men would be more than enough to deal with the 1,500 Sioux and Cheyenne that he anticipated finding in the area of the Little Big Horn River. Terry's offensive presumed that any one of the columns was more than a match for the Sioux—whose numbers and fighting ability he had underestimated (Crazy Horse had about 1,300 warriors, although many scouts thought the Indians had 5,000 braves).

Crook engaged the Sioux first, or, more accurately, the Sioux engaged him first. His Indian allies were engaged some distance from Crook's main body, but the gunfire warned Crook, allowing him to draw his forces up into position at Rosebud Creek. Even then, the experienced Indian-fighter Crook still underestimated the numbers and ferocity of the Sioux under Crazy Horse, who had lectured his forces on fighting Western style to destroy the enemy rather than obtain honor by counting coup or achieving meaningless, if flashy, victories. Worse, convinced the village was near, Crook dispatched three companies to find it, further depleting his force and stretching out his lines. A pitched battle ensued, but ultimately neither side was effective in killing the other's men—Crook's cavalry only lost 10 dead and 21 wounded, and the Sioux, about the same number—but the army had used up much of its ammunition. Even though Crazy Horse retreated and Crook claimed victory, he too, had to withdraw to resupply while the Sioux joined with Sitting Bull's forces to await the other columns.

Unaware of Crook's retreat, Terry continued to press ahead, and sent Custer ahead to scout. His vague orders to Custer left much room for the flamboyant cavalier to maneuver, but the intent seemed to be mainly for Custer to prevent the Indians from escaping, rather than forcing an attack:

> [Y]ou should proceed up the Rosebud until you ascertain definitely the direction in which the trail above spoken of leads. Should it be found (as it appears almost certain that it will be found) to turn towards the Little Bighorn, he thinks that you should still proceed southward, perhaps as far as the headwaters of the Tongue, and then turn the Little Horn, feeling constantly, however, to your left, so as to preclude the escape of the Indians passing around our left flank.[62]

It was, however, also clear that Terry did not expect Custer to wait for Gibbon's column or for Terry's forces, but rather to engage the Indians if he "thought he could whip them." But Custer, having already declined the Gatling guns and a battalion of the 2nd Cavalry, had never met an Indian force he "couldn't whip," so he forced his marches, arriving at the Rosebud/Little Bighorn rivers on June 25, and promptly divided his forces. His pack train, with 80 men, was already lagging behind. Then he sent Captain Frederick Benteen and 150 men farther south to scout, while dispatching Major Marcus Reno with 175 troops to attack the village. Custer promised to be on Reno's right, in support. In spite of numerous reports from his own trusted scouts that the Indian village was bigger than any he had ever encountered, Custer had divided his already outnumbered forces.

The Sioux and Cheyenne immediately reacted to Reno's approach and attacked, surprising and nearly overwhelming his forces. Reno's men were drawn up in a skirmish line when the first warriors appeared, but when Custer's promised support did not come, Reno ordered a retreat to the tree line along the Little Big Horn. (Custer's motivations for not immediately riding to Reno's aid have been the subject of numerous monographs.)[63] From a bluff, Custer could see the largest Indian encampment he'd ever witnessed, but characteristically was undaunted and though only in terms of attacking. He also could see Reno's skirmish line, and apparently thought Reno's men could handle the warriors in front of him. Or that by attacking the village farther downstream, he would force the Indians to leave Reno and defend their lodges.

Here matters get murky. Richard Fox, using archaeological techniques, has contended that Custer had information that the women and children—whom he needed to capture to force the surrender of the warriors—had already withdrawn, and that he took two troops still farther away from Captain Miles Keough to block their retreat before he realized they had escaped. Regardless, it is clear Custer set out to attack the village and not support Reno directly, as he had promised. He issued hasty orders, via two different couriers, to Benteen and to the pack

---

[62]Terry's orders appear at http://www.lbha.org/Research/terryord.htm.
[63]Robert M. Utley, *Cavalier in Buckskin: George Armstrong Custer and the Western Military Frontier* (Norman: University of Oklahoma Press, 1988); Edgar I. Stewart, *Custer's Luck* (Norman: University of Oklahoma Press, 1955); Evan S. Connell, *Son of the Morning Star: Custer and the Little Bighorn* (San Francisco: North Point Press, 1984); Stephen Ambrose, *Crazy Horse and Custer: the Parallel Lives of Two American Warriors* (Garden City, New York: Doubleday, 1975); and Richard Allen Fox, Jr., *Archaeology, History, and Custer's Last Battle: the Little Big Horn Reexamined* (Norman: University of Oklahoma Press, 1997).

train, urging them to *"come on ... Big village. Bring packs."* A postscript, "P. bring pacs [sic]," indicated Custer thought he would need every bullet in the train. Yet Benteen, who had separated from the Custer column earlier, did not know Custer had further divided his force, and would not have known whether he was joining Custer's units or Reno's, which were now in different places on the battlefield, until he got close enough to see the guidons. By that time, Benteen's own men were engaged by the Indians attacking Reno, who, convinced he couldn't hold the tree line, now attempted to retreat across the river. Custer apologists claim that had Reno not retreated, he could have tied up several hundred Indians, who now were free to join the forces attacking Custer's five troops. In fact, the Indians bungled this part of the battle, riding some fifty yards away from Reno's flank when a full attack would have overwhelmed his men as they scrambled for the river.

A controversy rages over how the battle developed from there, that is, whether there was a "last stand" or whether Custer's troops even fought from skirmish lines.[64] Although some methodological problems exist in his approach, archaeologist Richard Fox has employed a survey of cartridge dispositions at the battlefield to determine where soldiers and Indians were when they fired. He concluded that the absence of high concentrations of government spent cartridges in areas previously thought to be locations of a "stand" indicated that, in fact, no skirmish lines were ever formed, or if they were, they disintegrated quickly. Instead, Fox tells a convincing story of a regiment on the attack, with Custer's five troops further dividing at Keough Hill, where three troops remained. Custer, with two troops, moved rapidly to the northwest, parallel to the Little Big Horn River, to see if he could still block the Indians' escape. Finding he could not, Custer circuitously returned to the bluffs. But by that time (almost an hour, according to Fox), during which there seemed to be a lull as Keough's men remained on the ridge, the Indians began infiltrating their ranks and opening a harassing fire. Fearing he would be cut off from Custer, Keough sent a troop to the adjacent ridge (Calhoun Hill), still expecting Custer to return and order a full regimental attack. But the Indian infiltration grew serious, and soon Keough had thrown out a skirmish line. It was too late. The Indians, virtually on top of Keough's men, rose up and overwhelmed them. What few survivors escaped tended to run away toward Captain James Calhoun's (and, ultimately, Custer's) position, which would later be called Calhoun Hill. As they ran, and unit cohesion collapsed, they were easier to kill.

In short, the Custer debacle precisely illustrated the significance of the Western way of war, whose advantages derived from unit discipline, unit cohesion, and ordered volley fire. Spreading out not only the three main commands under Reno, Benteen, and himself (plus the pack company), Custer had also further dispersed his five companies in three main locations on the ridge, depriving them of their firepower and discipline advantage. Worse, some of the Indians were <u>armed with Winchester</u> 73 repeaters, meaning they actually outgunned the caval-

---

[64]Fox, *Archeology, History and Custer's Last Battle*, passim.

rymen. Frantic troopers with their slow-loading carbines were overwhelmed. In sum, Fox's archaeological evidence suggests a command on the offensive that stretched its cohesion to the limit. (This was almost precisely repeated in 1879 by the British at Isandlwana where 1,400 British troops, including only 800 regulars, were spread alongside the base of a hill that would have required twice that number to hold with western-style cohesion).[65] Custer's disaster demonstrated the downside of American military autonomy: even experienced commanders can (and occasionally do) make mistakes, or rely too heavily on autonomous subordinates to carry out their instructions (whether badly written or not). The *Cavalier in Buckskin,* however, was not the first accomplished cavalry officer to suffer a fatal lapse in judgment.

James Ewell Brown "Jeb" Stuart, the flamboyant Confederate cavalry commander of Robert E. Lee's Army of Northern Virginia, strutted his horse soldiers on a parade ground near Brandy Station in June 1863 while Union general Alfred Pleasanton moved his Federal cavalry across Beverly Ford to surprise the Rebels. Although Stuart's forces finally beat back the Union troopers, he was stung by editorials blaming him for a near disaster. Confederate cavalry, scolded the **Richmond Examiner**, "*was carelessly strewn over the country,*" and it fretted that the Federals were "*daily learning to despise the mounted troops of the Confederacy*" instead of fear them.[66] Without chastising Stuart by name, the paper warned that the Rebel forces must "*insist on more earnestness among the officers in the discharge of their very important duty.*"[67] The rebukes burned in Stuart's soul.

Even the Union forces knew, through spies, that Stuart's image had suffered. Southern papers, wrote General Daniel Butterfield to General Henry Halleck, "*call upon [Stuart] to do something to retrieve his reputation.*"[68] Given less flexible orders than those that would later undo Custer, Stuart allowed himself to be pulled far to the northeast, through Rockville, Maryland, while Lee's main body moved behind the Blue Ridge Mountains. He had compromised Lee's army by failing to adhere to Lee's order to "*take position on General Ewell's right, place yourself in communication with him, guard his flank, keep him informed of the enemy's movements, & collect all the supplies you can for the use of the army. [emphasis added]*"[69] It was absolutely clear that Lee intended Stuart to stay constantly in touch with Ewell, even to the point of "*guarding his flank.*" Once the confederate cavalier was out of Lee's reach, however, the lure of booty unraveled the discipline of Stuart's forces, who first captured several boats full of whiskey

[65]See Mike Snook, *How Can Man Die Better: The Secrets of Isandlwana Revealed* (Barnsley, South Yorkshire, ENG: Frontline Books, 2011).
[66]*Richmond Enquirer*, June 12, 1863.
[67]*Richmond Enquirer*, June 12, 1863.
[68]*The War of the Rebellion: A Compilation of the Official Records of the Union and Confederate Armies* (Washington: Government Printing Office, 1880–1901), 27, part 1, 41.
[69]Scott Bowden and Bill Ward, *Last Chance for Victory: Robert E. Lee and the Gettysburg Campaign* (Cambridge, MA: Da Capo Press, 2001), quoting Lee's letter of June 22, 1863, to Stuart, 105. The authors cover the controversy thoroughly on pp. 101–25, concluding that Stuart willfully ignored Lee's and Longstreet's specific orders to hew closely to Ewell, instead swinging far to the east to deliberately go on a raiding mission

on a canal, then, in front of the Federals' eyes, a massive Federal wagon train fully laden with oats, bacon, sugar, ham, and again, more whiskey. The 125 wagons waddled toward Rockville—right into Stuart's waiting hands. Along with the wagons came 400 prisoners that the Rebels had to parole, having no extra forces to guard them. Stuart's cavalry, usually swift and agile, had gotten a late start to begin with, and now moved as if in mud. His men then stopped yet again to rip up rails of the B & O Railroad, which chewed up half a day.

For an early nineteenth-century army, the cavalry was the scouting force, and deprived of intelligence provided by Stuart, Lee was blindly heading toward Gettysburg. Stuart's men, already six days in the saddle, were falling asleep on their horses. Near Carlisle, "*even in line of battle ... [men] would throw themselves upon their horses [sic] necks ... and fall asleep.*"[70] Having covered 210 miles, or about 26 miles per day, interspersed with destroying railroads and fighting, Stuart's men had simply taken themselves out of the picture. Lee's orders to Stuart to stay in touch with Ewell (and, thereby, with Lee) had been blown to the winds in the quest for wagons and glory. Not until July 2, when they die of a Union victory at Gettysburg had already been cast, did the weary Confederate cavalry reach Lee's headquarters at Seminary Ridge. Arriving at Lee's positions with "*hanging heads and trembling legs*," Stuart's exhausted troopers looked nothing like the proud regiments that had moved north several days before.[71] Of Stuart's arrogance in loosely interpreting Lee's orders, Douglas Southall Freeman wrote, "*Nothing was comparable to this in preparing the way for a tragedy.*"[72]

Stuart escaped Custer's fate. His command survived, and even managed to fight on July 3 at Gettysburg, at Rummel Farm. There a timely and critical charge by Union cavalry broke Stuart's cavalry advance and competed the defeat of Lee's forces. That change was led by a young Michigan officer yelling "*Come on, you Wolverines*"—George A. Custer.

Both Custer and Stuart had well-established track records of successful (even remarkable) independent action, and in both cases these commanders gave little evidence in advance that they would make such poor decisions (Custer less so than Stuart). However, it is entirely possible that fatigue played a crucial role in both outcomes. After Brandy Station, Stuart pushed his men on their raid into Pennsylvania, making them ineffective fighters even if they had arrived on the battlefield sooner—though, no doubt, Stuart would have provided Lee with the important intelligence and scouting he lacked. Custer, likewise, drove his men, and one of the most convincing accounts of the Battle of the Little Big Horn argues that fatigue exacerbated the unit disintegration of the 7th Cavalry.[73]

Other military failures (and a few disasters, such as the Fetterman Massacre where Captain William Fetterman, who boasted he could "*ride across the whole Sioux nation with 80 men*," was wiped out when his eighty-man wood train

---

[70]Bowden and Ward, *Last Chance for Victory*, p. 419, quoting George Beale in Colonel John Chambliss's brigade.

[71]Bowden and Ward, *Last Chance for Victory*, p. 422.

[72]Douglas Southall Freeman, *Lee's Lieutenants*, 3 vols. (New York: Charles Scribner's sons, 1944), III:170

[73]Fox, *Archaeology, History*, and *Custer's Last Battle*, passim.

was ambushed) derived from the American penchant for pushing autonomy down. At Kasserine Pass, poorly trained troops were led by unimaginative commanders, with the predictable result. Overall, though, the system has more than made up for abuses of autonomy, or poor command decisions, by empowering capable commanders who are flexible enough to adapt to unforeseen situations. For example, in 1898, Theodore Roosevelt, having raised his volunteer Rough Riders cavalry unit for action in Cuba in the Spanish-American War, literally commandeered a train of coal cars to get his men to Tampa for the limited ship space. Then, at the wharf, he and Leonard Wood seized the steamer Yucatan, virtually yanking it out from under the regiments assigned to it. *"That's our ship,"* said the flabbergasted members of the 71st New York, to which Roosevelt smiled and said, *"Well, we seem to have it!"* [74] However, the lack of shipboard space had already forced TR to choose whether to take the horses, and possibly miss the war, or abandon the horses. Roosevelt left the horses behind. The Rough Riders' greatest charge came on foot up Kettle Hill (frequently misidentified as San Juan Hill, which lies right next to it).[75]

Autonomy among lower-level officers also created a climate in which alternatives were raised, and possibilities opened. Grant, during his 1864 Overland Campaign, sat patiently while his officers debated his own battlefield conduct (whether to ride so close to enemy lines) in his presence. Such discussions alerted commanders not only to the ideas percolating up from below, but also to the mood of the troops and, in Grant's case, *"what common opinion was among ordinary Union officers."*[76] At the Ardennes in 1944, with German forces poised to smash through Allied lines and deal the war effort a massive setback, Dwight Eisenhower calmly listened to recommendations and suggestions not only from his own officers, but from British commanders as well, while hundreds of miles away, a dotty Adolf Hitler, having dismissed dozens of competent generals, exercised total control over Nazi forces without dissent. Eisenhower was largely saved in that circumstance by the autonomous actions of George Patton, who had already directed his staff to plan a staggeringly difficult ninety-degree turn to attack the German flank.

Certainly the king of capriciousness, Patton had a knack for timing his spontaneity so as to be in the right place at the right time. Ike, in his review of Patton, assessed him as *"a shrewd soldier who believes in showmanship [to the point of being] almost flamboyant. He talks too much,"* and his actions might have misled subordinates who lacked an understanding of *"the deep sense of duty, courage, and service that make up his real personality."*[77] In his first message to the troops as commander of the 7th Army, which was slated to invade Sicily, he said, *"When we land we will meet German and Italian soldiers whom it is our honor and privilege too attack and destroy."*[78] After landing, Patton saw the Brit-

---

[74]Alfred Nofi, *The Spanish–American War, 1898* (Conshohocken, PA: Combined Books, 1996), p. 114.

[75]Nofi, *Spanish–American War*, p. 150.

[76]John Keegan, *The Mask of Command* (New York: Penguin, 1987), p. 199.

[77]D'Este, *Patton*: pp. 500–501.

[78]D'Este, *Patton*, p. 504.

ish bogged down, and he flew into action, organizing a "provisional corps" that sliced straight through the middle of Sicily while other elements swung far to the west to capture Palermo, just ten days after Patton set foot on the island. Omar Bradley, ever sensitive to Patton's remarkable feats, dismissed the movement of armor and men across two hundred miles of mountainous terrain as "*great theater*," but Patton barely blinked before turning eastward toward the key city of Messina, which his troops captured on August 17, 1943. Even after the notorious slapping incidents, Ike moved to protect the man he said "*is indispensable to the war effort—one of the guarantors of our victory [emphasis in original]*."[79]

When the Germans launched their fierce counteroffensive through the Ardennes in the winter of 1944, they caught the entire Allied front by surprise, except for Patton, who had listened to Oscar Koch, the only American intelligence officer who had warned that the Germans were capable of mounting "a large spoiling offensive" precisely where they now struck.[80] More important, without asking Ike's permission in advance, Patton had his staff draw up plans to turn north and strike the Germans in the flank. Consider the remarkable speed with which Patton and his staff operated: On December 16 the Germans smashed through American lines. Three days later the Allied generals met, and Ike asked Patton, "*When can you attack?*" Patton replied, "*The morning of December 21, with three divisions.*"[81] (Actually, he struck on the twenty-second.) Just six days after an astounding counteroffensive that left the Americans dispirited and the British stunned, Patton drove three entire divisions into the Germans' side! Even Omar Bradley had to admire Patton's counterstroke: "*True to his boast at Verdun, Patton, having turned his Third Army ninety degrees, attacked on December 22. His generalship during this difficult maneuver was magnificent. One of the most brilliant performances by any commander on either side in World War II.*"[82] Patton's well-deserved praise obscured the phenomenal job of his logistics staff, who pulled the 3rd Army across two other armies' lines of supply and communication, which, even in the best of circumstances would have constituted a nightmare of planning. In the dead of winter, with an enemy assault under way, it was nothing short of miraculous.

Roach Motel

Patton's remarkable accomplishments contributed to a mythology about the general, solidified further by George C. Scott's portrayal in the 1970 Academy Award-winning movie, Patton. Like Custer and Stuart, Patton had serious flaws, but unlike Custer he never succumbed to overconfidence, and unlike Stuart, he never ignored his place in Eisenhower's broader strategy. Fittingly, then, our story of autonomy that began with armored units in Baghdad has returned to tanks

[79]Stephen E. Ambrose, *The Supreme Commander* (London: Cassell, 1970), p. 229.
[80]D'Este, *Patton*, p. 676.
[81]D'Este, *Patton*, p. 680.
[82]Omar N. Bradley, with Clay Blair, *A General's Life* (New York: Simon and Schuster, 1981), p. 367.

under Patton. In his 1999 book *The Soul of Battle*, in which one third of the analysis is devoted to Patton, Victor Hanson concluded with a pessimistic warning: that modern Americans might not again have the stomach for large-scale and costly military campaigns.[83]

Yet two years later it happened in Afghanistan, then, not long after that, again in Iraq. Al Qaeda's response in Iraq largely drew on Osama bin Laden's proposed "Mogadishu strategy," which promised that after a few casualties, Americans would withdraw. That failed miserably and was replaced by a new strategy—on the part of the Americans. One might call it the "roach motel" strategy, in which Iraq, whether by accident or design, has become a giant magnet for jihadists of every stripe. This same strategy was also pursued on a micro-level in the cities of Najaf and Fallujah, where so-called militants have holed up and drawn hundreds of jihadists to the cities. In response, the U.S. military has virtually surrounded the cities, secured local informants to identify bad guys, then stalked them at night or forced them out in one-sided firefights. In August 2004, for example, several hundred militants in Najaf were drawn into a heads-up battle with American forces, with the result being 300 dead insurgents and possibly as many as 1,000 wounded.

The simple fact is that no army or insurgency in history has ever sustained such losses, nor can they now. Despite claims in the media, the number of willing suicide bombers soon evaporates. Victor Hanson noted that at Okinawa, the lesson learned from kamikaze attacks were that the Americans *"could beat off the suicides, repair damaged craft, and replace lost ships faster than the Japanese could make up their own losses in planes and fanatical pilots."* [84] Moreover, the Japanese themselves began to detect that their suicide pools were drying up.

Indeed, most modern commentators—especially historians and journalists—have missed the central fact of modern asymmetrical warfare, which is that it is an admission by the jihadists that they cannot overturn the verdict of the battlefield. This alone places additional psychological stress on a culture that overemphasizes honor and male dominance, reminding the terrorists by their very acts (whether they acknowledge it or not) that they are already less than their foes. Two centuries of American warfare have taught us that the United States is willing to accept casualties to achieve victory. The bad news for America's enemies is that from World War II onward, technology and training have combined with old-fashioned Yankee heroism to steadily reduce those losses.

That ethos drove the planning for the first Gulf War and Operation Iraqi Freedom. Lieutenant General Anthony Zinni, the commander of I Marine Expeditionary Force who became commander of CENTCOM (Central Command, with authority over the Middle East) in 1997, and the commander of XVIII Airborne Corps, Lieutenant General Gary Luck, designed a plan to *"overthrow Saddam*

---

[83]Victor Davis Hanson, *The Soul of Battle: From Ancient Times to Present Day, How Three Great Liberators Vanquished Tyranny* (New York: Free Press, 1999), p. 412.

[84]Victor Davis Hanson, *Ripples of War: How Wars of the Past Still Determine How We Fight, How We Live, and How We Think* (New York: Doubleday, 2003), p. 44.

Hussein in a swift and decisive campaign."[85]   Zinni's replacement, General Tommy Franks, further refined the concept, meaning that "*the final plan for over-throwing the Iraqi regime owed its genesis to a complex interaction among military professionals at the highest levels.*"[86]   Misnamed Shock and Awe, the plan for Operation Iraqi Freedom was completely misunderstood, primarily because journalists, even more so than generals, have a bad habit of fighting the last war. ("Shock and Awe" was a phrase first used by Harlan Ullman, who taught at the National War College, in a 1996 book entitled *Shock and Awe: Achieving Rapid Dominance.*)[87]   Reporters, basing their experiences on Desert Storm, expected a massive aerial bombardment to open the campaign and were caught flat-footed when, aside from a "decapitating" missile strike on Saddam's location, the ground troops immediately swept across the Kuwaiti border. Instead of air-raid sirens and long lines of tracers across the Baghdad skies, stunned editors and anchors watched American infantry and armor rolling rapidly into the heart of Iraq.[88]

Frank's plan (named Hybrid 1003V OPLAN) resembled nothing of what was reported in the press. Indeed, the United States using an agent code named April Fool, who posed as a traitor selling deceptive (but realistic-looking) Pentagon documents to the Iraqis for months, had the Iraqis convinced that a major—if not the major—point of the invasion would be in the north, thus tying up some Iraqi divisions. Instead of a massive bombing effort, all operations would commence simultaneously, hence the first true large-scale joint invasion in American military history. Even the narrow sixteen-day "battlefield preparation" air plan that Franks originally anticipated was shrunk steadily until ground units actually moved into Iraq before air operations really commenced.[89]   Regardless of when the ground forces launched, the primary mission objective was to get to Baghdad as soon as possible and overthrow the regime, a plan Franks called the "inside-out" approach.[90] If resistance in Baghdad proved tenacious, Franks anticipated surrounding the city and using constant probes, mostly by 101st Airborne troops and Marines, to weaken resistance and "attrit" the enemy. As the U.S. Army's summary history of Operation Iraqi Freedom stated, the plan "for reducing Baghdad was necessarily vague," thereby providing commanders on the scene great flexibility in determining how to proceed.[91]   Initially, it was assumed armor would merely play a blocking role in this effort. Ultimately, though, if resistance continued, a block-by-block conquest of the city might be necessary—and would

---

[85]Murray and Scales, *The Iraq War,* p. 92.

[86]Murray and Scales, *The Iraq War,* p. 92

[87]Harlan Ullman and James P. Wade, with L. A. Edney, *Shock and Awe: Achieving Rapid Dominance* (Washington, DC: Center for Advanced Concepts and Technology, Government Printing Office, 1996).

[88]Reporters had been so completely taken in by the "shock and awe: mantra that even when it did not materialize, they tried to invent it. Watching only a handful of surgically precise explosions in Baghdad, one reporter said, "This is shock. ... And the sheer power of this bombardment is awesome." (Tommy Franks and Malcolm McConnell, *American Soldier* [New York: Regan Books, 2004],p. 481.) Virtually any Vietnam–era bombing campaign far exceeded Iraqi Freedom in its impressiveness (though certainly not deadliness). But the reporters were in a box, and they had to report a "strategy" that didn't exist!

[89] Franks, *American Soldier,* 441; Fontenot, *On Point,* p. 90.

[90]Franks, *American Soldier,* p. 391.

[91]Fontenot, *On Point,* p. 90.

be CENTCOM's worse nightmare. However, to conceal the tactics to take Baghdad, CENTCOM deliberately held the British back from occupying Basra for several days.

Although it was not apparent to troops in the field immediately, Franks quickly realized that the Iraqi army looked hopelessly confused, disorganized, and leaderless. This encouraged him to proceed with even greater haste. He calculated that the surest way to defeat enemy armies was to remove Saddam, and the quickest way to oust Saddam was to take Baghdad. The message went out: "*Bypass and haul ass!*" That, in turn, placed even more emphasis on midlevel officers exercising exceptional autonomy on the battlefield. There simply was no time to check and confirm every movement with headquarters. When Saddam's statue fell, a true "revolution in military affairs" had occurred, although not the one touted at the think tanks. Frank's troops had demonstrated, yet again, that the most revolutionary thing the American military offers is the best-trained, most independent-thinking troops in the world.

Americans involved in combat—even civilians, such as William Eaton in 1805—have exercised extreme autonomy unseen in history. It is telling that other military leaders have been mostly criticized for blindly following leaders or established doctrine: the Allies in World War I with their massed infantry attacks against trenches, the French knights at Agincourt for their futile cavalry charges against Henry's archers. Marshal Grouchy pursuing the Prussians from behind when his forces were needed between the enemy and Napoléon. On the other hand, with a few exceptions, Americans' most prominent defeats come when commanders use their autonomy recklessly or when they fail to innovate and adapt, as in Ambrose Burnside's case at Fredricksburg or Robert E. Lee's stubborn charge at Gettysburg.

American soldiers are expected to obey orders, but with the understanding that they can constantly innovate and modify orders to achieve objectives. Patton, in part, took Messina after ignoring orders to halt, claiming the messages were garbled in transmission, a favorite trick of the independent and autonomous leader. George Dewey owed much of his success at Manila Bay to the fact that Assistant Secretary of the Navy Theodore Roosevelt had taken advantage of the Navy secretary's absence for a dental appointment to order Dewey to Hong Kong in preparation for the war Roosevelt knew was coming.

Americans demand of their leaders that they think, exercise good judgment, and when appropriate, act independently. We instill in the nation's officers and enlisted forces the truth that it's easier to beg forgiveness than to ask permission. America's secret weapon has been that we push autonomy down, making the lowliest private a tactician and thinker, not a robotic killer. Indeed, the U.S. military has redefined the old maxim that deer led by a lion are more to be feared than lions led by a deer. A few good men who can think independently have proven themselves to be lions led by lions.

CHAPTER FIVE
If You Build It, We Will Win

Just as Americans willingly accept good ideas from lower ranks, so, too has the U.S. military embraced inventions and processes from the private sector, giving it an unprecedented advantage in wartime production.

The frothing horses had galloped through a drenching rain to Hoover's Gap, Tennessee, before their riders finally reined them in sometime around nine on the morning of June 24, 1863. They had ridden steadily from Murfreesboro as the vanguard of General William Rosecrans's Army of the Cumberland, and they had pushed their horses to the limit on the muddy roads. The artillery under Captain Eli Lilly attached to the brigade, saw its teams give out a mile up the road from Hoover's Gap, forcing the weary gunners to haul their guns into place on foot. By the time the artillerymen arrived, they deployed their cannon behind the 2,000 blue-coated soldiers, who had mostly dismounted and withdrawn their weapons from the sheaths, then taken up positions at the south end of the Gap on the hillside and along the road to Fairfield. These Union soldiers faced the 3rd Kentucky Cavalry of the Confederate Army in front of them, and farther behind them, the whole Army of Tennessee under Confederate general Braxton Bragg.

Normally, cavalry units without their own infantry support would be dispatched easily by masses of enemy infantry. But these were not cavalry troopers, and their weapons were not sabers: these men were from the Indiana Lightning Brigade—of infantry—and their rifles were not the traditional muskets carried by most Union infantrymen, but the new seven-shot Spencer repeating rifles. Colonel John Wilder watched calmly as his men deployed, much the way General John Buford's men would array themselves at Gettysburg a few days later. Methodically, each man worked the actions of the new Spencers, pushing forward on what normally would be a trigger guard, activating a rolling breech that drew a large .56 caliber cartridge from the tube inside the block and inserting it into the breech. The soldier then pulled the guard back, placing the cartridges into their case-hardened locks before using his thumb to manually draw back the S-shaped hammer. After firing, the block action of pushing the guard forward ejected the spent shell, and rammed in the next.[1]

Confidently, Wilder's mounted infantry waited for the Confederates, knowing they could fire seven shots in ten seconds, while their enemies could fire only once. Each man carried several preloaded tubes as well, making reloading the entire magazine a matter of seconds, not minutes. Wilder's troops had practiced with their mounts, which they had seized from Confederate cavalry or loyalists, by making practice runs all around Tennessee. The Lightning Brigade, which consisted of three Indiana regiments, two Illinois regiments, and Lilly's Indiana

---

[1] An excellent look at these mechanisms, and their operation, appears at http://armscollectors.com/mgs/spencer_repeating_rifle.htm.

artillery battery, designated one out of four men as a horse handler. His role was to move the mounts one hundred yards to the rear as the troopers formed into skirmish lines—not the traditional shoulder-to-shoulder massed infantry formations. Confederate brigades that arrayed in front of Wilder's men would soon counterattack. They would be traditional infantry, which, burdened by the inaccuracy of the musket, had to maintain dense order, counting on the volume of fire rather than the skill of the marksmen. (Indeed, in 1803, a German field marshal issued orders that forbade aiming while firing because it wasted time and detracted from firepower rates!)[2]

Many would have been stunned that Wilder's men even captured Hoover's Gap, much less held it. Wilder himself had a score to settle. The previous September, badly outnumbered, Wilder had surrendered at Munfordville, Kentucky, to Confederate general Braxton Bragg, whose men now marched to meet him. Nor did the unorthodox Lightning Brigade have the most imposing reputation. Wilder equipped his men not only with the new Spencers, but with hatchets, which in the style of the Roman legion, proved useful to dismounted infantry for cutting up wood for hastily constructed defenses. For that they were lampooned as the Hatchet Brigade, but no one laughed at Wilder's troopers that evening when reinforcements finally reached the dismounted horsemen. They had driven off Confederate infantry, losing less than half as many men as the Rebels. Wilder reported that *"the effect of our terrible fire was overwhelming to our opponents."*[3] Later, Major General James Wilson would equip an even larger force of 14,000 with Spencers and cut a swath through Alabama, made possible in part by Wilson's strict fire-control discipline that kept the men from expending their one hundred rounds of ammunition too quickly.[4] More than forty years later, former Confederate general E. P. Alexander observed that the war would have been *"terminated within a year"* if Federal troops had all been equipped with the 1861 repeater design.[5]

Wilder's troops demonstrated another aspect of why Americans win wars: they usually have better equipment, and more of it, than anyone else. Whether it was innovators of processes, such as Eli Whitney with his American system of mass production, or inventors who would not take no for an answer, such as John Holland with his submarine, American weapons suppliers used a free market and property rights to the advantage of soldiers who fight under the U.S. flag. And it is irrelevant whether the government was the customer, as with guns or other arms is often the case: the fertile fields of invention in America had already produced a bounty of clockmakers and other mechanics whose techniques and processes filtered into government armories or into the private arms makers who sold mostly

---

[2]H. Delbruck, *The Dawn of Modern Warfare: History of the Art of War*, vol. 4, translated by W. J. Renfroe, Jr. (Lincoln, NE: University of Nebraska Press, 1985), p. 450. Also see a. du Picq, *Battle Studies* (Harrisburg, PA: Military Service Publishing Company, 1946).

[3]Quoted at http://www.vectorsite.net/twcw50.html.

[4]J. K. Herr and Edmond S. Wallace, *The Story of the U.S. Cavalry, 1775–1942* (Boston: Bonanza Books, 1953), pp. 138–40.

[5]E. P. Alexander, *Military Memoirs of a Confederate* (New York: Scribner's, 1907), p. 53.

FIGURE 5

The Battle of Hoover's Gap

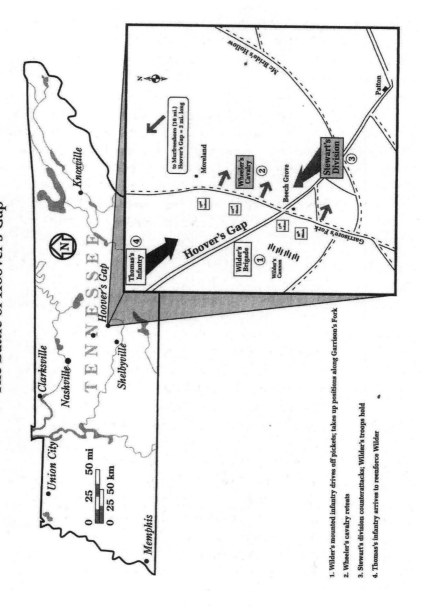

1. Wilder's mounted infantry drives off pickets; takes up positions along Garrison's Fork
2. Wheeler's cavalry retreats
3. Stewart's division counterattacks; Wilder's troops hold
4. Thomas's infantry arrives to reenforce Wilder

to Uncle Sam. Occasionally these businessmen/inventors had to fight through a military bureaucracy, but the fact that they succeeded so often says as much about the civilian side of American war fighting as it does the military. And for every Richard Gatling or Andrew Jackson Higgins who finally sold an important breakthrough weapon, dozens more had failed with lesser designs. That, too, represents a key strength in the military past of the Republic, for a willingness to tolerate failure—to permit experimentation, no matter how unorthodox— is essential to a climate of creativity that top-down totalitarians and non-Western warlords have lacked.

Private-Sector Power

The man who invented the decisive weapon that Wilder's men used at Hoover's Gap, Christopher Spencer, had encountered great resistance by the Union government to purchasing his advanced rifle, even though it had passed its tests with flying colors in 1861 and 1862. Part of the problem was that Spencer had to compete amid a blizzard of other private sector designs, and the War Department officials—mostly bean counters—had difficulty penetrating the numerous alternatives with any strategic insight. Joel Poinsett, the secretary of war in 1840, admitted that when it came to the introduction of breechloaders over muzzle-loaders, he "*discountenance[d]*" all "*new inventions*" unless "*long-tried experiments in the field*" convinced him otherwise.[6] Poinsett feared "*every attempt [at developing a breech-loading rifle] will fail… involving the government in great expense.*"[7] It is a recurring theme in American history that free-market entrepreneurs frequently think ahead of the establishment military hierarchy, often precisely because their invention allows them to conceive of new strategies. Consequently, Union generals and procurement officers failed to see the revolutionary impact of the Spencer, and instead pointed to its weight (ten pounds) and its expense (more than $40 per rifle, contrasted with the $18 musket that a dozen contractors offered). To the extent that they did think about the strategic implications, the War Department procurement staff obsessed over the rate of fire for the new weapon—as the Army would do again during the Vietnam era when the M16 was introduced—and they, correctly, fretted about the potential cost of ammunition. Only through a small contract with the Navy did Spencer's company stay in business (just as one hundred years later, it was only through the acquisition of the M16 by the Air Force that the U.S. Army got its new combat rifle).[8] Finally, General George B. McClellan placed an order for ten thousand, but Spencer fell behind an impossibly tight schedule, and it appeared his rifle was doomed.

[6]S. V. Benet, ed., *Annual Reports and Other Important Papers Relating to the Ordnance Department*, vol. 1 (Washington, D.C.: Government Printing Office, 1878), 381–82; I. B. Holley, Jr., *Technology and Military Doctrine: Essays on a Challenging Relationship* (Maxwell Air Force Base, AL: Air University Press, 2004), p. 58.

[7]Poinsett quoted in *Holley, Technology and Military Doctrine,* p. 58.

[8]Thomas McNaugher, *The M-16 Controversies: Military Organizations and Weapons Acquisition* (Greenwich, CT: Praeger, 1984).

By that time, Spencer held no financial interest in the company; he had sold his patent for $1 per weapon sold. Still, he worked to make the enterprise a success, designing the guns and even the equipment needed to manufacture them. And above all, he actively marketed his rifles, with his most famous sale coming just two months after Hoover's Gap when he met with Abraham Lincoln. Earlier, Lincoln had personally test-fired a Spencer on two occasions, and each time the weapon had malfunctioned. The president even halted the distribution of the Spencer to some units, but in August, after a preliminary meeting in which Spencer explained the specific earlier problems to the president's satisfaction, he and Lincoln fired the rifle for an hour near the Washington Monument, and Spencer closed the deal. Within two months, the company was selling not only large numbers of rifles, but also its new carbine model—the perfect cavalry weapon, as Wilder's men proved.

But it wasn't just Spencer: John Ericsson, Thomas Rodman, Richard Gatling, and dozens of other inventors and innovators churned out a seemingly unending stream of weapons that gave the North a decisive edge in the war. Their achievements, combined with Northern manufacturing advantages, testified to the power of private markets, even when the ultimate customer was the government. Richard Bensel has likened this to the Union government skimming off the top of a free-market bonanza, and has argued that the south, cosigned largely to government foundries, armories, and even salt production, lost the war in part because it suffered from "big government."[9] Not surprisingly, even the Confederacy, when it managed to top the North in creating a new weapon, purchased it from private inventors, not the government, as in the case of Horace Lawson Hunley's hand-cranked submarine that bore his name. Hunley developed the submarine design on his own, and had received a bill of marque from the Confederate government before being forced to flee from New Orleans as the Union armies approached. Hunley and other developers, including Richard McCormick, financed the Hunley themselves, although Hunley died during its sea trials. (Some sixty other Confederate sailors died during the sea trials as well.) Ultimatley, the North had more Hunleys—and Gatlings, Ericssons, Sharps, and Spencers—than did the Confederacy, which, all things being equal, would have produced a victory by itself. What the South did have was slavery, which discouraged both manufacturing and making marginal improvements on implements, as well as the idea of free men doing manual labor, thus putting the Confederacy at a significant disadvantage.

Unleashing the private sector proved a key weapon in the American way of war, dating back to the Revolution, when the British marveled at the colonial musket, "a handsome construction, and entirely manufactured in America."[10] More impressive was the Pennsylvania long rifle, a .50 caliber weapon deadly accurate at three hundred yards. Most early weapons came from private artisans,

---

[9]Richard F. Bensel, *Yankee Leviathan: The Origins of Central State Authority in America, 1859–1877* (New York: Cambridge University Press, 1990).

[10]Admiral Howe's secretary, Ambrose Serle quoted in David Hackett Fischer, *Washington's Crossing* (Oxford: Oxford University Press, 2004), p. 23.

but even before Eli Whitney's musket factory, small manufacturing operations churned out guns, cannons, swords, and other arms in significant quantities. More than any other entrepreneur, Whitney brought the United States onto an even field with England. His American System of mass production, based on innovative use of jigs, metal-cutting machines, and dies and molds allowed him to employ a largely unskilled (but trainable) workforce, using a simple design to crank out muskets. His most impressive machine, an iron-cutting gear with chisel teeth (known as a milling machine), would trace along the template and cut out parts, each one identical to the last because, like a pattern on a dress, each was cut to the same pattern. The device itself was a marvel, but the concept behind it was even more impressive. Nevertheless, Whitney failed to deliver the twelve thousand muskets at just over $13 per musket in two years as his contract required, but he did eventually deliver them and in the process revolutionized American production. (It should be noted that, like other manufacturers, Whitney suffered from the poor cost accounting that plagued early inventors and government contractors.)

Raised on his father's farm, where he spent a great deal of time in the workshop, the Yale-educated Whitney moved to South Carolina to tutor the children of Phineas Miller, a fellow Yalie. His first fame came when he developed a machine for separating the seed from cotton fibers, a process that previously had taken an hour per pound. Devising a machine with rollers that had teeth and another roller with a brush, Whitney invented the cotton gin and increased production fifty-fold.[11] He then moved back to Connecticut and opened a small shop. Ironically, Thomas Jefferson—no fan of a standing army—added impetus to Whitney's manufacturing concepts by cultivating interest in a concept he had seen in France, interchangeable parts. It had been Jefferson's advice that led presidents Washington and Adams to push through Congress a contract for Whitney in 1798. By then there were already two other private gunsmiths in New England who had started mass-producing muskets, including Simeon North, who built the first standardized milling machine. But like Henry Ford, who would come a century later, Whitney was superb at borrowing ideas and processes from anyone and everyone, mixing together a simple design with North's standardized parts and then mass-producing the guns.

Here was the private sector/government relationship at its best in weapons procurement: the government stated its need, and private businessmen met it. For a while, a cadre of revisionists claimed that federal armories originated the practice of mass production, which then spread to the private sector. In this thesis, "men left the arms business to set up the machine tool industry and [transferred the principles] to railroad equipment" and other products.[12] If this is true, virtually all governments would be like "America," and certainly the more centralized system of Germany would have led the way in the transfer of technology from the

[11]Constance McLaughlin Green, *Eli Whitney and the Birth of American Technology* (Boston: Little Brown, 1956).

[12]David F. Noble, "Command Performance: A Perspective on the Social and Economic Consequences of Military Enterprise," in Merritt Roe Smith, ed., *Military Enterprise and Technological Change: Perspectives in the American Experience* (Cambridge, MA: MIT Press, 1985), p. 337.

military sector to civilian uses. More important, the thesis falls apart under the weight of evidence. Donald Hoke has studied technology in early America and concluded that the "*American System is primarily and overwhelmingly **a private sector phenomenon** [emphasis in original].*"[13] In everything from clock technology to, later, typewriters, the private sector adopted concepts, processes, and structures that were the passed on to the government.

But in the early nineteenth century, there appeared a large network of private entrepreneurs, such as Samuel Colt, who designed new weapons and hoped to anticipate changes in the technology and government needs. Of course, many guessed wrong—Colt's revolver, for example, was not accepted for more than a decade after he introduced it. Born in Whitney's Connecticut, Colt showed mechanical genius at an early age. As a child he constantly disassemble and reassembled his father's rifles and pistols, then, on a trip to India in 1830, while observing the ship's paddle wheel, Colt carved a wooden model of a "revolver"—a handgun with a revolving cylinder capable of firing several shots without reloading.[14] He patented his design in 1836, but early demonstrations for the government failed to impress, partly because the Army's generals held a deep-seated dread that men with the ability to rapidly fire would waste ammunition. Well into the 1960s, the "marksmanship" school of Army thinkers battled the "firepower" school, with the former arguing that semiautomatic (then later, fully automatic) weapons would seriously harm the ideal of "one shot, one kill." Unfortunately for Colt, who when insufficient orders came in, had to close his factory in 1842, whereupon he toured the country as a chemical expert named Doctor Coult, giving demonstrations in nitrous oxide (laughing gas).[15]

Colt continued to work with firearms and an antiship mine, even staging a demonstration in 1844, when he used a telemagnetic cable to blow up a five-hundred-ton schooner sailing down the Potomac.[16] Still, Colt's revolvers had not found a significant market—until the Texas Rangers fought a battle with Indians where they were outnumbered five to one. Armed with Colt five-shot pistols made before the Colt factory closed, the Rangers drove the enemy off, and they sang the praises of the pistols so loudly that finally the War Department issued a contract for a thousand revolvers. Ironically, now that Colt lacked a factory, he leased one—from Eli Whitney, Jr. At his Hartford factory, Colt installed "*over a thousand belt-driven machines that allowed him to produce a revolver that was*

[13]Donald Hoke, *Ingenious Yankees: the Rise of the American System of Manufactures in the Private Sector* (New York: Columbia University Press, 1969), and his "Product Design and Cost Considerations: Clock, Watch, and Typewriter Manufacturing in the 19th Century," in Williams J. Hauseman, ed., E*ssays in Business and Economic History*, 2nd series, 18, 1989, pp. 119–28 (quotation on 120). Hoke effectively refutes David Noble, Merrit Roe Smith, and David Hounshell. See Smith, *Harpers Ferry Armory and the New Technology* (Ithaca: Cornell University Press, 1977) and Hounshell, *From the American System to Mass Production* (Baltimore: Johns Hopkins University Press, 1984).
[14]William B. Edwards, *The Story of Colt's Revolver: The Biography of Col. Samuel Colt* (Harrisburg, PA.: Stackpole Co., 1953); Henry Barnard, *Armsmear: The Home, the Arm, and the Armory of Samuel Colt, a Memorial* (New York: C. A. Alvord, 1866), p. 276.
[15]Larry Schweikart, *The Entrepreneurial Adventure: A History of Business in the United States* (Fort Worth, TX: Harcourt, 2000), pp. 73–74.
[16]Schwiekart, *Entrepreneurial Adventure*, p. 74.

80 percent machine made."[17]   Still, the bureaucrats remained intractable: one Ordnance Bureau colonel said that all of Colt's arms "*will ultimately all pass into oblivion*"—speaking of a carbine that fired fourteen thousand rounds before it broke![18]   His designs and production processes surpassed anything the British had, so much so that they invited him to establish a factory on the Thames. Colt obliged, and the British welcomed him as an industrial giant, labeling him "Colonel Colt, a Thunderbolt." Yet even before colt agreed to share some of his techniques with the British, Whitney had already declined such an invitation. Or, put another way, American production processes had already outstripped Britain's in gun making some twenty-five years before Colt traveled there!

Armed Americans

Even before Colt's revolvers appeared on the scene, Americans were awash in weapons. The only question is how well armed America's citizen soldiers were. In the highly discredited book Arming America, Michael Bellesiles made a splash with the antigun lobby by claiming that guns were far less common in the colonies and the young Republic than has been thought.[19]   Among other assertions, Bellesiles argued that marksmanship was poor and that most American males barely knew how to load a weapon.[20]   Clayton Cramer has dismantled Bellesiles' evidence, in the process providing an effective record of a truly armed America. In colonial times, statutes required that militiamen supply their own arms. Many colonies (then states) established fines for militiamen who did not have sufficient powder and a firearm. Some colonies provided for a general store of arms, although the public had full access to these guns, and in Massachusetts, Maryland, and Connecticut, individuals were required to have guns in their residences. By 1806, according to a federal census, there were at least 132,000 guns in federal armories, a number that did not include an additional 250,000 guns in private hands and all guns in state magazines![21]   And even that number is laughably low, as it only included those guns appropriate for militia duty, thereby excluding rifles, pocket pistols, and fowling pieces.

In short, half a decade before the War of 1812, there were probably half a million weapons in the United States in either private possession or government armories. Often, governors like William Claiborne, who fretted about having enough guns for their militias, would write entirely different reports after actually reviewing the militia: "*the prospect of having a well-armed militia, exceeds my most sanguine expectations*," Claiborne noted when the men finally arrived.[22]

[17]C. Joseph Pusateri, *A History of American Business,* 2nd ed. (Arlington Height, IL: Harlan-Davidson, 1988), p. 157.

[18]Benet, *Annual Reports,* vol. 2,pp. 3–4.

[19]Michael A. Bellesiles, *Arming America: The Origins of a National Gun Culture* (New York: Alfred A. Knopf, 2000).

[20]See Clayton Cramer's devastating critique of Arming America, "Firearms Ownership and Manufacturing in Early America," available at http://www.claytoncramer.com/ArmingAmericaLong pdf.

[21]Cramer, "Firearms Ownership," p. 125.

[22]Quoted in Cramer, "Firearms Ownership." p. 131.

The New Orleans militia had already been training twice a week by mid-October.[23] It is true some men showed up for muster without a musket or rifle. But that did not mean there were no guns, but rather that the militiaman had to purchase one owned by the state. In Louisiana, for example, unarmed recruits had to pay $14 for a musket obtained from the federal government. And while it is true that federal muskets requested by governors often arrived in a state of disrepair, again which did not mean that the soldiers went without guns. Quite the contrary, governors sold muskets in need of repair to local gunsmiths and purchased new, often better, rifled guns.

Far from an unarmed nation, a thriving arms market existed in the young Republic. Frontier Kentucky alone had six powder manufacturers in 1807, and in 1810, the United States exported 1.3 million pounds of gunpowder a year.[24] Census records were notoriously incomplete, and the amount of powder in the nation, both produced and held in private hands, was severely understated. In addition, firearms historian Cramer argues that the number of privately owned guns were seriously understated in public records.[25]

Moreover, the quality of American guns increasingly was the equal of anything made in Europe. For example, rifled barrels and sights on pistols were not present on British-made pistols. The arrival of the arms industry in America marked the final step in a journey of firearms manufacturing that began in China with gunpowder, traveled through the Muslim world to Italy, which, by the late 1400s, had become the crucible of early cannon manufacturing (due to its advanced brass-casting techniques, used in church bells).[26] Within two hundred years, the center of gravity shifted again, to northern Europe and Sweden, which became renowned under Gustavus Adolphus for its cannon making. Then the technological momentum moved to England, with its enormous coal reserves and ore deposits, on which the Industrial Revolution was based.

By 1814, however, the United States had rapidly closed the gap and, in some cases, surpassed Britain as the font of invention and the locus of cutting-edge manufacturing, not just in arms, but in entire fields of manufacturing. English advantages in textile production and milling started to erode even without help to American producers from the federal government. Of course, the essentially English nature of much of the United States facilitated a rapid technology transfer, but most of it seemed to flow from the British Isles to America's Atlantic Coast. Samuel Slater, for example, came to America from England in 1789 to start his own spinning mills. He eventually controlled half the spindles in the United States.[27] Slater had worked on Richard Arkwright's spinning machines in England, where he memorized the technology and learned the techniques. After

[23]Charles B. Brooks, *The Siege of New Orleans* (Seattle: University of Washington Press, 1961), p. 58.

[24]Albert Gallatin, *A Statement of the Arts and Manufactures of the United States of America* (Philadelphia: A. Cornman, 1812), p. 33.

[25]Cramer, "Firearms Ownership," p. 252.

[26]See William H. McNeill, *The Pursuit of Power: Technology, Armed Force, and Society Since A.D. 1000* (Chicago: University of Chicago Press, 1982).

[27]Schweikart, Entrepreneurial Adventure, 78; Barbara M. Tucker, Samuel Slater and the Origins of the American Textile Industry, 1790–1860 (Ithaca, N.Y.: Cornell University Press, 1984).

arriving in the United States, Slater worked in a small New York mill, then met Moses Brown, a Providence, Rhode Island, manufacturer who specialized in candles but who also specialized in capital. Brown and his associates saw in Slater the expertise they needed to mass-produce textiles. It is essential to understand to understand the interconnected nature of technology when it comes to civilian/military transfers: innovations in camshafts and crankshafts that powered the textile mills eventually found their way into other manufacturing processes (indeed, it was Swiss clock making's gear-and-tooth technology that undergirded western Europe's advantage in musket making in the first place). In the young United States, locksmiths, gunmakers, and clockmakers were often the same person! Dies and molds that enabled Slater to mass-produce cotton fabrics were easily adapted to musket production, then spun around conceptually to improve spinning technology, ad infinitum.

In the days of slater, Whitney, and Colt, there was time for a young nation to fall behind its enemies technologically and still recover. This was especially true of the United States. Americans found that even if their businesses were not producing weapons when a conflict erupted, they could rely on a growing industrial base of foundational materials, especially iron, coal, copper, than later, steel, to crank out the materials needed to manufacture weapons at astounding rates. But America was also unduly dependent on England for certain basics of arms manufacturing, including gunlocks, which were imported extensively. The U.S. government hoped to develop complete economic independence from England, and succeeded. Although the United States started later than England in the Industrial Revolution, by 1912, it produced twice as much steel as France, Great Britain, and Germany combined.[28] Advances in steel, especially, made it possible for the United States to rapidly catch up to European rivals in shipbuilding in the late 1800s.

More than iron and steel was involved in developing military-industrial dominance: it took visionary people, men like Herman Haupt, a West Point graduate who worked for J. Edgar Thompson's Pennsylvania Railroad, where he helped develop intricate, effective management systems. Haupt was one of those who appreciated the logistical value of railroads, although he never went so far as did Charles Caldwell, a Bostonian who saw the railroad as a deterrent to war. Caldwell claimed that the railroad would "do much toward the suppression of war in general, a thousand fold more than all the peace and Missionary Societies."[29] Haupt knew wars would come, and when they did, nothing could move men and equipment faster than a rail network. During the Civil War, he arrived in Washington to support General George McClellan's Peninsular campaign, quickly achieving a reputation for accomplishing the impossible. Haupt's men rebuilt a four-hundred-foot-long bridge over the Potomac Creek in nine days.[30] Promoted

[28]David Stevenson, Cataclysm: *The First World War as Political Tragedy* (New York: Basic Books, 2004), p. 27.
[29]Robert G. Angevine, *The Railroad and the State: War, Politics and Technology in Nineteenth-Century America* (Stanford: Stanford University Press, 2004), p. 55.
[30]Francis A. Lord, *Lincoln's Railroad Man: Herman Haupt* (Rutherford, NJ: Fairleigh Dickenson University

to colonel and put in charge of all military railroads under the Department of the Rappahannock, he thrived until General John Pope relegated his department to the Quartermaster Department in 1862. A disgusted Haupt left, only to be brought back when railroad traffic stalled and trains backed up. Given authority as a brigadier general over all the railroads under Union control in Virginia, Haupt gave the Union a consistent critical advantage in logistics. At Gettysburg, Haupt's railroad agents were the first to determine the intent of Lee's movements, leading Haupt to send the following telegram to General George Mead:

> Union Intelligence Report
> General Haupt to Baltimore & Washington. Information just received, 12:45 A.M., leads to the belief that the concentration of the forces of the enemy will be at Gettysburg rather than Chambersburg. The movement on their part is very rapid and hurried. They returned from Carlisle in the direction of Gettysburg by way of the Petersburg Pike.[31]

Haupt provided the Union with a massive logistical edge, and his railroad lines gave the North an important intelligence advantage. Just as Americans in World War II had an affinity for motor vehicles, Haupt frequently used professional railroaders, who needed no special training, saving the North countless hours of instruction. Like so many other northern West Point-trained engineers, Haupt went into private railroad construction after the war.

Maintaining an industrial base in times of peace always proved a challenge. Prior to the Civil War, the United States had kept abreast of naval technology, and at times even bested Great Britain in introducing new concepts or gadgets. After all, an American, John Fitch, had demonstrated the first steamboat in 1787, and another American, Robert Fulton, showed how to make steamships practical and profitable. Fulton was even designing a forty-four-gun steamship, the Demologos, for the U.S. government when the War of 1812 ended, leaving him with no funds—and no boat. John Ericsson, who designed the ironclad Monitor during the Civil War, sold his first iron-screw designs to the British Admiralty in 1842. An American steam warship plied even the Great Lakes in the 1840s, and the first battle of ironclads, of course, took place at Hampton Roads, Virginia, in 1862. Then, after the fury of war subsided, funds dried up. In the 1860s, one of the most advanced ships in the world, the USS Wampanoag, with its steam power, armored turrets, and seventeen-knot speed, was tied to a pier and left to rot. As Americans focused on issues of Reconstruction and Custer's travails on the Great Plains, the massive U.S. Navy dwindled into obsolescence, becoming a punch line in Oscar Wilde's Canterville Ghost. When Virginia, who befriends the ghost, says that Americans are boring because "*we have no ruins and no curiosities,*" the Canterville Ghost replies, "*You have your navy and your manners.*"

Over time, aggressive Navy secretaries and advocates of sea power re-

---

Press, 1969); James A. Ward, *That Man Haupt: A Biography of Herman Haupt* (Baton Rouge: Louisiana State University Press, 1973).

[31]Herman Haupt to George Meade, July 1, 1863, http://www.geocities.com/Heartland/Lake/3234/HaupttpMeade.html. See also Robert Angevine, The Railroad and the State, pp. 135–36.

started the industrial base for shipbuilding, finally passing the Naval Appropri-
ation Act of 1883, which funded the A,B,C,D ships (the light cruisers, Atlanta,
Boston, Chicago, and the dispatch vessel Dolphin). This act also established the
Army-Navy Gun Foundry Board to develop armor-piercing rounds for use against
ships.[32] Seven years later, the Naval Act of 1890 authorized funding for sea-go-
ing, coastline battleships, meaning they had a limited five-thousand-nautical-mile
range. Still, the Indiana, Massachusetts, and Oregon were impressive vessels,
each with four thirteen-inch guns. By 1896, six more battleships were authorized:
the Kearsarge, Kentucky, Iowa, Alabama, Illinois, and Wisconsin. Although these
ships' designs often came from abroad and had some serious flaws—they needed
constant refueling and road too low in the water—they were durable and more
advanced then what many of our enemies could deploy, and they provided the
basis for the naval victories in the Spanish-American War. It had taken close to
thirty-five years, but the U.S. Navy finally recovered the quality—if not size—that
it had at the end of the Civil War. Even when the British superbattleship Dread-
nought went into the water in 1906, the United States had several battleships under construction with designs that were every bit as advanced.

None of this would have been possible without the remarkable contributions of a die-hard pacifist, Andrew Carnegie. A Scotsman who came to America
penniless at age thirteen, he worked menial jobs as a bobbin boy, toiled twelve
hours a day for $1.20 a week, and, above all, kept his eye on the ball.[33] He al-
ready was earning more than his father at age sixteen, and impressed his boss,
Thomas Scott, the district superintendent of the Pennsylvania Railroad, with his
ability to translate Morse code without writing it down. Scott educated Carnegie
in the stock market and advanced him some money to invest. Carnegie quickly
made a small fortune, then, looking at trends, concluded that the boom industry
was railroads, which led him to bridges, which led him to iron and steel. Like
other brilliant entrepreneurs of the day (including Gustavus Swift and James J.
Hill), Carnegie was obsessed with cutting costs, and his managers applied his
principles. Charles Schwab, who became a leading steelman in his own right,
redesigned Carnegie's rail-finishing department so that it trimmed ten cents per
ton of steel, while Carnegie's other managers scoured far and wide for new techniques. Equally important, Carnegie's managers were all innovators, some of
them top inventors in their own right, including Julian Kennedy, who had more
than 150 patents on steel-related production. Another Carnegie manager, Captain
Bill Jones, who had learned from the great Alexander Holley, while hardly in
Kennedy's league as a tinkerer, nevertheless made significant technological contributions to steelmaking. His Jones mixer *"dramatically speeded up production
by eliminating sand casting and providing a virtually uninterrupted flow of pig
iron from the blast furnaces to the Bessemer converters."* [34]

[32]Harold and Margaret Sprout, *The Rise of American Naval Power, 1776–1918* (Princeton: Princeton University
Press, 1966).

[33]Joseph Wall, *Andrew Carnegie* (New York: Oxford University Press, 1970); Andrew Carnegie, Autobiography of Andrew Carnegie (Boston: Houghton Mifflin, 1920).

[34]Stuart Leslie, "Andrew Carnegie," in Paul Pascoff, ed., *Encyclopedia of American Business History and*

Thanks to his business savvy to acquire his own raw materials and hire exceptional managers, Carnegie rapidly drove steel prices down with higher production. Whenever his plants beat a record, Carnegie smiled, patted the men on the shoulder, then squinted at them, saying only, "*More!*" One superintendent wired him that his plant had turned out an unprecedented amount of steel in a week. Carnegie wired back, "*Congratulations. Why not do it every week?*" Along with the introduction of better steelmaking processes, such as the Bessemer furnace, Carnegie's steel company pushed down the cost of making rails from $28.00 to $11.50 per ton between 1880 and 1900. The cost for ship steel fell proportionally, most of it driven by Bethlehem Steel's efficient production. Did Carnegie want into that market? Until 1887, the Scotsman stayed away from steel-plate bids. He thought the profits too low, and it seemed counter to his pacifism. But by 1889, when construction of the New York and the Maine was delayed, the secretary of the Navy, Benjamin Tracy, appealed directly to Carnegie with an exceptionally large contract. Carnegie set aside his pacifism, admitting "*there may be millions for us in armor.*"[35] Still, he delayed entering the armor-plate market until Tracy threatened to buy steel from the British; Carnegie was in. Purchasing land close to the Homestead, Pennsylvania, steel plant, Carnegie built a new armor-plate forging plant, winning a contract for three battleships in 1890. When Charles Schwab quit U.S. Steel after J. P. Morgan bought out Carnegie, Schwab improved Bethlehem Steel so rapidly that within ten years it was U.S. Steel's major competitor, also specializing in heavy armor plating for the Navy.

Not surprisingly, the more that private entrepreneurs supplied to the government, the more that legislators feared they were being fleeced. Investigating "merchants of death," "speculators," and "gougers" provided high theater in Washington. Whenever politicians needed a target, arms manufacturers were an easy mark. Often, they threatened to build their own facilities, and did, usually at higher costs than the private sector had provided. When the U.S. Navy began its large shipbuilding program in the 1880s, only three steel companies—Carnegie, Bethlehem, and Midvale—made armor plate. Obviously, a potential for monopoly existed, but the bottom line was the bottom line: it cost much less to produce iron and steel for railroads than it did to make ship siding. Making appearances worse, domestic producers charged foreign customers less because the tariffs abroad were so high. All of that came out of the profit margins, however. The government countered that it would go into the armor-plate business itself, to which Charles Schwab warned that no government factory could make siding as inexpensively as private companies.[36] A further schism between the Navy and the builders occurred when a company submitted the lowest bid and won the contract—but not all of it. Frequently, the Navy offered the losers a small part of the

Biography: The Iron and Steel Industry in the Nineteenth Century (New York: Facts on File, 1989), p. 59.
[35]Peter Krass, *Carnegie* (New York: John Wiley & Sons, 2002), p. 259
[36]Burton Folsom, Jr., *The Myth of the Robber Barons: A New Look at the Rise of Big Business in America* (Hearndon, VA: Young Americas foundation, 1991), p. 75; Robert Seager, "Ten Years Before Mahan: The Unofficial Case for the New Navy, 1880–1890," Mississippi Valley Historical Review, 60 (December 1953), 491–p. 512.

contract (at the lowest bid) to keep them in business should the nation need them in the future. Here was one of the origins of the problems associated with the military industrial complex of the Cold War era: in private competition, one unstated goal is to become so efficient that you drive competitors out of business, but in matters of national security, the government could not afford to have monopoly providers.

Steel companies responded by submitting nearly identical bids, which on the eve of World War I convinced Josephus Daniels, Woodrow Wilson's secretary of the navy, that the government could make armor plate cheaper than the private sector, perhaps as low as $300 a ton (when the steel companies were charging $454 per ton). After a heated battle in which Charles Schwab attempted to defeat the bill authorizing a plate-armor plant, in 1917 the government chose South Charleston, West Virginia, as the winning location for a $17.5 million facility to make guns and armor. The plant was not ready for World War I, and by the time it opened in 1921, its prices were well above those of Schwab's Bethlehem Steel, just as Schwab had warned. Within a year, the plant shut down, a fitting testament to the superiority of the free market over government facilities.

Just as in the Civil war, when John D. Rockefeller (who had to support a sickly mother and six siblings, and paid a substitute) outfitted an entire regiment at his own expense and paid the living allowances of substitutes' families, in World War I the private sector also played a much-overlooked role in supplying the Allies. The Allied Purchasing Commission (a J. P. Morgan-originated bank) purchased $10 million in war material every day by private individuals for use by the Allies, making Morgan the single largest consumer in history, and, arguably, the one man who did the most to keep the troops supplied during the entire war.[37]

The Military Industrial Complex Bogeyman

Ensuring that competition existed in those industries that supplied weapons constituted one of the main problems of government/private sector relations when it came to maintaining a wartime industrial base in peacetime. Until the Cold War, Americans had been loath to spend on their military. In 1923, the United States spent six times more on soda and sugar than it did on the Army—by 2005 it had "shrunk" to only three times as much—and the experience of building weapons on a moment's notice in World War I led to the establishment of the Army Industrial College. Created to train officers in the techniques of procurement and mobilization, the Army Industrial College was later expanded to include other services as the Industrial College of the Armed Forces under the direction of the Joint Chiefs of Staff. With each successive war, Americans found that closing a technological gap became more difficult, and more expensive to catch up. Whereas in the 1700s, American Continentals could acquire enough weapons to equip and army in time it took British sips laden with troops to sail across the

[37]Mac Wortman, *The Millionaires' Unit: The Aristocratic Flyboys Who Fought the Great War and Invented American Air Power* (New York: Public Affairs, 2006), p. 47.

Atlantic, by World War II the capacity of industrialized enemies to steal a march on us technologically grew so pronounced that the threat of a Nazi bomb prodded Franklin Roosevelt to authorize the Manhattan Project. Later, of course, the potential capacity of rogue nations to make or acquire WMDs (weapons of mass destruction) led President George W. Bush to invade Iraq. And at no time was the response window, the time between when we learned of a new enemy weapon and developed a technological or conceptual counter to it, more acute than during the latter years of the Cold War, when each side raced to deploy cutting-edge technology.

Although President Dwight Eisenhower warned about the so-called military industrial complex, the Left picked up the slogan and embraced it. Perennial critics such as Frances Fox Piven have argued that military conflicts are just a subterfuge for, in essence, screwing the poor. *"The current wars,"* she contended, *"were promoted—and fed—by the powerful U.S. military establishment"* and the *"business interests backing [the neoconservative] agenda."*[38] *"War fever,"* she concluded, *"obscured the multiple ways that the Bush regime was the agent for business plunder."*[39] The good news is that screed such as Piven's has found smaller and smaller audiences. The bad news is, this kind of drivel is repeated by al Quaeda, whose propaganda assures us that the United States *"seeks to ravage the entire globe for the interest ... of corporate companies,"* and so kills the sons of Islam *"in Palestine, Afghanistan, the Balkans, Indonesia, the Caucuses, and elsewhere."*[40] *"War for oil"* is not only the mantra of the American Left, but, apparently, is also the staple of our terrorist enemies.

There is also this reality: if capitalism does not cause wars, then the only other culprit is government. World War I remains a stark reminder that even democratic majorities can push modern nations to war with little assistance from the "merchants of death." And while it is true that a few arms vendors make money preparing for war, an actual conflict only kills consumers and destroys factories, while at the same time resulting in government-imposed price controls (or worse).

Nevertheless, it remains a staple of left-wing ideology that there is a military industrial complex that pulls the strings behind most administrations (and all Republican administrations) and detonates periodic wars to boost profits. Little evidence exists to support either of those notions, save for the fact that some businesses do make money by supplying the government with arms, just as some make profits selling the government toilet paper. What is remarkable about the American system is its preference for using the private sector whenever possible. On occasion this has required innovative indirect forms of government support. Usually, if the market is pitted against a government-subsidized company or individual, the privately financed option wins. The Wright Brothers, having received no money from the government, bested Samuel Langley, who had a $50,000 sub-

[38]Frances Fox Piven, *The War at Home: The Domestic Costs of Bush's Militarism* (New York: New Press, 2004), pp. 1–2.

[39]Piven, *The War at Home*, p. 62.

[40]Quoted in Victor Davis Hanson, "Keep Quiet and Listen," National Review Online, August 12, 2005, at http://www.nationalreview.com/hanson/hanson200508120813.asp.

sidy, to make the first airplane. But in peacetime, maintaining an industrial base of defense-related products without government support was impossible. After World War I, for example, most aviation experts realized that air power would play a central role in any future conflict; therefore, maintaining the nation's aircraft manufacturing base was critical. Rather than directly subsidize a couple of aircraft builders, the government encouraged a higher level of private sector involvement by offering mail contracts through the U.S. postal system. This allowed the aircraft companies to build civilian planes rather than military aircraft and, in the process, begin to attract Americans to flying as a common type of transportation. That, in turn, supported infant airlines until the passenger market evolved, creating a civilian airline industry. Admittedly, the industry was heavily dependent on government mail contracts, and those came with a price; namely, the postmaster general attempted to influence internal management decisions and tried to dictate airframe and engine design on the grounds of reducing the government's costs.[41] Such interference was only acceptable on the grounds of national defense. By supporting the aircraft manufacturers in the tumultuous twenties, the government allowed the private sector to remain competitive long enough to build the desperately needed bombers and fighter planes of World War II. Mail contracts likewise later subsidized Juan Trippe's Pan American Airways as he forced-fed jet engines into the civilian airline business without notifying the government of his grand design.

On the other hand, the obsession with competitive bids, so as to ensure competition led to early errors in the contracting process. Howard Hughes's antics provided a constant challenge to the Army in the 1960s when his Hughes Aircraft Company put in abnormally low (indeed, intentionally fraudulent) bids on helicopters, offering them for about $19,000 each, or some $10,000 below Hughes's cost. Hughes planned a buy-in, which was a practice forbidden by the Department of Defense because it inevitably ensured that the manufacturer would raise prices after receiving the contract.[42] His competitor, Hiller Aircraft, submitted a bid 50 percent higher, so the Army gave Hughes Aircraft the contract—much to its dismay later when the company simply could not keep up with demand and, even then, only for much more money. Two years after receiving the sole-source contract, Hughes tried to bump his price up to almost $56,000, or nearly 200 percent over the contracted amount. Although slow to move, the government finally shifted production to Bell Helicopter, after Hughes had pumped his own fortune into the helicopter business. It was, he admitted, a "miscalculation"—of $90 million—but by that time Hughes was approaching the utter lunacy of his later life, when he had an assistant on call, twenty-four hours a day, merely to give him enemas![43]

The experience with Hughes and other companies who had mastered the

[41]F. Robert van der Linden, *Airlines and Air Mail: The Post Office and the Birth of the Commercial Aviation Industry* (Lexington: University Press of Kentucky, 2002), passim, but especially pp. 243–70.

[42]Donald L. Barlett and James B. Steele, *Howard Hughes: His Life and Madness* (New York: Norton, 1979), pp. 348–64.

[43]Barlett and Steele, *Howard Hughes,* pp. 537–40.

buy-in revived an old problem that vexed the government: if bidders who submitted higher bids are rewarded with some share of the winner's contract, why should lower bidders bid in the first place? On the other hand, if companies submitted bids that later proved to be disastrously low, but by virtue of being so, had driven other competitors out of the market, how could the government not keep other suppliers around? Congress and the Pentagon fixed part of the problem by law, whereby unrealistically low bids were rejected outright. While at times that might punish the innovator who had a brilliant new cost-saving process, most of the time it prevented contractors from "pulling a Hughes." New attention was paid to estimating costs of new programs, and to building reality into all proposals. While both contractors and the government still made mistakes, it was not for a lack of green-eyeshade types poring over proposals and bids.

For every Hughes who, at times, played the system, there was an Andrew Jackson Higgins or Henry Kaiser who delivered far more than the nation could have expected. Overall, the U.S. military benefited from the constant wave of investment, research, and innovation that came from the private sector. Just as it was Benjamin Holt's caterpillar tractor that led Colonel Ernest Swinton of the Royal Engineers to pioneer the first tank, so too it was a free-market idea from the American Bantam Car Company that led to the rugged Jeep.[44] In World War II, American entrepreneurs and builders would rise to the occasion as never before, burying the Axis powers in a tidal wave of production and invention. While mundane and unglamorous trucks and landing craft provided the critical advantage, the first, and most notable, application of American manufacturing might came in the skies over Europe.

Ulundi in the Air

When Lord Chelmsford returned to Zululand in 1879 with a new invasion force following the disastrous loss of the entire 1,400 strong British contingent at Isandlwana, he marched straight toward the kraal of King Cetshwayo, taking care to stay in formation in order to form into a square if attacked. Chelmsford actually hoped to provoke the Zulus into charging the British positions, as they had at Isandlwana, for he would not make the same mistakes as Colonel Henry Pulleine. Moreover, Chelmsford had 8,000 men, ample ammunition, cannons, and Gatling guns. Cetshwayo had to choose between seeing his kraal sacked and food destroyed or challenging the British in the open filed. He chose the latter, and his forces were decimated: no Zulu came within thirty yards of the British square. As odd as the comparisons seems, just over sixty years later, the United States Army Air Force would employ much the same strategy as Chelmsford did with the Zulus in its air assault on Nazi Germany, with much the same result.

Yet for years the Allied air success in Europe has been misunderstood or underestimated. In September 1945, the United States Strategic Bombing Sur-

---

[44]Niles White, "From Tractor to Tank," *Invention and Technology*, Fall 1993, pp. 58–63.

vey produced a dismal review of the effectiveness of the air campaign against Nazi Germany. Among pieces of evidence cited as proof of the limitations of air power, the survey noted that German production actually increased between 1942 and 1945.[45] The survey's conclusion provided grist for the mills of opponents of the Vietnam War, who, aware the United States did not intend to launch a ground initiative against North Vietnam, repeated the criticisms of strategic bombing as a means to force the United States out of Vietnam. It is one of the great myths that strategic bombing during the Second World War was ineffective, but what has clouded the discussion is the fact that the bombing campaign, in Europe especially, was effective, but in a far different way from that predicted or anticipated.[46] One recent analyst grudgingly admits that the German Ardennes offensive "sputtered to a halt" largely due to the air campaign—despite the presence of cloud cover that prevented direct air strikes during most of the Battle of the Bulge.[47] At the war's end, Stewart Ross notes that *the hundreds of brand-new German fighter aircraft, including jet-powered Messerschmitt 262s, that lined the fields alongside the Autobahns were paradoxes—testament to the inability of strategic bombing to disrupt their production, on the one hand, and to the bombers' successes in cutting off the fuel the Luftwaffe needed to train new pilots and fly defensive missions.*[48] In the Pacific theater, Japan had only five hundred modern fighters left by 1944, at a time when thousand-plane raids were occurring in Europe, forcing the Japanese to increasingly adopt kamikaze ramming missions in the air.[49] But even in Europe, American success was much deeper, and more complex, then even "realists" such as Ross admit. Misreading the "lessons" of strategic bombing therefore led Americans to misapply the history of World War II to Southeast Asia, in the process contributing to the fact that success there could never be achieved.

Proponents of air power often have been cast as unrealistic dreamers who saw the airplane as obviating the need for ground combat. The high priests of airpower—Billy Mitchell, Giulio Douhet, and Isoroku Yamamoto—seldom saw their views embraced by their contemporaries, and occasionally found themselves painted as fanatics. Douhet spent time in prison for criticizing the Italian government's policies in World War I, and Mitchell was court-martialed for charging the Navy and War departments with "criminal negligence" for failing to keep equipment maintained and refusing to provide weather stations for air bases.

Mitchell had already antagonized the Navy establishment when he staged a stunning demonstration of air power in 1921. His aircraft sank, in order, a submarine, a destroyer, a cruiser, then the supposedly unsinkable captured German battleship Ostriesland and the obsolete U.S. battleship Atlanta. Two years later he followed up those demonstrations with successful bombings on another pair of

[45]"The United States Strategic Bombing Survey: Summary report (European War), September 30, 1945," at http://www.anesi.com/ussbs02.htm.

[46]Stewart H. Ross, *Strategic Bombing by the United States in World War II* (Jefferson, NC: McFarland & Co., 2003).

[47]Ross, *Strategic Bombing*, p. 9.

[48]Ross, *Strategic Bombing*, pp. 9–10.

[49]Ross, *Strategic Bombing*, pp. 172–75

obsolete battleships. Yet just as Mitchell's superiors excused or explained away his successes, so, too, he tended to ignore or minimize the potential obstacles involved in attacking an enemy who fights back. Mitchell's impressive demonstrations, inflated further by his own bombast and ego, led him to proclaim, "*Aircraft now in existence can find and destroy all classes of seacraft under war conditions with a negligible loss*."[50]   Obscured in Mitchell's claim was that finding and destroying "all classes" did not equal finding and destroying all units, or even significant numbers of units.

Oddly, Mitchell's enthusiasm for air power did not extend to a full endorsement of the aircraft carrier, mainly because he thought carriers themselves would be vulnerable to ground-based air attacks. Nevertheless, he predicted that the Empire of Japan would one day launch a war against the United States by attacking Pearl Harbor through carrier-based aircraft. For all his vision, Mitchell underestimated the effectiveness of antiaircraft fire, the lethality of interceptor aircraft, and the difficulty of bombing hardened ground targets. There were limits to the armor ships could carry, but communications bunkers and even industrial targets could be covered by several feet of earth or hidden in caves.

Largely missing in the analysis of American bombing was the real devastation it wreaked on not only the Luftwaffe, but on German war resources overall. German munitions czar Albert Speer, while dismissing the effectiveness of the British night attacks, concluded, "*The American attacks, which followed a definite system of assault on industrial targets, were by far the most dangerous. It was in fact these attacks which caused the breakdown of the German armaments industry* [emphasis mine]."[51]   From 1942 to early 1943, this came at a high price: American bombers, without fighter escorts, suffered extreme losses. Even then, however, the Nazis found that they had to dedicate increasing resources to purely anti-bombing missions—not just fighter aircraft and fuel, but searchlights, anti-aircraft guns, intelligence, and so on. By mid-1943, the Germans had assigned nearly 21 percent of their fighters to interceptor missions alone, most of them on the western front; by 1944, the Americans and the British had a 30:1 aircraft advantage over the Luftwaffe in the skies above Normandy. This advantage had been gained through constant, often heavy, attrition in German ranks. In the "Big Week" bomber offensive of February 1944, nearly 700 German fighters were shot down and more destroyed on the ground, and between March and May of 1944, more than 2,400 fighters were destroyed in the skies and 1,500 lost to other causes.[52]

Worse for the Nazis, each time a German plane went down, there was a high probability that the pilot would be killed or wounded, and replacing pilots

---

[50]Russell Weigley, *The American Way of War: A History of the United States Military Strategy and Policy* (Bloomington, IN: Indiana University Press, 1973), p. 238.

[51]Charles Webster and Noble Frankland, *The Strategic Bombing Offensive Against Germany, 1939–1945*, 4 vols.; *History of the Second World War, United Kingdom Military Series* (London: Her Majesty's Stationery Office, 1961), 4:383.

[52]Kenneth Macksey, *Why the Germans Lose at War: The Myth of German Military Superiority* (New York: Barnes & Noble, 1996), p. 195.

proved increasingly difficult as the war went on because of training demands. (Similarly, Japan was never able to replace the three hundred pilots it lost at Midway.) One source estimates that 30 percent of German war resources went to anti-bombing efforts, a shift of strategic importance, siphoning off a critical portion of German air resources from the eastern front, where the Soviets handed the Germans a key defeat at Kursk in the summer of 1943.[53]

Consider the impact on this single pivotal battle, for example. As shown in Table 1, between December 1942 and June 1943—the pivotal point preceding Kursk—American aircraft flying in Europe increased the Allied total by 6,400 aircraft.[54]

Table 1		
American Combat Aircraft in the European Theater, 1942-43		
Year		**Number**
December 1942		**1,300**
June 1943		**5,000**

Source: James F. Dunnigan and Albert A. Nofi, Dirty Little Secrets of World War II (New York: Quill, 1994), 199.

Most of the new American arrivals were bombers, and the response of the German war industry is obvious in Table 2.

The staggering decline of aircraft available on the eastern front after the Americans began daylight bombing missions in 1943, as seen in Table 2, meant that "at Kursk, for the first time in the war, the Soviets contested the Germans in the air on an almost equal footing."[55] Soviet air power accounted for only between 2 percent and 6 percent of German tank losses. During the battle for the Orel bulge, German aircraft flew 37,000 missions, downing 1,733 Soviet aircraft at a loss of only 64 planes, while at the same time destroying 1,100 tanks and 1,300 trucks or tracked vehicles.[56] In short, while there is a tendency to look at Kursk as an inevitable Russian "win" because of the "advantage" in armor and manpower, at the time it was a close-run thing, decided, as most battle are, by control of the skies. It becomes an even closer-run scenario if the United States is out of the equation.

---

[53]See James F. Dunnigan and Albert A. Nofi, eds., *Dirty Little Secrets of World War II* (New York: Quill, 1994), pp. 195, 199.

[54]Larry Schweikart, "Kursk: a reappraisal," *Against the Odds*, 2 December 2003, pp. 20–23.

[55]David M. Glantz and Jonathan M. House, *The Battle of Kursk* (Lawrence, KS: University Press of Kansas, 1999), p. 270.

[56]Herman Plocher, *The German Air Force Versus Russia, 1943*, ed. Harry R. Fletcher (New York: Arno Press, 1967), p. 105.

Table 2		
German Deployment of Antiaircraft-Related Weapons		
Year	**Weapon**	**Number**
1940*	**Antiaircraft (AA) Guns/Searchlights**	**8,700/3,450**
1941*	**Heavy and Light AA Guns/Searchlights**	**12,908/3,905**
1942	**Heavy and Light AA Guns/Searchlights**	**15,472/4,650**
1943	**Heavy and Light AA Guns/Searchlights**	**26,020/5,200**

Source: James F. Dunnigan and Albert A. Nofi, Dirty Little Secrets of World War II (New York: Quill, 1994), 144, 246.
*Denotes western deployments only.

Table 3		
Percentage of German Aircraft on the Eastern Front		
Year		**Percentage**
1941		**64**
1942		**65**
1943		**42**

Source: James F. Dunnigan and Albert A. Nofi, Dirty Little Secrets of World War II (New York: Quill, 1994), 187.

Absent a serious American bomber threat from the West, the Germans could have deployed 350 more aircraft in the Kursk battle. If these numbers were divided between antitank and fighter aircraft, this would have added 175 more fighters and 175 more "tank killers" to the Luftwaffe forces deployed at Kursk. Such numbers would have affected virtually every aspect of the battle. Rudolph Hess, calculating the war's resource demand, concluded in late 1942 that Germany had to win in the next couple of years, and thus reallocated resources based on an American presence and a threat of invasion from the West. With no massive bombing raids in the West—at least, no daylight raids by American planes—it is reasonable to assume that the Germans would have been able to transfer 75 percent of their antiaircraft resources (including warnings, artillery, personnel, and so on) to the eastern front and Kursk. If one fifth of Germany's war resources went to the war in the skies, without a U.S. presence, as much as 10 to 15 percent of total German war resources could have been transferred to the East.

Counterfactuals or what-ifs are always dangerous, and never more so than in World War II, where the scope of operations resists alternate paths of history. Developments on the western front had an underappreciated impact on the Soviet success in the East. Historians make much of Soviet tank superiority (mainly because of the wide tracks, easy repair, and heavier gun on the T24 as contrasted with the Panzer IVs or the sophisticated—but highly temperamental—Panthers and Tigers), yet little mention is made of the fact that American industry provided nearly all of the soviets' trucks, armored personnel carriers, and Jeeps. To this day, there is no Russian equivalent of the "Veelees," and there is no Russian "Jeepski."[57] Patton raged that the United States supplied the Soviets with more six-wheel General Motors trucks than the Americans in Europe received. The United and Britain supplied 12 percent of all of the USSR's self-propelled guns and 100 percent of all armored personnel carriers.[58] On top of that, the United States supplied thousands of radios, miles of wire, tons of food, and other vital supplies that allowed the Soviets to concentrate almost exclusively on tanks, cannons, and aircraft.

America began the tsunami of production with a massive shipbuilding program, mostly directed at constructing transports to deliver men, arms, parts, and food to England, as well as the warships, submarines, and aircraft to protect them en route. Indeed, while the names Patton, Eisenhower, and MacArthur are familiar to most Americans, the names Kaiser and Higgins would likely warrant a response of Who? Yet when it came to shipbuilding, the USA had no equal to these two men. Henry Kaiser's magnificent shipyards turned out a Liberty ship in less than a week from scratch in late 1942, having cut the build time down from 126 days. Yet before he build a single hull, Kaiser had to import a new workforce wholesale, which he did by advertising in large urban newspapers, attracting to his California yards the first significant migration of blacks to the Golden State. Knowing that housing did not exist for such large numbers of people, Kaiser delved into prefabricated home construction, much as Andrew Jackson Higgins would do in his New Orleans facilities. Kaiser introduced new methods of welding, applied new organizational approaches, and steadily peeled time off the construction process. In 1942, when his builders set a record constructing the Robert E. Peary in an astounding four and a half days, Kaiser's yards used radical new modular construction techniques, dropping entire finished crew quarters into

[57]The United States and Britain shipped more than 20,900 armored vehicles to Russia, including 12,300 tanks, and provided 300,000 field telephones. See Richard Overy, *Why the Allies Won* (New York: Norton, 1995), pp. 182–90; Schweikart , *The Entrepreneurial Adventure,* pp. 378–79.
[58]S. J. Zaloga and J. Grandsen, *Soviet Tanks and Combat Vehicles of World War II* (London: Arms and Armor Press, 1984), pp. 128, 206.

hulls still under construction, adding superstructures while work still continued below decks. Kaiser's new welding techniques further chopped down production time.

Equally important to the war effort was Andrew Jackson Higgins, inventor of the famous Higgins boats used in virtually every Allied amphibious invasion of the war. General Dwight D. Eisenhower later called Higgins *"the man who won the war."*[59] Indeed, the prototypical "weapon" of World War II was not a cannon, airplane, or machine gun, but an unarmed landing craft. Higgins, a Louisiana boat builder, was born in landlocked Columbus, Nebraska, where he once designed an ice boat. Working a wide variety of jobs—lumber, clerk, banker, timber inspector and buyer, and truck driver—Higgins moved to Louisiana, where he ran a lumber export company. There he learned to build boats that could pull rafts of logs out of shallow streams, and after his initial lumber company failed, Higgins started a new one focused on building barges and other boats. His original breakthrough design, the Wonderboat, had a hull that solved the long-standing problem of cavitation—as so often happens in the free market—by accident. A pair of metal plates had pulled out of the molding floor, causing the hull to have a V amidship, which gave the boat higher speeds. Higgins called it a Eureka. This semi-tunnel drive was perfect for shallow water, and his accidentally designed and hardwood-reinforced hulls trapped air bubbles under the hull to create less resistance, giving the boat a roller-bearing effect. Soon his craft were adapted to lumbermen and fur trappers.

When Higgins took his designs to the U.S. Navy, however, he found little enthusiasm. The Landing Boat Development Board balked *"as though [it] feared that a more promising civilian design would be discovered before [the Navy] had a chance to complete its experimental craft."*[60] Such an attitude was common among bureaucracies, and could only have been defeated in a society that still believed that private enterprise had better ideas than government. Only the Marines, who were developing a landing manual, had any interest. A captain named Victor H "Brute" Krulak visited Higgins's yards and suggested adding a ramp to his boats. When the Marines' Tentative Landing Manual appeared in 1934, it concluded that Higgins's designs best fit the service's needs, although the Marines wanted the boats to be longer. General Holland "Howlin' Mad" Smith, commander of the 1st Marine Brigade, saw Japan as a growing threat. Looking at the string of Pacific islands, he knew Higgins's Eurekas gave his Marines the best chance to storm those beaches.

Nevertheless, the sleek, thirty-six foot Eureka, even though it had the designation Landing Craft Personnel (LCP), looked little like the landing craft in Saving Private Ryan. Rather, it resembled another craft Higgins received a contract to build in 1939—the wooden-hull patrol torpedo boat (PT boat). The

---

[59]For this quotation, and other information on Higgins, see John A. Heitmann, "The Man Who Won the War: Andrew Jackson Higgins," *Louisiana History,* 34 (1993), pp. 35–40.

[60]Jerry E. Strahan, *Andrew Jackson Higgins and the Boats That Won World War II* (Baton Rouge: Louisiana State University Press, 1994), p. 32.

Eurekas would blast up onto the beach, their long sterns still in the water, and Marines would jump over the side. It wasn't until mid-1939 that Higgins, looking for a better amphibious delivery system than the barges currently in use for tanks and artillery, was sent a photograph via the U.S. Bureau of Ships from Brute Krulak, who had photographed Japanese soldiers assaulting a Chinese position using ramped landing craft. A margin note said the ramps were the brainchild of "*some nut out in China*."[61] Here was a typically American weapons process in action, in which a Marine stationed abroad sees an enemy make use of a technology, then delivers the concept to an entrepreneur who works with the Marine to make an even better ramp, then applies American mass production to bury the foe that had the technology first. It was the twentieth-century replication of Charles Martel's use of the stirrup to defeat the Muslims at Tours or of Christian fleets use of superior gunfire to blow apart the sultan's fleets at Lepanto. In each case, the non-Western power had first what would be the superior technology, yet was unable to wed it to a mass-production system, remove fatal conceptual flaws, or establish it within a socioeconomic framework where it would flourish.[62]

The enemy of invention is often bureaucracy, which lives by static models of performance, largely unaffected by human will or determination. In most non-Western societies, rulers or their bureaucracies left no flexibility for entrepreneurs. In America, however, things were usually different, although Hiram Maxim, the inventor of the first true machine gun, encountered little interest from the War Department when he presented it, and, when combined with Maxim's rivalry with his brother, the inventor left for England, where he was knighted by Queen Victoria for his weapon. Fortunately, Andrew Jackson Higgins had a slightly better experience. When Higgins promised not only to deliver the ramped LCP for its scheduled test, but also to build an experimental version of a tank-landing vessel, Navy bureaucrats told him it couldn't be done. However, they agreed to a complete set of plans. Officials from the Marines and the Navy arrived from Washington for a test of a ramped Eureka, only to find not only the Eureka but also the ramped tank carrier, built and put into the water in sixty-one hours!

Higgins repeatedly went against the military grain, contracting with suppliers who were in the Navy's doghouse, resisting unionization, and committing the most unpardonable sin of consistently besting the Navy's own designs. Yet each time, reluctantly, the Navy not only extended contracts to Higgins's but also gave his vessels fair tests—and more contracts. Several times, Higgins's designs advanced only because a single officer (often Krulak) strategically intervened. Certainly, Higgins's boats were not perfect. Numerous modifications were required after early testing. Among other design deficiencies, the engine needed to be moved up, crewmen were exposed to fire, and so on. Yet the Higgins facilities quickly improved the vessels, and when engine shortages threatened to

[61]Victor H. Krulak, *First to Fight: An Inside View of the U.S. Marine Corps* (Annapolis: United States Naval Institute, 1984), pp. 90–91.

[62]Victor David Hanson, *Carnage and Culture: Landmark Battles in the Rise of Western Power* (New York: Doubleday, 2001).

shut down production of Higgins's remarkable integrated process, his workmen designed a faux engine the same size and dimensions as the real thing, complete with hookups, so that construction could continue until the actual engines arrived, at which time the substitutes were quickly shifted out. When Higgins observed in July 1941 that the Navy lacked sufficient training in piloting his unique boats, he opened the Higgins Boat Operators and Machine Maintenance School at the request of several Navy officers.

After Pearl Harbor, Higgins, bringing assembly-line techniques to landing craft construction, not only made LCIs (landing craft infantry), LSTs (landing ship tanks) and PT Boats, but following a key test in May 1942, in which the government's best other design was pitted against the Higgins boat, the government directed all American yards building landing craft to convert immediately to the Higgins design. When the U.S. 5th Army landed at Salerno, Italy, in 1943, and General Douglas MacArthur's men invaded New Guinea, of the fourteen thousand vessels in the Navy, 92 percent were designed by Higgins Industries and almost nine thousand of them were built at the Higgins plants in New Orleans.[63] His plants produced more than twenty thousand vessels during the war, cranking out an astounding seven hundred boats a month. Even at those rates, General Dwight Eisenhower fretted he might not have enough to invade Italy. When they buried him, Ike joked, his coffin *should be in the shape of a landing craft,* as they were *practically killing [him] with worry.*[64] Hitler knew Higgins's value, too, calling him the *new Noah.*[65]

Higgins's expansion brought him a remarkable new vice president, a Detroit race car owner and dreamer named Preston Tucker.[66] In 1942, Higgins acquired the Tucker Aviation Company of Detroit, and Tucker himself moved to New Orleans to work on Higgins's staff, although eventually differences in style would cause the two to break off their partnership. Nevertheless, Higgins had much in common with men like Howard Hughes, Henry Kaiser, and Preston Tucker, all of whom were welcomed as a part of the war effort and awarded generous contracts, but then to one degree or another were scorned or investigated after the war for profiteering. Tucker, Hughes, and Higgins especially, had advanced American military technology in ways that benefited the civilian sector mightily after the war, and all three were harassed by the government. Always a Roosevelt man, Higgins found that the very labor policies FDR had supported were dooming his post-war business. He came to support an open shop in defiance of the New Dealer pro-labor mentality. He wanted to hire veterans, whether they were members of unions or not, which brought the National labor Relations Board down on him. *"I consider the Wagner Act oppressive in its operation,"* he stated in an open

---

[63]Stahan, *Andrew Jackson Higgins*, p. 1

[64]Stahan, *Andrew Jackson Higgins*, p. 3.

[65]"Who's Afraid of the Big Bad Wolf? Who's Afraid of the Men of Higgins? No One Less Than Adolf Hitler Himself!" Eureka News Bulletin, 2, August 1943.p. 2.

[66]Charles T. Pearson, *The Indomitable Tin Goose: The True Story of Preston Tucker and His Car* (London: Abelard–Schuman, 1960).

letter called Give Me Liberty![67]   Rather than submit to union coercion, Higgins closed his plants and liquidated his company—the company that "won the war."

It would be unfair to suggest that the government forced Higgins to shut down his business, because in 1947 he was awarded a Reconstruction Finance Corporation loan of $9 million for his new business, enamel housing and refrigerator panels. Indeed, in some ways, the Democrat-dominated government had been caught between its newly found union friends and its wartime entrepreneur heroes. What Higgins had demonstrated was that when the shackles were removed, American innovators and rebels could out-design and out-produce fascist state businesses, Japanese Bushido corporations, and even Communist collectives many times over. An equally important lesson, though, was that not all those revolutionary businessmen hit home runs. For every Higgins, there was a Hughes.

Howard Hughes, having inherited his father's drill bit company, became fascinated with airplanes to the point where he produced his own movie, Hell's Angels (1930), so he could film aerial battles between World War I Spads and Fokkers. That had led him to form the Hughes Aircraft Company to build record-setting airplanes. By 1941, Hughes had the respect of many of the Army Air corps brass at Wright Field, and he had facilities and designs ready when Franklin Roosevelt called on the aircraft industry to produce fifty thousand planes a year in 1940. Hughes's problem was that he had radical concepts, but no airplane that fit into a specific category. His D-2, originally conceived as a wooden bomber, had to be repackaged as a twin-engined fighter. There were other problems: wooden planes laced armor; the D-2s landing gear was not durable enough; and the aircraft lacked a bullet-resistant windshield.[68]   Although, like all plants, Hughes's facilities manufactured a variety of war-related goods, including machine-gun feeders, the millionaire wanted to build airplanes. Convinced he had radical designs, he pulled every string until he won a contract for a twin-engine fighter, the XF-11 with its contra-rotating props. Over budget ad behind schedule, the sleek aircraft had already lost out to the P38 Lighting as a production airplane, and by July 1946, with all contracts canceled, Hughes hoped to redeem some of his political capital by flying the XF-11 and showing Washington what she could do. Instead, a malfunction caused the airplane to lose altitude until Hughes—who had insisted on test-piloting the airplane himself—crashed in Beverly Hills and sustained life-threating injuries.

If it had only been the XF-11, and if Hughes had had a record of success with other airplanes, he probably would have escaped the congressional investigation that followed. But along with the brilliant Liberty ship builder Henry Kaiser, Hughes had taken on a second revolutionary aircraft project. In 1942, when Nazi U-boats were sinking Liberty ships faster than even Kaiser could build them, the boat builder came up with a concept for ferrying troops to Europe by air on massive transport aircraft. Kaiser had no aircraft designers, however, and

[67] Andrew Jackson Higgins, "Give Me Liberty!" Dealers' and Salesmen's Bulletin, December 1, 1945, reprinted in Strahan, Andrew Jackson Higgins, pp. 296–99.
[68] Barlett and Steele, *Howard Hughes*, pp. 105–109.

in desperation he pitched the idea in a San Francisco hotel to a sickly Hughes, who reluctantly agreed to jointly build the world's biggest airplane. The result was a mixture of all the worst elements: Kaiser, thinking Hughes's aircraft team had the designs under control, kept his hand off, while Hughes—at best a novice designer and terrible manager—dabbled with blueprints and fell behind schedule. Their project, the HK-1 Hercules, was to be the largest airplane ever built, requiring eight massive engines to lift the monster flying boat aloft. Hughes sank his personal fortune into the Hercules, which by 1946 had lost more than $7 million of Hughes's money (as well as the government's investment). But the intricacies of layering the wood in Hughes's radical new laminating process were daunting, and the plane never would have been completed without Charles Perelle, whom Hughes put in charge of the project during its critical phase.

The size of the Hercules was beyond description. Merely moving its enormous wings, tail, and fuselage from Culver City in June of 1946 so that it could be assembled in Long Beach cost $80,000. Its wingspan was double that of the B-29, its hull thirty feet tall, and the engine's propellers were seventeen feet in diameter. Even after the advent of modern metals and better engines, as of 2005 the Hercules remains the heaviest aircraft ever built (four hundred thousand pounds), and it still has the largest wingspan. A man could stand inside the wings of the Hercules.[69]

Senators had, by that time, forced Hughes to testify in public (something he hated), but his flight of the Hercules in November 1947 had stunned everyone, and it was a remarkable achievement, even if the aircraft was delivered late and probably could not actually fly for more than a few minutes. In many ways, the Hercules resembled the original Wright flyer—breathtakingly advanced, yet so fundamentally flawed as to have virtually peaked technologically in its maiden flight. (The Wrights, however, did manage a demonstration in France that left French aviation experts embarrassed. One uttered, "*We are beaten. We just don't exist,*" and another mournfully added, "*We are as children compared with the Wrights.*")[70] No one walked away from Hughes's demonstration of the Hercules muttering "*we are children compared with Howard Hughes,*" and it is true that Hughes generated no breakthrough research. Still, the fact that he built a laminated wooden airplane larger than any that had ever got off the ground reflected the essence of the American entrepreneurial spirit, where even the failures contributed to the greater good with their drive, ambition, and constant prodding forward of the boundaries of the possible. It was a motif replayed in the story of Preston Tucker.

Preston Tucker's struggle with Uncle Sam, made famous in Francis Ford Coppola's film *Tucker: The Man and His Dream,* was even more dramatic. Having produced for the Army in the 1930s a prototype armored car that attained speeds of 117 miles per hour, which the Army rejected because it was too fast and

---

[69]Barlett and Steele, *Howard Hughes*, pp. 156–57.
[70]Richard P. Hallion, *Taking Flight: Inventing the Aerial Age from Antiquity Through the First World War* (New York: Oxford University Press, 2003), p. 233.

early tanks could not keep up with it, Tucker managed to sell the car's rotating ball turret for use in bombers during the war. After World War II, he attempted to make a revolutionary automobile replete with seat belts, a rear engine, and other bold features. Although he won a bid to build the cars in a massive government factory in Chicago, his battles with Senator Homer Ferguson of Michigan—and many of the same senators who relentlessly pursued Hughes—finally resulted in an SEC investigation for mail fraud. Tucker was acquitted, but he only made fifty of his remarkable cars before the factory was shut down. But like Hughes, Tucker proved that American produced enough dreamers, that somewhere, someone was getting it right. Top-down totalitarian societies condemned such failures to gulags or worse; but the American system, tolerant of failure as an engine of information, simply said, in so many words, "Try again." And in the process, American fighting men constantly had either better weapons, or more of them, than any other force in human history.

Consider the M4 Sherman tank, generally thought to be a mediocre armored vehicle at best. Hardly a match for the high-tech Panther or Tiger tanks on the western front in World War II, the Sherman nevertheless had tremendous advantages. It was simple and particularly easy to repair in the field. If a Panther had a malfunction with any of its middle wheels, the repair could involve removing all of the wheels on an entire side just to change one. A Sherman's wheels, on the other hand, came in pairs, and to repair any wheel required pulling only that wheel and its cover. Moreover, Americans learned from the Russians: if there is a problem, don't stop building while you fix it, because once you correct the problem, you'll have twice as many units, and more units are better. Over time, the 75 mm main gun was upgraded to a 90 mm gun that was sufficient to destroy German armor. The tank was relatively easy to operate, and with 95,000 of them produced, the United States could lose many and still outnumber the Germans, whose production fell so far behind that by 1944 they only had a total of 100 Tigers along the entire eastern front. Indeed, despite the apparent threat of the Russians, of the 2,300 tanks and assault guns produced by the Germans in the last two months of 1944, 1,379 of them went to the western front, where half of the German army was "pitted against a foe one-fifth the size of the Russian army."[71]

Far more important in winning the war than Shermans or bombers was the ability of the United States to feed and fuel its armies at the front, whether first by Liberty ships or later by truck. The famed Red Ball Express, created by General Dwight Eisenhower's logisticians, had 132 truck companies that moved along a four-hundred-mile route, providing some eight hundred thousand gallons of fuel a day. During Iraqi Freedom, the Army and 1st Marine Expeditionary Force logisticians aimed to more than double that accomplishment along a route of about the same length. Despite operating at time in enemy-controlled territory ("Ambush Alley" from As-Samawah to An Najaf), and despite a major sandstorm, the troops never ran out of gas—or ammunition, although delivering supplies to the tankers <u>inside Baghdad</u> on the Thunder Run proved dicey. The V Corps refueled about

[71]Victor Davis Hanson, *The Soul of Battle* (New York: Free Press, 1999), p. 326.

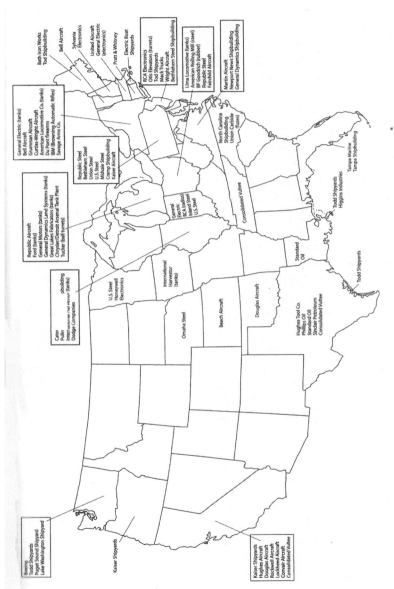

FIGURE 6 The Arsenal of Democracy

every hundred kilometers, or five times between the crossing of the departure line and seizing Baghdad.

Explaining the Arsenal of Democracy

One of the most significant advantages any private sector entrepreneur has over a government contractor is that he is free to use whatever materials best suit his particular technological challenge. Hence, in 1983, Burt and Dick Rutan, using composites and a radical design, would create an aircraft called the Voyager, which could circle the globe on a single tank of fuel.[72] Derided by Air Force and aerospace professionals as a stunt, the Rutans proved that the private sector could, in fact, meet any challenge as long as that challenge was clearly stated. In 2004, their spacecraft, SpaceShipOne, became the first private aircraft to reach space. These "stunts," in fact, confirmed what Hoke found in his study of clocks and typewriters: that the private sector solves the problem immediately in front of it. In contrast, as Jacques Gansler has pointed out in a study of how the Pentagon procures fruitcake, the multiple—often contradictory—regulations imposed by government on everything from arms to food tends to slow innovation, raise prices, and lower quality.[73] Some of Samuel Colt's early revolvers, deemed "inferior" by government inspectors, were snapped up on the open market.[74] Price is critical in the private sector, hence entrepreneurs constantly find lower-cost methods of production and substitute cheaper (or more reliable) materials, and employ better management than government armories.

Time and again, the superior firepower supplied by a free economic system provided the decisive edge over the nation's enemies. But technology alone did not ensure victory. History is full of examples of technologically superior armies who were defeated because of poor leadership, moral, or just bad luck. Weapons must be used in ways that make sense to create, in the military's jargon, "force multipliers," then combined with good moral and able leadership. Yet few armies in history have been better at bringing in decisive firepower at critical moments than America's. Whether at Breed's Hill or Belleau Wood, Yankee troops have proven themselves to be particularly adroit at massing fire. Once airpower and naval gunfire became available, this trait grew even more valuable. In Korea, a surrounded infantry battalion was rescued by box barrage artillery fire that completely shielded the unit with a curtain of lead until, at the appropriate time, the gunfire on one side was lifted, allowing the forces to fight their way out.[75] When artillery could not provide enough support, the Air Force flew more than forty-five hundred sorties in October 1952 alone to hold off superior numbers of Chinese

---

[72]For information on the Voyager, see http://www.centennialofflight.gov/essay/GENERAL_AVIATION/rutan/GA15.htm.

[73]Jacques Gansler, "How the Pentagon Buys Fruitcake," in Larry Schweikart, ed., *Technology and the Culture of War,* 2nd ed. (Boston: Pearson Custom Publishers, 2003), pp. 181–84

[74]Hoke, *Ingenious Yankees*, p. 261.

[75]Robert H. Scales, *Firepower in Limited War* (Washington, D.C.: National Defense University Press, 1990), p. 17.

soldiers.

A classic example of the benefits of air and artillery power can be seen in the 1965 Battle of the Ia Drang Valley in Vietnam. There, Colonel Hal Moore's 7ty Cavalry was nearly overrun on several occasions, but time and again the Air Force, Navy, and Marine pilots and several 105 mm howitzers rained death from above like a deluge of steel. Here is how Moore described it:

> The brave cannon-cockers in L[anding] Z[one] went without sleep for three days and nights to help keep us surrounded by a wall of steel. Those two batteries, twelve guns, fired more than four thousand rounds of high-explosive shells on the first day alone. [Battery C commander] Bob Barker said "On the first afternoon both batteries fired [directly on target] for five straight hours."[76]

When a Huey helicopter pilot set down briefly at LZ Falcon, the scene stunned him: "*stacks of shell casing, one at least 10 feet high, and exhausted gun crews. They had fired for effect for three straight hours ... without even pausing to level the bubbles. One tube was burned out, two had busted hydraulics.*"[77] When the 7th got into heavy night fighting, an Air Force C-123 gunship, Smokey the Bear, kicked out parachute flares so fast that Moore could call off his artillery illumination, saving those guns for high explosive rounds. Although the North Vietnamese tried to wait out the flares, it was impossible. Meanwhile, the artillery poured lead onto their positions nonstop. Later, at the battle of Landing Zone Albany, a sergeant related to Moore that his troops in the front of the perimeter called artillery in so close they were in danger of their own shrapnel, but it "kept the enemy away and kept the alive."[78] General James Van Fleet of the 8th Army in Korea expressed the same attitude toward firepower. Officers were ordered to "*expend steel and fire, not men.*"[79] Van Fleet continued, "*I want so many artillery holes that a man can step from one to the other.*"[80]

Just under twenty years later, a hundred Rangers and Delta Force members, surrounded in Mogadishu, and outnumbered nearly one hundred to one, managed to escape from the heart of the city because the precise firepower of their "little bird" air support. The helicopters ran missions all night, and knocked out several reinforcement waves by themselves.[81] As soldiers "painted" the targets with lasers, pilots warned, "*Keep your heads down*" and tore Somali positions apart.

Whether it was an eagerness and ability to embrace new forms of communication or the habit of employing firepower and force multipliers in an effort to save soldiers' lives, the American way of war consistently demonstrated a willingness to experiment with and, when feasible, implement the most radical tech-

[76]Harold G. Moore and Joseph L. Galloway, *We Were Soldiers Once ... and Young* (New York: Ballantine, 1992), p. 114.

[77]Moore and Galloway, *We Were Soldiers*, p. 114.

[78]Moore and Galloway, *We Were Soldiers*, p. 526.

[79]Michael Lind, *Vietnam: the Necessary War* (New York: Touchstone, 1999), p. 252.

[80]Lind, *Vietnam*, p. 253.

[81]Mark Bowden, *Black Hawk Down: A Story of Modern War* (New York: Signet, 2001), pp. 308, 310.

niques as a means to shorten conflicts. No example stands out more clearly than Ronald Regan's endorsement of a revolutionary new antimissile system in 1983.

Winning the Cold War with a Speech

The best weapon, a soldier will tell you, is the one that is never used. In the 1970s, the mere threat of producing what became the B-1 bomber forced the Soviet Union to commit substantial resources to countering it, resulting in the MiG-25P Foxbat interceptor, a very fast but highly limited aircraft. Western intelligence services learned that just by leaking a "proposed" new weapon system, they could provoke the Soviets into initiating all sorts of counterprograms. Without a doubt, though, the most important weapon never made (at least not until quite recently) was the antimissile system known as the Strategic Defense Initiative (SDI), popularly called Star Wars.

During the 1970s, advances in lasers (light amplification by the stimulated emission of radiation), charged particle-beam weapons, and other antimissile technologies made it possible for the first time to seriously contemplate attacking intercontinental ballistic missiles (ICBMs) in flight rather than (as was previously the case) in the terminal phase. Antiballistic missile systems (ABMs) were built in the 1960s, and they all shared one potentially fatal drawback: they could only be used in what was called the terminal phase of reentry, that is, when enemy missiles were over U.S. territory. That made for a tiny margin of error and, further, meant that the destroyed missiles would still land on American soil, causing civilian casualties. A number of sources, including both CIA agents and an Air Force special investigations team, concluded that the Soviets had moved rapidly into laser and particle-beam testing. Further, they warned, Soviet work had met with considerable success.[82]

Put another way, the Soviets clearly believed that some sort of Star Wars system would work, and they intended to deploy it first, but their technology screeched to a halt because despite their advances in beam weapons, they lacked a key technology needed for tracking and aiming: computers. Large computers, such as ENIAC and MANIAC, had been built in the United States in World War II, and after the war, companies such as International Business Machines (IBM) and Cray dominated the mainframe field. IBM, or Big Blue, became so dominant in the field by the late 1960s that competitors, foreign and domestic, sought legislation to shackle the giant. Tales of IBM's predatory practices convinced many that before long, IBM would, in science fiction fashion, control the world's computing.

Such hysteria, of course, ignored the reality of the market, where the leader in any particular industry is often standing on a precipice. Burton Klein's book *Dynamic Economics* traced the top fifty technological breakthroughs of twentieth-century America and found that not a single one came from the leader in the

[82]See the extensive sources in D. Douglas Dalgleish and Larry Schweikart, *Trident* (Carbondale, IL: Southern Illinois University Press, 1984), pp. 446–52.

field.[83]   One has to look only at such revolutionary machines as the automobile, developed by a Westinghouse worker named Henry Ford rather than the leading buggy manufacturer, or the airplane, which was built and flown by two bicycle makers rather than the leading balloonists, to prove Klein's point. Perhaps, according to popular logic, IBM should have pioneered the personal computer, but Big Blue, Hewlett-Packard, and others remained focused on making large mainframe computing machines and ignored the home computer market.

While it would distort the history of the computer industry to suggest that Steve Wozniak and Steve Jobs, two college dropouts, changed the course of the Cold War in their garage, it is certainly true that by the 1980s, it was the ubiquitous nature of small or minicomputers (generally categorized as PCs, or personal computers) that made Star Wars even thinkable. And while it would be incorrect to attribute all of this to the private sector—the National Security Administration (NSA) had, in the early 1960s, sought to achieve a thousand fold increase in performance in computing, and the Department of Defense had microprocessor programs in the works when Jobs and Wozniak started Apple—the civilian market energized the field and brought a multitude of geniuses into computing. The first home computers, the Altairs, were shipped in the mid-1970s, and in 1977, the Apple II was launched. IBM finally joined the parade in 1981, launching its competitor platform PC, but already chip sizes had fallen dramatically and computing power had started to surge. All of this made possible in the foreseeable future a vast network of engineers, designers, technicians, and military personnel all linked by computers that could perform tracking and aiming calculations unobtainable just a few years earlier. And with the speed of computing power growing geometrically (Moore's Law postulates that computing power doubles every eight months), the handwriting was on the wall or, in this case, on the monitor.

Like chess players planning twenty moves ahead, both President Ronald Reagan and the new soviet premier, Mikhail Gorbachev, began to calculate move and countermove. Gorbachev let the cat out of the bag in 1985 when he said: *"We know what's going on. ... You're inspired by illusions.* **You think you're ahead of us in information [technologies] [emphasis added].** *You think you're ahead of us in technology and that you can use these things to gain superiority over the Soviet Union."*[84] Already he saw the disparity in information and computing technology. At Geneva, Gorbachev blustered, *"Even now, due to computer technology, on side could get ahead in space.* **But we can match any challenge, though you might not think so"** [emphasis mine].[85]   Later at Geneva, Gorbachev again revealed, in Sovietspeak, what he feared most: the U.S. position *"was fed by an illusion that* **the U.S. was ahead in the technology and information systems on which space systems would be based"** [emphasis mine].[86] By 1986, Reagan adviser Ken Adel-

---

[83]Burton Klein, *Dynamic Economics* (Cambridge: Harvard University Press, 1977.

[84]George P. Schultz, *Turmoil and Triumph: My Years as Secretary of State* (New York: Charles Scribner's Sons, 1993), pp. 592–93.

[85]Paul Lettow, *Ronald Reagan and His Quest to Abolish Nuclear Weapons* (New York: Random House, 2005), p. 181.

[86]Lettow, *Ronald Reagan and His Quest*, p. 183.

man had concluded that SDI had become a bitter reminder of the gap between American technological strength and their own, and within a year, Soviet studies expressed concern that technological spinoffs from SDI would enhance yet other U.S. capabilities.[87]

If the Soviets overestimated some American capabilities, they demonstrated a good grasp of the vitality and sudden surges a capitalist entrepreneurial system could attain, often apparently out of thin air. Widespread use of computers—in the early 1970s the government's ARPANET (Advanced Research Projects Agency Network) was linking together universities and defense installations—made possible better antiballistic missile weapons, and, when combined with advances in lasers and particle-beam technology, meant that for the first time it might truly be possible to have a somewhat effective defense against ICBMs. At times even the CIA's reviews of Soviet progress (or lack thereof) in countering SDI seemed to miss the fundamental computer glue that tied everything together. Just as there was no Jeepski in the Soviet Union neither was there a Steve Jobski.[88]

Reagan had come into office thinking that the current strategy of mutual assured destruction (MAD) *"didn't seem to me to be something that would send you to bed feeling safe. It was like having two westerners standing in a saloon aiming their guns at each other's heads—permanently."*[89] Martin Anderson, Reagan's aide, said Reagan described MAD as *"the most ridiculous thing"* he had even seen.[90] Ed Meese, his chief of staff, recalled, *"Almost as long as I have known him ... Governor Reagan then, and later President Reagan, was very interested in some sort of defense against missiles—ballistic missiles— and nuclear warfare."*[91] He was determined to change the policy from one of *"assured destruction to assured survival,"* thereby making a paradigm shift of how the United States defended itself.[92] Reagan, whose fundamental insights still surprise liberals, who thought him an affable dunce, realized what military historian John Keegan understood, that in military history *"altogether more money and human labour has been expended [up to World War I] in fortification than in fighting."* [93]Consequently, he observed, *"Reagan's urge to realize a Strategic Defense Initiative, and so protect his United States against the threat of wholesale ballistic missile attack, belongs not to some utopian dream of the future but to one of the deepest and oldest of all human responses to military danger."*[94]

Having just two weeks earlier referred to the Soviet Union as the "evil empire," on March 23, 1983, Reagan gave the Star Wars speech, in which his

[87]Adelman cited in Lettow, *Ronald Reagan and His Quest*, p. 216

[88]One of the major factors in the West's unpreparedness for the fall of the Soviet Union was that even by 1990–91, analysts had still not come to grips with the way computers had started to fundamentally reorganize economic life and military operations, and therefore a society without a thriving computer industry and its attendant geeks was doomed.

[89]Ronald Reagan, *My American Life*, (New York: Pocket Books, 1990), p. 547.

[90]Anderson quoted in Lettow, Ronald Reagan and His Quest, p. 21.

[91]Meese quoted in Lettow, *Ronald Reagan and His Quest*, p. 23

[92]Reagan, *My American Life*, p. 552.

[93]John Keegan, *The Mask of Command* (New York: Penguin, 1987), p. 7.

[94]Keegan, *Mask of Command*, p. 7.

remarks on a strategic defense initiative were only part of a broader speech on national security. *"Tonight,"* he said, *"I am directing a comprehensive and intensive effort to define a long-term research and development program to begin to achieve our ultimate goal of eliminating the threat posed by strategic nuclear missiles."*[95] He did not use the words laser, Star Wars, particle-beam weapons, or in any way—not once—suggest that such a system was totally (or even predominantly) space based, nor did he even hint that such a system was foolproof or 100 percent impenetrable. These were all inferences made by leftist listeners who knew very well that such a system did not have to be anywhere near 100 percent effective to have its desired effect of eliminating the threat of ICBMs.

Certainly the Gettysburg Address, John Kennedy's Inaugural, and Washington's Farewell Address rate as some of the greatest speeches in American history. None, however, had the immediate and direct impact on world events that the Star Wars speech had. His own staff was shocked at how quickly he had announced the initiative. *"We weren't ready to announce it yet,"* recalled two of his subordinates, and the chairman of the Joint Chiefs said, *"We were surprised that it went that fast."* [96] Reagan knew that insiders who opposed any program could kill it, and he therefore played it close to the vest. By doing so, Reagan "got the first shot at making the national announcement," not the press.[97] Opinion polls, calls, and telegrams all reflected the public's approval of SDI.

Consider that almost immediately the Strategic Defense Initiative was renamed Star Wars in the press in an effort to ridicule the program, an effort historian Paul Lettow called "semantic subversion." By applying the Star Wars moniker to Reagan's brainchild, the media unwittingly gave the concept immediate credibility with the American people, who craved moral absolutes and who were weary of antiheroes. Virtually all Americans had seen on of George Lucas's Star Wars movies, and if they hadn't, they certainly were aware of the basic plot in which a simple farm boy (Luke/Reagan) defends the Republic (America) against the evil empire (the USSR) and its masters of malevolence Darth Vader and the Emperor (Gorbachev/Stalin/Lenin/any numbers of Soviet leaders). Reagan himself had set the table by labeling the Soviet Union the "evil empire" in 1982. Whether the Gipper actually meant to invoke images of Lucas's movies, it struck a chord in the American public instantly. Even the series of Soviet dictators leading up to Gorbachev—Leonid Brezhnev, Yuri Andropov, Konstantine Chernenko—all looked like the evil emperor, and all seemed a million years old! Here the leftist American media had stumbled into giving Reagan exactly the "point of contact" with the public that something as esoteric as SDI needed.[98]

[95] Reagan, My American Life, pp. 574, 575.

[96] Lettow, *Ronald Reagan and His Quest*, p. 106

[97] Lettow, *Ronald Reagan and His Quest*, p. 103.

[98] Predictably, a Massachusetts academic tried to claim that the movie Star Wars was a leftist parable in which Jimmy Carter was the farm boy, and the United States, under Reagan, the evil Empire because America relied on technology. Darth Vader, the author informs us, "was redeemable via love and faith, not power." However, anyone who knows the movies knows that it was the redeemed Darth's power, by the act of picking up the evil Emperor and throwing him into the Death Star's power generator, that saves the day. So perhaps power is necessary after all! See David S. Meyer, "Star Wars, Star Wars, and American Political Culture," Journal of

It is worth understanding that based on Soviet missile production rates, and the edge in numbers they already possessed, Reagan's advisers thought it impossible for the United States to catch up, using conventional methods, even with increased budgets. As Admiral James Watkins put it, given the ever-widening gap between the two superpowers, America was entering "a strategic cul-de-sac."[99] SDI constituted a strategic leapfrog of massive proportions. Yuri Andropov, the Soviet dictator at the time of the announcement, complained it was an attempt to "*disarm the Soviet Union*," so he clearly "got it."[100]   When Andropov died in 1984, Gorbachev—supposedly a different kind of Russian leader—took over and came to exactly the same conclusions.

Gorbachev, whom Strobe Talbott called the "man of the decade," was no fool, though he was not nearly as brilliant as the western media believed. He could see that his advantage—twenty years of investment in heavy ICBMs—was, in theory, rendered irrelevant by SDI. Moreover, from his nation's own research, he knew countering any functioning Star Wars system would be phenomenally expensive or perhaps impossible. The American Left leaped to his aid: the Union of Concerned Scientists (UCS) published a white paper claiming the SDI was impossible, offering ludicrous estimates for what the system would require. For example, the UCS claimed that protecting the United States would require twenty-four hundred satellites. Robert Jastrow, founder of the Goddard Institute for Space Studies, discovered that the UCS had assumed that a Star Wars system would have to, in Sherwin-Williams paint fashion, "*Cover the Earth*." In fact, Jastrow pointed out, Soviet missiles had to come over the North Pole through a "window," and protecting that window could require as few as fifty satellites.[101] Another error of massive proportions had a particle-beam satellite weighing an astounding forty thousand tons, when in fact all studies suggested the actual weight of a satellite would be close to twenty-five tons! These were not minor mathematical errors, but miscalculations of massive proportions—if they were, in fact, miscalculations. As Jastrow observed, the consistent pattern of errors could only yield one conclusion, namely, that the UCS had tainted its own "evidence" beyond the point of believability solely to discredit Star Wars.

Another straw man that critics constantly used was the 100 percent bogeyman, in which it was argued that no defense is 100 percent effective. The critics were absolutely right. Recent consumer tests of condoms has found that they fail at about a 15 percent rate. Does that mean no one should use condoms? Dale Earnhardt died when his safety belt failed. Does that mean that drivers should not use seat belts? Liberal critics of Star Wars constantly invoked the 100 percent effective test, but never mentioned deterrence, or the concept of the cost of overcoming a defense. Star Wars was part of a many-faceted strategy Reagan implemented in April 1982 (declassified in 1996). Its first principle was to "re-

Popular Culture, 26, 1992, pp. 99–115.
[99]Watkins quoted in Lettow, *Ronald Reagan and His Quest*, p. 94.
[100]Lettow, *Ronald Reagan and His Quest*, p. 115.
[101]Robert Jastrow, "The War Against 'Star Wars," Commentary, January 1984, pp. 19–25.

verse the expansion of Soviet control and military presence throughout the world [emphasis mine]," and to "*pursue the development of effective [ballistic missile defense] technology.*" As the document pointed out, "*Strategic defenses need not be impenetrable to enhance our nuclear strategy.*"[102] There it was. In the original planning documents, ballistic missile defense did not have to be 100 percent effective to be, well, effective.

Certainly, leftist scientists and journalists never believed they were part of a massive propaganda effort by the Communists, yet that was exactly the case. A CIA interagency report in September 1983 entitled *Possible Soviet Responses to the US Strategic Defense Initiative* stated that the Soviets would attempt to counter the deployment of SID with "*propaganda, diplomatic, and negotiation tactics.*"[103] In the 1990s, historian Jeffrey Herf found that even when the KGB did not orchestrate or organize nuclear freeze/anti—SDI demonstrations in Europe, it was deeply buried in all the freeze movements' leadership.[104] Recently released material from the KGB archives has revealed that the Soviets had infiltrated most of the peace groups and had quietly guided—if not outright directed—the nuclear freeze movement, in the West. Neither the propaganda offensive, the nuclear freeze movement, nor summit talks with Reagan at Geneva and Reykjavik could derail Star Wars. Despite the UCS's findings, Gorbachev's own ministers told him that overcoming a ballistic missile shield that was only partially effective could require hundreds, perhaps thousands, of new missiles. That, in turn, meant vast new expenditures for an economy that, by some accounts, was already spending 25 percent of the GNP on its military. Gorbachev's other alternative was to defeat Star Wars by "out-teching" it: using computers and technology to maneuver missiles in flight or otherwise jam American systems.

But Reagan had preempted that, too, by using the 1979 Export Control Act to prohibit sales of American computer technology to Soviet bloc countries. Meanwhile, the CIA, under Reagan, also "*coordinated the release of incomplete and misleading technical data*" to the Soviets, encouraging them to go down blind alleys in the attempt to keep up with SDI and other programs.[105] In one instance, sabotaged computer chips provided through CIA middlemen shut down Soviet military and civilian factories for weeks. Once again, Reagan's fundamental appreciation for the crux of a problem defied traditional analysis. His autobiography, An American Life, did not mention computers once in the context of Star Wars or SDI, yet it was precisely the growing American dominance in hardware, software, and networking that gave the United States its growing edge. Once engaged in the project, though, Reagan treated it like a Patton offensive. Within four years, the United States had collaboration agreements with Britain, Germany, Israel, Italy,

[102] Lettow, *Ronald Reagan and His Quest*, p. 67.
[103] Lettow, *Ronald Reagan and His Quest*, p. 130.
[104] Jeffrey Herf, *War by Other Means: Soviet Power, West German Resistance, and the Battle of the Euromissiles* (New York: Free Press, 1991).
[105] Peter Schweitzer, *Victory: The Reagan Administration's Secret Strategy that Hastened the Collapse of the Soviet Union*, (New York: Atlantic Monthly Press, 1994), p. 187. A 1983 CIA report concluded that the soviets would face "substantial pressures" trying to counter SDI technologically, and thus would divert their scarce resources into propaganda and diplomacy. (Lettow, *Ronald Reagan and His Quest*, p. 131.)

and Japan, all of whom had considerable scientific abilities to contribute to the program.

Unable to steal enough computer technology or to keep up with American advances, the Soviets found themselves in checkmate. SDI, one historian of the Soviet collapse observed, *"became an obsession"* for Gorbachev, and the "economic element" of Star Wars and the military buildup was "the number one preoccupation" of the Soviet premier.[106] After Reykjavik, according to one leftist writing about SDI, Gorbachev *"was angry that the American propaganda machine turned out to be far more effective than his own, and that the American public ... refused to believe his version of events and embraced SDI."*[107] Though all liberal scholars clung to the mantra that SDI "wouldn't work," Gorbachev spent an incredible amount of money trying to counter a "failed" system. In fact, as Bud McFarlane, one of Reagan's aides, observed, that the Russians had such a high regard for American technology that an investment in high technology paid off geometrically.

The Soviets knew from their own tests that the lasers and particle-beam weapons would work on a small level, and they were convinced that *"our investment ... would lead to discoveries that were bound to be enhancing to the American position in the world."*[108] Nikita Khrushchev had already written in his memoirs, "These 'rotten' capitalists keep coming up with things that make our jaws drop in surprise."[109] One Arms Control and Disarmament Agency study found that 70 percent of Soviet propaganda was directed at stopping SDI.[110] Richard Perle, a Democrat in the Reagan administration who later played a key role in formulating the case for the invasion of Iraq, recalled that Moscow's *"caterwauling deepened my conviction that it was the right program"* and that the U.S. was "doing the right thing."[111] Most of the Soviet leadership either directly or indirectly admitted that they were paralyzed by Star Wars. Eduard Shevardnadze, the new Russian foreign minister, conveyed an almost "desperate" underlying concern to Bud McFarlane for the impact of SDI on the Soviet economy when he met with Reagan in 1985.[112] At the Geneva Summit, Secretary of State George Shultz warned Reagan that Gorbachev, above all, wanted to stop the SDI program.[113]

Unable to shake Reagan—or the American public—the Communist Party of the Soviet Union developed a new five-year plan to catch the United States in electronics and computers, more than doubling the number of industrial robots and increasing funding for R&D by 50 percent, and instituted a plan to convert their liquid-fueled rockets to "fast burn" solid-fueled missiles (at tremendous

[106]Quoted in Schweitzer, *Victory,* 238.

[107]Frances FitzGerald, *Way Out There in the Blue* (New York: Simon and Schuster, 2000), p. 365.

[108]McFarlane quoted in Lettow, *Ronald Reagan and His Quest,* p. 90.

[109]Quoted in John Mueller, *Retreat from Doomsday: The Obsolescence of Major War* (New York: Basic Books, 1989, p. 205.

[110]Lettow, *Ronald Reagan and His Quest,* p. 140.

[111]Lettow, *Ronald Reagan and His Quest,* p. 141.

[112]Lettow, *Ronald Reagan and His Quest,* p. 169.

[113]Don Oberdorfer, *From the Cold War to a New Era: The United States and the Soviet Union, 1983–1991,* 2nd ed., (Baltimore: Johns Hopkins University Press, 1998), p. 139.

cost). Gorbachev glumly told the party faithful that *"the U.S. wants to exhaust the Soviet Union economically through a race in ... expensive space weapons."*[114] (At the same time, the Saudis increased oil output, forcing down the price of Russian crude oil, indirectly increasing U.S. businesses' profitability!) Reagan summarized the impact of SDI after he left office: "if we showed the political resolve to develop SDI, the Soviets would have to face the awful truth [that they] did not have the resources to continue building a huge offensive arsenal and a defensive one simultaneously."[115] SDI, Reagan said, was not a trade-off for arms control, it was arms control.

Only if one understands the trump card of Star Wars do other Soviet moves—and retreats—during this critical period become clear. As Gorbachev resigned himself to the inevitable disposition of the chessboard, the withdrawal from Afghanistan made perfect sense: why continue sustaining heavy losses in a country with no real strategic value or natural resources? Likewise, the unwillingness to use force to slam shut the door on Lech Walesa and his Polish labor union movement. To rephrase Stalin, *"How many computers do the Poles have?"* And the final acquiescence in the demolition of the Soviet empire, when the Berlin Wall fell without a shot, represented little more than Gorbachev knocking over his own king.

Did Gorbachev know more than the western media? Ironically, it appears many experts on both sides missed a critical component of the analysis. Disagreements over the effectiveness of any missile defense system, especially in the western press, inevitably focused on U.S. capabilities. Lost in the discussion was the reality of problems in Soviet technology. Simply put, their stuff failed often, far more frequently than did American technology. In a 1988 study of Soviet launch capabilities that applied known or estimated U.S. failure rates to Soviet missiles, a much different picture of the entire Star Wars debate appears. American missile tests failed about 15 percent of the time. Using known Soviet ICMB numbers, then applying a 15 percent failure rate—not only to the launch phase but also to the separation and impact stages—then calculating the capabilities of a defense that was only 80 percent effective, the study found that both pro- and anti-Star Wars camps were significantly overestimating the number of Soviet warheads that would leak through to an impact. For example, of the 1,400 Soviets ICBMs, based on known failure rates, fewer than 1,330 would have gotten off the pad; and at an 80 percent kill ration by the first layer of a missile defense system, only 266 would survive to the separation phase. After further space attacks by other layers, 15 percent of Soviet warheads would fail to separate the "bus" vehicles. And so on. In an all-out missile launch by the Soviets, fewer than 50 missiles would actually release their bus vehicles; and after the terminal attacks and the estimated number of duds, the use of dummy warheads, and accounting for the targeting "footprints," it is likely that fewer than five nuclear warheads out of a

---

[114]Gorbachev on soviet television, October 14, 1986.
[115]Ronald Reagan, "It was "Star Wars' Muscle That Wrestled Arms Race to a Halt," Los Angeles Times, July 31, 1991.

full-scale Soviet launch would have actually detonated! Even one or two nuclear explosions would be horrific—and result in severe loss of life and long-term ecological destruction—but that is not the point: as a deterrent, Star Wars would be overwhelmingly effective, making it impossible for the Soviets, even in a surprise attack, to have achieved any strategic advantage. (One should keep in mind that most testing occurred on remote islands in the Pacific Ocean, and there had never been a launch over the North Pole, with its uncertainties about magnetic pull affecting trajectories.) Reagan's purpose for a ballistic missile shield was never to eliminate all missiles, but to drive the cost and uncertainty of an attack up to such high levels that the enemy would never even consider it.[116] Certainly, both Reagan and Gorbachev had been briefed on the more accurate failure rates of Soviet technology. Gorbachev knew the score. His team lost, beaten by a single speech.

Here was a case of a technology not even being deployed yet having a war-winning effect. Later, as primitive elements of Star Wars wound themselves into the antiaircraft Patriot missile system, and were used in the Gulf War, the results were predictably mixed. Proponents of the Patriot may have jumped the gun touting its success: subsequent analysis significantly revised downward the claims of Patriot kills, but in the intervening thirteen years since Desert Storm, Patriot upgrades have proven exceptionally effective, and in Iraqi Freedom, Patriots performed extremely well, shooting down numerous missiles.[117] Errors still occurred: there was also a friendly fire incident in which a Coalition plane was destroyed. Nevertheless, as Karl Zinsmeister wrote, the soldiers thought highly of Patriot: "*We're gonna have to take those Patriot boys out on the town when we get home,*" said one trooper, and everyone came to appreciate the reassuring words from the loudspeaker, "*Missile destroyed.*"[118] Naturally, the media totally ignored the success of Patriot, despite the fact that it had, in real combat, validated the principal of missile defense.

Perhaps the greatest aspect of the Star Wars story is that even if, somehow, Gorbachev's Soviet empire had managed to acquire enough computer technology to compete, it was still doomed—by the very technology it needed to embrace. A nation linked together by webs of computers, all capable of allowing individuals to talk to each other through e-mails or primitive chat rooms, is the antithesis of state control, even when tightly monitored for security uses only. (A CIA study in 1985 assessed the Soviet system as capable of driving the country "*through forced-draft industrialization in the era of steel and coal, [but] it is highly unsuited to achieving the desired pace of technological advances ... under modern conditions.*")[119]

More than any weapon ever built—certainly more than the monstrously

---

[116]Larry Schweikart and D. Douglas Dalgleish, "What You Don't Know About SDI," Dayton Engineer, part 1, July 1988, and part 2, August 1988.

[117] Theodore A. Postol, "Lessons of the Gulf War Experience with Patriot," *International Security Review* (Winter 1991–1992), 119–71.

[118] Zinsmeister, *Boots on the Ground*, p. 57.

[119]Director of the CIA, document NIE, 11-18-85, "Domestic Stresses on the Soviet System, Office of Information Management, Washington, D.C.

destructive nuclear weapons it was designed to "kill"—Star Wars was scorned by the left. Here was a purely defensive system that sought at the simplest level only to keep nuclear warheads from exploding on American cities, yet it was lampooned and lambasted by leftists, who on the one hand, fumed that it would not work and on the other, wailed that it might, and in so doing, upset the fragile "balance of power" between the United States and the Soviet Union. Of course, what really gnawed at the left was not that they knew Star Wars would work, but that because it would work, it would bring about the final collapse of Soviet communism and discredit many of the principles on which the left had relied for years. Despite government funding, Star Wars was ultimately the result of free-market invention and innovation so thoroughly and convincingly defeating collectivism that it shook the leftist to their foundations. All in all, not a bad day's work for a B actor and a Buck Rogers space fantasy!

CHAPTER SIX
All for One

Better than anyone else, Americans have overcome a recurring and debilitating problem of military operations, which is that service branches and different units talk to each other, coordinate their activities, and fight together.

Men keeled over every hour, it seemed, overcome by malaria or dysentery. The Marine rifle companies had to locate fresh water, and the only source they knew lay at Cuzco Well, in the Guantánamo area—protected by the Spanish 6th Barcelona Regiment. It was June 10, 1898, and Captain George Fielding Eliot's two Marine rifle companies maneuvered into position, awaiting bombardment by the gunboat Dolphin, lying offshore. To their horror, shells started exploding among the Marines: the Dolphin, rather than laying down covering fire, was firing at them! The captain of the Dolphin had not been given the exact location of the Marines and now he threatened to wipe them out, just as the Marines had expected him to destroy the 6th Barcelona Regiment. Marine Sergeant John Quick detected a raised point from which he could flag the vessel, and amid shell bursts, he crawled up to the hill and waved a semaphore message to the Dolphin, which quickly shifted its fire to the Spaniards. Quick received the Medal of Honor for his actions.[1]

Some nineteen years later, as the American Expeditionary Force arrived in France to battle the Germans, General John "Blackjack" Pershing found communication difficulties insurmountable. He not only had to deal with mistakes in transmitting orders to Americans, but he had to coordinate with the French. One staff officer, a colonel, had the following conversation:

> *[American] Hello, this is Colonel Wilson, and I want to speak to Major Johnson in Tours.*
> *[French operator] pardon, je ne comprends pas. Repetez, s'ilvous plait.*
> *[American] I said Major Johnson in Tours and hurry up.*
> *[French Operator] Monsieur, quelest le nom, s'ilvous plait?[2]*

After the war, Patton, commenting on tank exercises held in the Carolinas, noted with disapproval, *"We still fail to use every weapon every time."*[3] His comment reflected a coordination problem, which, in turn, is a communication problem.

These episodes demonstrated the potential for disaster that existed when service branches could not communicate or coordinate effectively with each other. Poor communication and inadequate cooperation has been the ban of armies

---

[1] Joseph H. Alexander, *A Fellowship of Valor: The Battle History of the United States Marines* (New York: HarperCollins, 1997), pp. 20–21.

[2] John S. D. Eisenhower, *Yanks: The Epic Story of the American Army in World War I* (New York: Free Press, 2001), p. 57.

[3] Edward Coffman, *The Regulars: The American Army, 1898–1941* (Cambridge: Belknap Press, 2004), p. 393.

since ancient times. Gallic leader Vercingetorix, bottled up by the Romans inside his headquarters city of Alesia in 52 B.C., knew that a large relief force of Gauls waited just outside the Roman siege fortifications. Unable to coordinate his attacks with his rescuers, Vercingetorix was crushed by Caesar, whose Romans had the much-desired interior lines of communication.

Just the opposite result could be seen in Iraq, where the Marines of Recon Combat Team 5 (RCT 5), moving carefully along the Diyala River on April 4, heard incoming 122 mm Russian-made rockets. Within minutes, a Marine artillery battalion swept the zone with its antiartillery radar and tracked the rocket, instantly feeding back the coordinates to the Marines' six 155 mm guns. After just three rockets hit Leatherneck positions, Marine gunners rained down on the enemy 72 rocket-assisted projectiles, each one containing 108 bomblets: the Marines had responded to three rockets with 7,776 bomblets.[4] If the Marines had been willing to wait a few minutes, though, the Air Force would have pummeled the enemy location with its own bombs, and the Navy could have targeted the spot with cruise missiles, though that would have been a case of using a shotgun to kill a gnat.

Like almost all forces in the field in Iraq, the Marines of RCT 5 were connected by communications links to virtually the entire weaponry of the American arsenal. Although they still relied heavily on radios, new tracking computer chips, satellite imagery, and wireless e-mail now connected the foot soldier to the command, control, and intelligence behind the lines and to support firepower above and beyond his field of vision in ways undreamed of in previous wars. Joint communication was especially critical for the expected attack by Scud missiles and WMDs: theater air and missile defense in Operation Iraqi Freedom linked the services together in unprecedented ways. The USS *Higgins*, an Aegis destroyer, handled the early warning and linked the Navy's missile defense to that of the Army's Patriot batteries. Those defenses proved 100 percent effective in destroying Iraqi missile attacks on the coalition's forces in Kuwait.

Although the new technology united the armed forces in unprecedented ways, it was certainly not without glitches—consider the deadly Keystone Kop attempts by a column of American Humvees trying to escape Mogadishu, for example. Few operations in wartime occur without mishaps that bring death, but communications had advanced enough that it would be a rare occasion, such as the snafu that led to the 507th Mechanized unit taking a wrong turn in Nasariyah, when disaster would derive from inadequate contact with units.

The three-week war to topple Saddam constituted the most rapid major military campaign of conquest in history (as opposed to Israel's Six Day War, which was defensive), surpassing the success achieved by Operation Desert Storm in 1991. And more than the first Gulf War, the Battle of Baghdad represented the culmination of three dominant post-Vietnam/post—cold war military doctrines: joint operations (all services, operating in unison), combined arms (artillery, air,

---

[4]Bing West and Ray L. Smith, *The March Up: Taking Baghdad with the 1st Marine Division* (New York: Bantam, 2003), p. 169.

armor, infantry, intelligence units all working together), and full integration of the battlefield. Tanks and Humvees were connected not only to headquarters, but also to air support above. Rick Atkinson, traveling with the 101st Airborne in Iraq, noted, *"I could see that it was routine for colonels and captains and sergeants on the battlefield to summon the genies of the air and the earth and the sea, and to sic them on the enemy."*[5] It took mere seconds to call in counterbattery mortar or artillery fire, as gunners, using the AN/TPQ-36 Firefinder radar system, *"could detect an incoming artillery round and track it back to its source."*[6] Radar was linked to American artillery, which would instantly return fire. But there was low-tech methods that instantly calculated the trajectory of incoming shells based on crater locations, which also could be fed to the battery's guns. Either way, return fire was directed against the enemy within two minutes of the first shell impact. Virtually any enemy not fully drilled in "shoot and scoot" tactics, where a unit fires no more than three shots and packs up, would be dead.

Although still far from perfect, by the time of Operation Iraqi Freedom, American military forces, more so than any other in history, had overcome not only technological barriers to integrating air, ground, and sea operations, but more important, had eliminated institutional obstacles. The likelihood of a "Charge of the Light Brigade," brought on by hostile, elite officers who refused to talk to one another, had been virtually eliminated, and the plague of modern combat—death by friendly fire—has been reduced to previously unseen levels.

Talk to Me

Obtaining fire support with accurate target information highlighted a technology force multiplier of yet another type that united the services: communications. Since 1860, American commanders have appreciated the value of secure and rapid communications by, at the time, telegraph. Ulysses S. Grant and William Tecumseh Sherman used the telegraph better than any of their contemporaries—certainly better than George B. McClellan, who saw the telegraph only as an instrument of personal gain by which he could announce his latest victories to the press. *"Headquarters,"* Grant recalled, *"were connected [by telegraph] with all points of the command."*[7] Grant's Personal Memoirs revealed his facility for dispatching telegraphed messages, which required a certain word economy. Botched messages turned more than one battle, and Grant especially knew how to mix *"hard information, informed speculation and direct command"* in his messages.[8]

In France in World War I, the American Expeditionary Force notched perhaps its greatest accomplishment, not in the Argonne but in General John J. Pershing's Chaumont headquarters, which was connected by the Army Signal Corps to the coast by twelve thousand miles of telephone line leased from the French

---

[5]Rick Atkinson, *In the Company of Soldiers: A Chronicle of Combat* (New York: Henry Holt, 2004), p. 213.

[6]West and Smith, *The March Up*, p. 56.

[7]John Keegan, *The Mask of Command* (New York: Penguin, 1987), 211.

[8]Keegan, *Mask of Command*, p. 212.

and augmented by twenty-two thousand miles of new wire the Americans laid. Pershing also pressured the War Department for four hundred female American telephone operators fluent in French. The women, he predicted, *"will do as much to win the war as the men in khaki,"* and later he bragged that no civilian telephone service that he had observed beat the performance of the American operators.[9]   Again, however, this was made possible in part by Americans' preexisting familiarity with the technology. Just as in World War II, where 1 in 4 Americans owned a car, as opposed to 1 in 38 Germans or 1 in 130 Italians, (making truck and tank-driving techniques easy to teach), in World War II the United States boasted 14 telephones for every 100 people, while in France there were only 1.5 telephones for every 100.[10]

Nevertheless, the absence of integration and communication marked the First World War as fundamentally different from all wars previous—or since. Lieutenant Colonel C. F. Jerram of the Royal Marines commented on this, arguing *"the only thing that matters and without which you cannot begin to criticise [is] the fact that [World War I] was the only war ever fought without voice control."* [11]   Although Americans arrived too late to witness too much of this command "decapitation," examples abound, frequently involving the failure to exploit successes obtained by tanks. At Cambrai, for example, one veteran infantryman, who followed in the paths of a tank tread, recalled that the battle plan had called for cavalry to gallop through the openings (a first-day gash five miles deep, as it turned out) and turn the flanks. *"A child on a donkey could have ridden through,"* he mused. But without field telephones, walkie-talkies, or radio, the cavalry waited for confirmation that the holes had indeed opened, only to find the tanks knocked out by counterattacks by the time they received it firsthand from field observers.[12] Whereas in Grant's day, some degree of control of the battlefield was still possible through flags, bugles, and even riders or runners, by Pershing's time, the scope of the battlefield had grown so large that no one could exercise any voice control over anything. Even spotter aircraft had to land in order to make their reports.

Occasionally, what would later be deliberate inter-service cooperation between air and ground units, occurred strictly by accident. In Ocotal, Nicaragua, for example, in July 1927, a force of fewer than 50 Marines was under attack by more than 600 followers of Augusto Sandino. The Sandinistas were about to overrun the Marine positions when five DH-4 biplanes carrying bombs arrived on the scene. Pilots had flown over the scene earlier that day and reported the developments to headquarters, which dispatched the bombers. Marine major Ross Rowell then led his five bombers into what may be the world's first organized dive-bombing mission, terrifying the Nicaraguans and saving the Marines, who

[9]Eisenhower, *Yanks,* pp. 59–60.

[10]James Dunnigan and Albert Nofi, *Dirty Little Secrets of World War II: Military Information No One Told You About the Greatest, Most Terrible War in History* (New York: Quill, 1994), p. 26.

[11]John Terraine, *The Smoke and the Fire: Myths & Anti-Myths of War, 1861–1945* (London: Leo Cooper, 1992), p. 179.

[12]Quoted in "Tank: The Wonder Weapon of World War I," History Channel.

lost only one man killed.[13]   The following year, close to 200 Marines at Qualili, having suffered severe losses in ambushes, were besieged by hundreds of enemy. In what was possibly the first aerial resupply effort, U.S. Marines flew in some fourteen hundred pounds of supplies and took out the wounded.

During World War II, combined arms, as first demonstrated by Hitler's blitzkrieg tactics, relied upon pre-established rolling patterns of attack: dive-bombers and medium bombers would destroy hardened positions and supply depots; tanks would smash through the now-vulnerable softer defenses, and infantry would surround and mop up. Although infantry and armor could call for air support, it was a tedious and unreliable process. Radio signals usually went behind the lines to some unit at headquarters, where the Wehrmacht then communicated the need to the Luftwaffe, which in turn (if approved) dispatched air strikes in support of the ground forces. Even if everything went well, it might be hours before air support showed up—if ever. If a commander on the ground issued orders based on an expected strike that never came, he would look hesitant or even cowardly. If he attacked too soon, and air support showed up later, he would lose lives needlessly, or even risk putting his own men directly in the attack zone. Perhaps the only think more difficult for commanders on either side in World War II than calling in air support was calling it off if it was late, unnecessary, or worse, attacking friendly forces.

Thus, until the advent of forward-deployed, very fast airplanes linked to the ground with radios, calling in support fire almost always involved artillery, and even then it required a spotter on the ground with visual contact of enemy positions. This, of course, proved quite dangerous for the spotters, and by the time of the Korean War, it was common to use aircraft for spotting purposes, to the point where the Air Force even placed tactical air controllers for jet aircraft attacks in propeller-driven trainers that could direct the bombing.

Airpower, however, introduced the concept of vertical envelopment, possible in the past only by highly effective airborne drops. Not only could well-timed strikes destroy enemy supply lines, they also could cut lines of communication, leaving enemy forces isolated. In theory, paratroops and glider forces could be devastating. In reality, such lightly armed troops were fodder if they were not quickly reinforced by armor and artillery. Hitler's successful paratrooper conquest of Crete came at the expense of enormous casualties, effectively eliminating his parachute regiments for the remainder of the war. The infamous "bridge too far" of Operation Market Garden, following the successful use of paratroopers and gliders on D-Day, nearly did the same for Allied parachute forces. And paratroopers were ineffective in dense jungles or mountainous regions, where drops could be deadly.

After Vietnam, the potential for using helicopters to outflank or surround an enemy became a genuine alternative to parachute attacks. Once again, however, the key remained heavy lift, armor, and artillery support. Although troops

---

[13] Max Boot, Savage Wars of Peace: Small Wars and the Rise of American Power (New York: Basic Books, 2002), p. 238.

could be dropped deep behind enemy lines by helicopters, tanks could not be, and only a few helicopters could tote a piece of artillery—and even then, only one at a time. The solution? Find a way to increase the firepower of "overhead artillery," such as helicopters or C-47 "Puff the Magic Dragon" gunships, and by the end of the Vietnam War, it was common for gunships and artillery to cover the same "box," with air cover keeping a safe distance above projectile trajectories. This proved effective so long as the enemy did not have mobile antiaircraft units, as the Soviets discovered in Afghanistan and as we learned in Mogadishu. A cheap rocket-propelled grenade could destroy any multimillion-dollar helicopter.

Consequently, the most common and reliable form of unit firepower support remained the old standby, artillery. In Vietnam, artillerymen reorganized their guns from line to circular formations, so a battery could fire in any direction and surround a target with different trajectories. But with the renewed emphasis on mobility, the days of towed, emplaced artillery positions were limited, and in both the Gulf War and Iraqi Freedom, mobile artillery moved with the tanks. If a pause occurred, or a unit took up a fixed position for a night, artillery marked zones around the units and could respond to an enemy attack within seconds. All of this depended on instant communication—still iffy during the Vietnam War.

Future Force

"This is another type of war, new in its intensity, ancient in its origin— war by guerrillas, subversives, insurgents, assassins, war by ambush instead of combat; by infiltration, instead of aggression," John Kennedy stated in his 1962 address to West Point.[14] Even then, Kennedy, by creating the Green Berets, was demonstrating that he knew World War II methods would not be effective in this new war. And yet combined arms, or the ability of military forces to coordinate their efforts with different elements (that is, infantry with tanks and artillery), had been crucial to battlefield success dating to at least napoleon's time, and perhaps as far back as Alexander the Great. During World War I, when American commanders appreciated the lethality of the trench and machine-gun combination, they attempted to open up their tactical formations to reduce casualties and to take advantage of supposedly greater American expertise in marksmanship. But as historian Allan Millett concluded, these efforts often failed because many officers simply lacked the training to coordinate their units properly with barrages.[15]

American technological dominance, however, acted as a force multiplier in more ways than one, because, for the first time, it made truly joint operations feasible. To see how far we had come, consider that as late as the 1980s, the services, for all intents and purposes, still fought independently. For example, American military planners had prepared to stop a Soviet ground invasion of the Fulda Gap in Western Europe by defeating tank-heavy Russian forces through

---

[14] Kennedy quoted in Michael Lind, *Vietnam: the Necessary War* (New York: Touchstone, 1999), p. 103.
[15] Allan Millett, *The General: Robert L. Bullard and Officership in the United States Army, 1881–1925* (Westport, CT: Greenwood Press, 1975, p. 315

rapid attrition and sheer effectiveness. *"Fight outnumbered and win"* was a less than reassuring motto of the Cold War army in Europe, whose objective was to stay alive long enough for help to arrive from the states. Yet it was the challenge of planning to fight a foe that substantially outnumbered them that helped break down the walls with the other services and lead Army planners to relinquish their independence and to ask for help—and lots of it.

Therein originated the Air/Land Battle Doctrine that demanded close co-operation between the Army, Air Force, and, sometimes, Navy to overcome superior numbers through deadly efficiency of integration. Aircraft, using long-range air-to-ground missiles would destroy Soviet command and control vehicles and buildings; helicopters, using "pop up" tactics, would snipe at enemy columns on the move; then, finally, NATO tankers and gunners would engage a much-depleted enemy force. By necessity, anti-Soviet tactics stressed defensive deployment and accurate fire followed by immediate relocating to another spot, so as to steadily even the odds. Air support was to continue to conduct deep-strike attacks on Soviet staging areas—assumed to be protected by state-of-the-art antiaircraft missiles, guns, and interceptor aircraft—and to defeat the high-tech Red air force in head-to-head combat.

Much of this war-fighting doctrine became obsolete after 1991. America's new enemies fought in the deserts and mountains, not Europe's forests and farms, and although the new foes were low tech, they were even more committed to their cause than the Communists. Indeed, Americans had experiences with fanaticism of the jihadist type: perhaps the only examples that came close were the defense by Los Niños in Mexico City of the Japanese kamikaze attacks in World War II. Yet even these encounters were exceptions to the norm: most Mexican soldiers did not engage in suicidal last stands, and after Emperor Hirohito announced Japan's surrender, the empire's soldiers laid down their arms almost universally. (One of the striking differences between the Iraqi occupation and the occupation of Japan is the absence of attacks on GIs after September 1945, a difference that is entirely traceable to the Japanese culture and the incomparable role of the emperor in Japanese society.) Even fierce Sioux warriors did not assault the remaining 7th Cavalry forces on Reno Hill in suicide fashion, nor did most German units fight until the death. Bombers in Iraq came as a surprise precisely because of the previous, misleading experience with large numbers of surrendering Iraqi troops during Desert Storm. Suicide tactics in Baghdad demanded a new understanding of the enemy and appreciation for this deadly fighting style.

Traveling with the 3rd Infantry Division's tanks rolling into Baghdad on the "thunder run," David Zucchino captured the thoughts of Major Ricky Nussio as his Bradley's 25 mm gun tore apart an enemy combatant charging the column in a garbage truck. A garbage truck, he thought. *"It was as if they wanted to die,"* Zucchino wrote. At one point, the Iraqis' inept tactics and inferior training started actually to frighten American tankers, who were convinced they were walking into "a big trap. They really do have a plan. They're just luring us in with these haphazard, disjointed tactics. Sometime soon, they're going to get organized and attack with some serious tactics."[16] In this instance, the old maxim "if it's too good to be true, it probably isn't" did not apply. It really was too good, and it was all too true: the Iraqis were pitifully trained, and dying by the dozens.

They weren't the only ones. Stephen Biddle concluded that "*al Qaeda's inability to master the modern system in its entirety was instrumental in their rapid expulsion*," by which he meant their inability to handle combined arms and to employ the full spectrum of American training, concepts of freedom and adaptation, and autonomy as well as western weapons.[17] Joint operations, in which air reconnaissance is combined with ground forces, can provide deadly effectiveness, even when the enemy is aware that he is being watched. In Afghanistan, al Qaeda, aware of air surveillance, emerged to fire as soon as reconnaissance planes flew away, only to be hammered by well-timed American ground mortar fire. While the much-touted abilities of guerrillas to handle ground troops alone (as in Vietnam), or helicopters by themselves (as in Mogadishu) have been overemphasized, what is really important is that they have not dealt with, nor can they successfully deal with, joint operations, because that requires implementing the American way of war, and such coordination is, by definition, beyond such enemies.

One of the central problems of Vietnam was that combined arms/joint operations were not even conceptually applied. Deep strikes by the Air Force and Navy (and, today, by the Army's helicopter regiments) slows down reinforcements, makes movement behind the lines difficult or impossible, prohibits rebuilding of bridges and roads, and above all drives troops on the march into hiding. Eyewitnesses who had been in Vietnam reported to the author that they looked across the South Vietnamese border to see enemy formations within artillery or aircraft range, yet they were denied authority to engage because of political concerns. A North Vietnamese general, pointing out to an American that after a bridge bombing, entire villages would turn out with gunny sacks filled with dirt to rebuild a passage over a creek or river, noted, "*Caucasians have no idea what ant labor can do*." Yet such "ant labor" can do little if it is under fire from long-range artillery or ducking from overhead bombs. The battlefield in the Vietnam War was not just South Vietnam, it was all of Southeast Asia, and allowing the North Vietnamese to move troops through their own country or Laos or Cambodia was akin to the Union's allowing Robert E. Lee to march Pickett's division right up to Cemetery Ridge without firing a shot so as not to offend people living around Seminary Ridge!

Joint operations, combined arms, and system integration all offset another long-held military necessity, preponderance of power. Traditionally, armies had to mass sufficiently to ensure dominance at almost any point in the line, or, at least, at a point that could be attacked quickly by rapidly focused troops. Vast reg-

---

[16]David Zucchino, *Thunder Run: the Armored Strike to Capture Baghdad* (New York: Atlantic Monthly Press, 2004), p. 34.

[17]Stephen Biddle, Military Power: Explaining Victory and Defeat in Modern Battle (Princeton: Princeton University Press, 2004), p. 57.

iments had to stand in formation waiting, or move with ponderous baggage trains that themselves became targets. Using all the service arms in an integrated way, however, simulates a karate fighter concentrating all his power into the end of his fist or foot: it allows full maximization of military power, all the time. During Iraqi Freedom, the embedded "generals" repeatedly complained that there were not more troops, which would have defeated the purpose of having light, fast, fully integrated forces that were not required to conquer Iraq foot by foot. Indeed, *"a single 155-mm howitzer can kill any exposed infantry over an area of more than four football fields in just two minutes; massing more troops in the area would only raise the toll."*[18] A 1960s-vintage American tank could destroy ten to fifteen Soviet T-62s in just five minutes in open ground with proper targeting! During the Gulf war, in one engagement, the 2nd Armored Cavalry Regiment, consisting of 9 Abrams tanks and 12 Bradley fighting vehicles engaged and destroyed 37 Iraqi T-72s and 32 other armored vehicles (in defensive positions) in less than forty-five minutes. Three troops of U.S. armor had wiped out an entire Republican Guard brigade, totaling more than 110 Iraqi tanks or personnel carriers compared to the loss of a single Bradley and one crewman.[19] The "rigid and centralized" Iraqi command system with its *"nearly complete absence of initiative among junior officers"* and *"little ability to operate independently in small units"* ensured the doom of Iraqi forces.[20]

Operation Desert Storm, in fact, demonstrated conclusively the futility of non-Western forces (no matter how well equipped) duking it out with the American military in any semblance of a "traditional" war. Loss rates of the Coalition—the attacker, who is expected to have higher casualties than the defender—were the lowest in history, or approximately one fatality per 3,000 soldiers. A decade later, Operation Iraqi Freedom had a loss rate of one fatality for 2,500 military personnel, only slightly higher than in 1991, despite a much more difficult and complex mission. (Contrast this with the U.S. Marines' losses at Tarawa in 1943, which were a thousand times higher!) Clearly al Qaeda learned from Desert Storm. But has it learned enough? Arguing for a "new theory" of military capability, Army War College analyst Stephen Biddle claims that the *"modern system of force employment ... is extremely difficult to master,"* and the necessity to limit losses and physical exposure on the battlefield demand institutional and structural changes.[21] This is, of course, somewhat fancy talk for saying that to beat Americans in the American way of war, you have to adopt "Americanism." Put another way, *"America's military power is unsurpassed because it derives its strength not simply from technology but also from the voluntary consent to institutions and policies that have developed within democratic societies."*[22] Consider

[18]Biddle, *Military Power,* p. 69.
[19]Jesse Orlansky and Jack Thorpe, eds., *73 Easting: Lessons Learned from Desert Storm via Advanced Distributed Simulation Technology* (Alexandria, VA: Institute for Defense Analysis, 1992).
[20]Biddle, *Military Power*, p. 138
[21]Biddle, *Military Power*, p. 190.
[22]Douglas MacGregor, *Transformation Under Fire: Revolutionizing How America Fights* (Westport, CT: Praeger, 2003), p. 41.

that during World War II, Japanese admirals, under the code of Bushido, thought it beneath them, as warriors, to escort merchant vessels. Consequently, Japanese shipping was pillaged by American submarines, in contrast to the Anglo-American convoy system implemented in the Atlantic, which finally provided a defense against German U-boats.

That is not to say that the transformation is complete. As late as 2003, Douglas MacGregor of the National Defense University argued that of the five major questions facing the U.S. Army, three of them related directly to "integrating" the Army with other services or joint forces; organizing or commanding such joint forces; and retaining initiative with such joint forces.[23] Like so many other modern commentators, MacGregor finds the transformation too slow and predestined to stall. And like so many commentators, he is wrong. The fact that modern fighters still deal with intelligence that is "*frequently wrong or misinterpreted by commanders in the field*" is hardly a failure, but rather a commentary on conditions that have characterized combat from the beginning of time.[24] Paradoxically, one of the most serious problems to emerge from the new joint/integrated military is that individual soldiers and sailors increasingly lose a sense of the broad battlefield, of advance and retreat, of success and failure. Enemy units painted by lasers from an aircraft crossing a battlefield may not be physically observed being destroyed. Neither the pilot who identifies the target, nor the sailor who fires the cruise missile that destroys it, is likely to see his or her handiwork.

Overlying the new emphasis on joint operations and combined arms is another traditional concept made truly revolutionary by technology—mobility, mobility, mobility. During the Cold War, America had years to preposition men, vehicles, and supplies throughout Europe to resist a Soviet incursion there. Since 1991, however, new threats are likely to be smaller and more dispersed, meaning that reaction time matters more than ever. Prepositioning supplies was impossible in many of these potential trouble spots, and the United States lacked close bases to some regions. (Operation Enduring Freedom was only possible within the time frame that it actually took place because the Bush administration received permission to stage troops out of Uzbekistan and Kazakstan, and received overflight rights from Pakistan.) Such demands meant the military had to "get light and get fast." Weapons systems that could be dropped, airlifted, or floated onto a battlefield or beach got priority funding, including the Marines' new LAV (light armored vehicle), an eight-wheeled lightly armored semi-amphibious vehicle that carried Marine infantry or antitank weapons. In its most common form, the LAV featured a 25 mm chain gun capable of firing a variety of ammunition types, and while not nearly as resistant to enemy fire as a Bradley personnel carrier, the LAV was lighter.

New demands for mobility struck the Cold War—oriented Army particularly hard, forcing generals to reexamine its core of heavy tanks and long-range heavy artillery. Contrary to the claims of critics, however, no one suggested elim-

[23]MacGregor, *Transformation Under Fire*, p. 11.
[24]MacGregor, *Transformation Under Fire*, p. 21.

inating tanks. Indeed, there is no greater friend to the grunt on the ground than an M1A1 Abrams coming up to lend support. Even more impressive was the M1M2 upgrade, with its superior fire control and advanced thermal imaging.

In almost any scenario, however, the nearly invulnerable Abrams tanks posed a serious problem for rapid deployment. Each of the not quite five thousand Abrams tanks weighed sixty-nine and a half tons and was twenty-seven feet long and twelve feet wide. For long journeys, such as from ports to staging bases in Kuwait during Desert Storm, the Army used flatbed tractor trailers to haul the monsters and to save gas and wear and tear on treads and engines. Only the largest helicopter could lift one into battle, and the tanks consumed so much space that airlifting a tank brigade into position with C-130s was virtually impossible. Partly because of these deployment problems, and partly because the end of the Soviet threat meant that further upgrades to antitank capabilities for the Abrams were superfluous, the army canceled further purchases of the M1A2s after 2004. Nevertheless, there remained the lesson of Mogadishu: that Humvees cannot survive against rocket-propelled grenades (RPGs) and that they were highly vulnerable to heavy caliber fire. In response to the need for an armored vehicle that was lighter, and more easily transported, in 1999 the army announced production of a lighter armored vehicle, the Striker.

To obtain the Striker, the Army had to free up resources by canceling a number of programs, including a new command and control vehicle and a tactical rocket system, and restructuring the Crusader artillery system, which was eventually canceled. When listing it requirements for the new armored vehicle, the Army insisted that the vehicle be transportable in a C-130 aircraft and be able to exit the aircraft ready to fight. It settled on the Marines' LAV III vehicle, which can be reconfigured to include artillery.

The Striker represented a process of "incremental adaptation" to changing battlefield demands rather than a "revolution," and is fully in keeping with the American approach to deploying good new technology slowly but steadily.[25] Recall that the Union Army did not drop the Springfield rifle in favor of the Sharps carbine after Hoover's Gap, nor did the United States abandon the Sherman tank in World War II—rather, in each case, either a methodical replacement process was employed or consistent and significant upgrades were added until full modernization and effectiveness were achieved.

Limits and Lessons of Joint Operations

During the battle for Manila in February through March of 1945, the United States, having devastated the Japanese with combined arms, encountered a new challenge: urban warfare where the enemy routinely used civilians as shields. American doctrine for such urban warfare was *"grinding in nature,"* using *"overwhelming fire to get to a point of penetration in a strongpoint or building, make a*

---

[25]Biddle, *Military Power*, p. 206

penetration in the building, then painstakingly clear the building room by room."[26] Combined-arms teams of engineers, tanks, and artillery would blast through the walls for infantry to clear a building. Manila made two things clear: the kinds of infantry casualties needed for such house-to-house fighting would not be tolerated by the public, and indiscriminate firepower that leveled cities and slaughtered civilians was no longer an option. "*Artillery*," Kevin Benson, the author of "*Manila*" in a book on urban warfare, **City Fights**, argued, "*may not be able to play a large role once the fight inside a city is joined.*"[27] (Ironically, at Hue, cathedrals and churches that were off limits to U.S. bombers were routinely strafed and bombed by South Vietnamese aircraft.)

Nevertheless, by the Korean War, in the clearing of Seoul, a joint approach had been developed to fight through a city full of enemy obstacles:

> *First, navy and marine fighters conducted rocket and strafing attacks on the barricades and adjacent positions. Next, mortars and small arms provided protective fire while engineers went forward to detonate or disarm the land minds. Once a path was clear, tanks would move aheadand blast the enemy machine guns. ... While this was taking place, infantry riflemen would follow the tanks to give them protection from the suicidal satchel chargers. [All the while] ammunition was being brought forward and casualties were being evacuated almost constantly.*[28]

Even with improved firepower and with more coordination, the battle to retake the city was "bitter," as General Matthew B. Ridgway recalled. It introduced an old danger to the urban battlefield: fire, where smoke obscured and choked. Above all, the chaos of urban warfare underscored the need for disciplined reporting procedures, rapid support from other service branches, and synergy between different types of units. As Major Thomas Kelley observed of the urban battle in **Seoul**, "*a combined-arms approach to fighting in a city provides the range of capabilities needed to overcome complex defenses. ... [N]o single branch or type of unit can do it along. ...*"[29]

The battle for Seoul starkly contrasted with the battle for Hue City in 1968, where "*the lack of effective operational control ... resulted in haphazard and disjointed tactical actions.*"[30] American ground units had to deal not only with the U.S. Navy and Air Force, but also with the Army of the Republic of Viet Nam (ARVN) and, at the battle of Da Nang during the Tet offensive, with the Blue Dragons of the Korean Marine Corps. Hue highlighted the significance of having HUMINT (human intelligence, or people on the ground who could identify enemy soldiers and positions) as well as SIGINT (signals intelligence, or intercepting

---

[26]Kevin C. M. Benson, "Manila, 1945: City Fight in the Pacific," in John Antal and Bradley Gericke, *City Fights: Selected Histories of Urban Combat from World War II to Vietnam* (New York: Ballantine Books, 2003), pp. 230–50 (quotation on 245).

[27]Benson, "Manila," *City Fights,* p. 247.

[28]Thomas A. Kelley, "Seoul, 1950: City Fight After Inchon," in Antal and Gericke, *City Fights*, pp. 314–38 (quotation on 333).

[29]Kelley, "Seoul," p. 337.

[30]Norm Cooling, "Hue City, 1968: Winning a Battle While Losing a War," in Antal and Gerick, *City Fights*, pp. 339–74. (quotation on 358).

enemy radio signals). As American code breakers in World War II discovered, obtaining mountains of signals, transmissions, or other pieces of intelligence was often nearly useless unless someone on the ground could add specifics. At Pearl Harbor, for example, a single reconnaissance pilot who might have flown over the Japanese fleet that attacked the U.S. 7th Fleet on December 6, 1941, would have had an immediate impact, whereas intelligence being gleaned from listening posts and other spy stations in the Pacific had not only to intercept, translate, decode, then analyze signals and transmissions, but then had to forward them to the appropriate officer who could issue orders. In some cases, important Japanese messages, broken under the Magic program and related to Pearl Harbor, were not translated or decoded until 1945! This was, unfortunately, still true in the Vietnam War. At Hue, on January 30, 1968, an army intercept on Highway 1 south of the city indicated an imminent North Vietnamese attack, but procedures required that the message go to Da Nang for analysis rather than directly to commanders in the field—who did not get the "warning" until Communist troops were running through the city streets.[31]

Hue City revealed that *"the principle of unity of command is of increased importance in urban areas,"* and that both human and signals intelligence is even more important in an urban environment.[32]   Increasingly, an oft-ignored branch of the services, the spy and intelligence units, were viewed as the key to successful urban and, later, counterinsurgent warfare. A single friendly civilian who can identify a dozen locations with hostile forces, or point out enemy combatants, is worth a dozen air sorties or a brigade of combat troops. Moreover, all the success of combined arms, especially in urban warfare, reaffirmed the *"high premium on individual skill and initiative."*[33]   Nevertheless, in one study of thirteen battles involving urban warfare, the authors concluded that *"no single branch or type of unit can fight alone"* in urban settings without extreme risk." Combined arms were "essential," and were almost unbeatable when properly synchronized.[34] Since communication will play such a vital role in combined arms actions in the future, the authors of City Fights observed that no form of communications should be ignored, including human or animal couriers, civilian and military telephones, and , of course, radios. (It is worth noting that al Qaeda reverted to cell phones almost exclusively to avoid traditional SIGINT surveillance—until they discovered that we had tracked their cell phones as well.) And not surprisingly, General Tommy Franks noted that Operation Iraqi Freedom involved, for the first time, a full-spectrum war against computers, communications, and intelligence as well as traditional military forces.

---

[31]Cooling, "Hue City," p. 360.

[32]Cooling, "Hue City," p. 370.

[33]Mark J. Reardon, "Evolution of Urban Combat Doctrine," In Antal and Gericke, *City Fights*, pp. 388–415 (quotation on 395).

[34]John F. Antal and Braldey T. Gericke, "Lessons Learned from City Fights, 1938–1968," in Antal and Gericke, *City Fights*, pp. 416–30 (quotation on 423).

The Camptown Ladies Sing This Song, OODA, OODA

Communications offered the key to getting inside the enemy's OODA loop, the in-vogue catch phrase in the military for observation, orientation, decision, and action. Developed by Colonel John Boyd, USAF, the OODA cycle is the time it takes for a commander to receive battlefield information, process it, and respond. Boyd's two most famous briefings, *"Patterns of Conflict"* and *"A Discourse on Winning and Losing,"* which began as hour-long presentations, grew into fifteen-hour sessions that lasted two days.[35] In Boyd's loop, the actor—in this case, a leader—makes decisions based on observation and orientation. But a great danger exists if the leader fits observations into a preexisting mind-set or orientation, at which point he loses the capacity to adapt and instead becomes an echo chamber.[36] Unless careful, a leader can receive accurate battlefield information, yet consistently make the wrong decisions because he is interpreting it based on preconceived notions of what the opponent will do. To a degree, this was what occurred with the warnings about 9/11: those receiving signals fit them into hostage-taking scenarios, rather than flying-bomb scenarios.

Although developed by a USAF fighter pilot, the OODA loop, so far, has only been adopted formally by the USMC. Once again, cross-pollination of ideas among the services led to significant battlefield advances (it was Air Force MPs who first adopted the M16 as their standard weapon, prompting the Army to soon do so as well).[37] Boyd—known as Forty-Second Boyd because he won every dogfight in less than forty seconds—argued in his briefing "A Discourse on Winning and Losing":

> *Physically we can isolate our adversaries by severing their communications with [the] outside world as well as by severing their internal communications to one another. We can accomplish [the former] ... via diplomatic, psychological, and other efforts. To cut them off from one another, we should penetrate their system by being unpredictable.[38]*

Widely adapted to business, the OODA loop emphasized changing the enemy's behavior, not annihilating his forces, although in general, once the enemy is forced into operating outside his normal practices, he will make mistakes that allow him to be destroyed. It was important, Boyd argued, to orient the enemy into wrong deployments, strategies, and battlefield decisions. In such an environment, the side that has the most advanced communication and intelligence will usually be victorious. While primitive signaling, such as the smoking tires the Somalis used at Mogadishu, might be effective in some circumstances, unit coordination

---

[35]http://www.mindsim.com/MindSim/Corporate/OODA.html.

[36]John Coram, Boyd: The Fighter Pilot Who Changed the Art of War (Boston: Little Brown, 2002); *Grant Hammond, The Mind of War: John Boyd and American Security* (Washington, D.C.: Smithsonian Institution Press, 2001).

[37]Thomas McNaugher, *The M-16 Controversies: Military Organizations and Weapons Acquisition* (New York: Praeger, 1984).

[38]Keith R. Hammonds, "The Strategy of Winning and Losing," http://www.fastcompany.com/online/59/pilot.html.

and cooperation is a far better force multiplier. Had the United States wished to call in artillery on the clansmen pursuing American troops down alleys in Mogadishu (and inflict civilian casualties), it would have been easy to do so. Military necessity was overridden by the concern for civilian casualties, but the helicopters flying overhead could have radioed instant coordinates to artillery if such had been the objective. Such an action would have gotten inside the enemy's OODA loop, anticipating movements and shredding his soldiers before they even made eye contact with the Americans.

At Fallujah in March of 2004, the United States found itself at a disadvantage in using the OODA loop: the insurgents were prepared for a major assault; they had the civilians terrified into supporting them; and they anticipated provoking a scorched-earth attack that would produce heavy civilian casualties. Americans wisely held back, choosing to delay while using deception, probes, and psychological warfare to throw the enemy off balance. Once Fallujah was surrounded, American troops began winnowing the terrorists—in essence refusing to play on the terrorists' field, and making the enemy play on the Marines' home turf. Assured that they were not going to be made into human shields, Iraqi citizens began exiting the city at night to deliver tips to the Marines. As Colonel G. I. Wilson and others noted in a widely circulated briefing on OODA loops and "fourth generation warfare," money, food, and above all, information were all ammunition.[39] By November, when several roadblocks had been cleared, including an Iraqi transitional government and the reelection of George Bush, a steady policy of attrition had severely reduced the insurgents' numbers, eroded their support among the local population, and left them unsure as to what the United States planned to do. When the attack finally came, it was swift, overwhelming, and so rapid that American commanders were quickly inside the OODA loop.

Purchasing Power

If improvements in communication have enhanced "jointness," it is still a rocky road when it comes to willingly surrendering "turf." Ceding any operations to someone else may mean losing a budget line, regardless of effectiveness. In the case of the Army's twin-engine C-7 Caribou, a small cargo plane designed to deliver loads to remote, unpaved runways, the Air Force argued that such an aircraft infringed on its mission, and that it could provide the airplanes more effectively. Once the program was transferred to Air Force control, "*there appeared a spate of statistics, all showing that the Air Force had a much higher readiness rate for the Caribou, a much lower accident rate*," and other indicators of superior effectiveness.[40] However, the Air Force achieved this by doubling the manpower the Army had assigned to the job! Of course, that is not necessarily bad, in that

---

[39]G. I. Wilson, Greg Wilcox, and Chet Richards, "4GW and OODA Loop Implications of the Iraqi Insurgence," April 12–14, 2005, http://www.d-n-i.net/fcs/ppt./16th_strategy_conference.ppt.

[40]I. B. Holley, Jr. *Technology and Military Doctrine: Essays on a Challenging Relationship* (Maxwell Air Force Base, AL: Air University Press, 2004), p. 86.

the Air Force may have the available personnel for such duties, but it is indicative of the extent to which services will go to retain control over programs and operations.

Joint purchasing, the holy grail of economizing the military, has proven stubborn, mainly because the needs, mission, and even the service cultures differ so dramatically from Army to Air Force to Navy. Robert McNamara, in one of his most serious miscalculations, tried to force a jointly designed fighter aircraft, the TFX, on the Air Force and Navy. But the demands of the Navy for a study undercarriage, capable of sustaining carrier deck landings, and high-torque engines to get the plane off the carrier deck, were 180 degrees in opposition to the Air Force's need for top speed and a light undercarriage. The result was the predictable camel (a horse designed by a committee): the F-111B fighter bomber, which proved an excellent fighter bomber, but a completely inadequate aircraft for the purposes it was designed to meet, namely a fighter plane for each service.[41]

If services can agree on truly shared characteristics, there is more hope. In the 1980s, the Navy, the Defense Advanced Research Projects Agency (DARPA), the Air force, and NASA all combined to fund a research aircraft called the X-30 (later the National Aerospace Plane, or NASP). This revolutionary program was conceived by DARPA's mad-scientist genius, Robert Williams, and tackled staggering challenges every step of the way: a proposed scramjet-powered aircraft that would use slush hydrogen fuel, the airplane required materials that were not available at the time the contracts were let. An actual prototype plane had to be built in order to just test the scramjet characteristics, since no wind tunnels existed capable of testing any flight above Mach 8. Further, perceiving that the project would take years, Williams sought to cement long-term support from several services ad agencies on the assumption that if everyone had a little kicked in, it would be in no one's particular interest to kill the program for the funds.

Several factors killed the X-30, most notably the difficulty in getting the scramjet engine to work as hoped. There were great successes, including production, pumping, storage, and burning of the hydrogen fuel; radical new materials, including carbon-carbon composites and titanium aluminides; and breakthroughs in "computational fluid dynamics," in which computer models can be substituted for actual flight test data. (In the cases where the models were checked against actual flight data, they proved remarkably accurate.) Most important, however, Williams misread the services' parenthood of programs: if no one is the "father," no one makes the program a priority. In the case of the X-30, neither the Air Force nor NASA ever adopted the program as exclusively its own, so each willingly allowed it commitment to be cut in favor of other programs.[42]

Truly joint production items, such as missiles and ammunition, can be procured with little difficulty. But attempts to increase the government's purchas-

[41]Robert B. Coulam, *Illusions of Choice: the F-11 and the Problem of Weapons Acquisition Reform* (Princeton: Princeton University Press, 1977),
[42]Larry Schweikart, *The Quest for the Orbital Jet*, vo. III, *The Hypersonic Revolution*, ed., Richard Hallion (Washington, D.C.: United States Air Force, 1998).

ing power by streamlining the differences among the services down to nothing are fraught with danger. Each service branch has its own internal culture for a reason: the constant, familiar engineering give-and-take required by Air Force personnel working on a new fighter plane design would be stifled by the more rigid Marines, who must clear rooms full of terrorists. Service branches have their own rhythms as well: submariners work on rotations of ninety days under water—the extent to which sailors can be expected to hole up in a tin can—but three months is scarcely enough time to learn the ropes for a combat infantryman or a Marine. Where the services have minimized cultural differences they have been successful, as with the AGM-154A joint Standoff Weapon, developed by Raytheon for the Air Force and Navy, and capable of destroying land and sea targets, guided by the highly accurate Global Positioning system.[43] This missile includes both bomblet, anti-armor, and anti-ship variants, and scored successes in its initial tests. Perhaps the ultimate test in "jointness" will involve missile defense, where the Air Force, the Navy, the Strategic Defense Initiative Office, and the Army, with its theater antimissile defense, will all play a role in identifying, intercepting, and killing enemy missiles. So far, early tests—especially those in Iraq—have indicated that this multifaceted integrated system is indeed working.

Communications Breakdown

Some of our greatest disasters, or near disasters, have occurred because of misunderstood orders or poor communications. Understandably, only recently could ground, air, and sea units effectively communicate. But even when limited to a single service branch, poor communications or inadequately worded orders have resulted, at other times and in other armies, in the annihilation of the Light Brigade and in Marshal Grouchy's failure to reinforce Napoléon at Waterloo. In the South Pacific, in September 1944, another poorly worded order nearly handed the Japanese a naval victory that they desperately needed.

On September 27, 1944, Admiral Chester Nimitz transmitted the operation plan for the combined U.S. Army, Marines, and Navy assault on Leyte in the Philippines. Such orders routinely carried a letter or number in front of each sentence, but there was in this order an apparent late insertion. Nimitz commanded Admiral William "Bull" Halsey to support the invasion with his 3rd Fleet (in reality, Task Force 38). Halsey was to

> *"COVER AND SUPPORT FORCES OF SOUTHWEST PACIFIC IN ORDER TO ASSIST THE SEIZURE AND OCCUPATION OF OBJECTIVES IN THE CENTRAL PHILIPPINES."* [44] *Further, the orders instructed Halsey to "DESTROY ENEMY NAVAL AND AIR FORCES IN OR THREATENING THE PHILIPPINES AREA."*

<u>This too</u> was unambiguous. What caused problems was an unnumbered,

[43]"AGM-154A Joint Standoff Weapon [JSOW]," http://www.fas.org/man/dod-101/sys/smart/agm-154.htm.
[44]Orders from Nimitz quoted in Thomas J. Culter, *The Battle for Leyte Gulf, 23–26 October 1944* (Annapolis: naval Institute Press, 1994), p. 59.

FIGURE 7

The Battle of Leyte Gulf
October 23–26, 1944

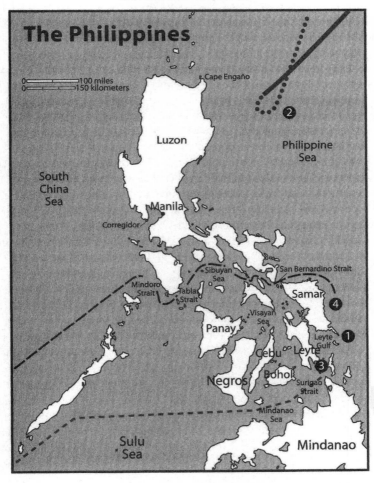

❶ Invasion forces in Leyte Gulf
protected by Halsey's 3rd Fleet
and Kincaid's 7th Fleet

❷ ▬▬ Ozawa's approach
●●●● Ozawa lures Halsey's 3rd Fleet
carriers and battleships to the north

❸ – – – Nishimura's forces defeated at the
Battle of Surigao Strait, but lures
Kincaid's battleships south

❹ ▬ ▬ Kurita's main attack against
"Taffy 3," "Taffy 2," and "Taffy 1,"
escort carriers and destroyers

unlettered sentence that *"was apparently a late insertion,"* according to Halsey's biographer, which commanded the admiral,

"IN CASE OPPORTUNITY FOR DESTRUCTION OF MAJOR PORTION OF THE EN-EMY FLEET OFFERED OR CAN BE CREATED, SUCH DESTRUCTION BECOMES THE PRIMARY TASK." [45]

E. B. Potter, Halsey's biographer, determined that Admiral Ernest King ordered the addendum, according to his assistant chief of staff, whom Potter interviewed, but later the same assistant was less sure of the origin of the added phrase. Further, Potter observed that the order was not characteristic of either King's or Nimitz's style, and that such an order should have been made clearer or given a priority status. Regardless, Halsey was all too happy to have the extra flexibility, and he wrote Nimitz saying *"Inasmuch as the destruction of the enemy is the principal task, [emphasis added], every weapon must be brought into play and the general coordination of these weapons should be in the hands of the tactical commander responsible for the outcome of the battle,"* namely, Halsey. [46] Yet the "principal task" of the 3rd Fleet was the destruction of the enemy only if *"opportunity ... offered or can be created."* Halsey clearly intended to create an opportunity!

Rear Admiral Jesse Oldendorf commanded the 7th Fleet Bombardment and Fire Support Group, which was to provide cover for the troops landing on the beaches. His ships opened fire on October 18, 1944, at which time Douglas MacArthur ordered 60,000 troops and one hundred thousand tons of supplies to hit the beaches. These forces were separate from Halsey's formidable 3rd Fleet, which consisted of tour task groups, totaling eight aircraft carriers, seven light aircraft carriers), six battleships, five heavy cruisers, nine light cruisers, and forty-eight destroyers, as well as submarines and auxiliaries. It was an impressive fleet. With no Japanese ships in sight, the frustrated Halsey rotated his task groups to Ulithi to re-provision.

Meanwhile, his carriers and battleships had been pounding Japanese airfields and land targets on Okinawa, Luzon, and Formosa. At Formosa, Admiral Soemu Toyoda, the commander of the Japanese combined fleet, attempted to fight it out in the skies with his remaining aircraft, only to watch the Americans destroy his airplanes in droves. Japanese pilots had virtually no training—their fuel shortages were so severe that they were often trained with movies shown on a screen attached to the front of the stationary aircraft. American pilots, who often had more than a year of training, easily shot down Japanese who had a maximum of two months' actual flying. Toyoda's subordinate, Vice Admiral Jisaburo Ozawa, who had command of the carrier strike force, emerged from the Formosa battle with only 110 airplanes for all of his carriers put together, and his impotence forced the transfer of his command to Vice Admiral Takeo Kurita, who was steam-

---

[45]Order quoted in E. b. Potter, *Bull Halsey* (Annapolis: Naval Institute Press, 1985), p. 279.
[46]Halsey to Nimitz, quoted in Potter, *Bull Halsey*, p. 279.

ing northward from Sumatra with his fleet to rendezvous with Ozawa and Admiral Shoji Nishimura.

Farther south, at Leyte, General Douglas MacArthur stood on the bridge of the USS Nashville, watching the shore bombardment as the invasion craft started for land. When he strode ashore on October 20, he had no way of knowing that three different Japanese fleets were converging on the Philippines. From the north, Ozawa's force included a heavy carrier and three light carriers, as well as two "hermaphrodites," battleships that had a short aircraft carrier deck in the aft section, capable of launching (but not recovering) aircraft. From the south, coming through the Mindoro Strait, came Kurita while also from the south, Nishimura sailed through the Mindanao Sea and the Surigao Strait. Ozawa was to occupy and distract the American surface fleet, while the two fleets under Nishimura and Kurita would attack from the south. They hoped to coordinate their efforts in order to strike the American simultaneously.

Japan's only hope for success lay in deception, and the Americans' only chance of defeat would involve poor communication. The Japanese counted on American poor intelligence about the condition of the aircraft forces on the carriers. Bluntly, there were none. Ozawa had a handful of planes left, but did the Americans know that? And would the rich lure of the fat carriers be enough to distract the main part of the American fleet (they were still unaware that Halsey was in charge), so that the other two pincers could destroy the landing force at Leyte? Another Japanese force, the 5th "Fleet" (a pair of cruisers and some destroyers that lagged behind the Kurita's force as it left Lingga in Sumatra) under Kiyohide Shima, also steamed northward to catch up to Nishimura.

Collectively, these fleets composed a significant fighting force, especially since Kurita's fleet included the massive new battleships the Yamato and the Mushashi, seventy-thousand-ton ships that were some thirty thousand tons heavier than the new American North Carolina-class battleships. Their eighteen-inch guns fired projectiles that weighed thirty-two hundred pounds, outranging the sixteen-inch guns on the Iowa. Yet in many ways, the battleships represented a horrendous misapplication of resources. Japan was investing in horse cavalry when Americans were producing tanks. The United States still needed battleships for gunfire support during island invasions. Japan had staged no invasions in a year and all but the most unrealistic Japanese leaders knew there would be no more. What Japan needed was aircraft carriers and, above all, new planes with trained pilots. Instead, they received these gargantuan floating hulks. Effectively using these behemoths was akin to a blind, one-armed boxer depending on his opponent two walk toward his good arm while wearing a cowbell. And, astoundingly, the United States almost entered the ring in October 1944.

Two Davids were the first to confront this Goliath's fleet: the submarines Darter and Dace. When Kurita sailed into their patrol zone, they immediately moved into firing position and promptly blasted two cruisers to the bottom, then damaged another. The Japanese offensive was scarcely under way and already it had sustained serious—though not critical—losses.

Meanwhile, the Japanese in the Philippines had scraped together a few hundred airplanes with ill-trained crews to use in simultaneous attacks on the American carriers supporting the invasion, providing a form of fire support for Kurita and Nishimura's vessels. It marked one of the few times that Japan's army and navy agreed to work together—a sign of desperation that contrasted starkly with typical American operations. Even then, the results were much the same. After spotting the incoming Japanese planes. American carrier aircraft rose to engage them, and in one case, a single pilot, David McCampbell, shot down nine confirmed Japanese planes and probably downed two others that could not be confirmed. His wingman, Roy Rushing, also became an ace that day, shooting down five enemy planes.[47]

After repulsing one foray by Kurita, damaging his monster battleship Mushashi, the Americans picked up Shima's third attacking force coming across the Sulu Sea, meaning that *"by midday Halsey and [Admiral Thomas] Kinkaid knew about all the Japanese forces approaching Leyte Gulf except the one that wanted to be discovered"* Ozawa's decoy fleet of empty carriers.[48] At that point, things fell apart for Halsey and the American forces. When reconnaissance aircraft finally found Ozawa's nearly empty carriers, Halsey turned northward with all of his task force, at the time designated Task Force 34, a newly formed group that included all of the full-sized carriers and four battleships and three heavy cruisers. Believing this was the main Japanese fleet, Halsey charged off, leaving the back door open through the San Bernardino Strait.

It was a delicately laid trap, involving four Japanese fleets converging on Leyte from different directions, with the key being Ozawa's ability to lure Halsey's carriers away. Little did Kurita dream that Halsey would leave the landing forces virtually unprotected from the northeast. While Admiral Jesse Oldendorf's powerful screen of battleships and cruisers sealed off the Surigao Strait to the south, decimating the combined fleets of Nishimura and Shima onthe night of October 24-25, everyone (including Nimitz) presumed that Halsey had left some of his capital ships to cover the three "mini" carrier task forces that were supporting MacArthur's invasion. These "baby" flattops, or escort carriers, in the three invasion-support task forces (known as Taffy 1, 2, and 3), were used more as auxiliaries to transport aircraft to battle zones than as main attack carriers. Designated CVEs, the baby flattops, had little antiship ordnance on them, and little armor, leading their crews to refer to them as "combustible, vulnerable, and expendable." [49] When Halsey left with the main combat forces of the fleet, his subordinate, Vice Admiral Thomas Kinkaid, did not know that all he had to defend the invasion force from Kurita's approaching heavy ships were the Taffy flattops, because Halsey had sent a poorly worded message suggesting that he had not taken all of the battleships.

[47]Cutler, *Battle for Leyte Gulf,* pp. 123–27.

[48]Cutler, *Battle for Leyte Gulf,* p. 154

[49]Cutler, *Battle for Leyte Gulf,* p. 58.

In short, Kurita's plan had worked well, completely exposing the U.S. invasion fleet to some of the largest guns in the Japanese navy. What followed was an event of incredible determination by American destroyer captains, poor combat decisions by Kurita, and a little luck. By the time U.S. reconnaissance planes identified Kurita's battleship force coming from the north, it was too late to acquire any anti-ship bombs or torpedoes. Taffy 3 under Rear Admiral Thomas Sprague met the enemy vessels first, and launched his planes without armor-piercing bombs or torpedoes. Sprague's aircraft could harass, but hardly damage, the large ships. At the same time, he turned his force south and fled, hoping to come under the cover of the nonexistent battleship force. Several of Taffy 3's heroic destroyers turned head-on into the Japanese fleet, closing in some cases so fast that they got under the guns of the bigger ships. Their small five-inch guns could hardly damage a heavy cruiser or battlewagon; and while their torpedoes were always a threat, before long several of Taffy 3's escorts had been sunk or badly damaged. Kurita was still coming, but he misjudged the slow speed of the creeping flattops and failed to observe that he was gaining on them. Then, briefly, a squall came up and further concealed Sprague's ships. After it lifted, however, his CVEs were pounded by the long-range guns of the Yamato and the Kongo.

Chasing Ozawa farther north, Halsey's planes were sinking the carrier Zuikaku and light carrier Chitose when the admiral began receiving panicked messages from Kinkaid begging for help. These messages also were received at fleet headquarters, where CINCPAC head Admiral Chester Nimitz was reading them. He ordered a message sent to Halsey asking his position with the famous phrase *"Where is rpt [repeat] where is Task Force Thirty-four."* In an unfortunate choice of code wording, wherein additional (supposedly meaningless) phrases were tacked onto the front end of every message, separated by two letters (for example, GG), the unidentified seaman transmitting the message added the phrase *"The world wonders"* after *"Where is Task Force Thirty-four."* He apparently did not see that it seemed to fit with the rest of the communique, nor, of course, did the sailor decoding the message on Halsey's ship—thus it was not removed before the admiral saw it. To Halsey, this was an incredible affront by his friend and superior, Nimitz. It appeared that Nimitz was mocking him, and he exploded in rage and embarrassment, throwing his cap on the deck. Even though it was too late to effect the outcome, he dispatched his battleship group to rescue the Taffys, which were under full attack by the Japanese guns by that time.

Halsey was not the only one to send help to Taffy 3. Farther south, Rear Admiral Felix Stump, with Taffy 2, mustered all the aircraft he could launch and sent them to strike Kurita. It was an ineffective force, but through the cloud of war, the additional aircraft convinced Kurita that he faced the main American carrier fleet. Then he received word of Halsey's force striking Ozawa to his north and, possibly, turning on him next. Simply put, Kurita lost his nerve. He had Taffy 3 dead in the water, and could have annihilated the exposed Taffy 2, and possibly even Taffy 1 before help arrived. Still thinking he was engaged with the outer fringe of the main American carrier fleet, however, Kurita ordered a retreat. Although Oldendorf had shredded Nishimura and Shima's fleets, Kurita escaped with many of his large ships, so both sides avoided giving—or receiving—the knockout blow.

Recriminations against Halsey were harsh. Samuel Eliot Morison's *History of United States Naval Operations in World War II* claimed that the Japanese came within a whisker of isolating MacArthur's army, and Bernard Brodie ridiculed Halsey in his article, *"The Battle for Leyte Gulf."*[50] The admiral did himself no favors by blaming Nimitz, however indirectly, for a poor command structure and Kinkaid for being unprepared. On the other hand, Halsey was following the main doctrine of American sea power at the time, namely, adhering to a concentration of forces, and he was in pursuit of what everyone thought was the main Japanese carrier fleet, the last real threat in the Pacific. No one, especially Halsey, suspected the Japanese were as low on aircraft and pilots as they were. Halsey should have left some capital ships in the north as protection from an approach through the San Bernardino Strait, but he sought the knockout blow that had evaded Rear Admiral Ray Spruance first at Midway, then again on the Philippine Sea. Although official criticism of Spruance was muffled, a concern existed among CINCPAC that he had let the Japanese off the hook, and Halsey was instructed directly not to allow that to happen again.

The Battle of Leyte Gulf therefore represented a great opportunity for the Japanese, with American lack of coordination and communication at its worst. But this is true only if viewed with blinders, as though the Japanese could have operated flawlessly, with their own communications intact. Instead, what happened was what usually happens in war when each side has equal numbers of missteps: the side with the simplest plan, the fewest orders, and the best technology wins. Halsey's failure to coordinate involved essentially one area of operations—the back door, so to speak, but one that could still be closed eventually. Sooner or later, Jesse Oldendorf's "heavies" would have swung back from the Surigao Strait if Kurita had pursued the Taffys too far south or east; or if he had hung around to destroy shipping and transports in the Gulf, Halsey's own dispatched units would have sealed off his retreat.

More important, whereas Americans had erred through badly worded messages and poor assumptions about their enemy (even over-estimating Japanese air power), Kurita's forces suffered from a worse problem, a deferential culture. One Japanese destroyer commander, Shigeru Nishino, having witnessed how Nishimura's lead ships were savaged when they attacked in column formation, did not bother to warn the follow-up forces under Admiral Shima because *"I had no connection with him and was not under his command [and] I assumed that*

[50]Samuel Eliot Morison, *History of United States Naval Operations in World War II*, 15 vols. (Boston: Little Brown, 1963), 12:337–38; Bernard Brodie, "The Battle for Leyte Gulf," Virginia Quarterly Review, Summer 1948, 455–60; Gilbert Cant, "Bull's Run: Was Halsey Right at Leyte Gulf?" Life, November 14, 1947, pp. 73–90; William D. Leahy, *I Was There: The Personal Story of the Chief of Staff to Presidents Roosevelt and Truman Based on Notes and Diaries made at the Time* (New York; McGraw-Hill, 1950), and his comments in the New York Herald-Tribune, October 31, 1953, "Leahy Hits Halsey on Leyte Battle."

Shima knew the conditions of battle. ... ."[51] While Americans of all ranks were desperately (even, at times, perhaps unprofessionally) begging Halsey for help, alerting him to the status of Kurita's force, the Japanese withheld information because it was "not their place" to pass on such information to superiors. Moreover, a standard rule of combat is that as communications become more difficult, and the chaos increases, a good commander simplifies plans and eliminates complexities that might introduce indecision in battle. Japanese admirals such as Kurita, steeped in their practices of intricate maneuvers and complicated plans, were foiled in large part by several American destroyer captains' decisions to, simply, charge. As at Midway, the Japanese suffered from inordinate deference on the one hand and rigid sclerosis on the other. As a recent analysis of the Midway defeat concluded of Japanese leadership, *"an inability to change their plans in midstride was endemic to the Japanese military as a whole."*[52]

The U.S. Navy learned the lessons of Leyte Gulf, as did the other services. Communication was essential; coordination highly desirable. The more the services worked together, the more each found important strengths in the other—and the more willing each became to loosen its control over battlefield situations in order to achieve success. Americans win wars because the lessons of cooperation among the units of a single service, after Vietnam, were absorbed by the commanders of all the branches. Americans win wars because we have, better than anyone else to this point, integrated our military and eliminated inter-service friction. "All for one" is more than the motto in Alexander Dumas's The Three Musketeers: it is the essence of modern inter-service, multiunit warfare that makes the whole far more than the sum of the parts. And it is another reason Americans win wars.

---

[51]Cutler, *Battle for Leyte Gulf*, p. 201.
[52]Jonathan B. Parshall and Anthony P. Tully, *Shattered Sword: The Untold Story of the Battle of Midway* (Washington, D.C.: Potomac Books, 2005), p. 103.

CHAPTER SEVEN

Protesters Make Soldiers Better

The United State has turned a perceived weakness—dissenters from the media, Hollywood, and universities who oppose almost every war—into an advantage by transforming their concern for human life into a devastatingly effective war machine that has relentlessly minimized its losses.

Warnings had already been sent to the troops: the forthcoming five days would be a "festival of blood."[1] The city, as one reporter noted, *"was washed with the air of battle*," and commanders knew that a *"hardcore element ... was ready for a fight*." Someone on the other side predicted, *"There will be slaughter. Just slaughter*." When one leader motored through a town on his way to the battlefield, the locals screamed, "Murderer! Killer!" and a mob attacked his vehicle at another town. The enemy threatened to poison the water supply; infiltrators brought in guns and strapped bowie knives to their bodies under their clothes; food supplies were tainted with feces; and one braggart said he would "roast" and "eat" the enemy leader. Staring a few hundred yards away at the opposing army, one guard said, *"You can smell them*." *"To the streets! The streets belong to the people*," screamed the generals. This was Chicago, and this was 1968. And this was a "peace" protest.[2]

Arrayed against some 8,000 to 10,000 yippies, hippies, and other protesters who had publicly threatened to poison the Chicago water supply with LSD, was a force of almost 12,000 Chicago police, supplemented by 5,600 Illinois National Guardsmen and 1,000 FBI agents, with another 10,000 guardsmen and regular Army soldiers standing by if things got further out of hand. Whether or not the police should have taken seriously the various threats to place razor blades on the ends of broomsticks or to throw real acid—not LSD—in cops' faces, the demonstrators hurling bottles and rocks at them hardly seemed "peaceful." Tom Hayden, later known mostly for marrying actress Jane Fonda, warned that his troops were coming to Chicago to *"vomit on the politics of joy*." He was *"expecting death, expecting the worst*." Hayden told the officer arresting him, *"We're going to take you into a dark alley and you're never going to come out*."[3] By such threats and provocations, the police had been pushed to the edge. One eleven-year veteran who had rarely drawn his gun in wild-and-woolly Chicago found that against the protesters he almost drew it, twice.

Several years later, when the United States had all but withdrawn the last forces from Vietnam, Hayden and his fellow protesters thought they had won. Many sincerely believed they had dealt the military a fatal blow. Little did they

---

[1]The Chicago Seed, quoted in Frank Kusch, *Battleground Chicago: The Police and the 1968 Democratic National Convention* (Westport: Praeger, 2004), p. 54.
[2]Kusch, *Battleground Chicago*, pp. 43–64, 74, and passim.
[3]Kusch, *Battleground Chicago*, p. 71, and passim.

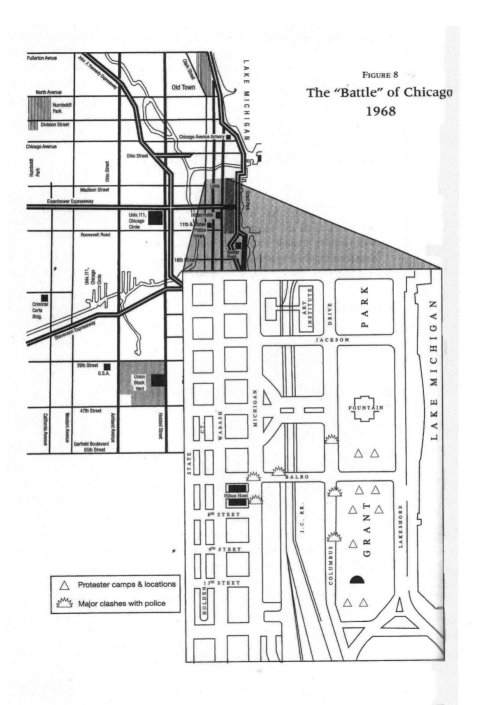

FIGURE 8

The "Battle" of Chicago
1968

know that they had laid the groundwork for victory in four consecutive wars. The media, which had assisted the protesters in their Vietnam "success," contributed to that victory by revealing itself for what it was: overtly hostile to the U.S. military.

Antiwar protesters, who have been present in every conflict, have increasingly found that their most successful strategy is not to emphasize the "morality" of war because most Americans (rightly) know that they usually fight only moral wars. Instead, antiwar movements have sought to play upon a casualty-sensitive American public by emphasizing the cost of combat to American families. This has backfired. Since the Revolution, American military thinkers have understood that soldiers have value, and that heavy losses are rarely acceptable, no matter how grand the victory. Even without prodding from protesters, therefore, the U.S. military has relentlessly sought to ensure the safety of individual soldiers as much as possible, whether through more effective tactics or better body armor, while at the same time guaranteeing that they have the best weaponry so that they can eliminate their enemies with dispatch. This preparation has served to make the American armed forces the most lethal in the world, yet at the same time it has steadily pushed down U.S. death tolls, leading to the ironic (and perverse) complaint by some media sources that American medical procedures were too effective in saving lives and returning wounded (read "damaged") soldiers to civilian life. One author referred to the "*darker side of increased survival rate,*" which leads one to wonder if an article on breast cancer advances would deal with the "darker side" for survivors.[4]

The Anti-military Press

None other than the firebrand propagandist Tom Paine recalled in 1803 the "*black times of Seventy-six.*" He wrote fellow pamphleteer Sam Adams that, in retrospect, the defeats suffered by Washington that year were "*no other than the natural consequence of the military blunders of the campaign.*" However, he worried that Americans might have seen them "*as proceeding from a natural inability to support its cause against the enemy, and might have sunk under the despondency of that misconceived idea.*"[5] Paine knew about the power of the press to influence civilian populations to support—or fail to support—a war, since it had been his stock in trade for several years. His pamphlet The American Crisis, which began with the famous line "*These are the times that try men's souls,*" constituted a pro-military propaganda masterpiece, without which the Revolution likely would have failed. More than two hundred years later, Paine would be described by contemporary mainstream journalists as a cheerleader for the war effort. He would not be taken seriously as an objective observer—even though he not only was at the front but was actually fighting! Indeed, few reporters ever

---

[4]Ken Fuson, "Technology, Medical Advances Raise Soldiers' Survival Rates," desmoinesregister.com, November 28, 2005, http//:demoinesregister.com/apps/pbcs.d11.article?/D=120051188/NEWS11/51A1280317.

[5]Paine to Adams, January 1, 1803, in Philip S. Foner, ed., The Complete Writings of Thomas Paine, 2 vols., (New York: Citadel Press, 1945), 1:434.

have suffered the same slings and arrows of military fortune as Paine, who survived Valley Forge.

What happened? Why did the media, especially the post-1960 mainstream media turn on the military? Were reporters always liberals? And why has an antiwar contingent been present in almost every conflict, yet have so little power until Vietnam? Are reporters inherently antiwar and, therefore, antimilitary? World War II, often held up as a model of good reporting, had episodes in which journalists seemed less than patriotic. Was the World War II experience different, and if so, why? Answers to these questions inevitably relate to deeper questions about the opposition to the use of the military in America, particularly in light of the Vietnam Template. Can war protesters be patriotic? If there actions endanger the lives of soldiers at the front, can they truly claim to support the troops? The answers may provide some surprising conclusions. Protesters' efforts to undermine the Vietnam War were, without a doubt, successful in the short run. But, ironically, protesters and antiwar activists have actually made American soldiers even more effective—a result that would, doubtlessly, trouble them greatly. Protesters have made the American military machine more lethal than even because, in their howls of concern over Americans being lost in Southeast Asia (most recently), they raised the premium on soldiers' lives, thereby increasing even further the emphasis on training, technology, and professionalism.

There have always been antiwar protesters—one could argue that the one third of the Tories who did not join (and even fought against independence) the Revolution were the first Jane Fondas, Tom Haydens, and Abbie Hoffmans. What has changed is the role of the media in its treatment of protesters. Press coverage of American wars in the past was uneven, mostly confined to the battlefield scribblings of a few on-site journalists and to the reposting of clipped stories from a few of the major papers that could afford reporters. James Bennett's New York Herald sent a single reporter to cover the Mexican War. But that soon changed, and by the Civil War the paper had sixty reporters in the field. One could hardly characterize their work as antimilitary, although reporters seldom shied away from publishing details of friendly and enemy troop movements and strengths. Robert E. Lee learned as much about Union troops from Yankee newspapers as from his own spies. Understanding the key role of the antimilitary media today requires a slight digression into the history of journalism and the rise, disappearance, and reappearance of the partisan press.

America has always had some partisanship among its journalists. George Washington and Thomas Jefferson felt the barbs of nasty writers, including the aforementioned Paine, who fifteen years later wished Washington dead, or Philip Freneau, who fifteen years later wished Washington dead, or Philip Freneau, who remained a constant critic of the Federalists.[6] Early papers, or broadsides, contained much local content and occasionally clipped news. Typically, such broadsides were posted in inns, saloons, and so forth, usually read aloud by a literate

[6]Larry Schweikart and Michael Allen, *A Patriot's History of the United States: From Columbus's Great Discovery to the War on Terror* (New York: Sentinel, 2004), p. 130.

person over a meal, with all of the patrons chiming in with editorial comments. This early practice of "reading the news" greatly resembled the modern Internet political Web site, where readers post comments, such as www.freerepublic.com or www.democratunderground.com. However, the early broadsides dealt mostly with local events and were substantially nonpartisan, with a few exceptions, such as the papers of John Fenno and Freneau.

That changed dramatically in the Age of Jackson, when the very purpose of a "newspaper" was to elect the party's candidate. Political parties subsidized all the major papers and expected them to toe the line when it came to editorials supporting party positions. Almost all papers needed party funding to survive, and subscriptions ran disastrously behind costs. Politicians routinely had entire speeches reprinted in a sympathetic partisan paper. Other important benefits attended those who remained loyal to the parties. For one thing, the nature of postal laws meant that newspapers could be sent through the mails at a fraction of the cost of books. This temporarily allied the papers, the post office, and the politicians, who could send speeches and other political material home to constituents virtually free. But in August 1846, Congress decided to give printing contracts to the lowest bidder instead of a partisan organ, and at the same time, ended most printing contracts to partisan papers. Fourteen years later, the final official link between the government and the press was severed when the Government Printing Office was founded.

The partisan press was challenged by the penny press of Bennett's Hearld and Benjamin Day's *New York Sun*, which began to move newspapers into more sensationalist and crime-oriented news, and as early as 1843 editors called for a national convention for the purpose of establishing standards, *"enter[ing] into mutual pledges ... [and] form[ing] a virtuous resolution, that they will hereafter control their passions, moderate their language," in order to "pursue truth."*[7] **The Herald** "pursued" such truth by, as one competitor noted, *"offend[ing] all parties and all creeds."*[8]   Clearly, however, the public had tired of the partisan press, because the "pennies" saw their circulations soar: within five years, Bennett's paper had a combined circulation of fifty-one thousand or fourteen thousand more than James Watson Webb's competitor, the New York Enquirer.[9]   The success of these papers was not lost on competitors. After 1850, journalists in larger numbers gravitated to a standard of scientific measurements of facts: *"Facts; facts; nothing but facts. So many peas at so much a peck; so much molasses at so*

[7]"American and British Newspaper Press," *Southern Quarterly Review,* 4 (July 1843), pp. 235–38.
[8]New York Tribune, June 3, 1872.
[9]Donald Lewis Shaw, "At the Crossroads: Change and Continuity in American Press News, 1820–1860," Journalism History, 8, Summer 1981, pp. 38–50; Thomas C. Leonard, The Power of the Press: The Birth of American Political Reporting (New York: Oxford University Press, 1996); Charles E. Clark, The Public Prints: The Newspaper in Anglo-American Culture, 1665–1740 (New York: Oxford, 1994); and Michael Warner, The Letters of the Republic: Publication and the Public Sphere in Eighteenth-Century America (Cambridge, Mass,: Harvard, 1990); Hazel Dicken-Garcia, Journalistic Standards in Nineteenth-Century America (Madison, Wisconsin: University of Wisconsin Press, 1898); and Gerald J. Baldasty, The Commercialization of News in the Nineteenth Century, Madison, Wisconsin: University of Wisconsin Press, 1992).

much a quart."[10]

It was the Civil War, however, that broke the back of the partisan press. "*Almost overnight,*" wrote L. Edward Carter of the American Civil War, "*it seemed that newspapers were quite different.*" The war contributed to the movement toward an objective, fact-driven press—a "*revolution in journalism.*"[11] Readers wanted to know what happened, and needed accurate news, not sugar-coated fables: "*the home front,*" noted Carter, "*wanted unvarnished facts.*"[12] The romantic, flowery writing style was replaced by the "inverted pyramid" of stating the most important facts first, then subsequent facts in descending order of importance. "*The 'lead' was war-born,*" meaning that the introduction, or news lead, was introduced during the war and that this led to increased sales. While considerable fluff still remained in the writing, one could learn the critical details of a story in the lead paragraph. Second, as people of all political stripes wanted war news, papers downplayed partisanship in order to report facts.[13] By 1866, Lawrence Gobright, the AP's Washington agent, concluded, "*My business is merely to communicate facts. My instructions do not allow me to make any comments upon the facts which I communicate. ... . My dispatches are merely dry matters of facts and detail.*"[14] Researchers found that in the decade after the Civil War, objective stories constituted about 40 percent of all news articles, and that share had risen to more than 66 percent by 1900. In contrast, stories that researchers labeled "biased" declined especially sharply after 1872.[15]

A second factor, technology, in the form of the telegraph, played an important role in changing the press during the war. Straight news reporting by the **Associated Press** out of New York gave it a distinct advantage in war reporting because AP writers already had pared their reports of excessive words and opinion, omitting, therefore, editorial comment. Anticipating the embedded reporters of Iraqi Freedom, Lincoln realized that non-editorialized reporting of his actions would receive higher levels of public support, and aimed to get battlefield reports to the people, bypassing the editors. By its very reporting style, AP came as close to a White House press office as Lincoln could have hoped for.[16] AP had not adopted its word economy because of administration pressures, but because of the technology of the telegraph, which "*was superimposed on a news-gathering system that already placed a premium on the apparent factual accuracy* [emphasis

[10]Michael Schudson, *Discovering the News* (New York: Basic Books, 1978), pp. 78, 86.

[11] L. Edward Carter, "The Revolution in Journalism During the Civil War," *Lincoln Herald,* p. 73, Winter 1971, pp. 229–34 (quotation on 230. See also J. C. Andrews, *The North Reports the Civil War* (Pittsburgh, Pennsylvania: University of Pittsburgh Press, 1955), pp. 6–34; Edwin Emery and Henry Ladd Smith, *The Press and America* (New York: Prentice-Hall, 1954); and Havilah Babcock, "The Press and the Civil War," Journalism Quarterly, March 1928, 6, pp. 1–5.

[12]Carter, "Revolution in Journalism," p. 231.

[13] Robert W. Jones, *Journalism in the United States* (New York: Dutton, 1947), p. 322.

[14]Gobright quoted in David Z. T. Mindich, *Just the Facts: How Objectivity Came to Define American Journalism* (New York: New York University Press, 1998), p. 109.

[15]Harlan S. Stensaas, "Development of the Objectivity Ethic in U.S. Daily Newspapers," *Journal of Mass Media Ethics*, 2, Fall/Winter 1986–87, 50–60, and Donald L. Shaw, "At the Crossroads: Change and Continuity in American Press News, 1820–60," Journalism History, 8, Summer 1981, pp. 38–50.

[16]Robert S. Harper, *Lincoln and the Press* (New York: McGraw-Hill, 1951), pp. 303–24.

added]."[17] The telegraph replaced verbose writers, who embellished their stories, with stringers who submitted bare facts.[18]

Commanders in the field appreciated both the threat and the promise of the press as much as Lincoln. General Henry Halleck denied reporters access to his camps. General Benjamin Butler threatened to shoot the reporter, and General George Gordon Meade shipped another out of his camp riding backward on a horse with a placard reading "Libeller of the Press."[19] War secretary Edwin Stanton became especially adept at skillful censorship, and most generals understood that reporters could be dangerous foes, and that their printed reports, however innocent appearing, might yield valuable gems to the enemy and result in battlefield deaths. (One publisher, Wilber Storey, with instructions that seemed eerily similar to the 2005 *Newsweek* Koran story, told his reporters, "*Telegraph fully all the news you can get and when there is no news send rumors.*")[20] Lincoln, while cognizant of the evil that publishers could do, nevertheless told his commanders that they should leave the reporters alone unless "*they may be working palpable injury to the Military in your charge; and, in no other case will you interfere with the expression of opinion in any form, or allow it to be interfered with violently by others* [emphasis added]."[21]

In the Confederacy as well, John Thrasher, the superintendent of the Press Association of the Confederate States of America, encouraged his association's reporters to submit clear and concisely written telegraphic stories, free of opinion or comment.[22] Thrasher insisted that correspondents eliminate extraneous words and to "*see where you can use one word to express what you have put in two or three.*"[23] He provided an example in which he underlined the words to be omitted:

> OKALONA, April 25—Our cavalry engaged the enemy yesterday at birmingham. *The* fight lasted 2 ½ hours. *The* enemy were completely routed, *with* 15 killed *and* a large number wounded. Col. Hatch *of the* 2d Iowa cavalry was seen *to* fall from his horse, which rant into *our* lines and *was* captured. Our loss was one killed and twenty wounded. *The* destruction of *the* bridge prevented pursuit.[24]

Lacking a press association, the Union government placed authority over

[17]Dan Schiller, *Objectivity and the News: The Public and the Rise of Commercial Journalism* (Philadelphia: University of Pennsylvania Press, 1981), p. 4.

[18]James Carey, "The Dark Continent of American Journalism," 144–90 (quotation on 161), in Evea Stryker Munson and Catherine A. Warren, eds., *James Carey: A Critical Reader* (Minneapolis, Minnesota: University of Minnesota Press, 1997

[19]Jeffrey Alan Smith, *War and Press Freedom: The Problem of Prerogative Power* (New York: Oxford, 1999), 104–5. See also David T. Z. Mindich, "Edwin M. Stanton, the Inverted Pyramid, and Information Control," Journalism Monographs, p. 140, August 1999.

[20]Smith, *War and Press Freedom*, 103.

[21]Abraham Lincoln to John M. Schofield, October 1, 1863, in Roy P. Basler, ed., *The Collected Works of Abraham Lincoln* (New Brunswick, New Jersey: Rutgers University Press, 1953), 6:452.

[22]Ford Risley, "The Confederate Press Association: Cooperative News Reporting of the War," *Civil War History,* 47, September 2001, pp. 222–39.

[23]Thrasher quoted in Risley, "Confederate Press Association," p. 231.

[24]Quoted in Risley, "Confederate Press Association," p. 231.

battlefield reporting under the Department of War, which, in the East, was controlled almost exclusively by General George B. McClellan. Soon after Edwin Stanton replaced Simon Cameron as War secretary in 1862, he reviewed the flow of information and concluded that the Union cause was not aided by McClellan's control of most telegraphic dispatches from the front. Stanton received authorization from Lincoln to have total control of the telegraphs shifted to himself, and within two weeks McClellan's personal telegraph office was dismantled and all lines routed through Stanton's office.[25] Peter Watson, Stanton's close friend, took over press releases, and Stanton started reviewing the daily reports, sending agents to sniff around telegraph bureaus and ordering Charles Dana to spy on General Ulysses Grant for signs of drunkenness or dereliction of duty. Lincoln was obsessed with the telegraphic reports from the front that rattled into Stanton's office, where the president had his own chair.

Stanton's dispatches, which papers disseminated as his "War Diary," often constituted the day's lead story. His terse, facts-only style, written in descending order of importance, helped establish the inverted pyramid technique. This ran contrary to the chronological style still used then by many reporters, which reserved the important facts for the end of the story.[26] Journalists lamented Stanton's control over the news, often forgetting that the slightest detail could result in death and carnage at the front. When the *New York Tribune* revealed where General William Sherman's forces were rendezvousing with their supply vessels, a Confederate reader of the *Tribune,* General William J. Hardee, learned of this rendezvous and attacked Union forces there. It wasn't the first time such a leak had occurred: Robert E. Lee learned of the movements of General Ambrose Burnside from the pages of the *New York Daily News,* and on another occasion withdrew from Richmond based on a *Philadelphia Inquirer* report about the location of McClellan's forces.[27]

Grant, for one, had little toleration for reporters' undermining of the war effort. He ordered Major General S. A. Hurlburt, in Memphis, to

> suppress the entire press of Memphis for giving aid and comfort to the enemy by publishing in their columns every move made here by troops. ... Arrest the Editor of the Bulletin and send him here a prisoner, under guard, for his publication of present plans via New Carthage & Grand Gulf.[28]

Grant's opponent, General Robert E. Lee, had no higher regard for the press, saying "they do not contribute to our self respect, or to a solution of the troubles of the country."[29] Lee further remarked, with rare sarcasm, to Confederate senator B. H. Hill that *"we appointed all our worst generals to command the armies, and all our best generals to edit the newspapers." "I am sorry,"* he wrote

---

[25]Mindich, *Just the Facts*, pp. 78–79.

[26]Mindich, "Edwin M. Stanton, the Inverted Pyramid, and Information Control," passim.

[27]Mindich, Just the Facts, p. 88.

[28]Quoted in Peter G. Tsouras, *The Greenhill Dictionary of Military Quotations* (London: Greenhill Books, 2000), p. 374.

[29]Quoted in Tsouras, *The Greenhill Dictionary of Military Quotations.*

his wife, "*that the movements of the armies cannot keep pace with the expectations of the editors.*"[30] Napoléon had warned "*four hostile newspapers were more to be feared than a thousand bayonets.*"[31]

If the telegraph and the terse writing style demanded by it contributed to more objectivity, so, too, did pressure from the market. Slowly but steadily this process favored an open exchange of ideas. A commercialized news business, oriented toward profit, sought to offer readers what they wanted. One editor likened a newspaper to a department store, which gave readers what they wanted "*just as the merchant gave his customers calico if they want[ed] it instead of silk.*"[32] Papers started to look just like other businesses, with "managerial hierarchies" focused on the bottom line and especially sensitive to attaining the broadest consumer base possible while simultaneously diminishing risk.[33] That meant avoiding unpleasant political positions that might alienate readers. News was separated from editorial comment, with the former, to a great degree, emphasizing facts. Horace Greeley, editor of the *New York Tribune*, established rules for contributors to his paper, assuring that "all sides" to an argument received attention.[34]

Even those editors who still championed partisan journalism tempered their positions: Richard White explained that a journalist was "*the advocate of a party,*" and should make the "*strongest argument*" he could, but was not "*at liberty to make intentionally a single erroneous assertion, or to warp a single fact.*"[35] This mainly took the form of separating news from editorial comment and emphasizing local stories that would appeal to mass audiences—a practice called the "new journalism."[36] The new journalism paid off: the *New York World* attained a readership of nearly three hundred thousand by 1893, generating advertising revenues proportional to its circulation.[37] Papers such as the *San Francisco Examiner* published massive special editions, such as the World's Fair edition in 1893, which brought in $70,000 in revenues.[38] Even then, publishers warned against sensationalism at the expense of facts: Arthur Dodge, of the *Madison (Wisconsin) State Journal,* warned, "*News is not gossip, nor romance, nor history, nor literature, nor opinion,*" and noted that newspapers could not perform their civic duty to educate citizens merely by holding up a "*mirror to social life.*"[39]

In 1889, an article criticizing the press use of the word ethics in the title

[30]All quotations by Lee in *The Greenhill Dictionary of Military Quotations*.

[31]Quoted in *The Greenhill Dictionary of Military Quotations*, p. 373.

[32]Quoted in Ted Curtis Smythe, "The Reporter, 1880–1900: Working Conditions and Their Influence on the News," *Journalism History*, 7, Spring 1980, 1–10 (quotation on 1).

[33]See Larry Schweikart, *The Entrepreneurial Adventure: a History of Business in the United States* (Ft. Worth:Harcourt, 2000), especially chapters 5 and 6.

[34]William g. Bovee, "Horace Greeley and Social Responsibility," *Journalism Quarterly*, 63, Summer 1986, pp. 251–59.

[35]Richard Grant White, "The Morals and Manners of Journalism," *The Galaxy*, 8, December 1869, pp. 840–47.

[36]"Gathering Local News," *Harper's Weekly*, January 9, 1891; Eugene M. Camp, "What's the News?" *Century Magazine*, June 1890, 260–62; and William Henry Smith, "The Press as News "Gatherer," *Century Magazine*, August 1891, pp. 524–36.

[37]"By-The-Bye," *The Journalist,* April 22, 1893.

[38]"About Mammoth Newspapers," *Newspaperdom*, June–July 1893, p. 152.

[39]Arthur J. Dodge, "What Is News—Should the People Get It all?" *Newspaperdom*, June–July 1893; "Col. M'Clure Discusses the Virtues of Journalism," *The Journalis*t, June 10, 1893.

for the first time, and a year later a code of conduct for journalists first appeared.[40] Adolph Ochs, who bought the struggling *New York Times,* symbolized the ascent of objectivity over partisanship when he arrived in New York in 1896 and instructed the staff *"to give the news impartially, without fear or favor, regardless of party, sect or interests involved."*[41]   Oswald Garrison Villard, publisher of *The Nation* and the *New York Evening Post,* reiterated the concept of fairness, emphasizing that the objective journalist had to report "both sides of every issue."[42] The American Society of Newspaper Editors, established in 1912, adopted a code of ethics that stated, *"Partisanship, in editorial comment which knowingly departs from the truth, does violence to the best spirit of American journalism; in the news columns it is subversive of a fundamental principle of the profession."*[43]

Soon, however, the commitment to fairness turned to cynicism, E. W. Scripps, of the *Detroit Evening News,* founded an effective chain of papers that rested on the premise "Whatever is, is wrong."[44]   This value-free approach was fraught with danger. It was inevitable with such an approach that the United States itself would have to be "wrong" merely by existing! And whatever foreign affairs the United States was involved in would de facto deserve criticism. What began as fairness—the technique became so prominent it has become a staple in journalism ethics textbooks as the get-the-other-side-of-the-story-rule—inherently assumed that there always was "another side" and that it was equally legitimate.[45]

It is easy to see why journalists, particularly the modern media, are anti-military. They can't help but be so: fairness, while well intentioned, presumes there is no truth, that one value is not better than another. "Who is to say who is right or wrong?" is the inherent question in every story. With no values present, it was inevitable that the "values" of the North Vietnamese were really no different from those of the United States. And if American principles or values are not inherently better than those of other nations, why should anyone fight for those values? Such views could only lead to comments such as Dick Durbin's equating Guantánamo Bay with a Soviet gulag or with Auschwitz. The journalistic principle that one must "get both sides of the story" leads inevitably to the position by the reporter that whatever an American president says can be his viewpoint only, and that there must be a opposite side to the story. Consequently, the press started down the road of legitimate skepticism about unverified facts to a confrontational position ensuring that the mainstream media would be antagonistic to any presi-

[40]W. S. Lilly, "The Ethics of Journalism," *The Forum,* 4, July 1889, pp. 503–12; George Henry Payne, *History of Journalism in the United States* (New York: D. Appleton, 1925), pp. 251–53. Also see standards in the *Minnesota Newspaper Association Confidential Bulletin,* no. 20, May 17, 1988, pp. 4–5, and those adopted by Will Irwin, published in Collier's magazine (1911), reprinted in Clifford f. Weigle and David G. Clark, eds., *The American Newspaper* by Will Irwin (Ames, Iowa: Iowa State University Press, 1969).

[41]Quoted in Bill Kovach and Tom Rosensteil, *The Elements of Journalism* (New York: Crown, 2001), p. 53.

[42]Oswald Garrison Villard, "Press Tendencies and Dangers," in Willard G. Bleyer, *The Profession of Journalism* (Boston: Atlantic Monthly Press, 1918), p. 23.

[43]See Paul Alfred Pratte, *Gods within the Machine* (Westport, CT: Praeger, 1995), p. 3.

[44]Marvin Olasky, *Prodigal Press: The Anti-Christian Bias of American NewsMedia* (Wheaton, IL: Crossway Books, 1998), p. 52.

[45]Philip Meyer, *Ethical Journalism* (New York: Longman, 1987), p. 51.

dent, but particularly one who did not share its worldview.

When the United States declared war on Germany in 1917, this worldview was still evolving, and was strongly tempered by concepts of responsibility and patriotism. President Woodrow Wilson called on Missourian George Creel to head the Committee on Public Information in April 1917, an agency that easily could have been called the News Management Bureau. Creel had been a reporter, professional boxer, and police commissioner. During his stint as a muckraker in Kansas City, he had attacked the infamous Pendergast political machine, so he did not back away from a fight. A modern press corps would have been instantly antagonistic to Creel, and spent most of its time attacking him rather than covering the news, but in 1917, Creel not only co-opted the journalists, he recruited them for his agency![46]

Reporters cooperated even beyond the government's expectations: when General John Pershing's ship, the Baltic, left New York Harbor in May 1817, newspaper reporters, familiar with the developments, easily could have printed stories, and German agents could have alerted U-boats to seek out the vessel. Even Pershing did not realize that the press had kept the departure secret out of patriotism.[47] Meanwhile, Creel's propaganda office provided material that he later claimed accounted for some twenty thousand newspaper columns, and he organized a cadre of pro-war speakers called the Four-minute Men, who gave talks at theaters and rallies. He even drafted the famous explorer Roald Amundsen to bolster support for the war.

More important, journalists identified with, well, Americans! After American troops saw their first action, large urban papers featured such headlines as *U.S. MARINES SMASH HUNS GAIN GLORY IN BRISK FIGHT ON THE MARNE, CAPTURE MACHINE GUNS KILL BOCHES, TAKE PRISONERS (**Chicago Daily Tribune**) and MARINES IN GREAT CHARGE OVERTHROW CRACK FOE FORCES (**New York Herald**).*[48]

Movie Madness

Journalism, and the mainstream media, represents just one area in which cultural elites have abandoned a traditional support of the military. The entertainment industry is another. The culture of heroic Hollywood stars who fought in World War II gave way to a crass, self-absorbed motion picture society full of do-gooders, hedonists, and shallow egotists whose understanding of sacrifice, commitment, and duty has all but disappeared.

Only recently has this development occurred among the entertainment elites. Prior to Vietnam, virtually all of the entertainment industry kicked in to support the military, and not just motion pictures, but Broadway and the music

---

[46]John S. D. Eisenhower, *Yanks: The Epic Story of the American Army in World War I* (New York: Free Press 2001), p. 20.

[47]Eisenhower, *Yanks,* p. 35.

[48]Eisenhower, *Yanks*, p. 145

business as well. In World War I, Tin Pan Alley, America's songwriting center, turned out famous standards such as George M. Cohan's *"Over There,"* Irving Berlin's *"Oh, How I Hate to Get Up in the Morning,"* and ditties such as *"KKK-Katy."* During World War II, songwriters came up with such catchy propaganda tunes as *"It's Our Pacific, to Be Specific," "Let's Put the Ax to the Axis," "When the Cohens and the Kellys Meet the Little Yellow Bellies,"* and *"Let's Find the Fellow Who Is Yellow and Beat Him Till He's Red, White, and Blue."*[49] Even during the 1960s, with the antiwar hippie movement, the music industry did not produce anti-Vietnam songs until around 1970, when public opinion polls had already turned against the war and when it was financially safe to do so. The number one song in America in 1965 was *"The Ballad of the Green Berets,"* sung by Sergeant Barry Sadler.[50]

Although few male movie stars were associated with combat in World War I, several led public rallies for bond sales, including Douglas Fairbanks and Charlie Chaplin. The brief nature of the war, and the relative novelty of films prevented the movie industry from contributing any propaganda movies or shorts. That was hardly the case in World War II. American motion pictures in the Second World War left no doubt about who the good guys and bad guys were. Paramount Studios' *Wake Island,* with Robert Preston and William Bendix, went into production in 1942 before Americans even knew the bastion had fallen. (Veterans of Wake later laughed at the movie's gross inaccuracies.)[51] One of the most effective World War II films for generating support for the war was ***Sergeant York*** (1941), with Gary Cooper as the Yank sharpshooting hero of the Ardennes. Despite wartime pressures, movies took time to produce, meaning that some of the best-known World War II movies were not released until well after the war, including John Wayne's classics *Back to Bataan* (1945), *Sands of Iwo Jima (*1949) and *They Were Expendable* (1949). *His Flying Leathernecks (*1951) came out during the Korean conflict. Only Wayne's *Fighting Seabees* (1944) and *Flying Tigers* (1942) really could affect morale during the Second World War. *Guadalcanal Diary* (1943) and *Thirty Seconds Over Tokyo* (1944) were possibly the best combat-related films to come out during the war, although many consider ***Casablanca*** (1942) the greatest of the World War II-era movies. The Humphrey Bogart classic highlighted courage and sacrifice from the periphery, without ever depicting the actual combat that had engulfed the world.

Bogart also played a Liberty ship captain in ***Action in the North Atlantic*** (1943) and a Nazi spy hunter in *All Through the Night* (1942). Spy thrillers were commonplace—*Background to Danger* (1943 and *The Conspirators (*1944), both with Peter Lorre, and *Across the Pacific,* with Bogart—as were many films dealing with the Canadians, such as *Corvette K-225* (1943) and *Captains of the Clouds* (1942), and the Atlantic crossing *Lifeboat (*1944) and *In Which We Serve* (1942).

[49]Schweikart and Allen, *A Patriot's History of the United States,* p. 599.
[50]Kenneth J. Bindas and Craig Houston, "Takin' Care of Business': Rock Music, Vietnam, and the Protest Myth," *Historian,* 52, November 1989, pp. 1–23.
[51]John Wukovits, *Pacific Alamo: The Battle for Wake Island* (New York: New American Library, 2003), p. 261.

*Desperate Journey (*1942) had Ronald Reagan and Errol Flynn playing American pilots trying to escape Nazi Germany; *Gung Ho* (1943) featured a, well, gung ho Randolph Scott launching a counterattack after Pearl Harbor. Cary Grant commanded a sub headed for Japan in *Destination Tokyo* (1943), and Flynn played a Norwegian resistance fighter in *The Edge of Darkness* (1942). *The Fighting Sullivans* (1944) depicted the deaths of the five Sullivan brothers on the USS *Juneau*; *Objective Burma* (1945) featured Errol Flynn on a desperate mission; *The Story of G.I. Joe* (1945) detailed the wartime experiences of correspondent Ernie Pyle; and *The Purple Heart* (1944) related the fate of the Doolittle crews who were captured.

Cartoons, however, could be produced much faster than full-length films, and Disney's cartoon factory released prowar propaganda shorts in a torrent. *Der Fuhrer's Face* (1943), an Oscar-winning Donald Duck cartoon, featured a German Donald working in a munitions factory, only to wake up from his nightmare back home in the United States. *Out of the Frying Pan Into the Firing Line* (1942) encouraged civilians to save bacon grease, while *Private Pluto* (1943) had Mickey Mouse's dog guarding pillboxes with the questionable help of the chipmunks Chip and Dale. Other Disney cartoons included Donald Duck in *Donald Gets Drafted, The Vanishing Private, Sky Trooper* (all 1942); *The Old Army Game, Fall Out, Fall In, and Home Defense* (all 1943); and *Commando Duck* (1944). Pluto also starred in *The Army Mascot* (1942), and Goofy appeared in *How to Be a Sailor* (1944). Disney characters preached the value of savings (*Thrifty Pigs,* 1941) and buying war bonds (*Seven Wise Dwarfs*, 1941), both of which were made for Canada prior to Pearl Harbor.

In what is called "the most unusual feature film" Disney ever made, *Victory Through Air Power* (1943), animators reviewed the history of aviation and the plan to use strategic bombing to bring Germany to its knees. An hour-long narrated movie dedicated to Billy Mitchell, *Victory Through Air Power* argued that the Nazis had the advantage in ground fighting and that the United States had to counter through superior American know-how. Disney's other training films, such as *Food Will Win the War*, 1942, and *Defense Against Invasion*, 1943, (about germs), addressed specific target audiences of farmers and children.[52]

Warner Brothers, not to be left out, starred Bugs Bunny in Bugs Bunny *Nips the Nip* (1944), and he fought Hitler, Tojo, and other enemies in a series of cartoons. Bugs also appeared in short films supporting war bond sales, and in a pro-war spoof on Disney, the rabbit is reading *Victory Through Hare Power* when he encounters a gremlin who tries to sabotage a plane in *Falling Hare* (1943). None of these cartoons leaves any doubt about which side was good and which was evil.

Even writers like the famed Dr. Seuss (later an antinuke protester) were unabashedly patriotic and promilitary. Seuss's cartoons, which appeared through 1943, displayed overt hostility toward the Nazis and Japanese, bordering on rac-

---

ism in the latter's case.[53]   In June of 1942, Theodor Geisel (Dr. Seuss's real name) lampooned Charles Lindbergh's isolationism, showing him petting a Nazi sea serpent while saying, "*'Tis Roosevelt, Not Hitler, that the World Should Really Fear.*"[54]   Dr. Seuss could be shockingly grisly: a July 1942 cartoon featured a forest of trees with lynched Jews hanging from them and Hitler singing "*Only God can make a tree to furnish sport for you and me.*"[55]   Right after Pearl Harbor, Dr. Seuss showed an Uncle Sam bird waking up in a rocking chair being smashed, shot at, and drilled by several heavily caricatured Japanese soldiers under the caption, "*The End of the Nap.*"[56]   Following Doolittle's raid, Seuss depicted "*The Old tobacco Juice Where It Counts!*" showing American flyers spitting in Tojo's eye.[57]   Dr. Seuss was hardly alone.   Regardless of the artist, American soldiers were depicted as heroes, Nazis and Japanese as grotesque villains, and even when Americans lost (as at Wake Island), the cartoonists still portrayed it as a moral victory.   Stars and studios, artists and actors, writers and musicians all supported the war with remarkable uniformity.

During the early decades of the Cold War, although some promilitary sentiments remained, an increasing number of cynical movies like *Dr. Strangelove* (1964), *Fail-Safe* (1964), and *The Bedford Incident* (1965) were being made.   There were a few pro-military exceptions in the late 1960s and 1970s: John Wayne's *The Alamo* (1960) carried clear Cold War overtones, and his *The Green Berets* (1968) was one of the very few pro-Vietnam War movies of the era.   Since Vietnam, however, the entertainment industry has moved even further in the antimilitary direction, again with a few exceptions.   *An Officer and a Gentleman* (1982) featured a handsome Richard Gere as a lower-class officer seeking validation through his grueling training by Lou Gossett, Jr., and his love affair with Debra Winger. While it contained impressive imagery of the discipline and dedication needed to succeed in the armed forces, there was little commentary on the necessity of war. *Red Dawn* (1984) introduced a brat pack of young stars who heroically fought off Cuban/Russian invaders in Colorado, but the cause of the war, summed up in Powers Boothe's "they-fired-one-we-fired-one soliloquy drove home the message of moral equivalence between the Soviet Union and the United States.   Perhaps the most successful pro-military movie ever, *Top Gun* (1986), has been lambasted as a recruiting tool by liberals.   Tom Cruise (Maverick) and Val Kilmer (Iceman), flying F-14s and bedding beautiful women, actually found time for combat, although against Libyans, not Russians.   Of course, that was pre-9/11, when it was still safe to portray Islamic terrorist states as "bad."   A little-known, but brilliant film, *The Siege of Firebase Gloria*(1989), featuring real-life former Marine staff sergeant R. Lee Ermey, probably captured the reality of the Communists' failed Tet offensive more than any other movie, but remains little more than a cult clas-

[53]Richard H. Minear, Dr. Seuss [Theodor Geisel], and Art Spiegelman, *Dr. Seuss Goes to War: The World War II Editorial Cartoons of Theodor Seuss Geisel* (New York: New Press, 1991).

[54]Minear, *Dr. Seuss Goes to War,* p. 34.

[55]Minear, *Dr. Seuss Goes to War,* p. 101.

[56]Minear, *Dr. Seuss Goes to War,* p. 144

[57]Minear, *Dr. Seuss Goes to War,* p. 149.

sic.[58]

After the Vietnam War heated up, however, the entertainment industry went overwhelmingly over to the Dark Side. Hollywood's most prominent and more frequent antiwar movies were not subtle with their messages. In *First Blood* (1982) a mentally unstable Vietnam vet, John Rambo (Sylvester Stallone) fought off an army of police in a small Oregon town. Stallone reprised the role in *Rambo II* (1985), where his Rambo character was pulled out of jail by Colonel Samuel Troutman (Richard Crenna) and taken to North Vietnam to release POWs still held by the North. Although Rambo II was nearly alone in depicting the horrors of the North Vietnamese POW camps and Russian-directed torture of prisoners of Hua Lo Prison, the *Hanoi Hilton* (1987), directed by a conservative, Lionel Chetwynd, was another. Rescuing POW's left behind in the North was also the subject of 1984's *Missing in Action*, with karate expert Chuck Norris. However, despite the heroic overtones, it is noteworthy that these movies depicted the U.S. government still lying about Vietnam years after the war ended. During the war years, no movies dealt with POW abuse (as a moral failing of the Communists) or torture. The closest one comes is in **Deer Hunter** (1978), where the Communist practice of forcing prisoners to play Russian roulette merely exacerbated the soldiers' preexisting instability, presumably due to the "immoral" war itself or, possibly, that nasty sport of deer hunting!

Hollywood dealt with antiwar messages in other ways, too. In *Coming Home* (1978), military wife Jane Fonda ditches her pro-war hubby for the paraplegic Jon Voight, whose main attraction (besides the ability to perform oral sex) appears to be his antiwar sentiments. Fonda's soldier husband (Bruce Dern), of course, goes crazy in the movie, possibly because of his wife's unfaithfulness or, perhaps, because she had taken up with Tom Hayden in real life.

A fairly clear antiwar pattern emerged from the Academy Award-winning triumvirate of the movies *The Deer Hunter, Apocalypse Now* (1979), and *Platoon* (1986). One might even argue that *Patton,* another Academy Award winner (1970), was antiwar, since it portrayed the general as unhinged and bloodthirsty. Certainly the antiwar message of *Gandhi* (1982) could not be missed, and was described in numerous editorials as a lesson for the warlike Reagan administration. Although it did not win a best-picture Oscar, Stanley Kubrick's antiwar *Full Metal Jacket* (1987) introduced R. Lee Ermeyas a caricature of his drill instructor self. Then Tom Cruise, perhaps to make up for his *Top Gun* appearance, starred in the Oliver Stone antiwar screed *Born on the Fourth of July* (1989), while Michael J. Fox (*Casualties of War,* 1989) highlighted the (in moviemakers' minds) prevalence of American atrocities. From there, Hollywood seemed to accelerate its attacks on American military actions. *Dances With Wolves* (1990), another Academy Award winner, taught that only the evil white cavalrymen practiced frontier violence. (One wonders what Hollywood would have done if members of the black 10th Cavalry, say had assaulted Black Kettle's village at Sand Creek.)

---

[58]Although Ermey is routinely called Gunny (for gunnery sergeant), he was awarded this anan honorary rank. He is medically retired as a staff sergeant.

Another favorite anti-military trick is to make a rogue military unit the hidden villain. The ever-reliable conspiracy theorist Oliver Stone used this plot device in his Oscar-nominated *JFK* (1991) somewhere in between seemingly hundreds of repetitions of "back, and to the left" by Kevin Costner. Somewhat more mixed messages could be found in the Oscar-nominated *A Few Good Men* (1992), depending on which character the viewer identified with. In the story of two Marines accused of killing a screw up fellow Marine in a Code Red disciplinary action gone awry, an attorney for the Marines' defense, Lieutenant Sam Weinberg (Kevin Pollak) makes no pretense of his disdain for his clients. Lieutenant Commander JoAnne Galloway (Demi Moore), on the other hand, empathizes with the two Marines. "*Why do you hate them so much?*" Galloway asks, and Weinberg snarls, "*They beat up on a weakling, and that's all they did. The rest is just smoke-filled coffee-house crap. They tortured and tormented a weaker kid. They didn't like him. So they killed him. And why? Because he couldn't run very fast.*"[59] Weinberg asks, "*Why do you like them so much?*" She replies, "*Because they stand upon a wall and say, 'Nothing's going to hurt you tonight, not on my watch.'*"[60]

In 1995, Hollywood gave its top award to a prowar movie, Mel Gibson's *Braveheart*. A bold, pro-war statement? Perhaps not. It is noteworthy that the villain in the movie was the English king seeking to extend his power over the freedom-loving Scots led by William Wallace (Gibson). Was this, in the mind of Hollywood, a comment on the recently completed Gulf War? Were Americans the evil English? Three years later another pair of war films won Oscar nominations, *Saving Private Ryan* and *The Thin Red Line*, the former with a somewhat amorphous theme and the latter with a clear antiwar message. "*War don't ennoble men,*" says the narrator of *The Thin Red Line*, Private Doll. "*It turns them into dogs ... poisons the soul.*"[61] The object of the literal manhunt in Steven Spielberg's *Saving Private Ryan*, a soldier whose brothers have already been killed and whom the War Department wants to save for public relations purposes, wonders at the end of the movie if his life was worth it. "*Earn this,*" Captain Miller says as he dies, having rescued Private Ryan. Miller philosophizes about losing 94 troops under his command:

> But that means I've saved the lives of ten times that many, doesn't it? Maybe even 20, right? Twenty times as many? And that's how simple it is. That's how you ... That's how you rationalize making the choice between the mission and the man.[62]

Increasingly, the message of most Hollywood war movies was not that principles were worth fighting for, or that there was a right and wrong in the world, but rather that when wars "*coming along,*" men fight "*for the man next to you.*" (Nevertheless, leftist historian Howard Zinn predictably fretted that *Saving*

[59]http://imdb.com/title/tt0104257/quotes.
[60]http://imdb.com/title/tt0104257/quotes.
[61]http://imdb.com/title/tt0120863/quotes.
[62]http://imdb.com/title/tt0120815/quotes.

Private Ryan "draws on our deep feelings for the GIs in order to rescue not just Private Ryan but also the good name of war.")[63] Fighting for the "man next to you" was again the message in Black Hawk Down (2001), where the advertising tagline was "Leave no man behind." Ironically, the most sensible assessment of war came not from the Americans trapped in Mogadishu but from Abdullah Hassan (Treva Etienne): *"Without victory, there will be no peace."*[64]

Leave no man behind soon dominated all promilitary movies. It was the main theme of *We Were Soldiers,* the 2002 movie interpretation of Joseph Galloway's *We Were Soldiers Once ... and Young.* Mel Gibson starred as Colonel Hal Moore, who promises his 7th Air Cavalry unit headed for Vietnam, *"I will leave no one behind. Dead, or alive, we will all come home together."*[65] Another Gibson character, south Carolinian Benjamin Martin in *The Patriot* (2000), struggles to avoid the war against the British that his son (the true patriot) embraces, rejecting the rhetoric of liberty and freedom, and fighting only for ... well, one never really knows.

As promilitary movies, these were lukewarm, but their message seems gung ho when contrasted with the drivel that undergirds almost all modern Hollywood plots. Just one example will suffice: in *XXX: State of the Union* (2005), the hero—a former SEAL named Darius Stone (ex-rapper Ice Cube)—is recruited by National Security Agency agent Augustus Gibbons (Samuel L. Jackson) to defeat a "military splinter group" headed by Willem Dafoe's evil Rumsfeld-esque secretary of defense, George Deckert. Deckert wants to assassinate the president (Peter Strauss), a New Englander who wants to change U.S. policy in order to "win the hearts and minds of our enemies" (!) and cut military spending. No reference is made to the War on Terror, and it should be noted that never was the phrase win the hearts and minds applied to America's enemies, only to civilians who were caught in the crossfire between the United States and guerillas or terrorists. At any rate, Ice Cube recruits thugs from "da hood," who manage to (of course) outshoot all of Deckert's supposedly elite military forces. Not only are America's best fighters worse shots than gansta rappers, but the ghetto "soldiers" manage to hijack a tank. The film ends with the rescued president quoting rapper Tupac Shakur: *"Wars come and go, but my soldiers are eternal."* Of course, Shakur was referring to street gangs and druggies who killed cops, not the valiant men and women in khaki (who were the buffoons in this movie).

"Rogue" or "splinter" military groups are the villains of other movies, including *Die Hard II* (1990), *Seven Days in May* (1964), and *Executive Action* (1973). A somewhat related plot line in *The Siege* (1998) pits a military officer

[63]Howard Zinn, "Private Ryan Saves War," *The Progressive*, October 1998, http://www.progressive.org/zinn1098.htm.
[64]Trevor McCrisken and Andrew Pepper argue that unlike the leftist *Three Kings* (1999) *Black Hawk Down* was "more representative of a troubling common approach to historical movie-making ... that largely eschews critical inquiry ...." (189). By "critical inquiry," of course, the authors only mean critical inquiry from the Left. They would not view it as "critical inquiry" to question whether, for example, we are being militaristic enough in the War on Terror. See McCrisken and Pepper, *American History and Contemporary Hollywood Film* (New Brunswick: Rutgers University Press, 2005).
[65] http://www.imdb.com/title/tt0277434/quotes.

played by Bruce Willis against a counterterrorism expert from the FBI. Once again, the clueless military was depicted as out of control. Hollywood, in such movies as *Pearl Harbor* (2001), attempted to look more realistic by using more special effects, but in the long run *"did not become more accurate [but] simply became different—bad history in a different way."*[66]   Most had abandoned what film historians Trevor McCrisken and Andrew Pepper call "begin meta-narrative," which is any story in which the United States is a force for good.[67]   By the 1980s, only a few old-timers, like Bob Hope or Charlton Heston supported the military. Most of Hollywood had aligned itself with the post-Vietnam media in their hostility to things military. Some, such as Jane Fonda and, later, Sean Penn, actively inserted themselves and their anti-American messages into hot war zones, raising profound questions about the very definition of treason itself.

Is It Treason?

During World War II, many Americans were indicted for making radio broadcasts for the Nazis or Japanese, and in 1948 the Supreme Court (*Chandler v. United States*) agreed with a lower-court decision that found such actions fit the definition of an "overt act" of treason.[68]   Axis Sally and Tokyo Rose were both tried for treason after the war, and despite claims that they were either forced into making such radio addresses or were attempting to slip secret messages beneficial to American forces into the broadcasts, both were found guilty and served time in prison. During Vietnam, the notion of giving aid and comfort to the enemy reached new heights when actress Jane Fonda visited North Vietnam and posed on an antiaircraft gun while American POWs, sick and tortured, languished in Communist prisons not far away. In 1988, Fonda issued an apology on the television show 20/20 for *"a thoughtless and cruel thing to have done,"* yet never linked her actions to the fate of the men in the POW camps. On another visit to 20/20 in 2001, she elaborated further: *"It just kills me that I did things that hurt those men,"* referring to the POWs, yet she never later communicated with the POWs or asked them why they refused to meet with her. Indeed, when some returned in 1973 and reported they had been tortured, Fonda called them *"liars and hypocrites."*[69] A year after her first apology, she "un-apologized," saying *"I did not, have not, and will not say that going to North Vietnam was a mistake ... I have apologized only for some of the things that I did there, but I am proud that I went."*[70]   Her autobiography, *My Life So Far*, featured a "history" of Vietnam that could only be described as clueless.[71]

[66] Kenneth Cameron, *America on Film: Hollywood and American History* (New York: Contiuum), 1997, p. 235.

[67] McCrisken and Pepper, *American History and Contemporary Hollywood Film*, p. 7.

[68] *Chandler v. United States*, 171 f. (2nd) 921 (C.C.A. 1st 1948), affirming 72 F. Supp. 231 (D. Mass. 1947).

[69] Henry Mark Holzer, "Jane Fonda's 'Apology': New Whine in Old Bottles," http://www.frontpagemag.com/Articles/ReadArticle.asp?ID=17632, April 7, 2001.

[70] Holzer, "Jane Fonda's 'Apology.'"

[71] Jane Fonda, *My Life So Far* (New York: Random House, 2005); Robert F. Turner, "The Fonda Fallacies," http://www.vvlf.org/default.php?page_id=41.

While in North Vietnam, Fonda, doing her best Axis Sally impersonation, made several live broadcasts containing pro-Communist, anti-American propaganda, taped for later replay.[72] If broadcasting propaganda for the enemy constituted treason in World War II, why would it not in Vietnam? And why would rebroadcasting claims today made by enemy puppets, such as Al Jazeera, not constitute treason today? Despite concerns over the Patriot Act and a stifling of public debate, never in human history has so much enemy propaganda been welcomed into the homeland of a country at war.

One of the first signs that the mainstream media opposed the War on Terror was when almost all the major networks—even the cable news channels— stopped running any video of the planes slamming into the World Trade Center on 9/11. Rationalizing the decision by claiming the material was too gruesome or unsettling to watch, the media made certain that the American public would not be reminded of the cause of war. During Operation Iraqi Freedom and its cleanup, they likewise refused to show the grisly beheading of Nick Berg. While these images are understandably gut-wrenching, they serve as important points of reference as to why the war was started, and by whom—and of exactly the type of enemy the United States faced. However, news organizations were perfectly willing to show American coffins returning from Iraq, under the guise of "informing the public." During World War II, censors refused to allow any photographs of dead Americans to appear until 1943, when Life magazine ran a cover photo of three dead soldiers.[73] Polls showed Americans favored more of the pictures run, as a means of remembering what they were fighting for. Photos of casualties could prove demoralizing, unless placed in the context of the casus belli.

In the post-Vietnam era, the antimilitary tendencies of the mainstream media were magnified, with its implications of being an intangible social threat in the long run increasing as it became a specific battlefield danger in the short run. These factors required challenging the briefings and reports of virtually all officers and government spokesmen; accepting as truth comments from enemies (without being able to verify them due to the closed nature of non-Western societies). In Vietnam, as reporters grew increasingly cynical about the Johnson and Nixon administrations' assessments of progress in the war, there was never an attempt to challenge North Vietnam's claims of bomb damage or prisoner treatment. Thirty years later, the ramblings of Iraqi "information" minister (the very title alone should have given reporters pause) Mohammed Saeed al-Sahaf (Baghdad Bob) were presented as at least possibly factual, while every comment by U.S. secretary of defense Donald Rumsfeld was challenged and criticized. Yet could any sane person in World War II have reported as even slightly credible—in the name of "fairness" or "objectivity"—the propagandistic blathering of

[72]Henry Mark Holzer and Erika Holzer, *Aid and Comfort: Jane Fonda in North Vietnam* (Jefferson, NC: McFarland, 2002).

[73]Thomas Fleming, *The New Dealers' War: F.D.R. and the War Within World War II* (New York: Basic Books, 2001), p. 380.

Joseph Goebbels?

The fact that virtually no one in the media even asks these questions is a testament to how far the mainstream media has fallen. It was almost inevitable that the perpetually scowling *USA Today* columnist Julianne Malveaux, called President Bush "a terrorist" and America, "a terrorist nation."[74] She went on to tell radio host Sean Hannity that *"George W. Bush is evil. He is a terrorist. He is evil. He is arrogant."* Is it any wonder that, as reporter/soldier Mark Yost wrote, *"most Americans, particularly soldiers, hate the media."*[75]

Increasingly, any protest against the military or a war deserves coverage, regardless of the protest's size or impact. In 2005, the networks covered a single mother, Cindy Sheehan, who camped outside President Bush's Crawford, Texas, ranch after her son was killed in Iraq. Sheehan, who had been a Bush supporter before linking up with MoveOn.org, an anti-Bush Web-based group, received news coverage on every network. Unfortunately for the antiwar left, Sheehan turned out to be a rather loopy spokesmom: in August 2005, she referred to terrorists allied with the forces that killed her own son as "freedom fighters," and claimed that President Bush was the real terrorist.[76] *"The polls are plummeting, people are dying, now's the time,"* a smiling Sheehan told a woman from the Austin Peace and Justice Center.[77] Sheehan also spoke at a rally in favor of Lynne Stewart, "my human Atticus Finch" for Stewart's role in enabling her client, Omar Abdul-Rahman, convicted of the 1993 World Trade Center bombing, to carry out other terrorist activities in prison.[78] The left quickly backed away from Sheehan with the she's-not-the-story, Bush-is-the-story template, but it was too late. Sheehan had severely damaged the antiwar movement to the point where mainstream media outlets had to disavow her.[79] At the same time, confidence waned in the mainstream media's ability to cover the real war news.[80] Responding to a poll that found a stunning drop in confidence in the media's ability to report war news, David L. Grange, executive vice president of the McCormick Tribune Foundation, who, along with Gallup, conducted the poll, concluded, *"The mass media gets negative points from the people because they think that the big media is taking a position and shaping stories to fit their agenda."*[81]

Contrast the media frenzy over Sheehan with the massive street demonstration by more than ten thousand in Baghdad on November 28, 2003—against terrorism and against the insurgency—which had almost no network news coverage. Once again, the Vietnam Template was in play: during the Vietnam War, a

---

[74]Carl Limbacher, "Julianne Malveaux: USA, Bush Are 'Terrorists,'" http://newsmax.com, July 11, 2005.

[75]Mark Yost, "Why They Hate Us," St. Paul Pioneer Press, July 12, 2005.

[76]Carl Limbacher, "Sheehan Calls Son's Killers 'Freedom Fighters,' August 24, 2005, http://www.newsmax.com/archives/ic/2005/8/24/90434.shtml

[77]Andrew Walden, "Sheehan Cheers On Terror in Iraq," at http://www.freerepublic.com/focus/f-bloggers/1469696/posts. Sheehan was recorded on video speaking to the "Veterans for Peace."

[78]http://www.discoverthenetwork.org/Articles/Stewartrally.htm.

[79]See Patt Morrison, "Looking for Wisdom in All the Wrong Places," http://www.latimes.com/news/opinion/commentary/la-oe-morrison24aug24,0,1427206.column?coll=la-news-comment-opinions.

[80]Josh White, "Confidence in Military News Wanes," http://www,washingtonpost.com/wp-dyn/content/article/2005/08/23/AR2005082301290.html.

[81]White, "Confidence in Military Wanes."

large majority of Americans consistently supported the war until the 1979s, when antiwar protests had garnered intense media coverage.

For the Left, all wars are Vietnam. Yet it is important to note that the Vietnam antiwar protests began early, long before it was a "quagmire." In other words, the Left was opposed to the Vietnam War merely because it was the United States acting to impede communism. The Committee for a Sane Nuclear Policy (SANE) and Students for a Democratic Society (SDS) both had protest marches in 1965, with the SDS march assembling eighteen thousand people, including Senator Ernest Gruening. This was not a response to Lyndon Johnson's "escalation" or Richard Nixon's "invasion" of Cambodia, but rather a kneejerk opposition to any U.S. military action. Students, far more than anyone else, were more likely to protest, not surprising given the radical leftward bent of the university campus in the 1960s.[82] Americans did not think too highly of the protesters: seven out of ten Americans had an unfavorable view of the protesters, and even of those who advocated a unilateral withdrawal from Vietnam; "more than half nevertheless placed Vietnam protesters on the negative side of the feeling scale."[83] Observers sympathetic to the protest movement candidly admitted, *The peace movement is not simply trying to mobilize an already existing mass feeling or sentiment; it is trying to create a radical change in the **national image** [emphasis added]."[84] Although more moderate protesters scored better reactions from the public, large majorities thought protesters were "disloyal."[85] Despite significant positive coverage by the media, the protesters were only partially successful in changing the views of the public. Although the number labeling themselves "hawks" (as opposed to "doves") decreased, polls consistently showed no enthusiasm for "complete" or "immediate" withdrawal.[86] However, the damage had been done: the antiwar movement had successfully labeled Johnson and Nixon as "murderers" and "baby killers," who engaged in a "holocaust." Without ever once having addressed the moral failings of communism in North Vietnam, the protesters, aided by the media, had demonized the United States, not the totalitarians.

Moreover, the media continued to spread myths after the war. Probably the most widespread Vietnam myth was that of the Rambo figure, the disturbed Vietnam vet. Tom Wicker, the *New York Times* columnist, claimed that "hundreds of thousands of Vietnam veterans" suffered from war-related psychological problems.[87] Wicker then, using statistics obtained from Penthouse magazine, alleged that in 1975, 500,000 Vietnam vets had attempted suicide (a number almost equal to the highest number of troops in Vietnam at the peak of the buildup).[88] In fact,

[82]Schweikart and Allen, A Patriot's History of the United States, 695–707; William Edward Hensley, "The Vietnam Anti-War Movement: History and Criticism," Ph.D. dissertation, University of Oregon, 1979, p. 26.

[83]Hensley, "Vietnam Anti-War Movement," 2; Howard Schuman, "Two Sources of Antiwar Sentiment in America," *American Journal of Sociology*, 78, November 1972, pp. 513–36 (quotations on pp. 516–17).

[84]Kenneth E. Boulding, "Towards a New Theory of Protest," *ETC: A Review of General Semantics*, 24, March 1967, pp. 49–59 (quotation on p. 55).

[85]Harris Poll, quoted in Hensley, "Vietnam Anti-War Movement," p. 249.

[86]Hensley, "Vietnam Anti-War Movement," p. 256.

[87]Tom Wicker, "The Vietnam Disease," *New York Times*, May 27, 1975.

[88]B. G. Burkett and Glenna Whitley, *Stolen Valor: How the Vietnam Generation Was Robbed of Its Heroes and*

psychiatric problems of Vietnam vets were one third of the rate of Korean vets (12 per 1,000 versus 37 per 1,000). Studies further showed a similar level of problems to World War II vets; a lower unemployment rate than the national average; and suicide and divorce rates only equal to the national average.[89]

Victor Hanson has written that *"the real problem for a democratic American army has never been defeat by the enemy, but rather the maintenance of a moral high ground,"* which is precisely what the moral equivalence of the mainstream media seeks to deny.[90]   American military forces in Vietnam, essentially an uncensored war, learned they could not win without the news media. It did not have to be "on our side," but if it substantially presented the enemy's point of view uncritically, the military's efforts—no matter how successful on the battlefield—would be futile. After Vietnam, the Pentagon "ran so scared" of the news media that it "virtually took over" coverage of Grenada, Panama, and the Gulf War.[91]   Reagan adviser Michael Deaver, just before the first Gulf War, wrote that *"television has absolutely changed our military strategy,"* then wrongly predicted that *"we will never again fight a major ground war."*[92]   Before combat operations in Kuwait even began, *USA Today* ran a story about George H. W. Bush's polling numbers, with the headline **BUSH SUPPORT SLIM.** Newspapers gleefully reported the comments of Democratic senator Daniel Patrick Moynihan, who said a war with Saddam "will wreck our military [and] will wreck [Bush's] administration."[93] Journalists felt disgusted by their own patriotism. A writer in the New Yorker confessed, *"Sitting in my home by my TV set, I had felt not only horror at Saddam Hussein's deeds ... but ... an unfamiliar pride in our armed forces and their commanders. And the arguments against the war, which had been clear enough to me before it started, had begun to seem unreal."*[94]   Within days, the writer had come to his senses and was "back on the side of the antiwar movement."[95]   *CNN's* Bernard Shaw left Baghdad because he could no longer be neutral. Peter Arnett, also of *CNN,* did not even wish to be neutral, saying, *"I am sick of wars, and I am here [in Baghdad] because maybe my contribution will somehow lesson the hostilities, if not this time, maybe next time."*[96]

To minimize the negative impact of journalists in the Gulf War, Central Command (CENTCOM) developed the pool system, in which small groups of re-

---

Its History (Dallas: Verity Press, 1998).

[89]Eric T. Dean, Jr., *Shook Over Hell: Post-Traumatic Stress, Vietnam, and the Civil War* (Cambridge: Harvard University Press, 1997), pp. 15, 18, 30, 40, 182–83; Burkett and Whitley, *Stolen Valor,* p. 30.

[90]Victor Davis Hanson, *The Soul of Battle* (New York: Free Press, 1999), p. 410.

[91]Herbert J. Gans, "Reopening the Black Box: Toward a Limited Effects Theory," in Mark Levy and Michael Gurevitch, *Defining Media Studies: Reflections on the Future of the Field* (New York: Oxford University Press, 1994), p. 276.

[92]Michael K. Deaver and Mickey Herkowitz, *Behind the Scenes: In Which the Author Talks About Ronald and Nancy Reagan ... and Himself* (New York: Morrow, 1987), p. 147.

[93]Bob Woodward, *The Commanders* (New York: Simon and Schuster, 1994), p. 324.

[94]"Talk of the Town," *New Yorker,* February 11, 1991, p. 25.

[95]Robert Donovan, Raymond L. Scherer, Lee Hamilton, *Unsilent Revolution: Television News and American Public Life, 1948–1991* (New York: Cambridge, 1991), p. 313.

[96]Lee Edwards, *MediaPolitik: How the Mass Media Have Transformed World Politics* (Washington: Catholic University Press, 2001), p. 80.

porters were allowed to enter the combat zone under strict control, then share their observations with others. General Colin Powell, chairman of the Joint Chiefs of Staff, instructed military briefers to be *"as truthful as possible within the necessary and reasonable constraints of security."*[97] Reporters disliked the pool system, but the public, again, sided with the government: 60 percent of Americans thought the Pentagon should exert "more control" over journalists.[98] The pool system worked well for the military because it exposed journalists as arrogant and anti-American. Daily press briefings contrasted *"well-groomed, neatly uniformed, confident, polite, and well-informed senior military officers [with an] often unkempt, rude, and absurdly ill-prepared press."*[99] One columnist noted that the *"adversarial antagonism toward just about everybody, self-satisfied arrogance in the face of authority, and ... incredible ignorance about other cultures and war"* told the public all it needed to know about the reporters.[100] Even the Washington Post's senior editor, Richard Harwood, acknowledged, *"Too many unprepared and dull-witted reporters demonstrated their incompetence day after day to television audiences throughout the world."*[101]

On some occasions, journalists divulged tactical information to the enemy, as when CBS cameraman David Green told Dan Rather that he had just come through a point on the Kuwaiti border and that the Iraqis could *"just walk in here."* That same night, the networks announced the commencement of air operations against Iraq fifteen minutes before many of the pilots had reached their targets, alerting the Iraqi antiaircraft defenses.[102] When General Norman Schwarzkopf learned that *Newsweek* had published a map showing a possible flanking attack through the western desert of Iraq—exactly Schwarzkopf's plan—Powell urged him not to react. *"Other magazines are full of maps showing other battle plans. They're all just speculating."*[103]

Powell and Schwarzkopf decided that rather than keep information bottled up, they would use the reporters' lust for a scoop to their own advantage. They carefully manipulated the media with an anticipated amphibious invasion on Kuwait City by the Marines, where frequent images and reports of Marine activities in the Gulf tied down ten Iraqi divisions waiting for an attack that never came. The diversion also occupied twenty-two of fifty-three pool reporters who salivated at the chance to storm ashore with the Marines.[104] Reporters probably would have been chagrined to know that they were little more than mud in the eyes of the troops: Chief Warrant Officer Eric Carlson said, *"We regarded them*

[97]Smith, *War and Press Freedom*, p. 203.

[98]Edwards, *Media Politic*, p. 77.

[99]William V. Kennedy, *Military and the Media: Why the Press Cannot Be Trusted to Cover a War* (Westport, CT: Praeger, 1993), p. 120.

[100]"Editors Told War Coverage Was Thorough," Portland (Maine) *Press Herald*, October 18, 1991.

[101]Georgie Anne Geyer, "Press Brought on Problems with Military, Public," Harrisburg (Pennsylvania) *Patriot-News*, March 6, 1991.

[102]Richard Harwood, "The Press At War," *Washington Post*, march 10, 1991.

[103]Powell quoted in Jeffrey A. Smith, *War and Press Freedom: The Problem of Prerogative Power* (New York: Oxford, 1999), p. 205.

[104]Smith, *War and Press Freedom*, p. 205.

as an environmental feature of the battlefield, kind of like the rain. If it rains, you operate wet."[105]   Journalists complained that the Pentagon defeated the press before it beat the Iraqis. ***The Wall Street Journal*** more aptly sized up the situation, noting that "the media is really a battlefield, and you have to win on it."[106]

Three factors counteracted the media's leftward and antimilitary bias during the first Gulf War. Ironically, the first was exposure. CNN's Peter Arnett, who brought pictures live from Baghdad, was son "unbiased" as to make clear his view that the Iraqis were victims. Arnett rushed to report stories of American bombs going astray, civilian deaths, or American aircraft shot down. Arnett's wartime reports bore the onscreen caution **CLEARED BY IRAQI CENSORS**, essentially telling the viewer that what followed was propaganda.[107]

A second factor that took the war out of the journalists' hands was the high-tech nature of war itself, which dictated the coverage in favor of American/Coalition success. If reporters, driven by the ever-present deadline and imagery, were going to cover action, the only action they could cover was that of American-led forces utterly destroying the enemy. Pictures of Tomahawk missile launches, aircraft leaving on missions or returning from sorties, or gun camera footage all dictated that reporters show American success. To produce "balance"—the "bad" side of the war—they either had to find Coalition casualties (which, for the total war, were under 150) or display evidence of American "brutality." When a few reporters managed to find bombs that went off target, it only made the Pentagon's case more solid: Americans were going out of their way to limit civilian deaths. For the most part reporters were overwhelmed by the hundreds of thousands of Iraqis surrendering, which itself made for tremendous television and which inspired public support even more. And despite the pool system, journalists missed the real story until it was all over: the wholesale slaughter or Iraqi armored units in the western deserts.

When the details of the western battles were learned, the evidence showed that smaller numbers of Americans repeatedly defeated a larger enemy who lacked sophisticated technology or, above all, skill and discipline. American forces easily defeated the Iraqis, which meant that American boys were safe and Iraqi soldiers were not. It was not a story the press could spin for ill, though many tried.

Third, the lack of military service among any of the journalists made them woefully unprepared to report. They compounded their deficiencies by their unwillingness to obtain any academic background in things military, which soon became apparent in the questions they posed in their press briefings. When a Rolling Stone writer engaged in an "*extended immersion in military life*," to his surprise, he found "*the Army was not the awful thing my [anti-military] father imagined*," and that it was "*the sort of American he always pictured when he explained ...his*

---

[105]Johanna Neuman, *Lights, Camera, War: Is Media Technology Driving International Politics?* (New York: St. Martin's Press, 1996), pp. 10–11.

[106]"U.S. Used Press as a Weapon," *Wall Street Journal*, February 28, 1991.

[107] Walter Goodman, "CNN in Baghdad: Danger of Propaganda v. Virtue of Reporting," *New York Times*, January 29, 1991.

best hopes for the country."[108] (Probably one of the most remarkable disconnects between the media and society was reflected in 9/11 polling, where the view of journalists continued to sink after 9/11 while the military has continued to rank high in public confidence.)[109] Peter Baestrup observed, *"Given the media's focus on conflict, deviance, and melodrama, most senior military med do not see the media as allies of civic peace and virtue. ... There is no counterpart in journalism to 'duty, honor, country,' or to the military leader's ultimate responsibility for life and death and the nation's security."*[110] The closest the media came to influencing the first Gulf War came at the end, when Coalition forces had successfully encircled the retreating Iraqis and had started a systematic devastation of the withdrawing convoys on the "Highway of Death." Images at first seemed to confirm that a massive slaughter was ensuing, but analysis showed that most of the vehicles were already abandoned when air strikes destroyed them. Pictures of apparent carnage, however, increased the pressure to refrain from obliterating the enemy. Schwarzkopf received calls from the White House expressing concern about public reaction.[111] *"I felt irritated,"* Schwarzkopf confessed. *"Washington was ready to overreact, as usual, to the slightest ripple in public opinion [while I] would have been happy to keep on destroying the Iraqi military for the next six months."*[112]

In retrospect, Schwarzkopf was right and President George H. W. Bush and General Powell, wrong. Enough of the Iraqi military survived to put down rebellions from the Kurds and Shiites in subsequent years, and Saddam remained in power, for another Bush administration to deal with. But the media had not "pulled a Vietnam," and had not converted a winnable war into a defeat. Meanwhile, the military (and the country) learned yet another valuable lesson about journalists in wartime: if they are removed from the action, they certainly will write critical stories, if for no other reason than dissatisfaction with their situation. The next time America went to war, the Pentagon would adopt a much more successful strategy toward reporters.

Embedded Journalists, Embedded Generals

Iraqi Freedom's lightning advance was captured by the embedded journalists, who illustrated yet another change in philosophy for the Pentagon. Following Vietnam, military planners realized that the speed of communications and power of the televised picture had changed warfare forever. More than one general admitted that if television had existed in 1944 or 1945, the horrific scenes of

---

[108] David Lipsky, *Absolutely American: Four Years at West Point* (Boston: Houghton Mifflin, 2003), pp. xii–xiii.

[109] David C. King and Zachary Karabell, *The Generation of Trust: How the U.S. Military Has Regained the Public's Confidence Since Vietnam* (Washington, D.C.: AEI Press, 2003), pp. 1–6.

[110] Cited in Edwards, *MediaPolitik*, pp. 87–88. See also Henry Allen, "The Gulf Between Media and Military," *Washington Post*, February 21, 1991.

[111] Woodward, *The Commanders*, passim.

[112] H. Norman Schwarzkopf, *It Doesn't Take A Hero* (New York: Bantam Books, 1992), pp. 468–70.

carnage at Normandy or Iwo Jima would have destroyed American morale and severely eroded support for the war at home. In Grenada (1983), the Reagan administration clamped down on all broadcasts and censored news coverage. But it was a short war, with minimal forces involved, and hardly set a precedent.

Reviewing media coverage in the first Gulf War, the Pentagon noticed that the most destructive characteristic of the pool system was that no matter how accurate a story was when filed, it could be "sanitized" and "framed" by the news anchors and editors in their cushy studios and offices once a reporter shipped it out. Countless studies have confirmed the left-wing bias of editors, writers, and producers of the news, to the extent that such bias is really beyond debate. The only question remaining among scholars is, "what impact does it have?"[113] In the minds of the mainstream media, their ability to turn an entire population against a war had been proved. Now they just had to demonstrate their power again. Meanwhile, the Pentagon knew that neither censorship nor "pooled" reporters had provided fair coverage of military actions. In 2003, military planners knew as they prepared for a conflict with Iraq that in the upcoming war, coverage was likely to be highly critical based on the biases of the press.

Already in the months leading up to war, journalists had produced a litany of doom-and-gloom prognostications:

• Chris Matthews, in the *San Francisco Chronicle,* August 25, 2002, *"To Iraq and Ruin"*: "This invasion of Iraq, if it goes off, will join the Bay of Pigs, Vietnam, Desert One, Beirut and Somalia in the history of military catastrophe."

• In May 2002, the *Los Angeles Times,* citing unnamed sources, had reported that planning for the war was "simplistic and myopic."[114] Among other inaccuracies, the *Times* article claimed that the war plan had never been fully discussed by the heads of the service branches.

• Former CBS News anchor Walter Cronkite issued a similar gloomy prediction, fearing "the military is always more confident than circumstances show they should be," and said that when he looked at America's future it was "very, very dark."

• R. W. "Johnny" Apple, in the *New York Times*, March 30, 2003, *"Bush Peril: Shifting Sand and Fickle Opinion"*: "With every passing day, it is more evident that the allies made two gross military misjudgments in concluding that coalition forces could safely bypass Basra and Nasiriya and that Shiite Muslims in southern Iraq would rise up against Saddam Hussein…. "Shock and awe" neither shocked nor awed.

• *The Washington Post* ran a front-page story on April 14 in which it said that the U.S. invasion force was "not large enough or powerful enough to take Baghdad by force."

• *The Post* just three days earlier had published a story in which it claimed officers were comparing Secretary of Defense Donald Rumsfeld to Vietnam-era secretary of defense Robert McNamara.

• CNN's Wolf Blitzer, on February 25, had a graphic at the bottom of the screen, *IF WAR HAPPENS, ANOTHER QUAGMIRE*?

• CBS News anchor Dan Rather, on January 24, intoned that "to win this time" U.S. forces would have to "wage a perilous battle in the streets of Baghdad" and warned that "civilians will fight, too." (U.S. troops took Baghdad in less than forty-eight hours with

---

[113]See Larry Schweikart, "First, the Bad News," manuscript in author's possession. Among the best books establishing media bias is Jim Kuypers, *Press Bias and Politics: How the Media Frame Controversial Issues* (Westport, CT: Praeger, 2002).

[114]Tommy Franks with Malcolm McConnell, *American Soldier* (New York: Regan Books, 2004), p. 384.

226

Minimal resistance.)[115]

The list of stunningly wrong predictions represents only a fraction of the torrential outpouring of defeatist news that descended from the press on a daily basis.

Pentagon planners were besieged by their own officers who had had experience with bad press in Afghanistan, and who suggested a new strategy to make an end run around the anchor desks and editors' offices. During an action in Haiti in 1994, special military units (made up of the 10th Mountain Division, Special Forces, and Rangers) took along four reporters, two from the *Christian Science Monitor* and two from *U.S. News & World Report*.[116] Although the brass viewed this as placating the media, the line troops, such as author and former major Bob Bevalaqua, found the reporters convenient because the press would have to take notice of U.S. soldiers ending human rights violations. The reporter teams in Haiti could not deliver live satellite pictures as would be possible in Iraq.

Enter Victoria "Torie" Clarke, the Pentagon's assistant secretary for public affairs. Applying the concepts used in Haiti, she fleshed out a plan for embedding reporters, in which individual reporters would be assigned to Army, Marine, Navy, Air Force, and headquarters units. These journalists would travel with their units, living, eating, and (when possible) sleeping with them, and be free to report anything within some broad guidelines about troop locations and numbers. All told, some five hundred reporters were embedded (90 percent of them Americans), operating with the most lax press restrictions in wartime history. They could not sue the U.S. government for injury or death, could not photograph POWs or detainees, and had to carry their own equipment; but other than that, they operated under few rules. Most of the time, they were free to release information that in the past would have been censored, including the size of the friendly forces involved in an engagement, description of the types of action (land-based or air-based), types of ordnance expended, and even operation code names.

Some journalists drew assignments at command centers, such as *The Washington Post*'s Rick Atkinson with the 101st Airborne, who listened with no restrictions to the generals' conversations about strategy, recording their doubts, their successes, their criticisms, and their celebration. Most, however, traveled in the field with combat units, such as Fox Television's Rick Leventhal, who provided gripping video of combat with the 3rd Light Armored Reconnaissance Unit of the 1st Marine Division, putting him at the forefront of many fights. Another Fox reporter, Greg Kelly, was an active-duty Marine pilot before becoming a journalist—and was the first reporter to ride into Baghdad. But most journalists

[115]The Media Research Center has compiled most of these excerpts: "Washington Times Documents Media's Doomsaying Predictions," April 15, 2002, at http://www.mediaresearchcenter.com/cybealerts/2003/cyb20030414.asp. Comments from Chris Matthews and Johnny Apple are found in "Hall of Shame," *National Review Online*, April 10, 2003, at http://national review.com/nr_comment/nr_comment041003.asp; Cronkite Voices Disappointment in Move to War," March 19, 2003, at http://www.dailyrecord.com/news/03/03/19/news6-cronkite.htm.
[116]Bob Bevalaqua and Bryan Fugate, *Major Bob Unvarnished: Why We Keep Making the Same Mistakes* (Salt Lake City: Millennial Mind, 2005), pp. 32–33.

had never served in the military, and few were even passingly competent on the basics of military organization, ranks, procedures, tactics, or weapons. Initially, as "embed" Karl Zinsmeister noted, *the vast number of reporters I've spoken to are scornful of this war's aims and execution.*[117]

However, as the journalists shared the dangers, setbacks, and successes of the troops—and saw, firsthand, what they were up against—their attitudes changed. Atkinson, no stranger to combat forces as a reporter, even while snidely dismissing the casus belli and the White House leadership, wrote of the 101st Airborne's soldiers:

> *The division's soldiers ... demonstrate[ed] competence and professionalism. Capably led—the division's brigade commanders and two assistant division commanders were uncommonly excellent—they took hardship in stride and refused to let bloodlust, cynicism, or other despoilers of good armies cheat them of their battle honors.*[118]

Reporters not only chronicled the heroism and tenacity of the troops, but suffered with them when they lost comrades. Instead of elite New York and Washington newsroom views of the world—those who thought France was a "reasonable voice" of international mediation—the embeds heard troopers joke frequently about the French ("How can you tell a military rifle on eBay is French? It's labeled, 'Never been fired. Dropped once.'") Karl Zinsmeister was also *"struck that [during prayer call in Protestant services] several requests for prayers for Iraqis were offered up by servicemen ... prayers for the safety of Iraqi civilians, and even for Iraqi soldiers, that they might recognize U.S. troops as 'liberators not enemies,' and not throw their lives away."*[119] David Zucchino wrote of the Assassins Brigade tankers, *"They slept on the decks, wolfed down lumpish MREs ... inside the turret, hunkered down in the cramped hatches on cold desert nights."*[120]

Even Evan Wright, a liberal reporter for the ultraliberal Rolling Stone magazine, painted a picture of Marines that could hardly be viewed as hostile:

> *The invaders drive north through the Iraqi desert in a Humvee, eating candy, dipping tobacco and singing songs.... The four Marines crammed into this vehicle ... are wired on a combination of caffeine, sleep deprivation, excitement and tedium.... [Two of the Marines] have already reached a profound conclusion about this campaign: the battlefield ... is filled with 'fucking retards.'... [O]ne retard reigns supreme: Saddam Hussein—"We kicked his ass once," says Person.... "Then we let him go, and he spends the next twelve years pissing us off even more.... What a fucking retard."*[121]

The Marines, it seems, came to some commonsense conclusions, if per-

---

[117]Karl Zinsmeister, *Boots on the Ground: A Month with the 82nd in the Battle for Iraq* (New York: Truman Tarley Books, 2003), p. 47.

[118]Rick Atkinson, *In the Company of Soldiers: a Chronicle of Combat* (New York: Henry Holt, 2004), p. 294.

[119]Zinsmeister, *Boots on the Ground*, p. 63.

[120]David Zucchino, *Thunder Run: The Armored Strike to Capture Baghdad* (New York: Atlantic Monthly Press, 2004), p. 1.

[121]Evan Wright, "The Killer Elite," *Rolling Stone,* June 26, 2003, pp. 56–68.

haps not, as Wright termed them, "profound." Martin Walker of UPI put it more bluntly: *"Those who have spent time on the front lines with coalition troops ... have learned to love the military."*[122] Zinsmeister recorded the pep talk of Captain Adam Carson of the 82nd Airborne:

> *I want you to remember something. You are Americans. Americans don't shoot women and children. They don't kill soldiers who have surrendered. That's what the assholes we're up against do. That's what we're fighting.*[123]

Embedding the reporters proved so effective at bringing the American soldier's viewpoint into the living room that ABC News scrooge, Sam Donaldson, called it a "stroke of genius." This was a coup, considering that most journalists (including those embedded) were predisposed to distrust and dislike the military. At the outset of the war, Secretary of Defense Rumsfeld had told the National Security Council in a memo, *"We need to tell the factual story—good and bad—before others seed the media with disinformation and distortions, as they most certainly will continue to do."* While Rumsfeld obviously meant Al Jazeera and Saddam's own state propaganda, he could have been referring to the American media when he used the term "disinformation and distortions." Instead, *"Our commanders can ensure the media get to the story alongside the troops ... [because] we will embed the media with our units [who] will live, work, and travel as part of those forces"*.[124] Slowly and sometimes reluctantly on the part of the media, the soldiers' stories started to dominate the news. People back home saw individual units fighting—and winning—rather than watching markers on a map being moved while a retired colonel on TV explained why the campaign was "bogged down." Average Americans knew that "bogged down" campaigns didn't blast ahead at forty miles per hour, all day, every day!

During a "pause," retired general Wesley Clark put the most negative spin possible on the situation, portraying it as a serious delay. (This same Clark, while supreme allied commander of NATO, had acknowledged that "avoiding losses" was his first "measure of merit" in achieving mission success—not accomplishing the mission or destroying the enemy; the same Clark who ordered Lieutenant General Michael Jackson to use his troops to stop the Russians from seizing Pristina Airfield in Kosovo—to which Jackson retorted, *"I am not going to start World War III for you"*; and the same Clark who, a year after running for president, was still insisting on more "resources" for Iraq.)[125] In fact, Major Bob Bevalaqua had it right on Fox when he said, *"The reason we've stopped is obvious. Before*

[122]Martin Walker, "Commentary: How the Media Changed," online at http://www.upi.com/view/cjm?Story-ID=20030408-071952-7876r.

[123]Zinsmeister, *Boots on the Ground*, p. 126.

[124]Joel Rosenberg, "Rumsfeld Memo to National Security Council: How to Win the Spin War," *World Magazine,* March 27, 2003, www.worldmag.com, excerpted on www.freerepublic.com/focus/f-news/877282/posts.

[125]Quoted in Evan Andrew Huefler, The "Casualty Issue" in *American Military Practice: The Impact of World War I* (Westport, CT: Praeger, 2003), p. xi; Jackson quoted in Tsouras, The Greenhill Dictionary of Military Quotations, p. 347; Wesley K. Clark, "Before It's Too Late in Iraq," www.washingtonpost.com, August 26, 2005.

a butcher gets ready to carve up a piece of meat, he sharpens his knife."[126] Beva-laqua's comments were a breath of fresh air among the embedded generals, most of whom were not even in the Army, but were retired from the Air Force or Navy! General Omar Bradley once said, "*I am convinced that the best service a retired general can perform is to turn in his tongue along with his suit and to mothball his opinions.*"[127] Marine general Al Gray put it differently: "*I can give you my opinion, but remember this is just Al Gray talking: I'm too junior to make policy and too senior to make coffee.*"[128] Even Winston Churchill sarcastically referred to the tendency of generals to release their memoirs when he said, "*I hear my generals are selling themselves dearly.*"[129]

Bevalaqua, one of the most clear-eyed analysts, commented at the onset of the war how bizarre it was that virtually all of the graphics of weapons systems that news departments were running were of aircraft, with few visuals of tanks, Bradleys, or infantry weapons—the equipment that would be handling most of the heavy lifting. The embedded reporters picked up these kinds of discrepancies fast, and the cameras picked them up even faster: Americans saw that we were not dropping bombs indiscriminately, but rather putting young men and women into dangerous situations, often with the "rights" of noncombatants and civilians placed ahead of their own lives.

When it dawned on members of the liberal media that Rumsfeld had out-flanked them, they howled. Neal Gabler of Salon moaned that the embedded reporters were "patsies" and "P.R. flacks" because they bonded with the troops. "*We need the 'larger picture,'*" he complained, and urged more "*context*," mean-ing more of a liberal slant on the obvious images of victory emerging from Iraq.[130] **The Los Angeles Times** chimed in, lamenting that the "embeds" were too close to the facts: "*these policies raise questions about the balance and sensitivity of wartime media coverage.*"[131]

Thus the war was simultaneously fought on two fronts, one with Amer-ican and Coalition soldiers pitted against Iraqis and their terrorist/foreign-fight-er allies, and a second in which the embedded journalists filed stories from the front that had to be explained away or "interpreted" by the liberal editors and anchors back home. (In this, the U.S. military had more openness than any of the mainstream media newsrooms!) Any spin that could explain American actions as failure was invoked, and the comparisons to Vietnam were endless: CBD warned that "*while Iraq has been seething, more than 90 people have been killed this week in Afghanistan's forgotten war.*" And CNN's Brian Cabell claimed the "*ar-gument*" over Iraq was "*likely to become louder in the months ahead: Is this truly a continuation of the war against terrorism, or is it possibly another drawn-out,*

---

[126]Bevalaqua, *Major Bob Unvarnished*, p. 107.

[127]Bradley quoted in Tsouras, *The Greenhill Dictionary of Military Quotations,* p. 341.

[128]Tsouras, *The Greenhill Dictionary of Military Quotations*.

[129]Tsouras, *The Greenhill Dictionary of Military Quotations*, p. 294.

[130]Gabler quoted in George Neumayr, "Embedded Patsies," *The American Prowler,* March 27, 2003, online at http://www.spectator.org/article.asp?_id-2003_3_26_23_14_27.

[131]Neumayr, "Embedded Patsies."

inconclusive Vietnam war in the making?"[132]   Every once in a while, though, the truth leaked out almost by accident. In April, 2005, *The Washington Post*, writing about the Fallujah offensive, recorded a terrorist who had been captured as saying "*We are fighting, but the Marines keep coming. We are shooting, but the Marines won't stop.*"[133]

Victor Davis Hanson has emphasized the significance of "civilian audit" in contributing to the success of western militaries.[134]   That civilian audit could, at the same time, encourage antiwar protesters during the Vietnam era and yet force the Pentagon into rethinking its war-fighting doctrines, leading, ironically, to an even more effective military machine. Now, in Operation Iraqi Freedom, the role of civilian audit was key, and it relied on accurate information getting out if the American electorate was to support the war. So the embeds battled (whether they wanted to or not) their editorial masters. UPI's Martin Walker admitted a "very different view" among journalists in the field from the "large and skeptical media corps" back at the headquarters briefings.[135]   Dartmouth journalism professor Jim Kuypers, who examined sixty-six stories from the war (twenty-six from embeds and forty from non-embeds), found a significant difference in the reports. Non-embedded reporters were "*less able to separate preconceptions*" and more often than not based their reports on domestic fears of potential resistance rather than actual instances of resistance.[136]

Later, a stunning journalism story emerged from the war when CNN chief news executive Eason Jordan wrote in the *New York Times* that CNN had deliberately buried negative stories about Saddam and his thuggish sons to stay in the good graces of the regime.[137]   Jordan justified lying to the American people about the nature and threat of Saddam's government on grounds that it would have "*jeopardized the lives of Iraqis, particularly those on our Baghdad staff,*" yet CNN never seemed to apply such concerns to American soldiers in harm's way. Later, *New York Times* writer John Burns would recount how journalists took the Iraqi information minister Baghdad Bob "*out for candlelit dinners, plying him with sweet cakes, plying him with mobile phones at $600 each for members of his family, and giving him bribes of thousands of dollars.*"[138]   Burns admitted that western reporters were accompanied by "handlers" at all times. Nevertheless, he argued, it was "*not impossible to tell the truth,*" even in Iraq, but rather his colleagues, "*rationalized [evil] away.*" When he reported on Uday Hussein's use of torture to punish the Olympic Committee ignored his evidence. Referring to jour-

[132]Mark Phillips, August 20, 2003, CBS "Nightline News," and Brian Cabell, September 8, 2003, CNN's "Newsnight."

[133]Washington Post, April 1, 2005.

[134]Victor Davis Hanson, *Carnage and Culture: Landmark Battles in the Rise of Western Culture* (New York: Doubleday, 2001).

[135]Martin Walker, "Commentary: How the Media Changed," online at http://www.upi.com/view/cfm?Story-ID=20030408-071952-7876r.

[136]Liz Ypsen, "Dartmouth College Prof.: Bias Influenced Iraq Coverage," *The Dartmouth Online*, October 22, 2003.

[137]Eason Jordan, "The News We Kept to Ourselves," *New York Times*, April 11, 2003.

[138]John Burns, "There Is Corruption in Our Business," *Editor & Publisher*, September 15, 2003.

nalists' unwillingness to confront the evil of Saddam Hussein, Burns concluded *"there was gross abdication of responsibility."* [139]

Slanted war coverage caused the public to steadily lose confidence in everyone in the media except the embeds. A May 2003 *USA Today* headline blared *TRUST IN MEDIA KEEPS ON SLIPPING[140]*. This marked a continuation of a downward spiral for news viewership and circulation among major papers, with only Fox News gaining substantially (its viewership rising 133 percent since 2001). And it stood in stark contrast to confidence in the military, churches, and the Office of the President, as measured by polls.[141] Surveys also showed that a majority of the public thought news organizations were biased and just under half thought the media was overly critical of the United States.[142] Whatever the manifold failures of the editors, anchors, and headquarters media, the embeds produced a constant stream of real-time news. Certainly not all of it was favorable, nor could it have been. Covering battlefield stories, by the very nature of field reporting, leads to an often murky, confusing picture. But the commentators in the studios turned normal military screwups, delays, mistakes, and battlefield confusion into strategic "setbacks," leading Rumsfeld to caustically refer to the "embedded generals" in the TV studios.

Such distortions of the real situation on the ground were not only untrue, but they also stunned the embeds once the field reporters found out about them. A BBC reporter, Paul Adams, blasted his organization for giving the war a negative slant, asking *"Who dreamed up the line that the coalition are achieving 'small victories at a very high price?... The truth is exactly the opposite ... the gains are huge and the costs relatively low."* Upon his return, Adams was "gobsmacked" to read a set of headlines that *"the coalition was suffering 'significant casualties.' This is simply **NOT TRUE** [emphasis in original]."*[143] And even the embeds failed to grasp the phenomenal progress, which exasperated Frank's officers back at CENTCOM. The embedded reporters had no Blue Force Tracker to reveal the stunning advance, or to understand that units were ahead of their objectives.

Almost universally, the "embedded generals" simply failed to connect the dots or discern the strategy. General Barry McCaffrey, for example, a self-promoting commentator, sharply criticized Rumsfeld for providing insufficient (in his view) forces to accomplish the task. Franks had deliberately "gone light" to gain the element of surprise, and he kept the 4th Infantry Division (ID) near Turkey an additional twenty-four hours just to keep Iraqi troops fixed in the north. Indeed, once the 4th ID did move, Iraqi intelligence was still convinced it would disembark at al-Aqaba and invade Iraq from the west. McCaffrey complained about bypassing Basra and An Nasiriva, but, in fact, the British had specifically been

---

[139]Burns, "There Is Corruption in Our Business."

[140]Peter Johnson, "Trust in Media Keeps On Slipping," USA Today, May 28, 2003.

[141]James L. Gattuso, "Who to Watch? The Iraq War and the Myth of Media Concentration," March 26, 2003, C:SPIN, online at http://www.cei.org/utils/printer.cfm?AID=3423.

[142]Jennifer Harper, "Public Wants Patriotic but Unbiased Reporters," *Washington Times*, July 14, 2003.

[143]Brent Baker, "BBC Reporter 'Gobsmacked' by BBC's Distorted War Refreerepublic.com/focus/f-news/876963/posts.

restrained from taking Basra out of concern that it would tip off Saddam to the tactics the Coalition would use in storming Baghdad. Nor did they seem to grasp that the strategy all along was to topple the regime, not conquer every city. Like William Tecumseh Sherman refusing to be drawn away from his March to the Sea to pursue Hood's offensive into Tennessee, the Army and Marines plowed ahead to destroy Saddam's regime, leaving follow-on units to mop up after the Coalition demonstrated the impotence of the Baathists. Risk-averse commentators repeatedly expressed concern that American troops were moving too fast, forgetting the lessons of Sherman's march. Ultimately—as is usually the case—rapid victory on the battlefield rendered mute the "embedded generals" and media critics.

"A Campaign Unlike Any Other in History"

No event in the brief war was more poorly interpreted by the "embedded generals" and journalists than the operational pause of March 24-26. Like other failures of the press, this stemmed from an incorrect understanding of the plan and an individual force's fighting capabilities. According to Bing West and Major General Ray Smith, General Tommy Franks *"planned a campaign with two main forces—and so had hedged against a setback to either one."*[144] The plan approved at a March 29 Camp David meeting stressed taking Baghdad over establishing secure supply lines and solidifying positions. It was true that by March 26, the Army needed more ammo and gas, but the Marines did not. Indeed, I Marine Expeditionary Force still was fully capable of offensive operations toward Baghdad.

At that point, two factors combined to give the impression the war had stalled. First was the genuine shortage of ammo and fuel with the tank-heavy Army in the west, combined with the extremely long lines of communication (LOCs) that had become unwieldy. The 3rd Infantry Division by that time was moving constantly, its five thousand vehicles moving at night without lights, and its drivers using night vision goggles. Some 20,000 men advanced along two routes converging at an area around An Nasiriya known as Ambush Alley. Ambushes were brief, deadly encounters in which fedayeen would place obstacles along the road to slow or stop the lightly armored column, then hit the vulnerable units with RPGs, mortars, and gunfire. On occasion, Iraqis in "technicals" actually rushed the column, only to be blown apart by 7.62 mm coaxial machine gun or 25 mm fire. Counterbattery fire could quickly pinpoint and destroy mortars. Nevertheless, Ambush Alley slowed down resupply, and General William Wallace decided to slow down to permit consolidation of the lines.

Troops of V corps had already moved ten thousand vehicles over three hundred miles, and many were running low on ammunition. Keeping the supply lines open was critical. Wallace did not have the same advantage that General William Tecumseh Sherman had had on his march through Georgia, where part of the objective was to strip the countryside. Sherman's army, as Admiral David

144Bing West and Ray L. Smith, *The March Up: Taking Baghdad with the 1st Marine Division* (New York: Bantam, 2003), p. 107.

Porter noted, *"was no respecter of ducks, chickens, pigs, or turkeys [and] one particular regiment ... could catch, scrape, and skin a hog without a solider leaving the ranks."* [145] The Americans moving through Iraq had to bring their own supplies along, and therefore Wallace brought the 82nd Airborne in to shore up logistics routes. Its arrival was a testament to the brigade's remarkable determination to get into the fight.[146] According to the Army's own "lessons learned," the 82nd was *"not favorably postured or located,"* but the paratroopers *"moved with fierce determination"* to get into action.[147] They had to derig for an expected jump into Baghdad International Airport and instead load up on vehicles, arriving north of An Nasiriya on March 29. But even during the repositioning of the 82nd, the Army's own summary pointed out that the so-called "operational pause" was "no time-out." For logisticians and combat troops alike, *"the pace slowed from outrageous to merely brutal."*[148] Franks relished the journalists' misreporting. When his director of communications fretted, *"They're filing stories that we've lost the war,"* Franks smiled and answered, *"Good.... We couldn't ask for better deception."*[149]

A second factor contributing to the pause was the shamal (sandstorm) that blew in on March 24, and even without a decision to bring in the 82nd or to resupply, operations would have been dramatically curtailed. Troopers had never seen anything like it. Winds gusted from twenty-five to fifty knots, blowing sand into every crevice scarves, even medical slings, around their mouths to reduce the impact of the dust, usually to no avail.

> *Most of the men had long since suffered through "the crud," that week-long period when the dust particles first infect the membranes of the lungs, choking off the vocal cords, causing constant coughing and the hacking up of enormous wads of yellow pus. After ... feeling miserable for several days, the body adjust to the dirt-filled air.* [150]

Helicopters were particularly vulnerable to the dust storm. Rotor blades had to be taped or specially painted to diminish the degrading effect of sand. When it blew at thirty knots, it found its way into helicopter engines and instruments.

To the Marines, who had fewer problems with logistics because they had adopted a plan called Log Lite (which imposed on them even more spartan food and equipment restrictions), the pause was an irritant. In one instance involving the offensive against the Baghdad Division of the Republican Guards, stationed in Al Kut, a deception movement by RCT 1 up Route 7, as if to attack the city from the south, was intended to hold the Baghdad Division in place. Then two other

---

[145]David D. Porter, *Incidents and Anecdotes of the Civil War* (1885), in Tsouras, *The Greenhill Dictionary of Military Quotations*, p. 278.
[146]Gregory Fontenot, E. J. Degan, and David Topa, *On Point: The United States Army in Operation Iraqi Freedom* (Washington, D.C.: U.S. Army chief of Staff, 2004), chap. 5.
[147]Fontenot, *On Point*.
[148]Fontenot, *On Point*.
[149]Franks, *American Soldier*, p. 504.
[150]West and Smith, *The March Up*, p. 51.

RCTs would sweep in behind the Iraqis. But just as RCT 5 started its encircle-ment, the pause order forced it to countermarch more than thirty miles. The Ma-rines were stunned: Baghdad seemed within their grasp, the entire Marine Expedi-tionary Force was either on or ahead of schedule, and yet they had to slow down. (The very presence of the Marines confounded the Iraqis, who were convinced the Marine Corps "never fights far from the sea.")[151]

Back in the United States, the "embedded generals" and the newsroom analysts *painted a grim picture and conveyed the tone of a ground offensive that was struggling and that could not continue without a pause.*[152]   Hundreds of stories suggested that fierce enemy attacks and high casualties had bogged down the advance, and there were renewed calls for more troops. Franks knew more troops would only muck up the process: already the 101st Airborne was offloading, with the 4th ID and the 2nd Armored Cavalry Regiment en route from the United States, threatening to back up still farther on the docks. In *American Soldier*, General Tommy Franks repeatedly ridiculed the notion that he needed more men. Quite the contrary, more men would have slowed down the plan and doomed it to failure.[153]   As he had briefed President Bush before the invasion, *"Coalition strength during decisive combat will derive from the mass of effective firepower, not simply the number of boots or tank tracks on the ground* [emphasis added]."[154]   Here was yet another example of the evolution of the western way of war, a karate-style interpretation of combat that emphasized total victory through overwhelming strength delivered at a well-defined point.

There had been some casualties, the most caused by two separate inci-dents of friendly fire. Ignored also was the fact that on March 23, an American sergeant—a disgruntled Muslim named Hasan Akbar—tossed a grenade into sev-eral tents of the 101st Airborne in Kuwait, killing 2 and wounding 14.[155]   But newsrooms downplayed Akbar's traitorous actions. Worse, they tended to over-look the rapid advance of the Marine Expeditionary Force to the east. This ad-vance was precisely what Franks had anticipated: that such fast-moving forces would get inside the "decision cycle" of the Iraqi leadership. Action so far had validated Franks' prediction that Iraqi Freedom was *"a campaign unlike any other in history."* More than a year after Saddam's fall, after hundreds of American ca-sualties to suicide bombers, booby traps, and mortar ambushes, many questioned whether the victory was as decisive as it had seemed on April 10. Editorials blared, *"Are we Losing the Peace?"*—virtually identical to columns written in 1945 and 1946 about the postwar Germany.[156]

A free press posed other dangers in wartime. As David Hackett Fisch-er noted, in America the press "demanded quick, clear, simple results that could

[151]Franks, *American Soldier*, p. 559.
[152]West and Smith, *The March Up*, p. 80.
[153]Franks, *American Soldier*, p. 475.
[154]Franks, *American Soldier,* p. 476.
[155]"Sgt. Akar Asks for Trial Delay," *Fayetteville (NC) Observer*, August 6, 2004.
[156]Larry Schweikart, "Three Occupations: There Ain't No Model, and None Are Without Problems," may 25, 2004 (misdated 2005, and reprinted in various places), http://www.freerepublic.com/focus/f-news/1142222/posts.

be summarized in eighteenth-century broadsides, nineteenth-century telegrams, twentieth-century headlines, and twenty-first-century sound bytes," and more important, it required military leaders "not merely to act but to give the appearance of action."[157] Yet this was precisely what made such American commanders as Washington, Grant, and Eisenhower superior soldiers in the strategic sense to Stonewall Jackson, Patton, or Maxwell Taylor: they looked beyond sound bites and press clippings, and understood that receiving bad press in the short run was insignificant if larger objectives were attained.

The Old Antiwar Strategy

Possibly because the antiwar demonstrations of the Vietnam Era were televised, there is a notion that previous wars lacked an antiwar movement. Nothing, of course, could be further from the truth. Lincoln faced massive draft riots in New York City; the Federalists sealed their political doom by opposing the War of 1812; and opposition to continued action in the Philippines divided the political parties in 1900, when Andrew Carnegie wrote letters on behalf of the New England Anti-Imperialism League against further occupation of the Philippines (although he had supported the liberation of Cuba in the Spanish-American War). Henry Ford, at the outbreak of World War I, chartered the ship Oskar II and filled it with pacifists before it sailed to Stockholm in 1916, predating Clark Clifford's goofy globetrotting during the Vietnam war (but the United States was not a direct participant in hostilities when Ford set off for Europe). Regardless, the "peace ship" was an exercise in floating futility, since no representatives of the belligerent parties showed up. (Some years later, Ford would contribute to the international support accorded to the German Nazi Party when he allowed publication of a series of anti-Jewish articles in the Dearborn Independent, which he owned). On the eve of World War II, Ford criticized the amendment of the Neutrality Act as enabling *"munitions makers to profit financially through what is nothing less than mass murder."*[158]

Enemies of America knew how to play the political card just as well then as now, and much of the Filipino insurrectionists' strategy depended on the "anti-imperialist" success in the 1900 election. There they pinned their hopes on William Jennings Bryan's winning the presidency.[159] Consequently, the insurrectionists goal was to *"use conventional (and later guerrilla) tactics and an increasing toll of US casualties to contribute to McKinley's defeat in the 1900 presidential election."*[160] But live by the sword—or in this case the ballot box—die by the sword: when McKinley won reelection, it demoralized the insurgents and con-

---

[157]David Hackett Fischer, *Washington's Crossing* (Oxford: Oxford university Press, 2004), pp. 370–71.

[158]"Ford Paints Peril in Lifting Embargo," *New York Times*, September 21, 1939.

[159]Timothy K. Deady, "Lessons from a Successful Counterinsurgency: The Philippines, 1899–1902," *Paramaters*, Spring 2005, pp. 53–68.

[160]John Morgan Gates, *Schoolbooks, and Krags: The United States Army in the Philippines, 1898–1902* (Westport, CT: Greenwood Press, 1973), pp. 161–63.

vinced many undecided Filipinos that the "Yanquis" were there to stay.[161]

America has always had an antiwar element. Occasionally it was populated by pacifists from the ranks of Christian churches, most notably the Quakers. At other time, it was war specific, deriving from either racism (Mexican War, Spanish-American War) or a sense of intellectual snobbishness (World War I). Protesters have almost always attempted to claim a moral high ground, from Henry David Thoreau to Martin Luther King, Jr. A few, particularly in World War II, differed sharply from most other groups in that they (generically known as isolationists) favored a strong and victorious nation, but thought the best way to achieve that was through a Fortress America, safe behind walls of water and curtains of airplanes. Few of those remain anymore. Whatever their political stripe, most are antinationalists and, by preference, globalists. In the late twentieth century, war protesters almost always came from the ultra–left wing of the Democratic Party, although more than a few self-professed "Libertarians" opposed the Iraq War and have written scathing attacks on Lincoln and Roosevelt for precipitating needless wars.[162]

For all their supposed pacifism, antiwar protesters throughout American history have tolerated, and even celebrated, the deaths of American soldiers. *"Oh, come now! That's too much,"* you say? In 1967 poet Allen Ginsberg wrote, *"Let the Viet Cong win over the American Army!"*[163]   Peter Collier, then a staff member of *Ramparts* magazine, recalled: *"We had a weekly ritual of sitting in front of the television set and cheering as Walter Cronkite announced the ever-rising body count on CBS."*[164] Mary McCarthy, a northeastern leftist writing for the *New York Review* in 1967 said, *"I confess that when I went to Vietnam early last February I was looking for the material damaging to the American interest."*[165]   On December 26, , 1972, after the Linebacker II bombing campaign against the North, presidential candidate George McGovern, on NBC, referred to the bombing as *"a policy of mass murder"* and *"the most immoral action that this nation has even committed."*[166] Anthony Lewis called it a "crime against humanity." The *"most terrible destruction in the history of man,"* apparently forgetting the Romans' leveling of Carthage and Jerusalem or the Japanese rape of Nanking.[167]

Surprisingly, one of those most opposed to war, especially the Mexican War, was Ulysses S. Grant, who thought it *"one of the most unjust ever waged by a stronger against a weaker nation,"* yet who fought at Palo Alto, Resaca, Monterrey, and Mexico City.[168] Years later, Grant wrote in his Personal Memoirs that

[161]Gates, *Schoolbooks to Krags*, pp. 204, 235, 273.

[162]See www.antiwar.com, for example, and any of the writings on that site by Justin Raimundo, or any of the work of Thomas DiLorenao.

[163]Quoted in Michael Lind, *Vietnam: The Necessary War* (New York: Touchstone, 1999), p. 128.

[164]Peter Collier and David Horowitz, *Destructive Generation: Second Thoughts About the Sixties* (New York: Summit, 1989), p.264.

[165]Lind, *Vietnam*, p. 128.

[166]Lind, *Vietnam*, p. 248.

[167]Martin F. Herz, *The Prestige Press and the Christmas Bombing, 1972: Image and Reality in Vietnam* (Washington, D.C.: Ethics and Public Policy Center, 1980). p. 47.

[168]Quoted in John Keegan, *The Mask of Command* (New York: Penguin, 1987), p. 182.

the "southern rebellion" was the direct result of the Mexican War in that it gave slavery new territorial legs. *"Nations, like individuals,"* he wrote, *"are punished for their transgressions. We got our punishment in the most sanguinary and expensive war of modern times."*[169]

Yet what did Grant do, even thinking as he did? He not only served, but fought well, to the point of chilling efficiency. After the fall of Fort Donelson and Fort Henry, Grant fumed that the separation of commands in the West prolonged the war, and that *"if one general ... had been in command of all the troops ... he could have marched to Chattanooga, Corinth, Memphis and Vicksburg."* [170] As commander of the Army, Grant praised Sherman's capture of Atlanta as *"one of the most memorable in history;"* despite the experience of the assault at Vicksburg still fresh in his mind, Grant did not hesitate to order the futile attack at Cold Harbor—probably his worst military move.[171] Still, by unleashing both Sherman and Phil Sheridan (who scorched the Shenandoah Valley), Grant coldly committed himself to "total war." His personal memoirs are mixed with orders to *"effectively destroy"* railroads, *"burn up"* bridges, round up and send South *"ten families of the most noted secessionists"* after every guerrilla raid. The Rebellion, he concluded, *"can only terminate by the complete subjugation of the south or the overthrow of the government."*[172]

Consider modern leftist critics of the war on terror. What were their first comments after the 9/11 attack? One Iraqi Freedom vet, who was at Pace Law School in the days after 9/11, recalled that his professor asked his students, *"Can you think of a time when the United States acted as terrorist?"*[173] Zbigniew Brzezinski, Jimmy Carter's national security adviser, said that the terrorist threat was stoked by "extreme demagogy," and the *International Herald Tribune* claimed that the United States was viewed *"as a greater threat than al Qaeda."*[174] After expressing gratitude that the "loonies" during the Cold War were powerless, Arthur Schlesinger, Jr., the perennial Kennedy/FDR apologist, wrote that *"in 2003, they run the Pentagon."*[175] Have any on the left hoped to "save lives" by demanding the *"complete subjugation"* of al Qaeda, or the *"overthrow"* of terror-friendly governments? Have any called for the rounding up of ten families of the most noted supporters of the PLO or Islamic Jihad in America and demanded that they be deported? One can learn much from Ulysses Grant, war protester.

Civilian Control

---

[169]Ulysses S. Grant, *Personal Memoirs of U.S. Grant*, abr. by Philip van Doren Stern (New York: Peter Smith, 1969), p. 38.

[170]Grant, *Personal Memoirs,* p. 96.

[171]Grant, *Personal Memoirs,* p. 291.

[172]Quoted in Keegan, *Mask of Command*, p. 220.

[173]Kieran Michael Lalor, "Forum: The Antiwar Movement Preceded War," July 3, 2005.

[174]Frances Fox Piven, *The War at Home: The Domestic Costs of Bush's Militarism* (New York: New Press, 2004), p. 10.

[175]Schlesinger quoted in Piven, *The War at Home*, p. 9.

One concept that infused Ulysses Grant was that the Constitution stated clearly the rights of individuals and the states, and secession was not one of them. Submission by the military to civilian authority was a principle that Grant never would have questioned. Indeed, while Americans have enthusiastically elected former military men to high office, only one time did a senior officer run for the presidency while retaining his position, and Winfield Scott was rejected by voters. More commonly, American soldiers have resigned their commissions to run for political office, and some, including Grant and Eisenhower, have been successful, while others, such as former NATO general Wesley Clark, have not. George Washington, of course, had resigned to return to civilian life, only to be "drafted" into becoming the first president.

The division between civilian and military—and, more important, the assumption that civilians should control the military—derived largely from George Washington, who established the framework of civilian control over the military by respecting the directives of the Continental Congress. Washington's efforts seemed destined to fail at first, as the legislators tried to run the military affairs of the war. The watershed occurred on December 27, 1776, when the Congress voted to give Washington virtually unchecked military authority for six months, putting *"the whole of the military department"* into his hands.[176] As David Hackett Fischer put it, *"Their grant of new powers to George Washington affirmed the rule of law, recognized the principle of civil supremacy over the military, and established the authority of Congress as representative of the states and the sovereign people,"* while asserting the primacy of the military to determine the conduct of military operations without congressional interference.[177] During the constitutional convention of 1767, civilian control over the military was reiterated and, as with all aspects of American government, power over the military was divided between the executive and legislative branches.[178]

On several occasions—George McClellan's snubbing of Abraham Lincoln or Douglas MacArthur's attempts during the Korean War to pull and "end run" around President Harry Truman's policies—American military officers have criticized civilian policies, though never actually challenged them. Most of the time, this occurs after the individuals have taken off their uniforms, as with George McClellan, but when an officer insists on his "free speech" while still a member of the armed services, he usually pays the price. More often, however, the problem is not that officers are too critical of the policy but that they imply to the press, through their comments, that they have more authority than they really do. For example, in the Gulf War, Air Force Chief General Michael Dugan outlined an impressive plan to the *Washington Post* that portrayed air power as the "only answer" to avoid a ground war. Dugan not only elevated his own service branch

---

[176]Fischer, *Washington's Crossing*, p. 144.

[177]Fischer, *Washington's Crossing*, p. 145.

[178]Richard Kohn, "The Creation of the American Military Establishment, 1783–1802," in Peter Karsten, ed., *The Military in America: From the Colonial Era to the Present* (New York: Free Press, 1980), 73–84; Richard Kohn, *Eagle and Sword: The Federalists and the Creation of the Military Establishment in America, 1783–1802* (New York: Free Press, 1975).

outside the plan accepted by the Joint Chiefs, but he delineated specific targets of the air offensive.[179]   Defense Secretary Richard Cheney listed nine separate violations of protocol by Dugan in relieving him, including the fact that Dugan made himself *"the self-appointed spokesman for the [Joint Chiefs of Staff]."*[180]

Dugan's behavior resembled on a much smaller scale the civilian-military confrontation of two earlier occasions, namely the provocative criticism of the U.S. Army and Navy by Colonel Billy Mitchell in 1925, which led to his court-martial a few months later, and the removal of Douglas MacArthur as the commander of allied forces in Korea in April 1951. Mitchell, the son of a wealthy Wisconsin senator, joined the Army as a private in the Spanish-American War, took flying lessons on his own, and organized the American air effort in World War I. During his eighteen months in France, he won high battle honors and was promoted to brigadier general, at the same time alienating most of his fellow officers with his personality (*"he was as subtle as a brass band,"* noted his biographer) but above all, because they did not share his insights into air power. Having nearly single-handedly organized the American air effort during World War I and having led some eighteen hundred aircraft in the Saint Mihiel offensive, after the war Mitchell fought with his superiors over the great advantages posed by air power, and despite proving his point in the well-known sinking of the *Ostfriesland* and other battleships (namely, that ships at sea were highly vulnerable to aircraft attacks), he was demoted to colonel and transferred to Texas. He continued his criticism, then elevated it to insubordinate levels when the Navy blimp Shenandoah crashed during a storm, and he accused his superiors in the Army and Navy of *"almost treasonable administration of the national defense."*[181]

President Calvin Coolidge, a sound-minded man who probably would have agreed with Mitchell's premise that airfields needed weather stations, nevertheless could not brook such a direct challenge to the chain of command. Worse, Mitchell's outburst came just as a political debate had erupted over the proper role for the government in supporting aviation. As Coolidge put it, *"We had to bring it rather sharply to the attention of men in the service that they ought to obey that regulation of the service which requires that they shouldn't volunteer to influence legislation,"* ordering the Army to bring charges against the colonel. A highly publicized court-martial resulted in Mitchell's being found guilty of insubordination, and he was suspended from active duty for five years. He resigned instead, an object lesson in civilian control over the military in America.

Mitchell's denunciations, while serious and impossible to ignore, nevertheless came during peacetime. General Douglas MacArthur's confrontation with President Harry Truman occurred in the middle of the Korean War. Several myths persist about MacArthur's actions: that he unilaterally made the decision to cross the 38th parallel, that he foolishly sought a land war with China, or that

[179]Woodward, *The Commanders*, pp. 290–94

[180]Woodward, *The Commanders*, p. 294.

[181]Billy Mitchell, http:www.airpower.maxwell.af.mil/airchronicles/cc/mitch.html. The fact that the Air Force's official history records this episode is itself a telling sign of the openness of the American system and the difference between ours and closed societies.

he entertained notions of overturning the established civilian control of the military. Instead, the problem was that Truman and MacArthur lacked the kind of face-to-face contact that existed between Grant and Lincoln or even Roosevelt and MacArthur. Truman's favorable views of MacArthur as the "Big General" slowly soured as it appeared MacArthur was shunning him. Worse, the general's criticism of U.S. Far Eastern policy convinced Truman of his disregard for orders, and MacArthur's unpopularity with the Joint Chiefs of Staff, particularly General Omar Bradley, who, in his view, already had dealt with one prima donna in Patton. It was as much MacArthur's rejection of control by the Joint Chiefs as by Truman that sealed his fate. At their meeting on Wake Island (where the general embarrassed the president by keeping him waiting, and then by shaking hands rather than saluting when Truman departed), Truman flatly asked if the Chinese would intervene, and MacArthur, relying on his own intelligence officers, replied they would not.

Here was a failure not only of MacArthur's judgment—to defer and say he did not know, or that it was not his call—but also his selection of staff. In a similar situation in 1944, Patton's own intelligence officers had discovered what no one else knew, namely, that the Nazis were about to attack. MacArthur's staff simply wasn't up to the job, and he lacked the good sense to say so. (That certainly did not absolve of failure the civilian intelligence agencies, whose primary task it was to unpattern in America history of civilian spy agencies repeatedly caught unawares by enemies of this nation.) As has been noticeable in the post-9/11 world, MacArthur's era witnessed the State Department often dragging its feet or otherwise inhibiting American military success. Secretary of State Dean Acheson had long battled MacArthur over his policies in postwar Japan, and worked stealthily to have him removed from his position as top administrator there. Matters were made worse by MacArthur's myopia regarding his subordinates General Edward M. Almond, who had command of X Corps, and General Walton Walker, who had the 8th Army, and further exacerbated by Almond's antipathy toward Major General O. P. Smith of the 1st Marine Division.[182] In short, MacArthur, at the time of his removal on April 10, 1951, was poorly connected both to his superiors and his subordinates, and he routinely pontificated on sensitive matters "far beyond his pay grade."

One can hardly imagine Grant, even in an age before telephones and radios, being so detached from Lincoln or from his generals. Part of the problem stemmed from a poorly worded instruction by General George Marshall to MacArthur to feel "unhampered" by the 38th parallel, and indeed, the United Nations resolution had endorsed a "united" Korea. MacArthur, however, went well beyond military comments to the media, arguing that Taiwan should send troops to Korea and advocated bombing Chinese cities. The cautionary tales of Billy Mitchell and Douglas MacArthur reiterate the fact that in America, civilians control the military.

---

[182]D. Clayton James, U.S. Air Force Academy, Harmon Memorial Lecture #24, November 12, 1981, at http://atlas.usafa.af.mil/dfh/harmon_series/docs/Harmon24.doc.

Of Freezes and Flops

Perhaps the biggest antiwar fizzle of all times was the nuclear freeze movement of the 1980s. Despite claims that the movement comprised a cross section of Americans, including *"homemakers and businessmen, clerks and doctors, clergymen, teachers, scientists, and even military men,"* the nuclear freeze movement originated with—and was dominated by—the radical left.[183] Praised by Ted Kennedy as a movement *"comparable ... to our movement for independence,"* or to the struggle for civil rights, the freeze movement supporters produced (largely bogus) polls showing that upward of 90 percent of Americans supported the freeze.[184] All the way through the campaign season of 1984, newsmen continued to affirm that nuclear war was at the top of the public's agenda, brightly beaming of citizens' radar screens. Political analyst Midge Constanza prophesied that the freeze might *"do to Ronald Reagan what Vietnam did to Lyndon Johnson."*[185] Perhaps it did: Reagan was reelected in a landslide.

The elections revealed the freeze movement to be, for its supporters, "a demoralizing flop."[186] Perennial peacenik Helen Caldicott glumly noted, *"In terms of pragmatic results, we haven't gotten rid of one weapon.... We haven't had any impact on Congress."*[187] One study of the freeze fizzle blamed the tendency of "both sides" in the debate of "oversimplifying" the issues. Complaining that Reagan's rhetoric was *"naïve and simplistic,"* in fact, Reagan understood precisely not only what the freeze movement's ends were, but he communicated that perfectly to the voting public.[188] Still, modern researchers miss the boat, with one claiming that the freeze movement "reformed" Reagan by making him *"return to ... bipartisan policies he had consistently eschewed."*[189] Of course, any reader of either Reagan's speeches or his autobiography would know this is silly. Reagan embraced bipartisanship when it was necessary in Sacramento, and he had come to Washington already determined to end MAD. The freeze movement had utterly no effect on him, but he had an effect on it by exposing it as a shallow, left-wing driven, and above all, dangerous campaign to enable the Soviets to maintain nuclear superiority. That was all the American people needed to know. Those writing the postmortems of the freeze movement did get one thing right, however,

---

[183]David M. Alpern, "A Matter of Life and Death," *Newsweek*, April 26, 1982, p. 20.

[184]J. Michael Hogan, *The Nuclear Freeze Campaign: Rhetoric and Foreign Policy in the Telepolitical Age* (East Lansing: Michigan State University Press, 1994), p. 1.

[185]Alpern, "A Matter of Life and Death," p. 21.

[186]Steve L. Hawkins and John W. Mashek, "Antinuclear Campaign Reawakens," *U.S. News & World Report*, January 27, 1986, p. 22.

[187]See Hogan, *Nuclear Freeze Campaign*, passim.

[188]Hogan, *Nuclear Freeze Campaign*, 5; G. Thomas Goodnight, "Ronald Reagan's Reformulation of the Rhetoric of War: Analysis of the 'Zero Operation,' 'Evil Empire,' and 'Star Wars' Addresses," *Quarterly Journal of Speech*, November 1986, pp. 390–414.

[189]David S. Meyer, *A Winter of Discontent: The Nuclear Freeze and American Politics* (New York: Praeger, 1990), pp. 269–72.

that the campaign substituted passion for argument and—a trait of the left that continues to this day—celebrity for expertise.[190]

Modern analysts, even those sympathetic to the freeze movement, have acknowledged that the freeze groups were "knit together" by an "interlocking directorate" and "*all shared pretty much the same worldview*," namely, that the United States was the font of all evil (with Israel a close second), and that the Soviets were just misunderstood.[191] So-called "religious groups" couched their language in neo-Marxist terms. Virtually all of them admitted that the freeze was a means to a total disarmament end, and while claiming a broad membership of supporters from Republicans, Democrats, and stream thinkers of all stripes, as Michael Hogan concluded, they "*remained for the most part a 'who's who' of the peace movement*," and included "stridently leftwing groups" in their coalition.[192] The Prominent Endorser's List contained the predictable names of leftist entertainers like Joan Baez and Paul Simon, as well as Vietnam retreads like Daniel Ellsberg and William Sloane Coffin, and the movement's propaganda arm toiled over language that appealed to most Americans, peppering its material with phrases such as "enjoys very broad support" or "bipartisan." When a planning session in 1982 brought this menagerie together, the cacophony was so loud, and the infighting so intense, that the attendees "*barely had time to print fliers*."[193] Some realists glumly admitted that many of those at the June 12, 1982, rally came to see Bruce Springsteen and Jackson Browne free, and that still others wanted to see what hundreds of thousands of people looked like. However, freeze proponents, believing their own press clippings, thought they had given birth to a broad-based movement that would change politics. After all, wasn't Jonathan Schell's anti-nuclear tome, *The Fate of the Earth*, a *New York Times* best seller?[194]

Unwittingly, of course, Schell had underscored Reagan's warnings: by describing in gory detail an all-out Soviet attack on the United States with ten thousand bombs, "*substantially the whole human construct in the United States ... would be vaporized, blasted, or otherwise pulverized out of existence*."[195] Schell's poorly written book full of elitist language surprised even his supporters with its seeming broad appeal until it was discovered that his books were sharply discounted almost immediately, and that antinuke groups were gobbling up thousands of copies for free distribution. For anyone who had read *Fate of the Earth*—all the vaporizing, incinerating, blasting, cremating, and so on—a simple question lingered: was it reasonable to think that Communist dictators, who did not have to answer to a voting populace, would disarm even if the United States

---

[190] Hogan, *Nuclear Freeze Campaign*, p. 7.

[191] Adam Garfinkle, *The Politics of the Nuclear Freeze* (Philadelphia: Foreign Policy research Institute, 1984), pp. 1–2.

[192] Hogan, *Nuclear Freeze Campaign*, p. 26.

[193] Dave Lindorfl, "War in Peace: The Fight for Position in New York's June 12 Disarmament Rally," *Village Voice*, April 20, 1982, p. 12.

[194] Schell was hardly alone: from 1977 to 1980 there were sixteen books published on nuclear issues; twenty-five in 1981, fifty-four in 1982, and eighty in 1983. See Nancy E. McGlen, *The Sources of Support of the Freeze Movement* (Niagara Falls: Niagara University, Department of Political Science, 1986).

[195] Jonathan Schell, *The Fate of the Earth* (New York: Alfred Knopf, 1982), p. 24.

did? And if not, who offered a better plan to protect America, the Democrats with MAD or Reagan with Star Wars?

Not to be left out, Hollywood obediently followed with *The Day After*, a made-for-TV movie from ABC depicting a nuclear attack on the United States. Giddy freezers passed out "viewing guides" and bought spots on local affiliates. *"It doesn't have to be the end,"* intoned Paul Newman in one of the ads. Although ABC sought cover from conservative critics who claimed it played into the hands of the freeze movement by claiming that it took no stand on either the freeze or deterrence, it *"did echo virtually every major theme of the freeze campaign: the inevitable end of deterrence, the futility of Civil Defense, and the corruption of all political authority."*[196] Yet phone banks set up to receive calls from terrified viewers had almost no business, and Reagans, job approval rose after the movie! One poll specifically examining Reagan's defense policies saw his approval go up by four points. Far from scaring people toward the freeze movement, the movie actually appeared to have caused them to seriously consider Reagan's policies.[197]

With each new hysterical screed, the nuclear freeze crowd appeared more bizarre and unhinged. Helen Caldicott, author of *Missile Envy*, employed medical terms to clinically diagnose Reagan as mentally unbalanced and included in her book a "history" of World War II that virtually ignored Hitler.[198] By the time a freeze resolution came up for a vote in the early summer of 1983 in the U.S. House of Representatives, it passed, but only after extensive amendments on verifiability and overall reductions in nuclear weapons (exactly what Reagan had called for). Moreover, polls showed that up to 80 percent of Americans opposed a freeze if either side could cheat, and since at least 80 percent of Americans expressed the sentiment to pollsters that the Russians would cheat, it was all moot. That March, Reagan outflanked the entire freeze movement with the Star Wars speech, and redirected Americans' thinking toward protection from nuclear weapons, not accommodation with them. Protestors had only succeeded in forcing a widespread popular debate about the necessity for missile defense, something people had not really thought about before.

Americans win wars because we tolerate protests and protesters, because almost every war entails bitter and acrimonious debate at home—debate that is not only permitted but structurally encouraged in the United States. One of the effects of this debate is to sort out those who actually want to see an American victorious from those who genuinely loathe their own country, usually resulting in the marginalization of many (though not all) of the war opponents. Although protests and protesters without doubt undercut morale, the practical effect of antiwar movements is that by emphasizing American casualties (the only strategy they have ever found that works to any degree at all), they continually improve the military. They do so by making battlefield effectiveness, as defined by quicker ac-

---

[196]Hogan, *Nuclear Freeze Campaign*, p. 48.
[197]Hogan, *Nuclear Freeze Campaign*, pp. 47–52.
[198]See Helen Caldicott, *Nuclear Madness: What You Can Do!* (New York: Bantam, 1980), and Missile Envy: The Arms Race and Nuclear War (New York: Bantam, 1985).

complishment of the mission with fewer losses, while exacting a high cost on our opponents. Because antiwar movements seek to invoke morality as a standard, they ironically lead most Americans to conclude that, in fact, American military involvement usually is moral. The paradox is that Americans win wars because, even though it is never their intent, protesters make our soldiers better than ever.

Conclusion

Since ground combat in Iraq began—best labeled the Battle of Iraq and not the Iraq War because, after all, it is one front in a much larger war—a predictable spate of military books has appeared. Many have sought to capitalize on the early success; others, to explain why works that surfaced after the first Gulf War, touting a "Revolution in Military Affairs," now seem so obsolete and irrelevant. Still others use Iraq to decry a "New American Militarism" or some similar nonsense, all well slathered with predictable villains such as the "military industrial complex," "corporate America," and (choose one) "imperialism" or "oppression" of non-Western people. A spate of academic books, replete with detailed technical models and impressive jargon, has also emerged, mostly stating the obvious: that suicide bombings and terrorism constitute the last gasp of dying ideologies, not the basis for successful mass movements. Little, if any, of the new analysis really seems to grasp why Americans win wars.

Flush with the rapid, and remarkable, victory over Saddam's forces in the Gulf War, in 1991, a group of military and civilian experts identified what they thought was a "Revolution in Military Affairs" (RMA), claiming the nature of military power was being transformed by technology to something wholly different than ever before.[1] According to proponents, in the RMA, "long-range precision air and missile strikes will dominate warfare, ground forces will be reduced to mostly scouts, and the struggle for information supremacy will replace the breakthrough battle as the decisive issue for success."[2] Like any new theory, RMA has been oversimplified and almost caricatured: advocates never claimed infantry would disappear, or that high-tech would replace foot soldiers. Still, a recurring theme in literature was the potential for laser sighting and targeting, long-range standoff weapons, and superior communication to greatly reduce the need for large-scale ground forces. Bruce Berkowitz, in a variant of the RMA theme, argued that "*the ability to collect, communicate, process and protect information is the most important factor defining military power.*"[3] Attaining superiority in information involves denying, destroying, deceiving, and exploiting. Using examples from World War II and the German bombing of England, Berkowitz contended that the British, having broken the Ultra code, constantly changed tactics—from jamming radio signals that directed the bombers, to attacking radio stations—to conceal the fact that they had broken the code.

Berkowitz is certainly correct that information processing and control will be key in all future wars, but this is nothing new. Napoléon and Grant both commented on the significance of controlling information, especially news from the battlefield to the public. Insofar as this new focus on information processing

---

[1]Stephen Biddle, *Military Power: Explaining Victory and Defeat in Modern Battle* (Princeton: Princeton University Press, 2004), p. 4.

[2]Biddle, *Military Power*, p. 4.

[3]Bruce Berkowitz, *The New Face of War: How War Will Be Fought in the 21st Century* (New York: Free Press, 2003), p. 21.

and control applies to the front lines, General Tommy Franks noted in Operation Iraqi Freedom that for the first time the United States used coordinated info attacks along with conventional ordnance. Overall, the RMA's value has been overstated. Stephen Biddle, another analyst, stated the obvious when he warned that "*force employment is a powerful ... determinant of capability.*"[4] Sheer technology must be wedded to national will, tactical mass, political determination, and conceptually sound strategy. In short, the real "revolution" involves using—and improving on—what we have, but employing it with innovation and audacity, exactly as Donald Rumsfeld has insisted all along.

This somewhat obvious theme is picked up in the work of an Israeli scholar, Gil Merom, in *How Democracies Lose Small Wars*. Democracies "*fail in small wars,*" he maintains, "*because they find it extremely difficult to escalate the level of violence and brutality to that which can secure victory.*"[5] Domestic culture, particularly the "*creed of some of their most articulate citizens*" (that is, antiwar protesters) and their very political structure that encourages participation and involvement, elevates the opportunities given to antiwar forces and endows them with an inordinate amount of credibility.[6] Merom identifies a correlation between the level of brutality and violence a nation is willing to accept and its success in conduction small wars, arguing that in larger wars, virtually all of society tends to agree on the ends, thus eliminating a persistent antiwar element that unravels consensus at home. Germany in Africa in the 1800s, he argues, although far more repressive in its colonies (killing some 400,000, with only about 18,000 troops deployed), lost far fewer soldiers than did the British in the Boer War, where the British only killed about 25,000, yet had to deploy almost 450,000 men and lost close to 8,000. As Merom concludes, "Indiscriminate annihilation requires relatively little investment and military skills, and produces long-lasting results."[7]

Or does it? Despite the fact that Germany's stay in Africa was brief, and that much of Africa remains in turmoil, which nation has had a longer-lasting influence on the Dark Continent, Britain or Germany? No matter how far short of British ideals countries such as Zimbabwe and South Africa have fallen, they have at least held what are viewed as "fair" elections, and are certainly no worse off than former German colonies. Is it not safe to say that, to the extent they do so, the African states look to Britain as a model, and not Germany?

Other explanations of what constitutes the new face of warfare come from Thomas X. Hammes, a career Marine officer who describes "4th Generation Warfare" (4GW) as guerrilla war that is different from previous generations of warfare.[8] Hammes mischaracterizes the Rumsfeld reorganization as about infor-

---

[4]Biddle, *Military Power*, p. 28.

[5]Gil Merom, *How Democracies Lose Small Wars: State, Society, and the Failures of France in Algeria, Israel in Lebanon, and the United States in Vietnam* (Cambridge: Cambridge University Press, 2003), p. 15.

[6]Merom, *How Democracies Lose Small Wars*, p. 15.

[7]Merom, *How Democracies Lose Small Wars*, p. 45. See also Thomas Pakenham, *The Scramble for Africa, 1876–1912* (London: Weidenfeld and Nicolson, 1991), and Bryon Farewell, *The Great Boer War* (London: Allen Lane, 1977); Martin Meredith, *The Fate of Africa: From the Hopes of Freedom to The Heart of Despair; A History of Fifty Years of Independence* (New York: Public Affairs Books, 2005).

[8]Thomas X. Hammes, *The Sling and the Stone: On War in the 21st Century* (St. Paul, MN: Zenith Press,

mation and high-tech warfare, and implies that the administration has ignored the political component of groups like Hamas, the PLO, and al Qaeda. The fact that George W. Bush's and Donald Rumsfeld's concepts of a new military strategy included, for the first time in thirty years, provisions for ground troops that did not possess overwhelming numbers or a clear (initially) preponderance of power suggests that Hammes missed the real revolution under his nose.

The Bush Doctrine, incorporated into top-level military documentation according to the Army, "*fundamentally changed the way the United States would ensure its domestic security.*" Rather than "respond" and "prepare"—the doctrinal mandates of the Clinton administration—the Army now was to "dissuade forward" and "decisively defeat" America's enemies. In its early review of Operation Iraqi Freedom, On Point, the Army noted that the Bush Doctrine had "*fundamental implications*" for how the military trained and equipped itself. It involved being able to deploy an expeditionary force capable of imposing America's will on hostile foreign soil, then maintaining a presence there long enough to secure the change. It was nothing short of a revolution in doctrine.[9]

And it has paid off. Despite journalists' fixation on suicide bombers in Iraq (whose number and frequency of attacks are steadily, if slowly, diminishing), was is on the decline worldwide, according to "*Human Security Report 2005,*" a study by researchers of the frequency and intensity of armed conflicts since the early 1990s.[10] Since 1990, the researchers found, more than 40 percent of all conflicts worldwide came to an end, and the numbers of genocides, human rights abuses, and military coups have all fallen significantly. This coincides perfectly with the rise of USA, Superpower. Pax Americana, anyone?

Then there is Anthony Bacevich, whose *New American Militarism* detects a "*marriage of military metaphysics with eschatological ambition.*"[11] Modern warfare in the Middle East, he opines, is all the fault of fundamentalist Christian fanatics who have hijacked American military strategy, made worse by toy maker's producing a George Bush aviator doll.[12] America's "new militarism" stemmed from bad application of historical lessons combined with a new Christianized military that see itself as virtuous. (What, after all, could be worse than an American military that thinks it is morally right?) Bacevich's concern with the use of the terms good and evilis echoed in **Battle**, by John Lynn, who warns that condemning terrorism as "*evil implies removing it from the category of war.*"[13] That, in turn, might "strip away" the past conventions that controlled or limited combat—as if those conventions did not disappear in twin infernos in the Manhat-

---

2004).

[9]Gregory Fontenot, E. J. Degan, and David Topa, *On Point: The United States Army in Operation Iraqi Freedom* (Washington, D.C.: Army Chief of Staff 2004), p. 23.

[10]Haider Rizvi, "War on Decline Worldwide—Report," October 21, 2005, http://news.yahoo.com/s/oneworld/20051021/wl_oneworld/45361209761129913324.

[11]Anthony J. Bacevich, *The New American Militarism: How Americans Are Seduced by War* (Oxford: Oxford University Press, 2005).

[12]Bacevich, *New American Militarism*, p. 31.

[13]John A. Lynn, *Battle: A History of Combat and Culture* (Boulder, CO: Westview Press, 2005) p. 318.

tan skyline on that September day.[14]

The *"new American militarism,"* Bacevich and others argue, has been formulated in large part by the neocons (translation, Jewish conservatives), led by Norman Podhoretz, Bill Kristol, Joshua Muravchik, and Charles Krauthammer. These writers indeed constructed a new view of the world, especially of the Middle East, that rejected the old Democrat/Republican orthodoxy in which despots were divided into "ours" and "theirs." Such an approach was not necessarily wrong in the Cold War, where the stakes of nuclear annihilation required compromises, at times, with the devil. But in a post—Cold War world, where the United States is the only superpower, they are unwelcome. There's a new sheriff in town, and today thugs and dictators no longer can harbor terrorists only because they themselves are not Communists.

The raft of new military literature—some of it impressive and sophisticated, some of it naïve, childish, or obvious—attempts to carve out positions based on potential book sales, not reality, and the reality is this: al Qaeda and the new enemies of freedom are much like the old. The abhor freedom, hate human liberty, and are incapable of long-term entrepreneurial investment. While they may push operational autonomy down—like, say, the Mongols—they dare not push conceptual autonomy down. There can be no protesters against radical Muslim fundamentalists, hence there can be no improvement of their military. Lacking true mechanisms of self-criticism found in the West, they cannot learn from loss, and can only learn marginally from victory (taking entirely the wrong lessons from Mogadishu). Toleration of protesters, whose message might force them into an even greater economy with their own fighters' lives, is entirely absent. As professional haters, and not professional soldiers, they cannot truly implement the training necessary to form long-standing bodies of committed troops—and, fortunately for us, their most committed men die in self-imposed explosive fireballs.

What is surprising is how some of the veterans of military history writing have missed the boat. Russell Weigley, arguably one of the best American military historians, was perhaps clouded in his judgment by proximity to Vietnam when he concluded in his classic, *The American Way of War* (1973) that *"after the experiences of Indochina, the idea that the United States can work its will in distant parts of the world by means of the measured, controlled application of punitive violence seems especially dubious."*[15] Weigley found *"no point on the spectrum of violence"* where *"the use of combat offer[s] much promise for the United States today."*[16] John Mueller, writing in *Retreat from Doomsday* (1989), theorized that the quest for prosperity had made war obsolete in the modern world.[17] Arguing that war *"lacks the romantic appeal it once enjoyed,"*

---

[14]Lynn, *Battle*, p. 319.

[15]Russell Weigley, *The American Way of War: A History of the United States Military Strategy and Policy* (Bloomington, IN: Indiana University Press, 1973), p. 476.

[16]Weigley, *American Way of War*, p. 477.

[17]John Mueller, *Retreat from Doomsday: The Obsolescence of Major War* (New York: Basic Books, 1989).

it *"has been substantially discredited as a method."*[18]   British military guru John Keegan, after assessing the significance of "the heroic" in famous commanders, similarly argued in his *Mask of Command* that mankind *"needs an end to the ethic of heroism in its leadership."*[19]   Even Victor Davis Hanson, whose understanding of most military affairs surpasses a raft of writers, including many who served, asked in 1999 if America still had the moral courage to use military force to defeat its enemies. Writing in *The Soul of Battle*, Hanson warned *"the great danger of the present age is that democracy may never again marshal the will to march against and ultimately destroy evil."*[20]   Since, then, especially after 9/11, Hanson has become one of the few stalwarts and clear thinkers of the military situation, but such is the nature of democracies that the barrage of the mainstream media and the antiwar left has become so pervasive as to sap the will from the most resolute and to dim the eye of the keenest of prophets.

Indeed, it was Hanson who, writing in *Ripples of Battle* (2003), pointed out the similarities between the suicidal Bushido-trained kamikaze pilots of Japan and the modern Muslim terrorists. Both faced a losing numbers game.[21] On Okinawa, where suicide planes had their most fearsome impact, large-scale attacks were over by late July and the Japanese found they could no longer entice "volunteers" to die for the emperor: *"there really was only a limited supply of a few thousand kamikaze pilots among millions of Japanese .... Some pilots ditched or tuned back. Others were intoxicated to the point of stupor."* Above all—in true bin Laden-like fashion—*"officers rarely, if at all, led the suicide attacks in person."*[22]   This early experiment with "asymmetric warfare" produced in the Americans a fury at the apparent fact that the Japanese knew they could not overturn the battlefield decision, instead seeking to kill as many Americans as they could. Predating the North Vietnamese assessments that the only really important statistic was how many coffins were sent back to the United States, the effort produced in the Japanese a nihilism that their lives counted for nothing and their honor for little more. In the case of Japan, this of course resulted in the atomic bombs, and one wonders if this isn't the "stripping away" of conventions that Lynn, Bacevich, and other fear: the possibility that America might once again use all of her military might, even on those who perhaps deserve it.

A crucial difference characterized the suicidal bombers of the Islamofascists from their kamikaze predecessors, however, in that the Japanese hoped to inflict such casualties that the United States would cease hostilities. The jihadists, on the other hand, hope to provoke increased brutality by the American military. As Gil Merom notes, *"The rise of human-rights agenda [which the jihadists reject], humanitarian intervention, ad hoc international indictment of senior officers and leaders for war crimes, and the establishment of a permanent interna-*

---

[18]Mueller, *Retreat from Doomsday*, p. 227.

[19]John Keegan, *The Mask of Command* (New York: Penguin, 1987), p. 350.

[20]Victor Davis Hanson, *The Soul of Battle* (New York; Free Press, 1999), p. 412

[21]Victor Davis Hanson, *Ripples of Battle: How Wars of the Past Still Determine How We Fight, How We Live, and How We Think* (New York: Doubleday, 2003), p. 62.

[22]Hanson, *Ripples of Battle*, pp. 62–63.

tional tribunal for the prosecution of individuals for war crimes" has changed the reality of modern military responses by democracies.[23]   As a result, terrorist attacks are often designed to provoke countermeasures of such ferocity as to "*attract the attention of international audiences*" and bring foreign pressure on, in this case, the United States to cease. Put another way, the terrorists are playing the PR game, hoping that a left-wing sympathetic press will focus on American "barbarity" rather than mass-murdering maniacs.[24]   In this vein, they are counting on the public's moral objections to its own military's actions over that of an enemy. Even in a quasi authoritarian state like Kaiser Wilhelm's Germany during the pacification of Africa in the 1890s, where top officials worried that the practice of not taking prisoners would affect Germany's standing among civilized states, the government's merciless subjugation of local tribes caused the famous Count Alfred von Schlieffen to contend that the policy would backfire.[25]

Islamic terrorists have acknowledged that they are also counting on something else: needling the United States into indiscriminate warfare against Muslims in order to unite all of the Islamic world against us. This was made clear in revelations by Jordanian journalist Fouad Hussein, who spent time in prison with Iraqi/al Qaeda kingpin Abu Musab al-Zarqawi, and who has outlined a seven-step plan for a "new Islamic Caliphate" as envisioned by the terrorist leaders. Of most relevance to my argument here is Phase 1:

> *The First Phase Known as "the awakening"—this has already been carried out and was supposed to have lasted from 2000 to 2003, or more precisely from the terrorist attacks of September 11, 2001 in New York and Washington to the fall of Baghdad in 2003. The aim of the attacks of 9/11 was to provoke the US into declaring war on the Islamic world and thereby "awakening" Muslims. "The first phase was judged by the strategists and masterminds behind al-Qaida as very successful," writes Hussein. "The battle field was opened up and the Americans and their allies became a closer and easier target."*[26] *Iran's delusional president, Mahmoud Ahmandinijad, has announced his intention to usher in the chaos needed to bring the "Twelfth Imam" to earth.*

So far, the United States not only has refused to play along, but has conducted its military activities in such a way that Afghans and Iraqis alike have fought with us against the terrorists. A massive anti-terror march for peace (and march against al Qaeda) in Baghdad went almost entirely unreported in the United States. In late 2005, stung by bomb blasts at a Jordanian hotel, a similar massive antiterrorist march in Jordan featured protesters chanting, "*Zarqawi, burn in hell!*" Cindy Sheehan, alone in a Crawford ditch, warranted more western press coverage than the antiterrorist marches in the heart of Islam. Not only had al Qaeda failed even to implement its first step, it had succeeded (at least partially) in turning Middle Eastern Muslims against the terrorist organization. Worse from al

[23]Merom, *How Democracies Lose Small Wars*, p. 250

[24]Merom, *How Democracies Lose Small Wars*, p. 205.

[25]Pakenham, *The Scramble for Africa,* p. 612

[26]YassinMusharbash, "What Al-Qaeda Really Wants," Spiegel, August 12, 2005, http://service.spiegel.de/cache/international/0,1518,369448,00.html.

Qaeda's viewpoint, asymmetric warfare usually results in massive losses for the force using asymmetric methods. In the Israeli invasion of Lebanon in 1982, for example, the Palestinian Liberation Organization lost, according to one estimate, an astounding twenty times as many troops per number committed as did the Israelis—not even counting the Syrians, who lost five times as many men per number committed.[27]   The French military in Algeria (1956-58) likewise succeeded in killing far more FLN terrorists than the organization could recruit.[28]

A taste of what would occur if Zarqawi's strategy was successful was seen in July 2005, when Colorado congressman Tom Tancredo, asked in an interview what might be done if the Islamofascist attackers struck American cities with nuclear weapons, replied that the United States could "*take out*" Muslim holy sites. Asked if that meant "*bombing Mecca*," he answered, "*yeah.*"[29]   In the swirl of outrage that followed, few assessed Tancredo's comments in light of history, wherein he had, in fact, aptly described the chain of events that followed a non-Western enemy whose obsession with death produces a removal of all civilized restraints, and it was precisely those restraints, in tandem with our highly skilled military, that had started to swing the pendulum. Ultimately, suicide attacks—whether kamikazes or truck bombers—reveal the impotence of an enemy, not his might, a point particularly piercing for societies based on shame and honor. John Mueller, Russell Weigley, Anthony Bacevich, and John Lynn are wrong: there are new threats, reincarnations of, yes, evil. These are individuals and groups that have revived a glorification of war, not as ennobling the human spirit, but as advancing a perverted variant of a religion. Prosperity and growth are meaningless to those whose every action is governed by shame and honor. Unwittingly, Private Lyndie England and the prison guards at Abu Ghraib, by placing a few panties on the heads of emasculated homicidal maniacs, did more to expose the impotence of Muslim radicalism than all the scholars who ever wrote. They should be given commendations, not jail terms.

We need more than ever to distinguish between the truly heroic and the culture of shame, honor, and death. We need to reaffirm what noble qualities combat does produce—brotherhood, courage, unselfishness, sacrifice, strength, discipline, honor, duty—while always acknowledging the horror and despair that accompanies any clash of violent people with lethal weapons. And in direct contradiction to Keegan's nostrums, we need more heroes, now more than ever. Fortunately, the United States is producing them every day. The American warrior ethos drove firefighters into the burning towers on September 11, led the passengers of Flight 93 to rise up and defy their captors, and spurred the armored units to run into Baghdad against all known military logic. It took particularly heroic leaders in America, Britain, Australia, Poland, Italy, and elsewhere to assess steely eyed the situation in the Middle East and conclude that a policy of bribing dictators and ignoring human rights violators could result in anything

[27]Merom, *How Democracies Lose Small Wars*, p. 157.

[28]Merom, *How Democracies Lose Small Wars*, pp. 84–85

[29]"Tancredo: If They Nuke Us, Bomb Mecca," http://www.foxnews.com/story/0,2933,162795,00.html.

other than future disasters. It took a warrior ethos of courage and decisiveness to invade Iraq, even without an absolute guarantee that Saddam had WMDs, and with no promise that the war would be short or casualties light. In the future, it will take even greater heroism to defeat Iran and Syria and crush Islamofascist fundamentalism once and for all.

At first it appeared that Hanson's 1999 observation about the absence of this heroic ethos in modern America was wrong, not just because American (and allied) forces crushed the Taliban in Afghanistan in a war that lasted but weeks, but because President George W. Bush mobilized a national will and an international coalition to invade Iraq and depose Saddam Hussein. Predictably, the Left has criticized him, harping on a "bait and switch" about WMDs, and complaining that there were no al Qaeda in Iraq (despite mountains of evidence linking the two). Some liberals, such as the 2004 presidential loser John Kerry, have clung fanatically to allusions of mysterious documents, such as the Downing Street memos, that, like the alien bodies at Roswell, will "prove" that "Bush lied" about the reasons for war with Iraq, and which, just as predictably, never seem to materialize.[30]

WMDs or not, al Qaeda or not (and there is plenty of evidence that the former existed, somewhere, in Iraq and overwhelming evidence of the latter's presence before the invasion), the removal of Saddam Hussein was a necessary step toward eliminating Islamofascist terrorism coming out of the Middle East. Unfortunately, it is only one step—the first step—and Hanson may be right after all. For wars are rarely won with a single battle. Ask the British after Brooklyn Heights, the Confederates after Fredericksburg, the Sioux after the Little Big-horn, or the Japanese after Wake Island. From the beginning of time, warfare demands an element of persistence and patience, a stick-to-itive-ness that late twentieth-century and early twenty-first-century Americans have had difficulty demonstrating. The Romans fought three wars over a period of half a century with the Carthaginians before obtaining ultimate victory; and Roman legions crushed uprisings by the Jews, but only after four years of bloody campaigning. Virtually every major twentieth-century insurgency or guerrilla war has lasted five to ten years, and military winners, such as France in Algeria or the United States in Vietnam, are often defeated by domestic politics.[31]

As of this writing, the Battle of Iraq, part of a larger—and longer—War on Terror hangs in the balance, though it steadily tips in our favor. Thanks to in-cessant, even gleeful, reports by the media on the number of Americans killed in Iraq, the "body count" has been the only number reported to the American public. It is indeed a number we should, and must, know. But there are other numbers that a society at war should, and must, know, that are almost as important—indicators of how we are faring against the enemy. If it is true that all Muslims are not ter-rorists, then it follows that the number of terrorists is most certainly limited; and if that number is finite, it is critical to know and report accurately the numbers of

[30] A Google search of the words Bush and impeachment yields more than 830,000 hits.
[31] Merom, *How Democracies Lose Small Wars*, passim.

enemy killed. Lingering Vietnam aftereffects now include the reluctance of our military to provide that information for fear of reviving the old "body count" exaggerations of Vietnam. The only problem is, this time, the numbers aren't exaggerations. If anything, they are underestimates.[32]

Arriving at exact numbers is difficult, but some estimate of our success in Iraq and Afghanistan can be gleaned from reporters filed in the July 26, 2006 **USA Today** and the June 7, 2006 *New York Times*, which both cite the statistic of 3,149 "civilians" killed in Iraq alone in June 2006. This is consistent with United Nations reports of 100 civilians per day killed in Iraq in June. Yet the Iraq Coalition Casualty Count put the number of "Iraqi Security Forces and Civilian Deaths" at 870 for that month. If there were 3,149 "civilians" killed, yet only 870 were genuinely civilians and security forces, what were the other 2,879 bodies? Terrorists and "insurgents," perhaps? It seems likely.

One of the difficulties that the United Nations and other "objective" observers have had is distinguishing civilians from terrorists. If the Iraq Coalition Casualty Count is anywhere near accurate, however, some 2,800 non-civilian bodies were in Iraq morgues in June, then in fact some 93 terrorists per day were being removed from the battlefield permanently. Put another way, since March 2003, it means that well over 100,000 non-civilians have been killed, and perhaps upwards of 120,000. To be safe, using United Nations/New York Times numbers, I arrive at 75 terrorists/insurgents per day, or 36,000 dead enemy fighters since operations began.

It's really much worse for the jihadists. Americans have experienced a killed in action/wounded ration of 13 percent (although as astonishing 55 percent of American wounded return to action in seventy-two hours). Does anyone think that the terrorists have the same level of medical care available to their wounded as we do? So it is reasonable to assume that if only 8 terrorists are wounded for every 1 killed that we find—because more die than ever recover—that suggests that 288,000 have been wounded since combat began, at the low end, to a high-end estimate of 960,000. And, again, many of those did not survive, but did not die in sight of American forces.

Add to that number of jihadists who quietly dropped their AK-47s and went home, never to fight again (which typically is a significant number in any war), and then factor in the 5,000 known al-Qaeda/Taliban dead in Afghanistan in Operation Enduring Freedom, and we are talking about momentous numbers of enemy combatants eliminated. Put simply, the argument I put forth in the earlier edition of this book, that Iraq was a "Roach Motel," has been proven beyond doubt by these numbers.

The real devastation still lay ahead for the terrorists. New offensives in Afghanistan in late summer 2006 resulted in 377 al-Qaeda/Taliban dead in a single month (another report said 1,000 during the month were killed), plus another 80 joined the government. At the same time, sweeps in Iraq netted another 134 in the months of August and September, meaning roughly 20 terrorists per

[32]Larry Schweikart, "The Real Body Count," www.frontpagemagazine.com, August 18, 2006.

day were being removed from the battlefields in the two fronts combined. These are astonishing numbers, indicating an utter collapse of the so-called insurgency. And if these recent estimates are lower than the per day average of the first three years, it is because, contrary to all press reports, we are overwhelmingly winning.

Further evidence is found in the Improvised Explosive Devices (IEDs) attacks. Press reports virtually celebrated the fact that attacks were up since 2005. In January through August 2006, there were 11,242 roadside bomb attacks, up from 10,953 over the same period a year earlier. Such devices accounted for 33 percent of all American fatalities, or 114 deaths. Further, the Marine Corps noted that accidents after IED attacks from drivers who lost control of their vehicles accounted for another one third of all casualties. American military forces responded to these tactics the way they always have: training, training, and more training. The Marine Corps, for example, established a new, difficult driving course at Camp Lejeune specifically to teach driving skills in combat. With Iraq-like sand and weak shoulders and narrow alleys and bridges, the training courses replicated wartime conditions (complete with simulated live fire). Marine analysts also learned that many post-IED accidents resulted from driving too fast, providing too little reaction time, leading the Marines to slow down their drivers. The adjustments paid off: 114 deaths for 11,242 attacks means that it took almost 100 such attacks to kill a single U.S. soldier—a better average for our troops than, say, flying B-17s over Germany in WW II, or flying an aircraft in WW I, where 50 percent of all fliers were killed, half of them in training accidents before even reaching combat.[33]

Reductions in our own casualties from IED attacks constitute only half of the story: the other half is that the enemy suffers losses merely attempting to set such devices. Some blow themselves up before they get to their detonation point. Others are killed while in the process of planting the devices, and so on. My back-of-the-envelope estimates are that for every one hundred IEDs set, the terrorists lose twenty—five dead and wounded. Put another way, from January to June 2005, 409 Americans were killed, while from January to June 2006, we lost 346, meaning that the death toll fell by about 15 percent despite the fact that the number of attacks rose by 300.

Bush had already sensed a mood change in the war, however, and had appointed the "Iraq Study Group" in early 2006 to suggest new directions and solutions.[34] When its report came out in late 2006, however, the findings had been widely leaked, and they generally fizzled. One recommendation that President Bush agreed to was a temporary surge in troop numbers for particularly violent sectors of Iraq. An estimated 21,000 ground troops would be inserted in 2007 to secure the Sunni Triangle and crush Moqtada al-Sadr once and for all. Still, more depended on the willingness of Iraqi Prime Minister Nouri al-Mailiki—a Shiite

---

[33]Larry Schweikart, "The Real Body Count," www.frontpagemagazine.com, August 14, 2006; Marc Wortman, *The Millionaires' Unit: the Aristocratic Flyboys Who Fought the Great War and Invented American Air Power* (New York: Public Affairs, 2006), p. 124.

[34]The findings of the Iraq Study Group's report are found at http://www.usip.org/isg/.

who seemed reluctant to rein in radical Shiite elements—than it did sheer U.S. force size. At the same time, however, events in Somalia showed that the War on Terror had spread. There, the Ethiopian government (with U.S. support) crushed al-Qaeda rebels attempting to hold Mogadishu and killed important al-Qaeda leaders. And shortly after the 2006 election, Secretary of Defense Donald Runsfeld resigned and several of Bush's top military advisers for Iraq were cycled out as the hard-charging General David Petreaus took over as the top American officer in Iraq.

Sectarian violence remained a problem in Iraq (although westerners—particularly Americans—often forget that English internal wars did not end until the 1600s, and after the French Revolution in 1789, fighting and civil wars continued until the mid-1800s). Nevertheless, the numbers say that not only are we winning, but that we are winning decisively.

Memo after memo, letter after letter, from or to Osama bin Laden to his al-Qaeda leaders in Iraq revealed the collapsing insurgency, which was capped by the death of Abu Musabal-Zarqawi, the leading al-Qaeda terrorist (and a foreign fighter) in Iraq in June 2006. Despite these successes, antiwar critics monotonously continue to try to liken Iraq (and before that, Afghanistan) to Vietnam. In fact, a better match was the Filipino Insurrection and the Moro Wars of the early 1900s, a fight against (often Muslim) foes that practiced barbarity—killing civilians, beheadings—and which tried to affect U.S. public opinion rather than win the war on the battlefield. Indeed, as a total percentage of all U.S. land forces, the land forces in Iraq and Afghanistan are roughly comparable to the ground forces in the Philippines, which, ostensibly, was a more difficult task, giving the jungle terrain and vast coastline. In each case, the number was between 12 percent and 17 percent, allowing for Air Force and Navy personnel who might be on the ground. Lest we forget, that war, too, was an American victory.

Only one thing can deny this now nearly inevitable success: leadership. Were a new administration to come into office today, one opposed to continuing the struggle (as were some Romans in their battles with Carthage), it would not be long before a new attack, in all likelihood for deadlier than 9/11, revived the spirit of determination needed to win decisively. It is precisely because Americans hate wars that they win them. War fighting requires frequent motivation, and if avoided too long, wars impose their own costly lessons that they are creatures that sometimes cannot be ignored, rationalized, or talked to death. The Beirut barracks truck bombing went without response; that begat the 1993 bombing of the World Trade Center, which again went without response; and that, in turn, led to the bombings of the African embassies, the Bojinka plot, and the attack on the USS Cole. None of those attacks proved sufficient to stir the martial spirit of Americans, so complete is their view that all humans "must be reasonable," and so deep is their distaste for large-scale combat that they know will be fought to an absolute and terrifying conclusion. As it took Pearl Harbor to finally shake the United States out of its lethargy in resisting fascism and Japanese imperialism, so it took 9/11 to rouse the slumbering giant once again.

America's victories come in large part because ending the war becomes the primary objective, not "dying gloriously." Precisely because our concern for preserving like—even of wounded comrades—exceeds our desire to end the lives of our enemies, Americans have mastered the techniques and training and the medicine and maneuvers needed to win with as few losses as possible. Even victories are measured in the cold light of the casualty list, and losses tempered by the potential of those who survived to fight another day. Americans win wars because this overriding concern for human life brings us full circle to a presumption that soldiers are free men and women with property rights, whose individual talents are encouraged as autonomy is pushed down, and whose value leads us to insist on fewer and fewer casualties, making fiercer and tougher warriors. Americans have been victorious because the constant pressure to eliminate casualties has produced unprecedented inter-service cooperation. American victories have resulted from training and preparing these tough warriors—equipped through our unmatched capitalist system—with unprecedented technology and weapons. Most ironically, Americans win wars because the most antimilitary among us unintentionally hones our soldiers' skills to even greater levels by forcing constant reassessment and refinement of training and tactics.

Yet all of this only works if the leadership at the top is sound, and completely committed to victory. If the commitment is to anything else, from LBJ's raising the cost on North Vietnam that it would stop its aggression to Barack Obama's odd phobia about using "Islam" in any term associated with terrorists, then the U.S. will encounter failure and most likely humiliation. According to "*Icasualties.org,*" which counted the number of American troops killed in Afghanistan and, since Obama took over the American missions there 1153 U.S. troops have been killed (compared to just 575 under Bush). Obviously U.S./coalition losses in Iraq fell when Obama withdrew all Americans in 2011. But American losses there were already falling quite dramatically. However, once the U.S. left, ISIS (the Islamic State of Iraq and Syria) picked up where al-Qaeda left off and staged major military operations all over Iraq, taking the cities of Mosul and Tikrit in June 2014. Mass murders ensued, and the Iraqi government begged for help from the United States. Obama, refusing to label ISIS as "Islamic," likened the terror group to the "jayvee team."

How the Middle East will be restructured after Obama's disastrous administrations remains to be seen. Certainly his April 2015 agreement to allow Iran to develop nuclear weapons has all the earmarks of a Neville Chamberlain-like Munich moment. Already the Saudi Arabians have insisted they will need nuclear weapons to protect themselves. The entire post-Bush trajectory of the wars in Afghanistan and Iraq have underscored the simple maxim that it is better to have an army of lambs led by a lion than an army of lions led by a lamb. No matter how good the American fighting man, or woman, is, we have seen from Bull Run to Kasserine, from Little Big Horn to Bladensburg that leadership counts. Perhaps it counts more than any other factor. And ultimately, Americans win wars only if permitted to fight . . . like Americans.

INDEX

Al Aaisi, Haj Ali, 32
Abd al-Hamid al-Ansari, 38
Abizaid, John, 65, 67
Abrams tanks, 180
Abu Ghraib
        Images, impact on Arab mindset, 31-32, 34, 38
        Liberal view of, 21
        News coverage, 21, 30-31, 43
        Participants as heroes, 251-53
        Women participants, 31-32, 38, 251
Abu Hanieh, Hassan, 31
Achenson, Dean, 239
Adams, Don, 91
Adams, Paul, 230
Adams, Samuel, 210
Adelman, Ken, 158
Adolphus, Gustavus, 133
Afak Dril, 98
Afgahistan, U.S. Invasion. See Operation Enduring Freedom
African Americans, in armed forces, 75, 81,82,85, 119-20, 123
Africa Korps, 60-61
Agar, John, 93
AGM-154A Joint Standoff Weapon, 189
Aguinaldo, Emilio, 27, 70
Air Campaigns
        Vietnam War, 69-70
        World War II, 52-53, 142-47
Air Force Magazine, 63
Aircraft, production of, 140-47, 152-53
Aircraft carriers, 144
Air/Land Battle Doctrine, 175-76
Air power, importance of, 140, 152-53
        Early airplanes, 140-41, 152-53
Akbar, Hasan, 236
Akin, Todd, 90
Alamo, 25
Albert, Eddie, 89
Alexander, E.P., 127
Alexander the Great, 24, 172
Ali, Muhammad, 105
Allawi, Ayad, 70
Allen, R. H., 56
Allied Purchasing Commission, 138
Almond, Edward M., 240
Altman, Robert, 93
Ambrose, Stephen, 125
American Bantam Car, Co. 147
American Crisis, The (Paine), 202
American military success
        Approach to combat, history of, 15
        Autonomy of military, 109-138
        And causes/stakes involved, 17
        And coalition forces, 22
        Fighting style, 14

And freedom of expression, 19
Loss, learning from, 13, 44-72
And military, members of, 73-108
Reasons, overview of, 15-16
Service branches, coordination of, 175-198
And weapons/equipment/technology, 15-18, 129-69
American Revolution. See Revolutionary War
American Society of Newspaper Editors, 210
American Way of War (Weigley), 243
Amundsen, Roald, 210
Anderson, Martin, 160
Andersonville Prison, 11, 32
Andropov, Yuir, 163
Antiballistic missile systems (ABMs), 150, 152-53
        Treaty conference, 160-64
Antiwar protests
        Antimilitary films, 214-16
        Civil War, 239
        Foreign enemies' view of, 18, 257
        Historical view, 240-41
        Media coverage of 208, 220-22
        Mexican War, 240
        Nuclear freeze movement, 245-48
        Operation Iraqi Freedom, 18, 36-37, 220, 221
        Revolutionary War, 206, 208
        Strategies of, 206-07
        Vietnam War, 15-16, 200-4, 210, 240
        War of 1812, 238
        World War I, 239
        World War II, 50, 239
Apple, R., "Johnny", 10, 67, 227
Arab-Israeli conflict, intifada, 25
Arab Mind Considered, The (Laffin), 29, 30
Arab Mind-set, See Muslims
Arafat, Yasser, 32
Arizona, 27
Arkwright, Richard, 138
Armed forces, members. See Military, members of
Arming America (Bellesiles), 139
Armitage, Leighton, 35
Armor-plate, 140-42
Army Industrial College, 48
Arnaz, Desidero "Desi," 85
Arness, James, 83
Arnett, Peter, 223, 224
Arnold, Henry "Hap", 50
ARPANET (Advanced Research Projects Network), 165
Arthur, Bea, 85
Artillery. See Firearms/artillery, development of
Assassins, 31
Associated Press (AP), 205

Atkinson, Rick, 172, 224
Atlanta, 148
Atomic bomb, 140
Autonomy of military, 100-130
    Civil War, 124
    Iraqi lack of, 117-18
    And Napoléon, 105
    And Operation Iraqi Freedom, 98-105, 115, 126, 125-30
    Post-Cold War, 116-119
    Versus arrogance, 120-26
    World War II, 110, 125-27, 130
Autry, Gene, 80
Axis, Sally, 225
Azzam, Abdullah, 32

Bacevich, Andrew, 25-26, 250, 253
Baker, Josephine, 85
Baghdad, battle of, 100-107, 133-34, 168, 180-81, 240-43
Ball, John, 18
Balsam, Martin, 80
Baltic, 215
Band of Brothers (Ambrose), 120
Barbary Pirates, 80, 85, 97-98
Barker, Bob, 87
Bataan, Philippines, Japanese Torture of Americans, 17-21, 35-36
Battle (Lynn), 251
Baxter, Ted, 89
Bell Helicopter, 155
Bennett, James, 210
Bennett, Paul, 118
Bennett, Tony, 90
Bensel, Richard, 145
Benson, Kevin, 195
Benteen, Frederick, 128-29
Berg, Nick, 8, 227
Berkowitz, Bruce, 258
Berlin Wall, 185
Bethlehem Steel, 153-55
Bevalaqua, Bob, 230, 231-32
Biddle, Stephen, 185-89, 255
Bigfoot, 370
Bin Laden, Osama
    Iraqi view of, 30, 250
    Underestimation of U.S. by, 18 – 19, 29, 55
    On U.S. in Mogadishu, 20, 28, 54, 139
Bin Sabbah, Hasan, 35
Biscari, Sicily incident, 28
Black Hawk Down (Bowden), 29
Black Hawk Down (film), 95, 220
Black Hawk Down incident, 29, 54
Blitzkrieg, 195
Blount, Buford, 108, 109, 112
Blue Dragons, 190
Blue Force Trackers, 238

Blumenson, Martin, 58
Boer War, 72-73
Bogart, Humphrey, 86, 218
Bond, Kit, 92
Boomer, Walter, 30
Boone, Richard, 89
Borgnine, Ernest, 89
Bowden, Mark, 29
Boxer Rebellion, 29, 58, 85
Boyd, John, 197-98
Bradbury, Ray, 85
Bradley, Omar, 119, 136, 236, 240
Bragg, Braxton, 139-45
Branch for Service, 67
Bremer, L. Paul, 69
Brevet, 111-12
    Civil War, 111
    Confusion related to rank, 111
    Defined, 111
    Napoléons Army, 110
    Revolutionary war, 1112-13
    Significance to American military, 112
Brezhnev, Leonid, 178
Brodie, Bernard, 200
Bronson, Charles, 83
Brooklyn Naval Yard, 25
Brooks, Mel, 88
Brown, Jacob, 85
Brown, Moses, 150
Broyles, William, 92
Byran, William Jennings, 244
Brzezinski, Zbigniew, 248
B-17 bomber, 55
Buckmaster, Elliot, 125
Buckner, Simon Bolivar, 127
Buford, John, 125, 147
Burns, John, 237
Burnside, Ambrose, 141, 215
Bush, George H. W. 20, 227, 228
Bush, George W.
    Bush Doctrine, 72, 255-57, 260
    Irag War. See Operation Iraqi Free dom
    As Nazi label, 35-36
    War for money accusation, 155-60
Bushido, 25, 28-29, 35, 195
Butler, Benjamin, 208
Butler, Smedley, 120
Butterfield, Daniel, 135
Button, Red, 91

Cabell, Brian, 238
Calwalader, John, 85
Caesar, Julius, 33, 185
Caldicott, Helen, 248, 249, 250
Caldwell, Charles, 150
Calhoun, James, 136
Callaghan, Daniel J., 132
Calley, William, 42

Cameron, Simon, 210
Camp O'Donnell, 24-5
Cannons, 145-46
Capra, Frank, 80, 83
Carey, Drew, 88
Carlisle Barracks, 67, 100
Carlson, Eric, 228
Carnegie, Andrew, 150-52, 240
Carney, Art, 89
Carson, Adam, 234
Casualties
    Civil War, 50, 58, 132
    Low, U.S. Efforts, 51, 55, 57, 135-136
    Media reporting of, 22, 27, 45, 70, 207
    Officers, 128
    Reducing, See Casualties, reducing
    Vietnam War, 40-45, 69-78
    Wake Island, 48, 58-59
    World War I, 50, 51, 53
    World War II, 55, 130, 154-55
Casualties, reducing, 43-45
    And air campaigns, 46-50
    Intellectual self-evaluation, 64-66
    Losses, study of, 65-67
    And military training, 44-45, 55-58
    Operation Iraqi Freedom, 60, 65-67,
    71, 238
    Overestimation of troops, avoiding,
    60-62
    Pearl Harbor lessons, 50-51, 158, 194
    With preparedness, 48-49, 55-56
    Revolutionary War, 60, 63
    And service branch coordination, 190,
    203-205, 200-8
    And tanks, 51-52, 56, 110-5
    U.S. Goals, 40, 51, 52, 53, 56, 70,
    135-37, 208
    World War I, 50-53, 55, 57, 98
    World War II, 1, 55-56, 60-61, 194
Cell phones, 63, 195
Chaffee, Adna, Sr., 115
Chamberlain, Joshua, 82-83, 95, 122, 126
Chandler, Jeff, 90
Chandler v United States, 220
Chaplin, Charlie, 91, 217
Chechnya, 65
Chelmsford, Lord, 160
Cheney, Richard, 248
Chennault, Claire, 53
Chernenko, Konstantine, 178
Chicago, Vietnam anti-war protests, 200-8
Chin, Edward, 105
China, Japanese atrocities in, 50
Chippewa, battle of, 85
Chitose, 201
Churchill, Ward, 20, 23
Churchill, Winston, 17, 55, 56, 238
City Fights, 190
Civil War
    Anti-war protests, 240

Armed forces, members of, 80-81,
84-86, 112-15
    Arrogance of military, 126-29
    Autonomy of military, 132
    Brevet, 115
    Casualties, 60, 62, 126
    Communications, 183, 184
    Draft, 81-82
    Hoover's Gap, battle of, 140, 143
    Lessons learned, 60
    Little Big Horn, 49, 51, 60, 64, 109,
    126-31
    Military overconfidence, impact of, 60
    Military training, 95-97, 100
    Press, coverage of 210, 211-14
    Prisoners of war, 27-8, 25, 28, 36
    Rockefeller's financial support, 152
    Service branches, coordination of,
    183
    Weapons/equipment/technology 140-
    42, 150-51
Civilians, control of military, 246-47
Claiborne, William, 79, 97
Clark, Wesley, 45, 236
Clarke, Victoria "Torie", 230-31
Clay, Henry, 120
Clifford, Clark, 240
Clinton, Bill, 55
Clinton, Hilary, 20
Clodfelter, Mark, 60-61
Club G'itmo, 28. See Guantánamo Bay prison
Coalition forces, as secondary units, 22
Cobb, Lee J., 98
Cochrane, Alexander, 108
Code breakers, 205
Coffee, John, 108, 110
Coffin, William Sloane, 245
Cold War
    End of, 170-71
    Reagan's influence on ending, 175-76
    Star Wars, 172-85
Cole, 252
Collier, Peter, 20, 240
Colt, Samuel, xviii, 140-41, 160
Command of the Air (Douhet), 52
Combined arms, See service branches,
    Coordination of
Command and General Staff School, 42
    Committee on Public Information, 215
    Committee for a Sane Nuclear Policy
    (SANE), 221
Common Sense (Paine), 100
Communications
    Breakdown, Leyte Gulf, battle of, 195-
    99
    Civil War, 179, 182
    Code breakers, 190
    Korean War, 180
    OODA loop, 190-92
    Operation Iraqi Freedom, 178-82

And service branches, coordination of, 179-81, 190-91
World War I, 180-81
World War II, 179, 180, 181-82
Computers
ARPANET, 168
Military use, 166-69, 170-76
Computer tracking chips, 180
Conrad, William, 100
Conyers, John, 105
Coogan, Jackie, 95
Coolidge, Calvin, 240-42
Cooper, Jackie, 105
Coppola, Francis Ford, 165-66
Costanza, Midge, 246
Cotton, Joseph, 105
Crazy Horse, Sioux chief, 130
Creel, George, 210
Crete, invasion of, 180
Crockett, Davy, 90
Cronkite, Walter, 230
Crook, George, 130, 135-36
Crusader system, 195
Cuba and Spanish-American War, 28, 140, 228
U.S. withdrawal from, 23
Also see Guantánamo Bay prison
Cummings, e.e., 61
Cunningham, William, 41
Curtis, Tony, 107
Custer, George Armstrong
Little Big Horn, 51, 55, 57, 62, 105, 118-19
Ranking, 108

Dace, 198
Daley, Richard, 92
Dana, Charles, 210
Darter, 198
Dash, Mohammed, 109
Davis, Ossie, 90
Day, Benjamin, 210
D-Day, 195
Dean, Dudley, 90
Dean, Howard, 40
Deaver, Michael, 225
Defense Advanced Research Projects Agency (DARPA), 190
Del Vecchio, John, 95
Dellinger, David, 24
Delta Force, 56, 62, 170
Demologos, 152
Desert Rogue, 112, 116
Desert Storm, See Gulf War
Detroit Evening News, 210
Dewey, George, 140
DeWitt, J. L., 36
Dietrich, Marlene, 90
Dinwiddle, Robert, 118
"Discourse on Winning and Losing"

(Boyd), 198
Dodge, Authur, 210
Doherty, George, 80
Dolphin, 175
Donaldson, Sam 230
Doolittle, James, 120
Dos Passos, John, 45
Doughboys, 46-47
Douglas, Kirk, 97
Douhet, Giulio, 48, 150
Al-Douri, Mohammad, 110
Draft
Avoiding, 107, 109
Civil War, 81-82, 240
Seven Years' War, 115
Vietnam War, 120
World War II, 85, 91
Dragon Eye, 68
Dragon Runner, 74
Drinkwine, Brian, 73
Dudin, Khaled, 74
Duffy, Patrick, 90
Dugan, Michael, 245-46
Duke of Wellington, 75, 101, 118
Durbin, Dick, 25-26, 28, 43, 210
Durning, Charles, 90
Dynamic Economics (Klein), 160

E-mail communication, 182
Earnhardt, Dale, 174
Eaton, William, 84, 97, 104, 140
Eckel, Kyle, 101
Eisenhower, Dwight D., 61, 120, 136, 155, 168, 171, 176
Eliot, George Fielding, 180
Ellsberg, Daniel, 247
Embedded journalists, 235-40
Employment of Combined Air Forces, 45
England, Lyndie, 250
ENIAC, 175
Entertainment Industry
Celebrities in armed forces, 90-101
Movies on military, 215-20
Nuclear freeze movement, 250
Equipment, military. See Weapons/equipment/technology
Ericsson, John, 148, 155
Ermey, R. Lee, 220
Eurekas, 158-60
Everett, Edward, 120
Evil Empire, 172, 173
Ewell, Richard, 101
Export Control Act, 175
Fairbanks, Douglas Jr. 87, 89, 215
Fallujah campaign, 62-66, 71, 125, 188
Fenno, John, 210
Ferguson, Homer, 164
Fetterman, William, 130
Fetterman Massacre, 130
Field Manual, 105-10, 125

Field Promotion, See Brevet
Firearms/artillery, development of 133-43, 165-66
Firefinder radar systems, 175-77
Fish, Hamilton, 96
Fisher, David, Hackett, 98, 238, 240
Fitch, John, 145
Fleet Manual 1: Warfighting, 132
Flying Tigers, 50
Follet, Ken, 47
Fonda, Henry, 80
Fonda, Jane, xx, xxiv, 207, 210, 220, 225
F-111B bomber, 189
Force multiplier approach, 48-49, 165
Ford, Glen, 87
Ford, Henry, 169, 240
Ford, John, 85
Forrest, C.R., 91
Forrest, Nathan Bedford, 27-28
Fort Benning, 58, 94
Fort Leavenworth, 49, 62
Fort Benning, 68, 90
Fort Leavenworth, 59, 62
Fort Mims, 70
Four-minute Men, 115
4th Generation Warfare (4GW), 255
Fox, Richard, 72, 133-34
Fox News, 230, 234
Franks, Tommy, 76, 78, 84, 104, 123, 130, 185, 250
    Baghdad, battle of, 117-20, 170, 188-89, 240-43
Franz, Dennis, 95
Freakley, Benjamin, 110
Fredendall, Lloyd, 55-56
French and Indian War, 76
Frost, Holloway Halstead, 130
Fulton, Robert, 155
Future Force, 125

Gable, Clark, 96
Gabler, Neal, 237
Gaddafi, Muammar, 21
Gallagher, Bill, 68, 96
Gansler, Jacques, 166
Gatling, Richard, 140, 145
Geisel, Theodore (Dr. Seuss), 198
Geneva Summit, 174-76
Germany
    North Africa campaign, 65-66
    Parachute attacks of, 186
    U.S. air campaigns against, 59-60,
    152-57
Gettysburg Address, 168
Giap, Vo Nguyen, 55
Gibbon, John, 125
Ginsberg, Allen, 246
Girl's Radio Unit, 93
Global Positioning system, 193

Gobel, George, 96
Gobright, Lawrence, 210
Goddard Institute for Space Studies, 170
Godfrey, Arthur, 87
Goebbels, Joseph, 25
Goering, Herman, 43, 44
Going After Cacciato (O'Brien), 90
Gold Star Mothers, 44
Gorbachev, Mikhail, and Star Wars, 170-71, 172, 173-78
Gore, Al, on Bush (George W.), 43-44
Gorshin, Frank, 88
Grange, David L., 225
Grant, Ulysses S., 17, 24, 38, 67, 94-95, 118, 120, 122, 135, 183, 246-47, 250
Gray, Al, 124, 231
Great Britain
    American Independence from. See Revolutionary War
    Aristocracy in military, 122
    War of 1812, 83-86, 90
Greeley, Horace, 210
Green, David, 224
Green Berets, 76, 180
Greene, Nathaniel, 86-88, 118, 122
Greene, Shecky, 97
Greenfield, Kent, 64
Grenada, xxiii-xxiv, 228
Groom, Winston, 100
Gruening, Ernest, 225
Guantánamo Bay Prison
    As Club Gitmo, 28
    Koran abuse, 36
    Liberal descriptions of, 25-26
    Torture allegations, 26-28, 50
    Also see Club G'itmo
Guidry, Roland, 67
Gulf War
    Iraqi prisoners-of-war, 32
    Liberal opposition to, 21
    Media coverage, 223-26
    Mobility, 190
    Service branches, coordination of,
190, 192-93
    Weapons/equipment/technology, 188
Gunpowder, 152-53
Guthrie, Woody, 53
Gutmann, Dave, 38-39

Hadges, Chris, 92
Hadley, Arthur, 92
Haiti, 230
Hale, Alan, 87
Haley, Alex, 89
Halleck, Henry, 130, 210-11
Halsey, William "Bull", 38, 195-6, 200, 201-2
Hamady, Sania, 39
Hamas, 52
Hamilton, Alexander, 118
Hammes, Thomas X., 250

Hancock, Winfield Scott, 122, 126
Hannity, Sean, 226
Hanson, Victor Davis, 15, 120, 228-30, 238-40, 246, 249-50
Hardee, William J., 210
Harwood, Robert, 225-30
Hassan, Nasra, 40
Haupt, Herman, 96, 154-55
Hayden, Sterling, 87
Hayden, Tom, 115, 210, 215
Heflin, Van, 85
Helicopters
        Destruction of, 180
        Hughes Development, 151
        Mogadishu, 34, 64, 168, 186, 190-92
        Vietnam War, 167, 185
Hell's Angels (film), 162
Hemingway, Ernest, 57
Hendrix, Jimi, 90
Hennings, Chad, 91
Hepburn, Audrey, 89
Herald, 210
Hercules aircraft, 166
Herf, Jeffrey, 175
Hess, Rudolph, 156-57
Hesse, Kurt, 83
Heston, Charlton, 88
Higgins, 182
Higgins, Andrew Jackson, 18, 138, 155, 157-58
        Higgins boats, 157-62
Higgins Boat Operators and Machine Mainte-nance School, 160
Hill. A. P., 126
Hill, B. H., 210
Hill, George Roy, 88
Hill, James J., 140
Hiller Aircraft, 151
Hirt, Al, 89
Hitler, Adolf, xix, 185
Ho Chi Minh, 55
Hoffman, Abbie, 24, 210
Hogan, Michael, 250
Holden, Josh, 91
Holden, Williams, 86
Holland, John, 140
Holley, Alexander, 145
Hollings, Ernest "Fritz", 104-5
Holt, Benjamin, 150
Homma, Masaharu, 22
Horror/shame
        Bushido, 25, 27-28
        In the Christian world, 31
        In the Muslim world, 26-33
Hoover's Gap, battle of, 138-39, 145
Hooper, Dennis, 90
Hornbuckle, Harry, 128
Horseshoe Bend, Battle of, 83-85
How Democrats lose small wars (Merom), 251-2
Howell, Patton, 39
Hudson, Rock, 87

Hue City, battle of, 184-85
Hughes, Christopher, 60, 130
Hughes, Howard, 161-62, 171-73
Hughes Aircraft Company, 151-52, 162-63
Hummer, Steve, 110
Humvees, 179, 190
Hunley, 145
Hunley, Horace Lawrence, 148
Hunter, Duncan, 92
Hurburt, S.A., 210
Hussein, Fouad, 257
Hussein, Saddam, 100-101, 112, 254
Hussein, Uday, 240

Ia Drang Valley, battle of 52-54, 55, 167-68
Imperial Japanese Navy, 37
Industrial College of the Armed Forces, 149
Infantry in Battle, 34
Infantry Drill Regulations, 90
Infantryman's Guide to Urban Combat, An 105
Influence of Seapower Upon History (Mahon), 51
Integration of battlefield, See Service
        Branches, coordination of
Intercontinental ballistic missiles (ICBM's), 169, 171, 172, 177
International Business Machines (IBM) 169-70
Iran, Operation Eagle Claw, 66-67
Iraq War, See operation Iraqi Freedom
Isandlwana, 152
Islam, Koran on suicide, 42
Islamic terrorists
        Arab antiterrorists marches, 265-66
        Background of, 40
        Honor/shame, code of, 36-33
        Islamic Caliphate plan, 265
Jihad, 42
Women as, 36, 39-40
        Also see Suicide bombing

Jackson, Andrew, 24, 55, 73-76, 97-104, 107-8, 115
Jackson, Michael, 240
Jackson, Thomas "Stonewall", 82, 122, 126
Japan
        American POWs. Torture/killing of, 21-5, 31-33, 35-36
        Bushido principals, 25, 37-38, 49, 185
        Kamikaze, 37-38, 129, 153, 188, 258
        Leyte Gulf, battle of, 199-208
        Racism of, 45
        Soldier self-annihilation, 37-38
        Wake Island invasion, 31, 43, 56-57
        Wartime atrocities by, 24-5, 49-51
        White flag trick, 33
Japanese-Americans, internment of, 48-49
Jason, Rick, 88
Jastrow, Robert, 173-74
Al Jazeera, 75, 229, 240

Jeep, 152
Jefferson, Thomas, 61, 84, 140, 210
Jerram, C. F. 184
Jersey, 30-31
Jihadists. See Islamic terrorists; Suicide bombing
Joan of Arc, 30
Jobs, Steve, 170
Johnson, Lyndon, 68-69
Johnson, Russell, 85
Johnson, Tim, 86
Johnston, Albert Sidney, 115
Joint Operations. See Service branches, coordination of
Joint purchasing, 195-97
Jones, Bill, 148
Jones, Edgar L. 33
Jordon, eason, 240
Journal of Military History, 61

Kaiser, Henry, 18, 152, 157-58, 161-63
Kamikaze, 37-38, 130, 153, 188, 254
Kanaly, Steve, 90
Kaplan, Fred, 97
Kasserine, battle of, 55-56, 70
Keegan, John, 88, 171, 255
Keeshan, Bob, 80
Keith, Brian, 80
Kelly, Thomas, 194
Kelly, Greg, 230
Kennedy, Edward, 21, 26, 253
Kennedy, George, 88
Kennedy, John F., 170, 184-85
Kennedy, Julian, 148
Keough, Miles, 128
Kerry, John, 260
Kettle Hill, 130
Al-Khash, Suleiman, 33
Khrushchev, Nikita, 176
Kidd, Issac, 127
King, Bill, 105
King, Edward P. Jr., 22
King, Ernest, 200
King, Martin Luther Jr., 245
Kinkaid, Thomas, 200
Klein, Burton, 169
Klemperer, Werner, 88
Knights of Bushido (Russell), 39
Knotts, Don, 85
Knox, Henry, 115-6, 120
Koch, Oscar, 138
Kongo, 200
Koran
    Guantánamo bay abuse, 36
    On suicide, 42
Korean War
    Communications, 185
    Officer violations, 250-52
    Outcome of, 13
Seoul, battle of, 190-1

    Service branches, coordination of, 185, 191-2
    Urban warfare, 192
    Weapons/equipment/technology, 168
Kosovo, 238
Krauthammer, Charles, 257
Kristol, Bill, 255
Krulak, Victor "Brute", 122, 155, 158
Kuhl, Charles, 113
Kulp, Nancy, 89
Kurita, Takeo, 200-4
Kursk, battle of, 155-7
Kuypers, Jim, 240

Laffin, Jim, 39, 41
Lafitte, Jean, 85, 89-91, 95
L'Amour, Louis, 80
Lancaster, Burt, 79
Landing Boat Development Board, 158-9
Landing Craft, 158-61
    Higgins Boat, 158-63
Landing Zone Albany, battle of, 168
Langley, Samuel, 150
LAV, (light armored vehicle), 190, 191
Lawrence, T.E., 39
Lebanon, Marine barracks bombing, 54, 256
Lechner, James, 125, 126
Lee, Charles, 118
Lee, Robert E., 57, 59, 118, 121, 121, 126-8, 131, 189, 210
LeMay, Curtis, 14
Lemomon, Jack, 87
Lender, Mark, 85
Lenin, Vladimir, 63, 170
Lennox, Williams, 93
Lettow, Paul, 170
Leventhal, Rick, 228
Leyte Gulf, Battle of, 199-208
Lexington, 128
Liberals
    Anti-war activities, See Antiwar protests on George W Bush as Nazi, 43-44
    On Gulf War, 21
    On military industrial complex, 149-50
    On monetary benefits of war, 23, 149-50
    News media, See Mainstream media on 9/11, 20, 44, 248
    On Operation Enduring Freedom, 21, 67-68
    On Operation Iraqi Freedom, 43
    On prisoners of war, 25-26, 33, 36
    On Star Wars, 170-171
    War as a quagmire view, 20-21, 43, 67-68
Liberty Bonds, 89, 89
Liberty Ships, 157-58, 162-63, 166
Life of an Enlisted Man in the United States Army, 85

Liggert, Hunter, 58
Lightning Brigade, 135-37
Lilly, Eli, 135
Limbaugh, Rush, 28
Lincoln, Abraham, 24, 81, 136-37, 215-17
Little Big Horn, 54, 55, 67, 62, 118, 125-26
Lombard, Carole, 89
Longstreet, James, 67
Los Niños, 188
Loss, learning from. See casualties; casualties, reducing
Loudon, Lord, 78
Luck, Gary, 140
Ludendorff, Erich, 19
Luftwaffe, 155, 156, 185
Lynn, John, 37, 253, 256

McAndrew, James, 56
MacArthur, Arthur, 58
MacArthur, Douglas, 38, 47-48, 48, 50, 52-53, 160, 200, 250-52
MacCaffery, Barry, 240-41
McCampbell, David, 200
McCarthy, Kevin, 86
McCarthy, Mary, 245
McClellan, George B., 140, 154, 180, 210-13, 250
McCormick, Richard, 140
McCoy, Brian, 105
McFarlane, Bud, 175
McGovern, George, 245
MacGregor, Douglas, 190
Machine guns, 161
McKinley, William, 70
McMahon, Ed 80
McNamara, Robert, 68, 195, 235
Magic program, 194
Magna Carta, 30
Mahan, Alfred Thayer, 60
Mailer, Norman, 89
Mainstream media
        On Abu Ghraib, 21, 36, 47
        Antimilitary position, 15, 210-11, 215-17, 220-22, 225-28, 230-33
        Antiwar protest coverage, 210, 220-22
        Casualties, reporting of, 27, 35, 65, 210
        Embedded journalists, 230-38
        Gulf War coverage, 230-34
        Language of reporting, 22
        Movies, 215-20
        Nuclear freeze movement, 250-51
        Operation Iraqi Freedom coverage, 226-28, 230-35
        Pentagon control efforts, 233-34, 237-39
        Press, historical view, 216-218
        Radio broadcasts, 226
        Riots resulting from reports, 36
        Sheehan, coverage of, 34-35, 228-

30,260
        And Vietnam Template, 20-24, 228-30
        On Vietnam vets, 230
        Vietnam War Coverage, 45, 228-30
Maintenance Units, 55
Malone, Paul, 94
Malveaux, Julianne, 228
Managerial approach, U.S. military, 51-52
Manchester, William, 89
Manhattan Project, 150
Mao Zedong, 19, 20
March, Peyton, 48
March Up, The (Bing and West), 34
Marines, competency Level, 58, 66
Marshall, George, 57, 120
Martel, Charles, 165
Marvin, Lee, 85
Massey, Jimmy, 27
Matthau, Walter, 86
Matthews, Chris, 230
Mattis, James, 115
Mature, Victor, 85
Maude, Timothy, 125
Maulden, Karl, 86
Maurice of Nassau, 102
Maxim, Hiram, 159
            Machine gun, 159
Meade, George, 57, 65, 115, 144-45. 210
Media, see Mainstream media
Media bias. See Mainstream media
Meese, Edwin, 171
Meredith, Burgess, 86
Mermon, Gil, 250-51, 253-54
Mexican War
        Antiwar protests, 247
        Armed forces, member of, 77, 80-81, 120-121
        Press, coverage of, 210
        Underestimation of militia, 80-81
        U.S. victories, 57, 72
Myers, Oscar W, 128
Midvale Steel, 155
Midway, battle of, 160
MiG-25P Foxbat interceptor, 172
Military members of, 73-98
        African Americans, 75, 76, 82, 85, 110-15, 123
        Civil War, 78-79, 79-81, 111-13
        Decline in (2005), 106
        Educational level of, 91, 93, 122, 123
        Equality of all, 117-25
        Hollywood figures, 86-91
        Mexican War, 87, 90-91, 123-24
        Native American, 85
        Non-commissioned officers (NCO's), 124-26
        Officers in combat, 126-27
        Operation Iraqi Freedom, 123
        Promotions, 117-8, 125-26
        Revolutionary War, 76-78, 85, 95,

118-9
Social ranking, 92, 119, 121-24
Sons of political figures, 91-92
Vietnam War, 83, 122, 123
War of 1812, 83, 85-86, 90, 93-94, 97-104
Women, 68
Also see Draft
Military Industrial Complex, 149-52
Military promotions
Equality of members of military, 124-26
Field promotion. See Brevet
Modern procedure, 126
Military success. See American military success
Military training/education, 93-96
Air power doctrine, 59-60
Army, improvement of 68
And autonomy of leadership. See Autonomy of military
And Bush Doctrine, 78
Civil War, 93-94, 96
Command and General Staff School, 59
Competency levels, 67-68, 76
Courses, types of, 58-59, 71, 96
And infantry, 57
Iraq War, 59-60, 94
Post-World War I, 48-49, 56
In procurement and mobilization, 149
Revolutionary War, 86-89
And tank operation, 96
Technical writing manuals, 58, 60-61, 94, 105, 115, 139
War of 1812, 79, 80
West Point, 48-49, 61-62
And women in military, 68
World War II, 94
Miller, Glenn, 89
Miller, Phineas, 139
Millett, Alan, 185
Missiles
Antiballistic missile system (ABMs), 169, 171-72
Intercontinental ballistic missiles (ICBMs), 169, 171, 172, 177
Patriot, 178, 182
And Star Wars, xix, 168-79
Surface-to-air (SAM) missiles, 68
Mitchell, Billy, 59, 153-54, 252-53
Mitchell, Cameron, 86
Mitchell, David, 75
Moffatt, Billy, 59
Mogadishu
Battle of, 34-35, 63-64
Bin Laden view of Americans, 20, 35, 64, 135
Black Hawk Down incident, 34, 64
Service branches, coordination of, 180, 195

Weapons/equipment/technology, 168
M1 Garand, 59
Monetary gain
Military industrial complex, 149-52
War for money view, xxiii, 149-50
Monitor, 145
Montgomery, Bernard Alexander, 76
Montgomery, Robert, 87
Moore, Hal, 54, 65, 125, 167-68, 225
Morgan, J. P., 147
Morison, Samuel Eliot, 33, 57, 200
Motor Sport School, 96
MoveOn.org, 44
Movies, 210-11
Antimilitary films, 220-21
Promilitary films, 218-20, 225-26
Moynihan, Daniel Patrick, 230
Mucci, Henry, 46
Mueller, John, 258, 260
Muravchik, Joshua, 258
Mushashi, 198, 199
Muslim Brotherhood, 31-32
Muslims
Abu Ghraib, reactions to, 36-37, 39, 43, 256
Arab mind-set, descriptions of, 35, 39-42
Education and conformity, 40-41
Honor/shame, code of, 46-43
Terrorists. See Islamic terrorists; Suicide bombing
Women, view of, 36, 39-40, 43
Mutual assured destruction (MAD), 170, 250

Najaf campaign, 129
Napoléon, 101, 110, 120, 185, 200, 215, 250
Nashville, 198
Nasser, Gamal Abdel, 41
National Aerospace Plane (NASP), 195
National Defense Act (1920), 48
National Defense University, 190
National Guard, 58, 88, 90, 91
National Labor Relations Board (NLRB), 161
National Security Administration (NSA), 170
Native Americans
Little Big Horn, 54, 55, 67, 111, 120-24
Red Stick uprising, 74-75
In U.S. militia, 85
Naval Appropriations Act, 145-46
Naval War College, 52, 120
Nazis
Bush (George W.) compared to, 43-44
Hitler, 19, 161, 185
Also see Germany
New American Militarism (Bacevich), 254
New Deal, 52-53, 55, 73, 160
New England Anti-Imperialism League, 243-45
New England Chronicle, 78
New Guinea, invasion of, 160

New Orleans, battle of, 73-76, 97-104, 107-108
New Orleans Committee on Defense, 97
New York Daily News, 210
New York Enquirer, 208
New York Evening Post, 215
New York Sun, 210
New York Times, 21, 235, 238
New York Tribune, 215, 217
New York World, 217
Newman, Paul, 87
News Management Bureau, 215
News media bias. See Mainstream media
News reporting. See Mainstream media
Nicaragua, service branches, coordination of, 184-85
Nimitz, Chester, 57, 198, 200-1
Nishimura, Shoji, 198-99, 200
Non-commissioned officers (NCOs), 110-12
Norden bombsight, 50
Nordland, Rod, 45
Nromandy, 155
North, Simeon, 149
North Carolina, 200
Northern Alliance, 84
Northern Ireland, 38
Nuclear freeze movement, 174, 248-53
Nussio, Ricky, 188

O'Bannon, Presley, 84
O'Brien, Tim, 80
Ochs, Adolph, 210
Officer Candidate School, 120
Oldendorf, Jesse, 200, 202, 205
On Point, 255
On the Wings of Eagles (Follett), 37
O'Neill, Bucky, 120-21
OODA loop, 195-97
Operation Eagle Claw, 66-67
Operation Enduring Freedom
        Liberal view, 21, 67-68
        Northern Alliance forces, 84
        Service branches, coordination of, 189, 191
        Staging of troops, 191-92
        Taliban defeats in, 21, 74
Operation Iraqi Freedom
        Anti-war protests, 20, 34-35, 225, 228
        Armed forces, member of, 115
        And autonomy of military, 105-110, 120, 129, 130-32
        Baghdad, battle of, 109, 105-110, 130-31, 166, 182-83, 240-42
        Casualties, reporting of, 23, 27, 45
        Causes/stakes involved, 17
        Civilian deaths, 45
        Communications, 180-81
        Enemy fighting style, 185-86
        Fallujah campaign, 62-66, 71, 195
        Hussein statue toppled, 99-100

        Iraqi soldier, lack of modern system, 120, 188-89
        Iraqi soldiers, training of, 128
        Lessons learned, 70, 75-77, 81, 240
        Liberal view, 20, 43-45
        Media coverage, 225-28, 233-40
        Military training for, 59-60, 94
        New weapons, 64
        OODA loop, 197
        Prison scandal. See Abu Ghraib
        Ramadi campaign, 65
        Republican Guard, 128
        Roach motel strategy, 129-30
        Sandstorms, 240-42
        Service branches, coordination of, 181-83, 190, 197
        Shock and Awe, 135
        Tanks, 101-7, 182, 192
        Thunder runs, 110-15, 165
        Weapons/equipment/technology, 64, 165, 175
        Wounded, survival of, 23
Operation Market Garden, 185
Operation Torch, 55
Oskar II, 245
Ostfriesland, 154
Othman, Muhammad Rafat, 42
Otis, Elwell, 71
Ozawa, Jisaburo, 200-4

Pace, Peter, 125
Padilla, José, 29
Paine, Thomas, 95, 210
Pajota, Juan, 46
Pakenham, Edward, 95-97
Palance, Jack, 86
Palestinian Liberation Organization (PLO), 42, 260
Pan American Airways, 150
Panay, 53, 54
Panzer IV's, 155
Parachute attacks, 185-86
Parameters, 70
Parker, John, 81
Particle-beam satellites, 173-74
Particle-beam weapons, Star Wars, 19, 168-79
Patriot missiles, 178, 182
"Patterns of Conflict" (Boyd), 190-93
Patton, George, 14, 17, 18, 25, 33, 57, 61, 63, 66, 76, 95, 110-12, 127-28, 175, 181
Peace of God, 30
Pearl Harbor, 55-56, 60, 150, 156, 190
Peckinpah, Sam, 88
Pender, William, 126
Pennsylvania Associators, 77-78
Penny Press, 210
Perelle, Charles, 163
Perkins, David, 114, 115-7
Perle, Richard, 176
Perot, H. Ross, 47

Perry, Oliver Hazard, 74
Pershing, John J., 34, 56, 115, 180-1, 183-84, 215
Persian Gulf War, See Gulf War
Petraeus, David, 76, 127
Philadelphia Inquirer, 210
Philippine Constabulary, 84
Philippines
    Bataan Death March, 21-25, 45-46
    Japanese atrocities in, 49-50
    Leyte Gulf, battle of, 195-201
    Philippine Insurgency, 70-71, 82, 245
    Philippine Sea, Battle of, 36-37
    POW camp rescues, 35-38
    Urban warfare, 190
    U.S. withdrawal from, 23
Philippine Scouts, 84
Pickett, George, 67, 120
Pickford, Mary, 91
Pinckney, Thomas, 74-75
Piracy, 75, 84, 97-98
Piven, Frances Fox, 23, 26, 43
Podhoretz, Norman, 258
Poinsett, Joel, 140
Pope, John, 150
Porter, David, 240
Poston, Tom, 87
Potter, E.B., 200
Powell, Colin, 56, 230, 233
Powell, Lee, 87
Powell, Doctrine. See Reagan Doctrine
Power, Tyrone, 87
POW's. See Prisoners of War
Press
    Civil War Coverage, 210, 211-15
    And Revolutionary War, 210, 211
    And telegraph, 210-15
    Also see Mainstream media
Preston, Robert, 86, 217
Prisoners of War
    Abu Ghraib prison scandal, 35-37, 39, 43
    Biscari, Sicily incident, 33
    Civil War, 27-28, 31, 38, 46
    Guantánamo Bay prisoners, 26-28, 36, 50
    Humane treatment, Greco-Roman roots, 29-30
    Human rights, U.S. respects for, 29, 31-32, 34, 48, 51
    Japanese torture/killing of Americans, 21-25, 31-33, 45-46, 49-50
    Liberal view of, 25-26, 33, 36
    Persian Gulf War, 32
    Revolutionary War, 30-31
    U.S. attempt to rescue, 34, 45-48, 51
Proceedings, 60, 120
Promotion. See brevet: Military promotions
Psychiatric problems, war veterans', 230
PT Boats, 159, 160

P38 Lightning, 162
Puerto Princesa Prison Camp, 25
Puff the Magic Dragon gunships, 186
Pulleine, Henry, 155
Puller, Lewis "Chesty", 120
Pyle, Ernie, 107, 220

Al Qaeda, 21, 195, 252-55. Also see Islamic terrorists
Al-Qaradawl, Yusuf, 42-43
Quakers, 245
Quezon, Manuel, 32
Quick, John, 180
Quth, Sayeed, 41-42

Radar systems, 180-81
Radio broadcasts, 225
Radio communications, 182, 185
Rahman, Omar, Abdul, 228
Railroad, Civil War, 144-45
Ramaldi campaign, 65
Rangel, Charles, 26, 100
Rangers, 57-58, 66, 168
Rape of Nanking, 49
Rather, Dan, 44, 234
Raye, Martha, 89
Raymond, Gene, 86
Raytheon, 195
Reagan, Ronald, 56, 88, 168, 170-71, 172, 173, 174-78, 220, 250, 255
Reagan Doctrine, 18
Reconstruction Finance Corporation, 158
Red Ball Express, 160
Red River War, 117
Red Stick uprising, 74-75
Reed, Robert, 87
Reeves, George, 86
Reiner, Carl, 88
Reno, Marcus, 125-26
Republican Guard, 120, 190, 245
Reserve Officer Training Corps (ROTC), 93, 104, 120
Reserves, 68, 93, 95
Retreat from Doomsday (Mueller), 258
Reuben James, 63, 64
Revolutionary War
    Anti-war protests, 210, 211
    Armed forces, members of, 76-79, 85, 94, 110-1
    Brevet, 110-1
    Lessons learned, 67
    Militia training, 86-89, 95
    Press, impact of, 205, 210
    Prisoners of war, 30-31
    Weapons/equipment/technology, 138-39, 141
Revolution in Military Affairs (RMA), 252-55
Reykjavik conference, 175
Riady, Richard, 29
Riall, Phineas, 79

Ridgway, Mathew B., 194
Ripples of Battle (Hanson), 260
Roach Motel strategy, 128-30
Robards, Jason, 86
Robert E. Peary, 158
Robertson, Cliff, 87
Robertson, Dale, 86
Robinson, David, 91
Rockefeller, John D., 98, 145
Rocket-Propelled grenades, 186, 192
Rodes, Robert, 120
Rodman, Thomas, 138
Rolling attack pattern, 185
Rolling Thunder, 68-69
Rommel, Erwin, 65, 76
Roosevelt, Franklin D., 48-49, 60, 64, 149, 161-62
    New deal, 62-63, 65, 73, 161
Roosevelt, Theodore, 24, 82, 86, 92, 127, 132
Rosecrans, William, 133
Ross, Sherwood, 60
Ross, Stewart, 153
Rough Riders, 130-31
Rowell, Ross, 185
Royal Engineers, 152
Rumsfeld, Donald, 78, 235, 239, 240, 256
Rupprecht, Crown Prince of Bravaria, 83
Rushing, Roy, 200
Russell, E.F.L., 49
Russell, John, 87
Rutan, Burt, 166
Rutan, Dick, 166
Ruxton, George F., 124

Sadler, Barry, 220
Al-Sadr, Ayatollah, 43
Al-Sahaf, Mohammed Saeed (Baghdad Bob), 114, 115, 228, 235
Sajak, Pat, 80
Sakaibara, Shigematsu, 31
Salafists, 41-42
Salafiyya Jihadiyya, 42
San Francisco Examiner, 210
San Juan Hill, 130
Sandanistas, 184-85
Sandino, Augusto, 184
Sangeman, Marc, 40
Santa Anna, Antonio López de, 80
Sapolsky, Harvey. 56
Satellite, images, 182
Savalas, Telly, 88
Scales, Robert H. 34, 56
Schell, Jonathan, 250
Schlesinger, Arthur Jr., 67, 248
Schmidt, Randall, 26
Schwab, Charles, 149-51
Schwarzkopf, Norman, 22, 230-34
Scott, George C., 87, 130-2
Scott, Norman, 130

Scott, Thomas, 146
Scott, Winfield, 62, 77, 79, 250
Scripps, E.W., 215
SEALs, 66
Seoul, battle of, 193-94
September 11, 2001, liberal views of, 20, 249
Serling, Rod, 88
Service branches, coordination of, 180-208
    Air/Land battle doctrine, 187-88
    Civil War, 183
    And communications, 181-86, 196-97
    And communications breakdown, 199-208
    Gulf War, 190, 192-93
    Joint purchasing, 197-99
    Korean War, 185, 193-94
    Lessons learned, 187, 193-95, 200
    Military doctrines, 181
    And mobility, 191-92
    Mogadishu, 182, 196
    Nicaragua invasion, 184-85
    Operation enduring Freedom, 188, 191
    Operation Iraqi Freedom, 181-83, 190, 195
    Spanish-American War, 180
    Vietnam War, 186, 189
    World War I, 183-84, 187
    World War II, 180-81, 184, 185-86, 191, 193, 194
Seven Pillars of Wisdom (Lawrence), 39
Seven Year's War, 109, 110, 111
Shame-based cultures. See Honor/Shame
Shapiro, Jeremy, 56
"Sharp Corners" (Spiller), 59, 60
Sharp's rifle, 138
Sharraf (honor), and jihadists, 36-43
Shaw, Bernard, 230
Sheehan, Cindy
    On Americans as terrorists, 20, 230
    Bush ranch sit-in, 44-45, 230
    Media coverage, 44-45, 230-31, 255
Sheridan, Phil, 250
Sherman, William T., 46, 115, 183, 217, 243, 245
Sherman tanks, 164, 166
Sheverdnadze, Eduard, 176
Shima, Kiyohide, 200, 205
Shipbuilding, 145-46, 148, 157-61
Shock and Awe, 130
Shock and Awe: Achieving Rapid Dominance (Ullman), 130
Shoup, David, 35
Schultz, George, 176
Shy, John, 85
SIGINT surveillance, 194
Silver, Ron, 91
Simons, Arthur "Bull", 46-47
Sims, William, 52, 92
Sinese, Gary, 91

Sistani, Ayatollah, 125
Sitting Bull, Sioux chief, 128
Six Day War, 182
Slater, Samuel, 143
Slayer One, 74
Smith, Holland "Howlin' Mad", 159
Smith, Jack, 52, 54
Smith, O. P. 250
Smith, Ray, 34, 240
Smith, Zachary, 104
Smokey the Bear, 168
Snipers, 63
Solzhenitsyn, Alexander, 50
Somalia. See Mogadishu
Soros, George, 44
Soul of Battle, The (Hanson), 129, 264
Soviet Union
       Afghanistan failure, 67-68, 176
Evil empire reference, 172, 173
And Star Wars, 168-79
Technical problems, 171, 174-79, 187
       World War II, 157
SpaceShipOne, 166
Spanish-American War
       And Cuba, xxiii, 127, 249
       Service branches, coordination of,
       180
       U.S. unpreparedness, 56
Special Operations Forces, 63-64, 66, 84
Speer, Albert, 154
Spencer, Christopher, 19, 136, 138
Spilling, Roger, 59, 60
Sprague, Thomas, 200
Springfield rifle, 59
Spruance, Ray, 204
Stack, Robert, 87
Stalin, Joseph, 19, 172, 177
Stanton, Edwin, 216-17
Stanton, John, 44
Star Wars, (Strategic Defense Initiative), 19,
168-79, 256
Staubach, Roger, 91
Steamboats, 145
Steel Industry, 146-48
Steiger, Rod, 87
Stewart, jimmy, 86
Stewart, Lynne, 230-31
Stimson, Henry, 64
Stoneman, George, 46
Storey, Wilbur, 215
Stowe, Frederick W., 110
Strategic Defense Initiative (Star Wars), 168-79
Strikers, 192-93
Stuart, James Ewell Brown "Jeb", 120, 125,
126-27
Students for a Democratic Society (SDS), 230
Stump, Felix, 205
Submachine guns, 62
Submarines, 135, 138, 199, 203
Suicide bombing

Boys raised for, 43
Compared to kamikaze, 256
Desired impact of, 39, 257
Historical view, 41-43
And honor/shame code, 39, 43
Koran on suicide, 42
And Operation Iraqi Freedom, 185
Surface-to-air (SAM) missiles, 68
Swift, Gustavus, 146
Swinton, Ernest, 152

Taffy 1, 2, 3, 200-4
Talbott, Strobe, 173
Taliban, U.S. defeat of, 21, 84
Tancredo, Tom, 255
Tanks
       Operation Iraqi Freedom, 105-10,
       157, 192
       Training for use, 96
       World War II, 61-62, 66, 164, 166
       Also see Weapons/equipment/tech
       nology
Taylor, Robert, 86
Technology, military. See Weapons/equipment/
technology
Tecumseh, Shawnee chief, 84
Telegraph
       Battlefield, messages, 180
       And press, 210-15
Telephone lines, 180-83
Tentative Manual for Landing Operations, 62,
160
Terrorists, Muslim. See Islamic terrorists
Terry, Alfred, 115, 123
Tet Offensive, 55, 194
Thayer, Sylvanus, 71
Thompson, John, 62
Thoreau, Henry David, 249
Thornton, William, 101
Thrasher, John, 210
Thunder Run (Zucchino), 34
Thunder runs, Operation Iraqi Freedom, 105-7,
166
Tillman, Pat, 91
De Tocqueville, Alexis, 89
Tokoyo Rose, 225
Toyoda, Soemu, 200
Tracy, Benjamin, 147
Training of the military. See Military training/
education
Trainor, Bernard, 73
Trenchard, John, 95
Tripoli, battle of, 94
Trippe, Juan, 151
Truce of God, 30
Truman, Harry, 250
Tucker, Preston, 52, 161, 163-4
Tucker Aviation Company, 161
Tucker: The Man and His Dream (film), 164

U-boats, 57, 63, 162, 215
Ullman, Harlan, 130
Union of Concerned Scientists (UCS), 174
United States Strategic Bombing Survey, 152-53
Urban warfare
    Chechnya, 59
    Fallujah campaign, 62-66, 71, 129, 197
    Korean War, 194
    Philippines, 193
    Vietnam War, 194-5
U.S. Naval Institue Proceedings, 70
U.S. Naval War College Review, 70
U.S. Steel, 147

Van Fleet, James, 168
Vercingetorix, Gallic leader, 181
Victory through Air Power (film), 60, 220
Vietnam Template, 20-24
    On demonizing the enemy, 22
    On U.S. coalition building, 21-22
    War as quagmire view, 20-21, 43, 67, 231
Vietnam War
    Air power, 78-79
    Anti-war protests, xvii-xviii, 205-09, 210, 250
    Armed forces, members of, 93, 115, 118
    Casualties, 52-55, 78-79
    Celebrity soldiers, 90-91
    Films about, 224-26
    Helicopters, 167, 187
    Hue City, battle of, 194-95
    Ia Drang Valley, 52-54, 62, 167-68
    Khe Sahn, 54-55
    Lessons learned, 54
    Media coverage, 55, 230-31
    Rolling Thunder, 68-69
    Service branches, coordination of, 186, 189
    Urban warfare, 194-5
    U.S. loss of, xiii, 54-5, 78-9
    Vets, media reporting on, 230
    And Vietnam Syndrome, 56
    Weapons/equipment/technology, 167-8
Villa, Pancho, 82
Villard, Oswald Garrison, 219
Vincennes, 70
Vincent, Strong, 120
Von Boehm, Max, 93
Voyager, 166

Wagner Act, 161
Wainwright, Jonathan, 21-2
Wake Island
    Japanese invasion of, 31, 55
    Japanese murder of civilians, 31-33
    Lessons learned, 66-67

Military training, lack of, 95
Walesa, Lech, 177
Walker, Kenneth, 117
Walker, Martin, 240, 243
Walker, Walton, 255
Wallace, William, 246
Wallace, William (Braveheart), 30, 120, 225
Wampanoag, 145
War of 1812
    Anti-war protests, 245
    Armed forces, members of, 73, 75-76, 80, 83-84, 97-104
    Militia training, 89, 90
    New Orleans, battle of, 83-86, 97-104, 107-08
    White House, attack on, 84
War Relocation Authority, 38-9
Warden, Jack, 88
Warner, Jack, 88
Waronker, Alvin, 95
Warrant Officer School, 120
Washington, George, 19, 24, 31, 57, 61, 65, 76-78, 110-1, 210, 250
    Farewell Address, 172
Washington Post, 238, 239, 242
Watkins, James, 173
Wayne, "Mad" Anthony, 78-79, 115-116
Weapons/equipment/technology, 18-19, 135-69
    Aircraft, 150-57, 162-63, 166
    Armored plate, 146-48
    Atomic bomb, 149
    And bureaucratic rigidity, 159-61, 166-67
    Civil War, 133-38, 144-45
    Computers, 169-71, 175, 177
    Firearms/artillery, 133-43, 167-68
    Gulf War, 178
    Korean War, 167
    Military industrial complex, 149-52
    Mogadishu, 168
    Operation Iraqi Freedom, 74, 166, 178
    And private sector, 18-19, 140-41, 151-52, 165-66
    Private weapons ownership, 141-42
    Railroad as, 144-45
    Revolutionary War, 138-39, 141
    Shipbuilding, 145-46, 148, 157-61
    And steel industry, 146-48
    Strategic Defense Initiative (Star Wars), 168-79
    Submarines, 135, 138
    Tanks, 51-52, 56, 96, 152, 164, 166, 184, 192
    Vietnam War, 167-68
    Weapons of mass destruction (WMD), 149
    World War II, 152-58, 160-66
    Also see specific types
Weapons of Mass Destruction (WMD), 149,

182, 267
Weaver, Dennis, 87
Webb, James Watson, 210
Webster, Daniel, 116
Weigley, Russell, 14, 52, 76, 255, 256
West, Bing, 34, 62-63, 65, 240
West Point
    Branch for Service, 67
    Establishment of, 61-62
    Post-World War I improvement, 48-49
Westmoreland, William, 44-45
We Were Soldiers, 93, 120, 225
Wheeler, Joseph, 46
White, Richard, 215
Whitmore, James, 97
Whitney, Eli, 139, 141
Whittlesey, Charles, 34, 86
Wicker, Tom, 230
Wilder, John, 134-35
Williams, Robert, 198
Wilson, G. I., 197
Wilson, James, 135
Wilson, Joe, 92
Wilson, Woodrow, 220
Winchester, Jesse, 105
Winged Defense (Mitchell), 59
Wolff, Tobias, 90
Wolford, Philip, 110
Women
    In Abu Gharib images, 36-37, 43, 254
    In Arab societies, 36, 39-40
    As jihadists, 36, 39-40
    In U.S. military, 68
Wonderboat, 158
Wood, Leonard, 56, 120, 130
Woods, James, 91
World Trade Center
    9/11, 20, 250
    1993 bombing, 255-56
World War I
    Anti-war protests, 245
    Army, strength of, 82-83
    Casualties, 58
    Communications, 183-84
    Lessons learned, 57-60, 65, 94
    Liberty bond rallies, 91
    Morgan's financial support, 147
    Officer casualties, 120
    Officer violations, 250-53
    Service branches, coordination of, 183-84, 187
    U.S. unpreparedness, 57-58, 63
World War II
    Air campaigns, 59-60, 152-57
    Antiwar protests, 57, 245
    Autonomy of military, 115, 130-31, 132
    Casualties, 66
    Celebrities in armed forces, 86-91
    Communications, 181, 184, 185-86

Draft, 83, 90
Films about, 220-23
Japan, atrocities by, 24-5, 49-51
Japan and American POWs, 21-5, 31-3, 45-6
Japanese internment, 48-9
Kasserine battle, 65-6, 72
Lessons learned, 55-6, 66-7
Military training, 94
And New Deal policies, 62-3, 65
Officer casualties, 120
Pearl Harbor, 55-6, 154
Philippines campaign, See Phillip pines
Service branches, coordination of, 180-81, 184, 185-86, 191, 194
Tanks, use of, 61-2, 66, 180
Victory Plan, 64
Wake Island, 31, 55
Weapons/equipment/technology, 59-60, 152-58, 159-60
Wozniak, Steve, 170
Wright, Evan, 91, 237
Wright Brothers, 150, 163
Wyler, William, 88

X-30 scramjet, 195

Yale Battery of the Connecticut National Guard, 92
Yamamoto, Isoroku, 35, 153
Yamasee War, 95
Yamashita, Tomoyuki, 49-50
Yamoto, 38, 200, 203
Yorktown, 120
Yost, Mark, 228
Yucatan, 130

Zanuck, Daryl, 98
Zappa, Frank, 100
Al-Zarqawi, Abu Mussab, 36, 76, 256
Zhukov, Marshal, 35
Ziff, William, 60
Zinni, Anthony, 130
Zinsmeister, Karl, 32, 91, 92, 178, 235-9
Zucchino, David, 34, 185, 235
Zuikaku, 200
Zululand, 152

About the Author

Larry Schweikart is the coauthor of *A Patriot's History of the United States: From Columbus's Great Discovery to the War on Terror* and is a professor of history at the University of Dayton. He has written more than twenty books on national defense, business, and financial history. Professor Schweikart lives in Centerville, Ohio, with his wife Dee, and his son, Adam.

Look for more books from Winged Hussar Publishing, LLC – E-books, paperbacks and Limited Edition hardcovers. The best in history, science fiction and fantasy at:

https://wingedhussarpublishing.com

or follow us on Facebook at:

Winged Hussar Publishing LLC

Or on twitter at:

WingHusPubLLC

For information and upcoming publications